The Official Guide to Informix®/Red Brick® Data Warehousing

The Official Guide to Informix®/Red Brick® Data Warehousing

Robert J. Hocutt

M&T Books

An imprint of IDG Books Worldwide, Inc.

Foster City, CA • Chicago, IL • Indianapolis, IN • New York, NY

The Official Guide to Informix®/Red Brick® Data Warehousing

Published by
IDG Books Worldwide, Inc.
An International Data Group Company
919 E. Hillsdale Blvd., Suite 400
Foster City, CA 94404
www.idgbooks.com (IDG Books Worldwide Web site)

ISBN: 0-7645-4694-5

Printed in the United States of America

10 9 8 7 6 5 4 3 2 1

1O/RZ/RQ/QQ/FC

Distributed in the United States by IDG Books Worldwide, Inc.

Distributed by CDG Books Canada, Inc., for Canada; by Transworld Publishers Limited in the United Kingdom; by IDG Norge Books for Norway; by IDG Sweden Books for Sweden; by IDG Books Australia Publishing Corporation Pty. Ltd. for Australia and New Zealand; by TransQuest Publishers Pty. Ltd. for Singapore, Malaysia, Thailand, Indonesia, and Hong Kong; by Gotop Information, Inc., for Taiwan; by ICG Muse, Inc., for Japan; by Intersoft for South Africa; by Eyrolles for France; by International Thomson Publishing for Germany, Austria, and Switzerland; by Distribuidora Cuspide for Argentina; by LR International for Brazil; by Galileo Libros for Chile; by Ediciones ZETA S.C.R. Ltda. for Peru; by WS Computer Publishing Corporation, Inc., for the Philippines; by Contemporanea de Ediciones for Venezuela; by Express Computer Distributors for the Caribbean and West Indies; by Micronesia Media Distributor, Inc., for Micronesia; by Chips Computadoras S.A. de C.V. for Mexico; by Editorial Norma de Panama S.A. for Panama; by American Bookshops for Finland.

For general information on IDG Books Worldwide's books in the U.S., please call our Consumer Customer Service department at 800-762-2974. For reseller information, including discounts and premium sales, please call our Reseller Customer Service department at 800-434-3422.

For information on where to purchase IDG Books Worldwide's books outside the U.S., please contact our International Sales department at 317-596-5530 or fax 317-572-4002.

For consumer information on foreign language translations, please contact our Customer Service department at 800-434-3422, fax 317-572-4002, or e-mail rights@idgbooks.com.

For information on licensing foreign or domestic rights, please phone +1-650-653-7098.

For sales inquiries and special prices for bulk quantities, please contact our Order Services department at 800-434-3422 or write to the address above.

For information on using IDG Books Worldwide's books in the classroom or for ordering examination copies, please contact our Educational Sales department at 800-434-2086 or fax 317-572-4005.

For press review copies, author interviews, or other publicity information, please contact our Public Relations department at 650-653-7000 or fax 650-653-7500.

For authorization to photocopy items for corporate, personal, or educational use, please contact Copyright Clearance Center, 222 Rosewood Drive, Danvers, MA 01923, or fax 978-750-4470.

Library of Congress Cataloging-in-Publication Data
Hocutt, Robert J., 1961–
    The official Informix/Red Brick data warehouse bible / Robert J. Hocutt.
        p.   cm.
    ISBN 0-7645-4694-5 (alk. paper)
    1. Data warehousing. I. Title.
    QA76.9.D37 H63   2000
    248.4'7--dc21   00-057548

ABOUT IDG BOOKS WORLDWIDE

Welcome to the world of IDG Books Worldwide.

IDG Books Worldwide, Inc., is a subsidiary of International Data Group, the world's largest publisher of computer-related information and the leading global provider of information services on information technology. IDG was founded more than 30 years ago by Patrick J. McGovern and now employs more than 9,000 people worldwide. IDG publishes more than 290 computer publications in over 75 countries. More than 90 million people read one or more IDG publications each month.

Launched in 1990, IDG Books Worldwide is today the #1 publisher of best-selling computer books in the United States. We are proud to have received eight awards from the Computer Press Association in recognition of editorial excellence and three from Computer Currents' First Annual Readers' Choice Awards. Our best-selling ...For Dummies® series has more than 50 million copies in print with translations in 31 languages. IDG Books Worldwide, through a joint venture with IDG's Hi-Tech Beijing, became the first U.S. publisher to publish a computer book in the People's Republic of China. In record time, IDG Books Worldwide has become the first choice for millions of readers around the world who want to learn how to better manage their businesses.

Our mission is simple: Every one of our books is designed to bring extra value and skill-building instructions to the reader. Our books are written by experts who understand and care about our readers. The knowledge base of our editorial staff comes from years of experience in publishing, education, and journalism — experience we use to produce books to carry us into the new millennium. In short, we care about books, so we attract the best people. We devote special attention to details such as audience, interior design, use of icons, and illustrations. And because we use an efficient process of authoring, editing, and desktop publishing our books electronically, we can spend more time ensuring superior content and less time on the technicalities of making books.

You can count on our commitment to deliver high-quality books at competitive prices on topics you want to read about. At IDG Books Worldwide, we continue in the IDG tradition of delivering quality for more than 30 years. You'll find no better book on a subject than one from IDG Books Worldwide.

John J. Kilcullen
John Kilcullen
Chairman and CEO
IDG Books Worldwide, Inc.

VIII
WINNER

Eighth Annual
Computer Press
Awards ≥1992

IX
WINNER

Ninth Annual
Computer Press
Awards ≥1993

X
WINNER

Tenth Annual
Computer Press
Awards ≥1994

XI
WINNER

Eleventh Annual
Computer Press
Awards ≥1995

Credits

ACQUISITIONS EDITOR
Debra Williams Cauley

PROJECT EDITORS
Barbra Guerra
Terri Varveris

COPY EDITORS
Chrisa Hotchkiss
Robert Campbell

PROJECT COORDINATORS
Danette Nurse
Joe Shines

GRAPHICS AND PRODUCTION SPECIALISTS
Robert Bilhmayer
Jude Levinson
Michael Lewis
Victor Pérez-Varela
Ramses Ramirez

QUALITY CONTROL TECHNICIAN
Dina F Quan

MEDIA DEVELOPMENT SPECIALIST
Travis Silvers

MEDIA DEVELOPMENT COORDINATOR
Marisa Pearman

PERMISSIONS EDITOR
Carmen Krikorian

BOOK DESIGNER
Jim Donohue

ILLUSTRATORS
Karl Brandt
Clint Lahnen
Gabriele McCann

PROOFREADING AND INDEXING
York Production Services

COVER ILLUSTRATION
© Noma/Images.com

About the Author

Robert J. Hocutt has focused his consulting expertise on large-scale decision support systems since 1990. He began working with Red Brick Decision Server products in 1993 while in charge of data warehousing for a convenience store chain with 450 stores. He was subsequently employed at Red Brick Systems, using his knowledge and experience to ensure successful customer implementations.

Mr. Hocutt has designed, implemented, or tuned over 100 data warehouse implementations in key industries such as retail, package goods, finance, insurance, telecommunications, and healthcare, to name a few. This level of customer involvement makes him intimately familiar with gathering complex business requirements; analyzing, designing, and managing applications; resolving complicated data-modeling issues; and overcoming the challenges of very large data warehouse implementations. In addition to these tasks frequently seen at implementation, Mr. Hocutt's involvement with customers has included the longer-term tasks of project management, training, performance tuning, problem solving, and troubleshooting.

While at Red Brick Systems, Mr. Hocutt's expertise made him a much sought after resource. For the development organization, Mr. Hocutt would translate a customer's challenges into new product enhancement descriptions. He was responsible for the programs and internal training components implemented by the Red Brick Professional Services Organization. These included an internal benchmark class, a Data Warehouse Implementation Methodology, and new hire training. Mr. Hocutt was also a very popular speaker at several Red Brick Builder Forums, Red Brick's annual user conference.

Mr. Hocutt continues to consult on all aspects of large-scale decision support systems. His depth of knowledge of the Red Brick Decision Server products and practical experience in all aspects of planning, designing, project management/oversight, implementation, and deployment of data warehouses make him uniquely qualified to author this publication.

To Grandpa

Foreword

Too often, technology gets ahead of the marketplace, and companies spend an inordinate amount of money to try and convince people that they really need the "next new thing" that is the "latest innovation." That hasn't been the case in the data warehousing market, where customers were looking for fast loads and even faster queries long before database technology supported those demands.

The traditional relational databases had focused on transaction processing, which required fast record inserts/updates and rollback/commit data integrity. But that meant that these traditional relational databases were very slow at retrieving data, used lots of resources for querying, often conflicting with resources needed for transaction processing, were complex to administer, and, in general, didn't serve two masters (OLTP and data warehousing) very well. The need to analyze data quickly, along with huge increases in the volumes of data available for analysis, drove an entire new industry: relational databases built specifically for decision support and business intelligence.

When I went to work for a consumer product company after I got my Master's in Management at MIT in the late 1970s, I found out that most of the quantitative analysis I had learned in school could not reasonably be done in real life. Companies just weren't keeping the information needed to do this analysis. Information was available for a point in time but very little history was kept (i.e., no trended information), and what was available could be accessed only from stacks of paper reports that came out periodically. While doing a post-execution analysis of an $8 million promotion, it took four months after the promotion was over before I had enough information to determine that we had generated incremental volume, but on unprofitable package sizes. It cost us $8 million to run the promotion and we lost $4 million in profit, resulting in a total loss of $12 million to the bottom line. Marketing was well on its way to planning and executing a similar promotion when this analysis pulled the plug. At that point, 95 percent of my time was spent locating and retrieving information, while only 5 percent was spent on the actual analysis. But the good news was that this type of analysis made management aware of the value of maintaining historical information, so transaction systems were now asked to maintain archival information.

The second major change was the advent of scanner data in the package goods industry in the early 1980's. Up to this point, companies like AC Nielsen and IRI provided competitive sales information in various product categories; in this industry, careers are made and lost on tenths of a market share point. One category might have 800 brands reported for 40 markets aggregated over a two-month time frame. With scanners, products were reported down to the UPC level representing 15,000 items for 40 markets, but available within some of those markets at the chain level, in weekly and monthly aggregates. Instead of managing almost 200,000 records per year, the number increased 1000-fold to almost 200 million records a year. This explosion of data challenged the loading, storage, and retrieval abilities of existing database systems, and business analysts started looking for new ways to work.

Over 250 companies discovered the Metaphor data storage, retrieval, and visualization system (now known as IBM's IDS [intelligent decision system] package). The analysts at these companies designed their databases to represent the way they thought about their businesses. They built dimension tables that described the dimensions and granularity of their business, like time period, products, markets, and they composed fact tables that contained quantitative information, like sales units, sales dollars, and price. This dimensional model made user access to the data much easier than the classical relational modeling espoused by Codd and Date (i.e., third or fifth normal form) because the data was stored the way the user thought about the business. The business benefit was that users could easily query the database themselves and get the right answer. As part of the Metaphor user community, we came to see many similarities in how different companies dimensionalized their business. These dimensionalized database designs would come to be known as star schemas in later years.

After designing and implementing a Metaphor system at my employer, I became a consultant working for Ralph Kimball, who invented the Metaphor capsule. Working with clients to design decision support applications and tune databases for query retrieval, we saw many database designs across different industries that either were best suited to or had already implemented a dimensional, or star, design. The problem was that people still had to use traditional database technology with its poor query performance. Why did the database have to read 15,000 pages, with each page containing multiple records, when it only needed information from 1500 records? The time required to process simple queries seemed excessive, and systems bogged down when too many queries were submitted. We would discuss lunch queries, meeting queries, overnight queries, weekend queries, and the queries from hell that we could never seem to get to return. We knew there was a lot of data locked into the databases – some very important – that we couldn't even get to.

Kimball realized that the existing relational engines were resolving the queries by executing pairwise joins and creating temporary tables with interim results until the query could be fully resolved. Kimball began to consider the benefits of an optimizer technique that resolved the dimensions first, then made just one pass of the fact table, eliminating temporary tables for query resolution in the bargain. Since the dimension tables were relatively much smaller than the fact tables, resolving them first and then going to the fact table would result in significantly fewer records read for query retrieval. This concept was the foundation of the Red Brick database engine.

As the small group of consultants and engineers designed and built the database engine, we remembered our own, often painful, experiences with other databases. Many of us had managed our own databases with little or no IT support, so we wanted to make Red Brick easy to install and administer. We had also dealt with database loads that would go on for days and then required indexing before the data was available for querying. I remember doing monthly loads of 26 syndicated data tapes; 36 hours and 19 tapes into the load, it failed and I had to start the load again from the beginning. At a time when companies were just beginning to understand that fast access to information and action could lead to competitive advantage, this kind of delay was stressful, expensive, and potentially career limiting.

Red Brick's loader was designed to make the process of loading, creating indexes, and checking referential integrity as efficient as possible. And our frustration with writing applications in SQL led Red Brick to create language extensions to easily do year-to-year comparisons (now supported in SQL through correlated subqueries) and the ability to rank responses (top 10), among others. These Red Brick extensions predated the new SQL OLAP extensions by more than half a decade, leading the way for business analysis long before other databases had even seen the need for such specialization.

Once Red Brick began to develop a customer base, those customers were vocal in both their appreciation of the database and in their requests for new features. Our first health care customer helped us expand the concepts of dimensionality and schema complexity. Large retailers and Internet-based customers helped to expand our ideas about how large dimension tables, particularly customer tables, could become. One customer, whose business was providing information to other businesses, gave us a new appreciation of how much data had to be loaded nightly and how small and fragile the load window could be. If they had any significant problems in loading the data, they could miss their contractual data availability obligations to their customers. Their experience caused us to reexamine use of memory, disk, caching, and multitasking during the loading process.

With the advent of data warehouses and database engines like Red Brick Decision Server, which provide fast and easy access to the information in those data warehouses, analysts can now spend the vast majority of their time analyzing the data, finding problems, and identifying solutions that will favorably impact their businesses. They are no longer bogged down in a tedious and time-consuming process of locating and retrieving data.

For Red Brick, necessity has always been the mother of invention. It began when the other relational database vendors didn't have a concept of data warehousing, or when they believed it was just a niche application, and it has evolved based on customer needs and changes in the way businesses work. You are holding the latest in a long line of customer-focused Red Brick productions: *The Official Guide to Informix/Red Brick Data Warehousing*, which will help you get the most value from the only database designed specifically for data warehousing.

Mona Pinette
Red Brick Systems Employee #4
September 1, 1988–December 31, 1998

Preface

Welcome to Red Brick! Those were the words that started what has turned out to be the *best* professional experience of my career. What began as concepts and ideas eventually became a top-shelf technology. However, it didn't stop there; it became a way of doing business, a way of interfacing with customers – in short, it was the Red Brick way.

Part of our Red Brick "way," if you will, was how we trained our field people to implement our technology. Even so, technology is only part of the solution. It takes people to make it work, and that was perhaps the most valuable asset Red Brick ever had. Because Red Brick started out as a consulting company, we understood the consulting paradigm and brought those lessons, values, and skill sets to our technology.

Those lessons continue today through this volume on Red Brick Decision Server technology. This book is designed to provide a level of knowledge sufficient to make you successful in a very practical way at not only the technology, but also some of the "soft skills" required to implement a data warehouse. Much of the material is the result of the combined field experience of my Red Brick (now Informix) colleagues and me in implementing Red Brick data warehouses. I have also thrown in a good dose of general consulting know-how for good measure.

Over the years, I have been intimately involved with scores of Red Brick data warehouse projects. From business analysis and logical modeling to implementation and performance tuning, I've applied Red Brick technology in a wide variety of situations and vertical applications. And in all that time, I've noticed a recurring theme: there are often several "correct" answers to many of the implementation questions you will face in Red Brick.

Accepting this from the outset will go a long way towards your success. If you let yourself get sidetracked over trying to find the "perfect" answer, you may not complete the project. At some point, after you've done due diligence, you may just have to adopt one of the solutions being considered and move on. Don't let that disturb you.

Will you get everything "right"? Perhaps not, but by applying the information presented here, you should be directionally correct at the very least. Could some components be done differently or better? Possibly, but that comes only with experience, which is something you don't get until just after you need it. The key thing is to take it one step at a time. Everyone has to start somewhere, so welcome aboard!

Intended Audience

The primary audience for this book is those of you who have or who are going to implement a Red Brick Decision Server warehouse. It doesn't matter if you are a project manager, project sponsor, DBA, or other team member – if you are involved in an implementation of a Red Brick data warehouse, you should read this book. Those of you who already have a Red Brick warehouse installation should find much of the information on segmentation, indexing, and Vista to be particularly useful.

This is also a book for consultants. Each of you has customers that you must support, be they internal or external to your organization. Consultants tend to have more customers than those of you who are the "customer"; however, everyone can benefit from the lessons and illustrations. As you will learn, there is a very close relationship between the technology of building a Red Brick warehouse and the process of gathering the necessary information.

The material here is designed in a tutorial fashion to walk you through the process of implementing a Red Brick Decision Server data warehouse using many of the same methods to instruct the Red Brick field resources many of you have come to know so well. As such, many of you will recognize the chapters on modeling and segmentation.

Assumptions About You

As with any technology book, it's necessary to discuss the assumptions made in writing it. Before I list them, however, I want to say a word about implementation frequency. As you read, please keep in mind that there are several types of readers. Some of you will implement a large number of warehouses in many different situations. You are most likely the consultants in the group.

Some of you will implement a half dozen or so, and still others will implement only one or two, at the most. I've tried to strike a balance in the level of information presented so that each of you will find it useful, but not at the expense of the others. It's an impossible task, but I felt compelled to give it a try anyway!

In writing this book, I've made the following assumptions:

◆ Access to Red Brick installation – You have access to a Red Brick environment where you have the ability to create/drop database objects and "play around." The best way to learn how Red Brick Decision Server works is to use it. I strongly suggest a development area separate from any production systems – no sense becoming famous yet; wait until you've built something they *want*, not crash something they *need*.

◆ Working knowledge of SQL databases – A large part of Red Brick Decision Server is based on SQL. It is beyond the scope of this book to teach you SQL and its concepts; however, I will discuss those SQL extensions that are Red Brick-specific. You should have a working knowledge of SQL in general. There are many good books available on ANSI standard SQL. You should probably have one anyway.

◆ Not a replacement for Red Brick documentation – The Red Brick documentation is a super resource. It's one of the best documentation sets I've worked with (when the pages don't fall out!). I will not spend much time rehashing the documentation. If that were all this entire book contained, there would be little value in it for you. If you read nothing else, read the *Warehouse Administrator's Guide* for your chosen platform (UNIX or NT) and the *SQL Reference Guide*. If you are feeling particularly studious, the *RISQL Self Study Guide* is a good resource to work through.

◆ Have read Warehouse Administrator online help – I'm also assuming that you are familiar with the Red Brick's GUI Administrator tool. Unfortunately, there is no printed documentation for the Administrator tool; however, it's a fairly easy application to pick up. Throughout the book, you will find a number of screens that show the Administrator performing a specific function. Everything you might need to do to maintain and administrate your Red Brick environment can be done both from the command line and from the Administrator.

What You'll Learn

The goal of this book is to teach you what you need to know to identify, design, and build a Red Brick Decision Server data warehouse. In addition to learning the basics of Red Brick Decision Server technology, you will also learn fundamental "soft skills" required to gather the necessary requirements from the business users. You should read the chapters in order, as each builds on the previous one. The following list is just a few of the things you will learn:

◆ How Red Brick technology components work together

◆ Red Brick project fundamentals and how to get started

◆ How to identify a first data warehouse effort

◆ How to collect user requirements

◆ How to properly develop the logical and physical data models

◆ How to implement the model in Red Brick

◆ All about Red Brick indexing technology

◆ How to employ Red Brick Vista technology

◆ How to maintain a data warehouse

Throughout the book, I'll discuss a sample database. On the CD, you will find everything necessary to create, load, and query the sample database in your existing Red Brick environment, including instructions on how to make it bigger by loading more data. This includes the DDL scripts, the TMU scripts, the base data, and a set of Perl scripts you can use to generate more data.

Book's Organization

The book is laid out in four major sections to roughly mirror the flow of a typical data warehouse project. This should help you identify major work segments and provide some context to the material presented.

Section I – Getting Started

This section contains Chapters 1, 2, and 3 and discusses selecting Red Brick as a technology, project fundamentals, and what to look for in a project. It concludes with an in-depth discussion on gathering requirements.

Section II – Modeling

Once you have the requirements, you must render a logical model that represents the business and how it works. Chapter 4 provides the details about the logical modeling process and walks you through the components of a dimensional model and how best to create one from the requirements you've gathered. Chapter 5 talks about turning the logical model into a physical instance that you can then load and query.

Section III – Planning and Implementation

This section includes Chapters 6 through 9 and covers everything you need to know to define the proper indexes, evaluate appropriate aggregate tables by implementing Vista, size the database, and implement a segmentation plan. There is a lot of information here, so don't rush through it. You may find it helpful to refer to the Red Brick documentation set from this section forward.

Section IV – Building and Maintaining the Data Warehouse

This section covers Chapters 10 to 14. Here is where you install the Red Brick products (if you haven't already) and actually build the warehouse. You'll also learn all about parallel queries, how to load the database, and finally, how to maintain a Red Brick data warehouse once it's populated.

In addition, most chapters have two special sections: "Lessons from the Trenches" and "Sample Database." The "Lessons from the Trenches" section is designed to give you the benefit of all the field experience Red Brick has accumulated over the years – from the sales engineers, technical support, and consulting folks alike. Many of the lessons might seem simplistic, but don't be fooled. Frequently, it's the little things that trip you up.

The "Sample Database" section included in most chapters is designed to discuss the sample database in light of the subject of the chapter. For example, in Chapter 9, "Segmentation," you'll read about the segmentation plan for the sample database in this section.

Feedback

This book is the end result of the efforts of numerous people. We have tried our best to be as accurate as possible; however, it's possible we might have missed something. If so, please accept our apologies and let us know. As a first-time author, I am very interested in feedback – positive and negative. I believe that there is always something to learn from others; so I encourage you to submit comments and questions.

You can provide feedback to the publisher and myself by registering this book at `http://my2cents.idgbooks.com` Web Site. (Details are listed on the my2cents page in the back of this book.)

You can also contact me directly. I can't guarantee an immediate reply, but I'll do my best. I only ask that you be professional and constructive in your comments. My e-mail address is the following:

`rjhocutt@penn.com`

Many years ago, I was introduced to this "thing" called a Red Brick. "What's a red brick?" I asked. It's a question whose answer brought all sorts of challenges and opportunities and has provided me with the most excellent professional experience of my career. My association with Red Brick (now Red Brick Decision Server) and the people who have made it possible continues with this volume on Red Brick fundamentals. I sincerely hope that you too will find Red Brick Decision Server to be as exciting and rewarding a technology as I have.

Good luck!

Bob Hocutt

Acknowledgments

I would like to thank my wife Rhonda and my son Buddy for all the support, encouragement, and sacrificed family time throughout this project. Much of what I am today is a direct result of the love and commitment we share for each other. I love you both very much.

I'd also like to thank Mona Pinette for the many years of mentoring, encouragement, advice, and – above all – friendship. You introduced me to Red Brick and changed my career direction forever, and I'm thankful for it. More than that, you taught me how to mentor others and to see the big picture – skills I hope to pass on to others.

To Sandy Tucker, Joe Kaminski, Bill Gates, and Liz Benevidas – all from Informix: Thank you for all your hard work, encouragement, ideas, expectation management, and most of all humor. Do you think we'll be allowed back into the ice cream place? You folks are truly great at what you do. A special thanks goes to Sandy Tucker for getting me involved in this project and for helping with other resource issues.

To Bob Rumsby, who graciously provided the bulk of the material for Chapters 6 and 7: I had no idea how large a project this was and I'm glad you were able to help. To Mojo Nichols, who can do amazing things with code: Thank you for the Perl scripts and all the work that went into them.

To Annie Wynn: Thanks for supporting the project every way you could – good luck!

To John Masarik, Crystal Wong, Tim Collins, John Muller, Steve Wysham, Paul Rosenthal, Elizabeth Duke, Laura Sensabaugh, and Richard Wyckoff, all from Informix: Thanks for all the help in testing the ddl, scripts, and loading the data. Your help was invaluable. To my brother Ross Hocutt: Thanks for providing video of past training sessions, other printed material, and the joke-of-the-day (where do you get those?).

To all those at Informix who have contributed to this effort, especially the developers Fred Ho, Rick Cole, Latha Colby, and Qi Jin: Thanks for all your help and support in keeping the material technically accurate.

And finally, a big thank you to all of the great folks at IDG Books: Debra Williams Cauley, Barb Guerra, Terri Varveris, and Chrisa Hotchkiss. You've all been tremendous to work with. Thank you for improving my spelling, grammar, and overall writing ability, and thanks for teaching me more about Microsoft Word than one person has a right to know.

Contents at a Glance

Contents

Part I

Getting Started

Chapter 1

Why Red Brick Decision Server?

IN THIS CHAPTER

- ◆ Data mart or data warehouse?
- ◆ Overview of Red Brick Decision Server technology
- ◆ How to get started

THIS CHAPTER INTRODUCES Red Brick Decision Server technology components and some of the broad concepts of data warehousing. Much has been written on implementing data warehouses and data marts, but there has not, until now, been anything to help you implement a data warehouse in Red Brick Decision Server.

First, you must determine which to build first – a data mart or a data warehouse. It's a question that is often mired in politics and marketing, but it is really a fairly fundamental question to answer. This question is often the subject of debate; this chapter presents a line of thinking to help you address the issue is a realistic and practical way.

Next, there is an overview of Red Brick Decision Server technology components to provide a baseline for the rest of the material, followed by a discussion on how to start looking for a potential project. This includes a brief discussion of business pain, sponsorship, and other elements necessary to make you successful.

The chapter concludes with "Lessons from the Trenches," where the most critical issues raised in this chapter will be addressed again. As in all the chapters, the material in these lessons has been collected from the actual field experiences of my colleagues and I, with hundreds of data warehouse implementations and several hundred years of consulting experience. I hope you will find it useful as you embark on your own data warehouse project. Good luck!

Data Mart or Data Warehouse — Which Do I Build?

The future belongs to those who can first identify and then exploit business opportunities, and data warehouse technology is the key to doing both. This Decision Support System (DSS) technology provides essential information for understanding and managing the future. As a result, corporations become more adaptable to rapidly changing market conditions, and in today's business environment (characterized by short product cycles and volatile markets), that can mean the difference between success and failure or success and *more* success.

There are as many definitions of data warehousing as there are "experts," so it's important to understand that this book is intended to support the implementation of data warehouses/data marts for decision support. Decision support, or online analytical processing (OLAP), is a concept that provides multidimensional analysis of business information. This multidimensional concept is a method of organizing data in terms of business rules, not data rules. Before I go any further, I should define the terms *data warehouse* and *data mart,* as there is often confusion on the definitions.

◆ A data mart is a subject-specific database and is usually built by whomever "owns" or is responsible for the data. Data marts are dimensional in nature, are loaded infrequently but on a fixed schedule, and are extremely queryable.

◆ A data warehouse is a company-wide data store that crosses business units. The data warehouse can be a collection of your data marts, or, in an enterprise situation, a completely separate and distinct object that houses all the data from across the company and serves as a capacity data source for subject-oriented data marts. It's just about that simple.

Notice I made no distinctions as to size and capability between a data mart and a data warehouse. That's because in reality, there aren't any. In the final analysis, it doesn't matter *what* you call it, as long as it works and solves your users' business problems. In my experience, size makes no difference relative to what you call it. One of the most impressive and complex data warehouses I've ever seen was a mere 10 gigabytes in size. I'm also aware of data marts approaching 4 terabytes of real data. To characterize warehouses or marts based on size is just plain inappropriate.

The answer to the question of which to build is academic: start with a subject-specific, single-source data mart. This approach has a number of advantages. First, if this is your first foray into data warehousing land, you have enough to learn without making your project any harder on yourself than necessary. Second, you probably have limited time and money to spend on the project, so start with something that will show value quickly.

I must also say a word about *stovepipe* data marts. These are data marts that are built in a vacuum of sorts—each data mart is unaware of the other(s), or, more accurately, the project teams are unaware of each other and critical decisions are not made in a unified manner.

This idea has been a very effective sales tool to dissuade many folks from starting in the right place. Eventually, they either give up or see their mistake and do it right the next time around. The only way you will end up with stovepipe data marts is if you build them that way. It is the project team and project sponsor's responsibility to be aware of what others are doing and work accordingly.

It's All About the Users

The confusion over the terms data warehouse and data mart is (in my opinion) largely the result of marketing efforts of different entities competing for market share. These characterizations, more often than not, are less reflective of actual practice and are more geared towards technology differentiation. This is not bad, but after a while, the marketing messages tend to loose sight of the real problem.

People have a tendency to assume that anything that confuses them or that they know nothing about is inherently bad—so it is with the whole question of warehouse/mart. Lot's of software has been sold based on nothing more than fear. Building a data warehouse or data mart is not about technology for technology's sake; rather, it's about the users.

Don't lose sight of the fact that data warehousing started with and should still be focused on the users and their ability to answer common business questions in a timely fashion. In the final analysis, the users don't care about which technology you use, how it was designed, or any other technical issue—all they want to know is when can they get it, understand it, and use it easily.

Data warehousing as a market segment started when the existing technologies of the day were applied to general business reporting problems and found to be lacking. You really have two choices: you can stand on the soapbox and argue data warehouse versus data mart until you are blue in the face, or you can do something really useful and implement a solution for your users' business problems. The reality is, it doesn't matter what you call it, as long as it works.

Overview of Red Brick Decision Server Technology Components

Informix Red Brick Decision Server is a relational database management system (RDBMS) that is designed for data mart, data warehouse, and OLAP (On-Line Application Processing) applications. Many of the technology components in Red Brick Decision Server existed nowhere else for a number of years, and although the merchant databases have caught up, there are still a few things that exist only in Red Brick Decision Server.

Many of the people responsible for the technology components were leaders in their fields with other databases such as Teradata, Oracle, and DB2 Parallel Edition. They are responsible for the leading-edge technology that is Red Brick Decision Server today. What follows is a brief discussion of the major technology components found in Red Brick Decision Server to give you a basic understanding of how it all works together. (I provide more detailed information in later chapters.)

STARjoins and indexes

A dimensional model contains fact tables (which hold the quantitative data about a business – the facts being queried) and dimension tables (which hold data that describe the dimensional attributes). A dimension table is connected to a fact table by means of a foreign key reference, as illustrated in Figure 1-1.

Figure 1-1 illustrates the relationships between fact and dimension tables and the foreign keys that connect them. These tables are from the sample database. The Billing_CDR table is a fact table; the rest are dimension tables.

As you most likely know, all databases join tables in pairs in what's known as a *pairwise join*. Red Brick recognized that they could improve relational databases by building an index that would improve performance: hence, the close relationship between the STARindex and its STARjoin algorithm. The STARjoin technology allows multiple relational tables to be joined in a fast, single pass operation to yield extremely fast query times.

Dimensional Models

There has been a lot of confusion and misinformation recently about exactly what a STAR schema is, what it's good for, and what it contains. STAR schema is a term Ralph Kimball coined to illustrate the concept of how the dimension tables surrounded the large fact tables and formed a star-type of pattern. (See Figure 1-1.) The terms *dimensional model* and *STAR schema* are used interchangeably throughout this book to convey the following notion: a STAR schema is a dimensional model and, as such, has no limitations on the number or type of tables that compose it. It can be used to accurately model any business process over which you wish to build a data warehouse.

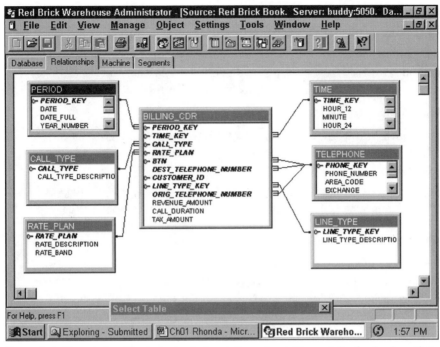

Figure 1-1: The relationships between fact and dimension tables and the foreign keys that connect them

Pairwise Joins

Pairwisejoin is the name given to the way the merchant databases join tables — and it means two at a time. If you have been associated with Red Brick for any length of time, you may have heard this referred to as The Pain of the Pairwise Join problem, and it is a multipass solution in that there are multiple passes to join the tables. This problem falls out of the technology limitations the merchant databases had (and in some cases still have) when data warehousing was young. This method of joining tables is the major reason that truly dimensional models do not perform as well in various merchant databases as they do in Red Brick Decision Server.

The idea behind the Pairwise Join problem is that the technology is not data-warehouse aware and goes about answering warehouse queries the way it goes about answering On Line Transaction Processing types of queries: two tables at a time.

Let's assume you have a Sales fact table with 500 million rows, a Period dimension table with 1,200 rows, and a Customer dimension table with 8,000 rows. Let's say you want to see the sales revenue for last quarter for all your customers in Pennsylvania.

Continued

Pairwise Joins *(Continued)*

The merchant database servers might solve the query by picking two tables (at random?), generating a temporary result set, getting the next table, generating another temporary result set, and so on, until all the necessary tables have been joined.

In actual practice, it might look like this:

Start with Sales and Period. It just joined a 1,200-row table with a 500 –million-row table and came up with 100 million rows, which are overflowing to disk and using up tons of memory.

Next, it takes that temporary result set and joins it to Customer. It just took the 100-million-row table and joined it to an 8,000-row table and maybe came up with 50,000 rows in the result set. As you can see, the process has excessive I/O and heavy CPU use — generally a bad idea.

The merchant databases have gotten smarter over time and built various optimizers that join the smaller tables and create a Cartesian product first before joining to the huge fact table. However, this is still pairwise join and tends to break down as the complexity (read number of tables) increases.

TARGETindex and TARGETjoin

TARGETindexes and TARGETjoins make up Red Brick Decision Server's bitmap index technology. *Bitmap index* (also known as *bit vectored index*) maintains information by tracking each unique column value in a compact bit representation, with a pointer (or vector) back to each row in the table with that specific value. Most (if not all) of the commodity database vendors have something like this type of index, but Red Brick Decision Server has taken the time to implement it as an integral part of the server, not an add-on piece of technology.

TARGETindexes exist on single columns that are weakly selective. A weakly selective constraint returns many rows from a table. For example, the GENDER column in a customer table would have two values: M/F. This weakly selective condition can also occur with higher domains as well, especially if there is a significant amount of *skew* (meaning the data is not evenly spread across the domain). Age would be a good example of this type of situation.

TARGETjoin is a join algorithm that uses target indexes to identify lists of candidate dimension rows; rows that exist on each list are then retrieved from the fact table. Target join will also be covered in more detail in Chapter 6. Figure 1-2 illustrates how TARGETindexes are used in Red Brick Decision Server.

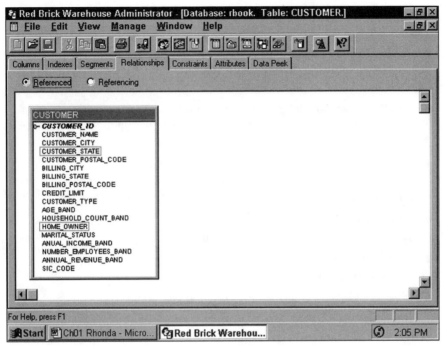

Figure 1–2: Target indexes used in Red Brick Decision Server

TARGETindexes are used to index columns with weakly selective constraints. A constraint on Home Owner, which has perhaps three values (Yes, No, Unknown), would be weakly selective and bring back large numbers of rows out of a 10–million–row table.

RISQL

One of the interesting outcomes of the data warehousing market is the idea of performing standard business analysis with standard Structured Query Language (SQL). As you probably know, SQL is the standard for accessing SQL databases and is based in relation set theory. However, this basis in set theory does not provide the necessary functionality to answer practical business problems such as ranking, moving averages, and running totals. You have no doubt run across or used extensions to the standard SQL language in other relational database engines, and Red Brick Decision Server is no exception. Red Brick extensions are designed to solve real business analysis problems that are frequently very difficult (if not impossible) to do using traditional database technology. Red Brick Decision Server Intelligent SQL (RISQL) extensions simplify the expression of common and frequently asked business functions and return values and sets of rows by performing sequential calculations. A list of the RISQL extensions follows. A more complete explanation can be found in the SQL Reference Guide (available at the Informix Web site).

- ◆ CUME: Calculates a running total by row for a set of values. It can be reset using the RESET BY component of the ORDER BY clause.

- ◆ MOVINGAVG: Calculates an average over an interval of *n* rows for a specific set of values. It can be reset using the RESET BY component of the ORDER BY clause.

- ◆ MOVINGSUM: Calculates a sum over an interval of *n* rows for a specific set of values. It can be reset using the RESET BY component of the ORDER BY clause.

- ◆ NTILE: Ranks the results into a range of tiers that you define. TERTILE places the results into three tiers (low, medium, and high), whereas NTILE can generate as many tiers as necessary. See NTILE and RANK.

- ◆ RANK: Determines rank (1–10, low to high, and so on) relative to the rest of the values. This is done hierarchically.

- ◆ RATIOTOREPORT: Calculates the ratio of a value in a relationship to the sum of a group of values.

- ◆ TERTILE: Determines a three-tiered rank (high, middle, low) relative to a group of values.

- ◆ RESET BY: Reinitializes the computed value of a RISQL display function to zero based on the columns referenced in the ORDER BY clause. RESET BY is a subclause of the ORDER BY clause.

RISQL REPORTER
RISQL reporter is a command-line interface that allows you to format the SQL output by adding totals, subtotals, and custom column headings. You can also format the width and spacing of the columns.

WEB-ANALYTIC STANDARDS
The "Spiderman" project that you may have read about in recent Informix press releases brings Web-analytic capabilities to Red Brick Decision Server to meet the challenging demands of Web and e-commerce applications. These standards provide a platform on which to build true one-to-one marketing, e-commerce, and CRM applications.

QUERY EXPRESSIONS
Red Brick Decision Server implements all the standard query expressions: SELECT, FROM, WHERE, GROUP BY, HAVING, and WHEN. You should be familiar with most of these; however, here's a word on the WHEN clause: WHEN places a condition on a result set after all the set functions have been performed, any HAVING clause has been evaluated, and all RISQL display functions have been applied. More information is available in the SQL Reference Guide.

SCALAR FUNCTIONS AND MACROS

The RISQL extensions also include a rich set of scalar functions that provide you with the ability to create compound expressions. Scalar functions operate on a single row at a time. They can be nested and take RISQL display functions as arguments. The scalar functions break down into the following groups:

- Conditional functions
  - CASE
  - COALESCE
  - DECODE
  - IFNULL
  - NULLIF
- Numeric scalar functions
  - ABS
  - CEIL
  - DEC
  - FLOAT
  - FLOOR
  - INT
  - SIGN
  - EXP
  - LN
  - SQRT
  - LENGTH
- String scalar functions
  - CONCAT
  - LOWER
  - LTRIM
  - RTRIM
  - STRING
  - SUBSTR

- TRIM
- UPPER
- ◆ Datetime scalar functions
  - CURRENT_DATE
  - CURRENT_TIME
  - CURRENT_TIMESTAMP
  - DATE
  - DATEADD
  - DATEDIFF
  - DATENAME
  - EXTRACT
  - TIME
  - TIMESTAMP
  - CURRENT_USER
- ◆ Macros for statistical functions
  - Power
  - Log
  - Log10
  - Variance
  - Standard deviation
  - Population variance
  - Population standard deviation

Referential integrity

While not a technology component, it's necessary to discuss the concept of *referential integrity* because it is so fundamental to Red Brick Decision Server's technology. Referential integrity (RI) is the process of checking each foreign key against the appropriate master table to validate the existence of that key. I cannot stress the importance of this validation enough.

Typically, RI checking is done as part of the load step. Often, this RI checking is what causes the merchant databases so much trouble and adds significantly to the overall load time. To get the data in, the RI will be frequently turned off. This forces you into a situation where you have to choose between load performance and clean data. If RI checking is turned off, in effect, you have compromised the quality of your data warehouse.

In Red Brick Decision Server, you do not have to choose. The RI check is built into the load process; it's very fast and guarantees that related rows are truly related. Perhaps the best way to illustrate the value of RI is with a real example.

A retailer requires updated inventory levels to be available every week for each store to determine product reorder quantities. A popular database took approximately two days to perform the load, during which time they lost just over 10 percent of the 110 million input rows because they had suspended the RI checks. Red Brick Decision Server was able to load the data in about six hours and accounted for every row: both the rows that were successfully loaded and the rows that failed either the RI or data validation checks.

 Occasionally, someone will suggest that because the RI was validated at the time the data was written to the transaction database, it is unnecessary to recheck it when the data is loaded into the warehouse. Don't believe it! While it's true that there *may* have been *some* type of RI check, the fact that the data has been realigned to conform to business rules instead of data rules almost automatically makes it suspect. In this case, it's guilty until proven innocent.

Table Management Utility

All the data you will store in your data warehouse exists in external systems. This might be patient visit records, call-switch data, retail data, or purchased data of one type or another. Collecting and preparing all this data for loading into the warehouse is a primary step and places a number of requirements on the process:

1. You must be able to read from a variety of data sources including disk drives, networks, magnetic tapes, and mainframe connections.

2. You must be able to convert the data from numerous external formats into the internal database format. These external formats include but are not limited to EBCDIC data, packed and zoned decimal data, fixed and variable length rows, and so on.

3. You must be able to filter and reject invalid data, duplicate rows, or other corrupt data.

4. You must be able to write the data to physical storage within the configuration requirements for segmentation and physical disk placement.

The *Table Management Utility* – TMU – is used to load data and maintain tables, indexes, and the relational integrity of the database. It provides the necessary functionality to meet the preceding requirements, and although its primary task is the loading of data, it also provides the following functionality:

- Unloads data

- Rebuilds tables/indexes

- Generates DDL

- Upgrades the database

The most important point to remember is that the TMU is an application designed to address significant data-handling issues inherent in building a data warehouse. It's not an afterthought or something cobbled up and held together with marketing. It really works!

There are four basic steps to loading a Red Brick Decision Server database:

1. Convert data

2. Perform Referential Integrity (RI) check

3. Build/update the indexes

4. Write/update the data

In the data conversion step, Red Brick Decision Server converts the data types in the input file to the corresponding column data type. This includes validating ranges, dates, times, and so on. The next step is RI checking, which is critical to the success of any warehouse.

The indexes are then incrementally built followed by the update to the data. Several options are available that tell the loader how to handle duplicates and new rows. These options are referred to as load modes, and they are as follows:

- APPEND: Inserts new rows into an existing table. Any rows from the input stream that already exist in the table are discarded, as are rows with missing primary keys.

- INSERT: Loads data into an empty table. If the server knows the table is empty, it can then make some assumptions on how to build the indexes. Again, any rows that do not have the appropriate foreign key reference will be discarded.

- REPLACE: Destroys the content of the table and then proceeds to load a now-empty table. Use this mode carefully. You should expect to have problems at least once with this one. You've been warned!

- MODIFY: Inserts new rows or updates existing rows.

- UPDATE: Updates only existing rows. Any new rows are discarded.

A number of configuration parameters can increase the performance of these steps. Note that you have the option of saving all rows that are discarded for any reason. Once the problem has been corrected, these rows are then available for reloading. It's interesting to note that many Red Brick Decision Server customers have purchased Red Brick Decision Server purely because of the load performance.

AUTO ROW GENERATION

Everyone's data is dirty (it's one of those unchangeable laws of life — right up there with death and taxes), and very often in the early stages of building a warehouse, you will have trouble loading a complete set of data because there are so many missing dimension rows. Other database products will discard the offending rows (if they even bother to check RI at all). After the initial load, the offending rows must be examined, the appropriate dimension rows must be added, and the previously discarded rows must be reloaded. This is a time-consuming and often annoying process.

The Automatic Row Generation (autorowgen) feature of Red Brick Decision Server gives you the ability to automatically generate rows in the referenced (dimension) tables while the data is being loaded. With autorowgen, when a row is automatically inserted into a dimension table, the primary key is populated with the missing value, and the rest of the columns are populated with the default value defined for them. This functionality provides three distinct behaviors:

1. Generates missing dimension rows to maintain referential integrity

2. Replaces any values that violate RI with default values in the referenced tables

3. Provides a combination of these behaviors that can be used on a table-by-table basis

AUTO AGGREGATE

Data warehouses vary greatly in their use of aggregations or summary tables. Red Brick Decision Server has long maintained that you should build aggregates only if they are needed, and the Red Brick Decision Server Vista functionality has made this guessing game much easier for the DBA. The basis for the Auto Aggregate function is that all aggregates are built from detail data. Since the loader processes every detail row as it's loaded into the database, it can also build the aggregates at the same time, rather than later in the load cycle. Building aggregates in this way means that only the changes represented by the new data must be made; the entire aggregate table does not have to be rebuilt.

VERSIONING

Versioning is the Red Brick Decision Server facility that provides real-time update capabilities to a data warehouse by allowing data to flow into the warehouse without affecting query response times of the users. The versioning technique permits data modification transactions to occur on a separate version of the same data, while queries are in process. When the data is available for update, the versioned updates are then made the base data.

Warehouse Administrator

Red Brick Decision Server's Graphical User Interface administrator tool allows you to connect to any Red Brick Decision Server database via ODBC and perform most DBA tasks. Figure 1-1 shows the main screen of the tool and how you interface with it. The list of operations you can perform is quite complete and includes the following:

◆ Re-creating DDL

◆ Managing users, roles, and macros

◆ Administering tables and indexes (adding/dropping columns, etc.)

◆ Maintaining views, hierarchies, and synonyms

◆ Updating the settings that control VISTA, the aggregate technology in Red Brick Decision Server

◆ Performing Vista Advisor analysis

◆ Viewing the system tables

◆ Submitting SQL commands and queries via an interactive SQL window

However, you cannot do performance monitoring through the administrator, although I understand it's scheduled for a future release. You also can't monitor concurrency (the versioning functions) through the administrator.

Vista

Red Brick Decision Server Vista is the mechanism that manages precomputed aggregate data. With VISTA, the users always query the base (detail) tables. This is useful for two reasons:

◆ You don't have to educate the users about how/when to use aggregates — it's transparent.

◆ If the business changes, you can change the aggregates without retraining anyone at all.

When a user submits a query, a cost-based analysis determines whether the query can be intercepted and rewritten to use an existing aggregate table and thereby improve its performance. The server logs statistics about query execution that enable you to evaluate the current aggregation strategy. Red Brick Decision Server Vista consists of two components:

- The query rewrite system – This is referred to as Aggregate Navigator and is the component that intercepts and rewrites queries (when possible) to use aggregate tables.

- The Advisor – This is the logging and analysis component that collects information that you can query to help understand the costs and benefits of existing aggregates as well as aggregates you might want to consider building.

DST/ECC

Dynamic Statistic Tables (DSTs) exist only as long as the server is up and running. These tables allow you to monitor database activity, and they exist only in memory and are updated periodically; however, they do show up and act like any other table in Red Brick Decision Server. They can be queried and joined like anything else.

The DSTs are as follows:

- DST_COMMANDS: Contains cumulative information about each command sent to the server.

- DST_DATABASES: Holds information that relates to the overall activity of a database. Also contains the database locations.

- DST_LOCKS: Contains information about locks that each session is either holding or waiting for.

- DST_SESSIONS: Contains information on each session connected to the database and includes cumulative as well as session peak statistics.

- DST_USERS: Contains information about each user who has accessed the database since the server was started.

The Enterprise Control and Coordination component of Red Brick Decision Server provides the mechanisms that allow you to control the database, users, and passwords, all with a nice graphical interface of the administrator, or from the command line of the RISQL prompt.

Connectivity and security

Red Brick Decision Server provides two ways to connect to the server: either ODBC or JDBC. When Red Brick switched to ODBC as the standard connectivity, there were lots of discussions and worries about it being slow. Well, as most of you know, if you have used Red Brick Decision Server for any length of time, it's not slow and, in fact, performs rather nicely. Most recently, JDBC support has been added.

ODBC

ODBC is a standard database connectivity protocol, and is the mechanism that allows almost any client tool to connect to Red Brick Decision Server. In addition, all the Red Brick Decision Server client tools (RISQL and the Warehouse Administrator) use ODBC to communicate with the server – on all platforms, both UNIX and NT.

JDBC

Java database connectivity (JDBC) is a standard application programming interface specification that allows Java programs to access Red Brick Decision Server databases. These interface standards allow you to write applications in Java that can connect to a database, send QL queries, and process the results returned by the server. The Red Brick Decision Server JDBC API supports both two- and three-tier configurations to give you the maximum flexibility in your JAVA development efforts. For more information, please refer to the Red Brick Decision Server JDBC Connectivity guide.

What's new on Red Brick Decision Server

There has been a long list of innovative and value-adding enhancements made to the Red Brick Decision Server product since its inception, and that tradition continues with Informix. What follows is a chronological list of the major improvements made to the product, by version number, including a peek at what's new for versions 6.0 and 6.1.

- ◆ New in Version 5.1.4 and Version 5.1.5:
  - Query-priority concurrency
  - Parallel query processing on Windows NT platforms
- ◆ New in Version 5.1.6:
  - New byte-oriented string functions LENGTHB and SUBSTRB
  - Ability for Red Brick Vista to rewrite queries that use a CASE statement in the SUM function
  - New TMU ROUND function to convert floating-point inputs to decimal or integer values
  - Improved processing of very large IN lists (more than 10,000 entries)
  - Support for the AIX 4.3.2 64-bit operating system
  - Intersolv® DataDirect® Connect ODBC™ SDK available for UNIX-based ODBC client applications
- ◆ New in Version 5.1.7:
  - New CHECK TABLE and CHECK INDEX server commands
  - Support for the Solaris 7 64-bit operating system

- New in Version 6.0 – changes to aid Web-enabling:
  - JDBC Type 4 driver support
  - Query "frozen" view of data while loading
  - Space-efficient processing of Web data
  - High-speed export for query results
  - Parallel Loader now with versioning
  - Faster RI checking during loading
  - Version Log viewer utility
- New in Version 6.0.3:
  - Multiple PSUs for default segments
  - "Read" level locking
  - Windows 2000 support
- New in Version 6.10 – GA Q3 2000:
  - Automatic Update of aggregates
  - ODBC 3.0
  - JDBC 2.0
  - Parallel MODIFY
  - Better memory management for RI Checking
  - Query Re-write for SET operator
  - Random Sampling
  - Optimize Index Building for MODIFY and UPDATE

How to Get Started in Red Brick Decision Server

So how *do* you get started in Red Brick Decision Server, anyway? Identify a problem that must be solved, build the warehouse, be extremely successful, get a promotion and a raise, and then retire early to (your favorite place in all the world). Okay, so some of the details were left out in between all that, but briefly, that's what you need to do. Actually, this is the first of many places where you need to pay particular attention to the business problems being considered.

Single source or subject specific

The absolute best place to start is with a single-source data warehouse. This has been proven repeatedly by the success of Red Brick Decision Server customers. Starting with a single source avoids a number of normally complicated data issues right up front. These will have to be addressed at some point, but usually there is enough going on in a first project that it makes no sense to complicate things unnecessarily.

Actually, a more appropriate phrase might be "delay the complicated data issues." As it turns out, you can't ignore the multiple data source issue, or you'll end up with data islands.

 I realize that it may not always be possible to start with a single data source project — reality happens. However, what I am suggesting is that if you can identify a single data source project, you should defiantly take advantage of it, if for no other reason than to increase your chances of success, especially if it's your first Red Brick Decision Server warehouse.

The other characteristic you want to strive for if possible is a subject-specific project to start. *Subject specific* means just that — one subject, such as marketing, claims analysis, or sales. If this is your first warehouse implementation, a subject-specific project is by far the easiest. This is not a requirement of Red Brick Decision Server. It is an intentional simplification of a complicated process designed to increase your chances of success. Red Brick Decision Server is fully capable of handling the full range of data warehouse installations — from a subject-specific data mart to a full-blown enterprise data warehouse. Multiple related subjects are frequently taken on as an initial project with just as much success, although they require a little more planning.

 Starting with a subject-specific data mart is not a Red Brick Decision Server requirement. It is for your benefit because it allows you to show value earlier, control your resources and costs easier, and increase your chances for success. Once you complete your first data warehouse, larger projects can be taken on with confidence.

Notice I did not say single fact table. You may (unlikely, put possible nonetheless) end up with a business problem that requires only a single fact table, but don't count on it. Many people make the mistake of assuming that a one-to-one correspondence exists between subject areas and fact tables.

Let's look at a simple situation and walk through how you might approach it. Assume a retail company with four major processes: Shipments, Orders, Invoices, and Returns. Each process has customers, products, and so on. The company wants to build a data warehouse to analyze data from these four processes. How would you build it? There are several ways you can attack the problem.

- Build one at a time – This is the easiest. You would select one subject (perhaps Shipments) and build the data mart. You then select the next subject (Orders), build it, and so on. As a matter of reference, the second and following "marts" can (and perhaps should) reside in the same database as the first one.

- Build by related subjects – This is a tad more complicated in that there is more data to deal with (which is the largest unknown, by the way), and you have more upfront work to do to understand the business issues and problems. In this example, you might choose to combine Shipments and Orders into the first project. They are related and have common business dimensions so it would work well.

- Build all at one time – This is the most complicated because you now have to spend lots of time looking at the relationships between the four areas. There are four times as many interviews, business questions, and participants; it can easily get out of control if you've never done this before.

Notice that in each of these scenarios, a number of tasks must still be accomplished – the only difference is that you have the opportunity to spread them out over a longer period. Being able to spread them over a longer time frame can be a big advantage, especially in a distributed environment where the individuals required are physically separated by distance. Here's what needs to happen:

- You must understand the dimensions in light of all the organizations.

- You must evaluate and select the data sources.

- You must identify business issues.

- You must define the measures for success.

These tasks don't go away. They apply to every subject area in the warehouse. What's different is that by looking at the big picture but building a smaller component, you avoid a tremendous amount of pain and confusion.

Many have looked at this approach and labeled it *stovepipe*. That is a gross misunderstanding of the process involved. Data warehouses evolve because your business evolves. It has to, or you won't be in business for very long. So must the process by which you build warehouses. It's iterative by nature, so the day you turn the warehouse over to the users, it starts to evolve. You have a responsibility to be aware of larger issues and develop database objects with a cross-business definition, but this approach does not, by default, lead to a stovepipe warehouse.

> ### Single Source
>
> A single-source data warehouse is defined as having only one source for the data. This simplifies the amount of work required because many data issues associated with multiple source systems are avoided. However, you must exercise due diligence to investigate potential data sources to choose the best one for the project at hand, and to avoid the stovepipe situations discussed earlier.

TIP Think big but start small. Building a warehouse one component at a time is almost always more successful than building it all at once.

Appropriate sponsorship

This is another area where due diligence pays off. More projects fail because there is insufficient sponsorship, or sponsorship at too low a level. Data warehouse projects by nature cross department and group boundaries. Without appropriate sponsors high enough in the organization, there is little incentive for these folks to cooperate.

It's a good idea to get multiple sponsors for the project to give appropriate coverage and not make the project solely dependent on the ideas and efforts of just one sponsor.

TIP Multiple sponsors will make your success less dependent on the participation of a single individual.

Obviously, you want to look for those people with the authority to make decisions who are well respected within the organization, and who have a history with the company. This gives them the edge over newer managers who may not know the culture, politics, or history of the company.

Try to identify sponsors who have the following qualities. The success of your project is directly tied to your sponsors, so it's worth the effort to look for these people. Notice that I've been talking about multiple sponsors.

◆ Vision – Effective sponsors have a long-range vision of the business and are able to articulate it well. They are able to see the warehouse as part of the solution, although there may be short-term problems to be addressed in building it.

◆ Realistic approach – Vision and expectations are one aspect, but they must be tempered with a large dose of reality about the business, the resources available, the data sources, and the scope of the project. Projects with unrealistic goals generally fail and waste gobs of time and money in the process.

◆ Accountability – Building data warehouses often requires making tough decisions on which functionality, reports, or other components of the warehouse are built first, which resources are assigned to the project, as well as a host of internal political and organizational issues to be decided. These decisions are not always easy, and the sponsors who can make them and be accountable for the results are the best sponsors to have.

Identify business pain

The best data warehouse projects start with a significant amount of business pain. If there is no pain in the problem you want to solve, why bother? One way you might ascertain how much business pain a given problem represents is to consider the following profiles:

1. **The Business Growth Profile** – This is the desire to build a data warehouse solution to achieve a specific business objective. Typically, these projects are born out of expansion activities, new products, services, and so on. Typically, these are more fun than the others.

2. **The Business Dilemma Profile** – This is the need to correct a critical business process or address shortcomings in existing functionality. Frequently, these types of projects come out of acquisition or reorganization. In other instances, they might be the result of a process that can't scale any further and hits the (Red Brick Decision Server) wall. In any event, the key word here is *need*.

3. **The Status Quo Profile** – This starts to move onto dangerous ground. This is where the customer wants a data warehouse but doesn't really know why and can't explain what's driving the decision from the business side. Be wary of these situations because they fail frequently.

4. **The Brash Profile** – This is the most dangerous of the four. Overconfidence is the primary characteristic of this group of people. Generally, they have limited experience in data warehousing, they think they can do it themselves, and they are often "experts" on whatever is printed in the trade magazines this month.

Of these four profiles, successful data warehousing projects come out of the first two. The latter two usually end up costing a lot of money for little if any measurable results.

TIP Be wary of projects that cannot be justified by significant and definable business issues. Keeping the status quo and/or building a warehouse "just because" are not sufficient reasons to engage in the process.

Supporting data

The next item you need to zero in on is the existence of supporting data. You're primarily interested in identifying the source and its availability. The more detailed analysis of the data happens later in the process. To solve a business problem, you must have the relevant data to load and analyze. For example, if you are building a data warehouse to analyze the sales function of your business, you must have sales data.

The correct number and type of resources

Another often-overlooked step is the identification of appropriate numbers and types of resources. Frequently, you will read a shopping list of individuals who are required to deliver a data warehouse project. This is great if you have all sorts of individuals in your organization with the appropriate skill sets. Most of us, however, do not have scores of resources standing around with nothing to do.

Recognize that even with the correct sponsorship, the appropriate business pain, and a willingness on the part of the project team to "get it done," you can do nothing unless you have the correct resources. I'll discuss the roles necessary in the next chapter.

Measurable results

Finally, while you are looking at the potential projects, or evaluating the chosen project, you want to understand how the project will be measured. Very often, you will run across measures that are so subjective that they are useless. There are subjective elements in a warehouse solution; however, these cannot and should not be used to measure the success of the project.

An example might be "increased customer satisfaction." What exactly *is* that? It differs enormously from company to company. It's too subjective to be useful. However, if you look at it for a second, you can see how it might be reduced to more specific and measurable components. The bottom line here is being able to definitively identify success factors for the project. If you don't know what the definition of success is, how can you build it?

Lessons from the Trenches

There are as many ways to go about finding a data warehouse project as there are readers of this book. Experience has shown, however, that the most frequent mistakes are those of starting with too big a project, overestimating what can reasonably be accomplished in a given amount of time or resources, and not having the correct sponsorship. Knowing to avoid these scenarios is the key to your success.

Think big, start small

Starting with a project that is too big or too complex is the most fatal mistake you can make, especially for a first attempt. However, starting small without the larger picture can be equally as unsuccessful in the longer term. Take the time to understand the long-term goals of the company and ask yourself how the current project fits into that vision. If the answer is not clear, perhaps the long-term vision and direction are not clearly defined or understood.

Don't underestimate

This is another critical area when it comes to getting started. In many cases, estimates tend to be guesses. Estimates as to complexity, data availability, resources required, time lines, and expectations are sometimes based on incomplete knowledge. The good news is that once you've delivered a few data warehouses, this gets easier, but for the first-time person, it can be a daunting task.

Strive to be as accurate as possible. Often, the estimate is not as important as the assumptions made in providing it. Always try to back up your estimates with the assumptions on which they are based. This will dramatically illustrate to all involved the dependencies that exist and how a change in one assumption can affect the entire project.

Be sure of your sponsorship

The sponsorship of your project must be brought in to the idea of a warehouse. There is no substitute for having accountable, realistic, and willing sponsors for your project. Multiple sponsors for different areas of the organization provide an extra measure of security, bring a more balanced view to the project, and should be encouraged whenever possible.

Summary

The future does indeed belong to those who can see it first. Data warehousing technology, while once a novelty, has now become "night-vision goggles," so to speak. It allows you to "see" your information in ways that were not possible before.

Red Brick Decision Server brings a tremendous amount of innovation to its technology that enables you to build a warehouse that is functional, useable, and maintainable. You are no longer forced to choose between performance and data quality. The necessary tools to answer routine business questions are at your disposal. Finally, there is a technology available that understands the tough issues of large warehouse installations, parallel queries, and the concept of performance from the users' point of view.

Even with all this artillery in your arsenal, it's important to start with an appropriate-sized objective. You must understand the big picture, but start small enough to show value early and mitigate your risk of failure as much as possible.

Your project's success or failure is directly tied to the project leadership and sponsorship. Spending the necessary time to find the right kind of sponsors is key to a successful project. The cost of failure is often many times the cost of success. Make sure you can measure your success; if you can't, how do you know when you're done?

Chapter 2

Red Brick Decision Server Project Fundamentals

IN THIS CHAPTER

- ◆ A typical project
- ◆ Projects resources and roles
- ◆ Staffing from within
- ◆ Lessons from the trenches

DEVELOPING AND STAFFING a data warehouse project is the next step in the process of implementing a data warehouse. There are so many different ways to run a project that it can be somewhat confusing. In this chapter, I'll discuss a basic Red Brick Decision Server project and the documents that I consider fundamental to the process. If you work in an environment that has a methodology spelling out in detail how to run a project, then use it. It might be a good exercise in due diligence, however, to review this chapter to be sure any project methodology you are using addresses the elements listed here.

Next, I'll tackle project scope and scope creep. These are the gremlins of projects everywhere and must be managed very closely if you are going to succeed. This discussion will offer some tips on how to identify out-of-scope issues and suggest a method for dealing with them.

From there, I'll discuss some basic project roles required in a data warehouse project and suggest some ways to staff these roles from existing staff you may have. I'll also point out a few pitfalls to avoid in staffing your project. Finally, I'll discuss some lessons from the trenches that include how to manage expectations and scope creep.

A Typical Project

You might be tempted to laugh at the word "typical," and I don't blame you. You could rightly argue that it doesn't exist because every project is different. True enough. However, what every project has in common are the steps they go through.

It's beyond the scope of this book to discuss project management in detail. However, several components of a project are worth reviewing. These are what I consider standard components of any project and should be used at a minimum. From time to time, I run across customers who have fully developed project methodologies that outline in detail how their projects are to run. These are the best situations to be in because much of the guesswork is eliminated. In cases where no such methodology exists, you may have a harder time picking your way through the project management minefield.

 While it's beyond the scope of this book to teach project management, I'm assuming that you are familiar with the basic concepts.

The initiation of the project begins once final approval is granted from the sponsors or other decision makers (the folks who spend the money). It concludes with the start of actual project work. There are several operational issues to be addressed, including the following:

1. **Assigning a project manager** – This is the resource person who will guide the project through to completion. All other project resources report up to this person.

2. **Developing the project scope** – This is a document that identifies exactly how much work is to be done.

3. **Developing the work plan/project plan** – This document is a task-level breakdown with resource assignments, task dependencies, milestones, and timelines.

4. **Conducting the kickoff meeting** – This is the initial meeting with the project team where the roles and goals of the project are discussed with the project team.

Components

A minimum of four components is essential to any Red Brick Decision Server project. It's not practical to attempt a data warehouse project without these four items. There are many good project management resources available that go into the minute details of project management and the instruments required; however, you need just enough information about running a Red Brick Decision Server-specific project to be successful. Therefore, I'll discuss only the components necessary for success. This discussion is not a replacement for a true project management or data warehouse implementation methodology; rather, it's a discussion of the minimum components required for you to succeed.

 The components listed here are the minimum number you need to be successful. Do not consider this list to be a complete set of documents needed for a data warehouse project methodology.

The four basic components you need to run your project are listed in the following sections. If you are a consultant, you've no doubt seen these before, with perhaps a dozen or so other documents as well. I take a little shortcut here with the project notebook, which I'll discuss shortly.

SCOPE DOCUMENT

I'll discuss scope in more detail in a moment; however, this is the first basic document you need. This defines the project and what is to be accomplished. If, during the project, you find yourself working on something that is not explicitly in the scope, stop and figure out why — either you are wasting valuable time on something out of scope or perhaps the scope has to be changed.

PROJECT PLAN

This document has the high-level phases of the project broken down into task-level details with timelines, resource assignments, milestones, and dependencies. This is the document that the project manager uses to track progress and to assess the impact of missed milestones and deadlines.

DIMENSIONAL MODEL

This is perhaps the one document that most often comes to mind when folks think about a data warehouse project. It's impossible to build anything without the data model. The how-to of dimensional modeling will be discussed in much more detail in Chapters 4 and 5. For now, just keep in mind that the model is a key component of a project and is to be considered an integral piece of project documentation.

PROJECT NOTEBOOK

The project notebook is the "book of record" for your project. It contains all the important information about a project and is retained for a time in case any questions arise during or after project completion. Generally, the project manager maintains the notebook. There are several sections to a project notebook, and each requires different documentation.

Do not underestimate the value of the project notebook. The project components presented here are minimal in nature. As such, you need a mechanism that compensates for the lack of a true project methodology. The project notebook fills this need by providing a repository for all project information collected or generated, organized in a simple but effective fashion.

Here is the shortcut mentioned a moment ago. In situations where a project methodology is in place, you will find many documents that are required as part of a project. There are formats for each of these deliverables and rules for gathering the information required on them. This type of methodology usually exists at companies whose primary focus is consulting or project management.

Companies engaged in other types of business don't normally have such a methodology, hence the inclusion of the project notebook in this section. The bottom line is that you want to document everything. The notebook is a place where you can gather all this documentation and not worry about the logistics of 30 types of documents, formats, and so forth. It's more important that you capture the information than spend gobs of time making it look pretty. A good notebook should contain at least the following eight sections.

- **Project notebook status** – This section serves as a sort of index or checklist for each section for the entire notebook. As documents and information are added to the notebook, the project manager checks them off in the status section. This allows the project team to understand where the project is at a glance.

- **Scope/design documentation** – This section contains the scope document, the out-of-scope issues and resolutions, and all the design documentation generated over the life of the project. The scope document should also include any project assumptions, individual or group responsibilities, and a risk assessment of the project.

- **Work plan** – This can be a detailed Gantt chart, task list, or spreadsheet that outlines the phases, steps, and tasks along with the expected resource assignments and time estimates for each task.

- **Acceptance measurements** – This section contains the acceptance criteria and project milestones to be achieved. It's vitally important that any measurement criteria be just that – measurable.

Be certain that the measures defined in the scope document are just that — measurable. Any other subjective or ambiguous criteria will put you into a position of not knowing if you are done — the dreaded never-ending project.

◆ **Time sheets** – This is good information to keep "just because." Often, the cost of implementing a data warehouse does not include the in-house resources. This gives you a way to attach value to all the time expended. If you are a consultant, this is a must because you will most likely end up billing the customer for this time.

◆ **Data mapping documents** – This section will probably be the hardest to develop and the most heavily used of all because, as you will learn in later chapters, data, its quality, and availability represent the lion's share of the work associated with a data warehouse. There should be a document for each data object in the warehouse that indicates where each piece of data is coming from and what must be done to it to correctly load it into the warehouse. It's common to go to a client and underestimate the time it takes to get the data. Sometimes it is not your problem, but eventually, you will be where the data is stored, so if it's not there because of some extensive delay or oversight in the transformation or cleansing phase, you ultimately pay a price – most often in missed milestones and deliverables.

◆ **Correspondence** – This section contains any other information relevant to the project and may include e-mail, status reports, meeting agendas, and minutes. Additionally, you should keep copies of everything presented at meeting and interview sessions.

◆ **Additional documentation** – This section is for additional documentation that doesn't seem to fit anywhere else. This could include data models, SQL code, diagrams, user-application documentation, and so on.

As I already stated, the important point is that you document everything and have a place to put it that's easy to find and review.

Scope and scope creep

Project scope is the mechanism that limits the amount of work to be done. Everything else comes in this "box." The scope document also identifies which individual or group will be responsible for carrying it out. Once all the parties involved have accepted the scope of the project, the budget and time frames for the project are set. From this point on, you start managing the scope because almost before the ink is dry, you will start to receive new ideas and functionality requests.

Project scope is what your project lives and dies by. Mismanage the scope, and you'll greatly complicate your project, possibly to the point of failure.

The scope document should also define the procedures to be used to determine if a proposed change to the project is in scope or out of scope. If the change is out of scope, that doesn't mean that it can't be done; that's what the change request process is all about. I have included a sample scope document on the CD-ROM that you can use as a template for your project. It has the following sections:

◆ **Overview** – This explains the business drivers behind the project, why it is being undertaken, and what the resulting expectations are.

◆ **Definition of scope** – This is a high-level discussion of the project and should include a description of the business or subject areas involved, the number and type of users expected, and any platform or configuration information necessary.

◆ **Tasks to be performed by (vendor/party/group)** – The specific tasks for each group are listed in this section. It's helpful to have separate headings for each group or individual. You should include information for external groups or individuals as well (outside consultants, vendors, and so on) so that everyone associated with the project knows what they are responsible for and when.

◆ **Items excluded from the project** – This section lists the tasks that will *not* be included in the project. This is your first opportunity to manage expectations. By deliberately calling out what is not going to be done, everyone involved should now be on the same page. Do not make the mistake of assuming that these items are common knowledge to the project team. Once listed here, there can be no question about what's in scope and what's out of scope.

◆ **Project assumptions** – Every project has a number of assumptions associated with it. Again, listing assumptions deliberately avoids any misunderstandings and puts everyone on the same page. Do not hesitate to include any assumptions, no matter how trivial or obvious they may seem. The only bad assumption is the one you don't list. Examples might include assumptions such as building access, work areas, reports, resource availability, and so forth. The list could be endless; however, be reasonable and above all, be clear.

◆ **Critical success factors/acceptance criteria** – Once you have determined the scope, you must decide how to measure acceptance of the tasks outlined in the scope document. Each task that is performed must have a mechanism for being accepted as complete – usually, by the client. Avoid ambiguous acceptance criteria. If there seems to be no way to make a certain item measurable, it should not be used as criteria for acceptance. Acceptance could be criteria like the creation of a document, qualities of data, load windows, query response times, or other items that result in a tangible or directly measurable metric. Every discussion you have here is worth weeks of project time later on.

◆ **Risk assessment** – It's a good idea to do a risk assessment prior to starting any data warehouse project. More than one project manager has had long sleepless nights because of not understanding the risk factors. This process is designed to be an objective measure of the factors that threaten the success of the project. The risks are sorted according to project priorities, probability of occurrence, and severity of their consequences, and a plan is then developed to address the most critical issues. Risk factors can include infrastructure, data access or availability, technical ability of users, the users understanding of data warehousing, or issues driving the project (tactical vs. strategic). Be as realistic as possible when assessing your environment.

◆ **Change management** – It's normal for issues to arise during the course of a project that require a change in the scope to include a previously out-of-scope item. This process must be managed closely, however, or the project will get out of control very fast and you may not be able to get it back under control.

 Change management is included in the scope document for two reasons: to clearly communicate the process and to underscore the seriousness of changes to scope.

SCOPE – THE ULTIMATE ENEMY

One of the project manager's most important jobs is managing expectations and project scope. Without a scope document and a change request process, it's almost impossible to stay on track and build a warehouse that meets users' requirements. In addition, you will usually find that there is no shortage of ideas and requests for enhanced functionality. (And you've hardly even started!) As the project team gets their arms around the problem and the users start to understand where you want to take them, the ideas will start to flow.

These ideas and requests are extremely valuable for the next iteration(s). However, you must take the time to evaluate each request to determine if it really should be in scope; if so, you must then process a change request so that all parties know what's going on.

The biggest problem you have to deal with here are the "water cooler conversations" where functionality issues are discussed and something gets committed to because it only takes an hour. Add enough of these hours together, and you're off in the weeds before you know it.

IDENTIFYING OUT-OF-SCOPE ISSUES

The obvious question is, "How do I identify out-of-scope issues?" It's not all that complicated, but it can be time-consuming. Generally, these types of issues come out of the user interviews. You will have a group of people in the room, and they will get stuck on an issue and be unable to resolve it for some reason. If you've made no progress after ten minutes or so of conversation, it's best to move on and investigate it after the meeting. Other signs of out-of-scope issues might be items that have little or no justification or whose value can't be easily determined. Frequently, these issues are out of scope, but not always.

There are several ways to manage changes in scope. You can expand the scope, accept the new functionality by dropping something else, or not accept changes at all. If you do expand the scope, you must also expand the timelines and budget to accommodate it. Exchanging functionality is often accompanied by an expansion of the timelines and budget when there is a significant difference in time and effort between the two items exchanged. Keeping the scope frozen is great for the project team but not always possible. In general, you should consider scope changes only under the following circumstances:

♦ You have the appropriate resources available.

♦ You have enough time to research the feasibility of the requested changes and their impact on the rest of the project without jeopardizing the timelines.

♦ The changes being asked for are technically feasible.

♦ Your budget can accommodate the changes.

♦ The project sponsors and the powers that be are willing to extend the schedule due to the requested changes and research if necessary.

If these conditions are not possible, then you probably don't want to consider the change.

There are three ways to manage scope: accept the changes with the appropriate expansion of the timeline and budget, exchange functionality (new for old) with small changes in timeline and budget, or hold to the original scope definition. The choice depends on your circumstances.

MANAGING SCOPE CREEP

Every scope document should include change management rules. *Change management* is the process by which the project team is made aware of changes and their potential impact on the project's cost and time. The first part of any change management process is gaining the understanding of the project team about why change management is important. It's important because while changes are being requested, you are still expected to produce quality deliverables, on time and on budget.

If your project's scope is continuously expanded to include new functionality, it rapidly becomes impossible to deliver your project on time and on budget; therefore, the scope must be preserved. However, this desire must be balanced with the users' desire to get as much as possible by pushing the scope to the limits.

THE OUT-OF-SCOPE DOCUMENT

A natural outcome of the change management process is all those requests that didn't make it. This is extremely valuable information both in terms of follow-up projects and understanding how the users are learning to leverage the warehouse. These items are collected in an out-of-scope document that is a summary of the change management documents. This provides an easy reference to review for the next iteration or entirely new efforts. All this documentation should end up in the project notebook.

Critical areas to monitor

While you are getting started with your project, several issues bear watching. Even at this early stage, you will have to resolve some conflicts with goals and directions. Getting started is perhaps the most difficult stage because a lot of the politics and internal issues are addressed here. Once the major issues are decided, it gets easier because the direction is set.

SCOPE

I've talked a lot about scope in this chapter, but it bears repeating – you must pay attention to the scope of the project from its inception. It doesn't take long for the scope to expand beyond your ability to deliver. It's much more difficult to get it back under control than if it's controlled from the start.

PROJECT GOALS

Project goals are another common source of strife between groups involved in the project. This is natural and is to be expected by the project team. Conflicting goals can be difficult to resolve, especially if the sponsors are divided on the issues. If you do find yourself in this situation, the faster you can get it resolved, the faster you can move ahead.

Resolving these conflicts is not always easy, and you may have to make some tough decisions. Communicating to the respective groups is key to their understanding and reaching an agreement about the priority of each goal and when it will be implemented (if at all). You want to come out of the process with the group's participation intact, even though they may have had to temporarily give up a benefit.

How data warehouse projects differ from traditional IS projects

As I pointed out earlier, the basics of managing a data warehousing project are not that much different from any other type of IS project. They are both based on sound and accepted project management fundamentals; however, there are some differences between the warehouse projects and other types of projects that need to be expanded upon.

ITERATIVE

Data warehouse projects are iterative by nature. One of the primary reasons for this is that your business changes over time. These changes are brought about by external influences such as changes in the business climate or programs and initiatives undertaken by your competitors. Additionally, as the users understand how to use the data warehouse, they then start to leverage it. The users' increased understanding gives rise to new functionality, requests for data, and so on.

LARGE AMOUNTS OF DATA

Data warehouses store large amounts of data. In many instances, the amount of data in the warehouse is exponentially larger than the source systems. This large amount of data, as well as the multiple sources from which it comes, leads to a tremendous number of data issues. I suspect that, on average, at least half the issues that arise in a data warehouse project revolve around the data in one way or another.

The frequency and sometimes the sheer size of the data issues can negatively impact an otherwise perfect project plan; it may be practically impossible to accurately estimate the amount of time required to load the data. It's not *if* you have data problems, but rather *how many* data problems you will have and to what extent you will have them.

DATA ALIGNMENT

Data alignment refers to how data is related to other data in the model for a particular application. In On Line Transaction Processing (OLTP) applications, data is related to other data via what I call *data rules*, the standard rules of normalization or normal forms. These ideals have been around since the dawn of relational databases and have a place in the transaction world. This alignment is necessary to achieve the transaction speeds necessary to run a business in the modern marketplace. The price for this speed is no data redundancy, multiple join paths, and very small transactions.

In a data warehouse, data is related to other data via *business* rules. Some of these rules are expressed as the foreign key relationships between fact tables and dimension tables, for example. It's not quite as simple as that, but the point is that the data is realigned over business rules that automatically make the data relationships suspect until it has been successfully loaded into the warehouse. The moment you realign the data with the business relationships, you introduce some potentially large issues that must be addressed.

For instance, many times, the project team finds themselves producing reports with numbers that can't be easily matched to existing reports from the operational systems. This is expected because you have aligned the data along the business process. Data quality, sparsity, and most of all, relational integrity are the three issues that send more projects into the data dumpster than anything else.

Note that the data evaluation will happen one way or the other. It usually *can't* happen without the business users because they know the data best and understand what it means. It sometimes *does* happen without the project team because they skipped this step and released it to the user community. Now the business users find all sorts of issues with reports and results that can't easily be explained.

There is a *big* difference between knowing the data and knowing *about* the data. The business users generally know the data; the IT folks generally know about the data.

Sometimes the warehouse is wrong, and if it is, you fix it. However, remember that many of the source systems that the data is coming from may have never had any other external validation, either. In other words, the system being used to source/compare/measure the results from the data warehouse has become the accepted standard, when, in fact, it may have had errors in it from the day it was put online.

It is not as important that the numbers match as it is that the difference can be explained in a logical and reasonable way that is consistent with the way the business runs. Don't lose sight of what's happening when warehouse reports and totals don't match to production reports. Sometimes they will, but often they won't. Look for the reasons why. If they make business sense, move forward with the team and educate the users.

It's more important to explain any differences between reports when validating the warehouse than it is to be able to match numbers exactly. It's nice when they do, but often they don't. Search for the reasons why they are different; if the reasons are valid and are consistent with the business rules, make the appropriate adjustments, educate the appropriate people, and move on.

This is one area where expectation management can play a BIG role in how the success of the project is perceived. Remember, you can be technically perfect but still lose the war by unrealistic expectations. Ironically, the business users hold the key to the validation/evaluation phase. However, if they do it on their own, it's very likely they will not fully embrace the warehouse in the same way again (if at all).

INFORMATION SHARING

Information sharing is the situation where the data from one group is suddenly available and useable to another group. This is a good thing – usually. The reality is that every so often, you find a group that feels threatened and doesn't want to play nice. Don't underestimate the level of data ownership some people will feel about their data and their unwillingness to share with others.

Data Owners and Junk Data

Every project has data issues — that's just normal. Occasionally, however, you may run into a situation where the data is in terrible shape. This can present a problem if not handled carefully. It's one thing to discuss the status of the data, but quite another to make a federal case out of it. The keepers of the old data will often become offended if you start to point out flaws in their data, and it is sometimes taken as a "You've been doing it all wrong" statement. Suddenly, you can find yourself alienating some valuable members of the team and perhaps feel a bit intimidated to boot.

When you have a situation like this, you must communicate to the sponsors as to what you've found, and assess the impact on the scope and timelines of the project. These types of situations often take a lot of time (that you probably don't have) to resolve, so it's important to understand the impact as soon as possible. Do not dwell on how bad the data is, but rather look closely for what the data can support. In most cases, the idea that the data is less than perfect is old news to the people who use it every day; however, they may not know the extent to which it's "bad."

As far as dealing with the people responsible for it, consider this: in many cases, the people you are dealing with didn't design or implement the system they are now responsible for, but inherited it from others who did the actual damage. Very often, they know (better than you do) where the flaws are and what it takes to fix them. Nevertheless, knowing what must be done and getting the OK from management to address those issues is not just an IT matter. In most cases, they would fix it if they could.

Accepting the data as it's presented and adopting an attitude of "let's see how we can fix things" will get you much farther than continually pointing out data issues. It's more a matter of attitude and how you approach it than the actual status of the data. If you put yourself in their shoes for a minute and see the problem from their point of view, you foster a mutual understanding that allows you to move on.

You must be careful not to compromise the scope, but if the data won't support what you are trying to do, you must be up-front with the team and look for other data sources, modify the scope to fit the data available, or solve another problem entirely.

Sharing information between different parts of the company is a fundamental principal of a data warehouse; however, it comes with some baggage. Often, people feel threatened because of what others may find in the data. This can be a sensitive issue because it could point out deficiencies in the data, holes in a business process, and otherwise expose it for what it is. The sponsors should be able to address this problem for you.

EXPECTATIONS

Finally, there are the expectations of all involved. Data warehouse projects are generally more visible than most other IT projects. Because of this, the expectations of the company as a whole tend to be on the optimistic side – meaning that they are usually higher than is reasonable. This is a chronic problem that you must manage head on – from day one. The only way to manage this is to communicate clearly and frequently with all levels of the company.

Project Resources and Roles

The project team will most likely vary from project to project. It's important, however, that as a project team is put together, each member understands his or her role(s) within the team. Although the team is temporary, there must be a clear and established reporting structure so that the project team can function within the organization as any other group or department.

In general, a minimal project team requires just a handful of roles. Several of these roles may be assumed by a single individual, which occurs often. Keep in mind that the more people you have on the project team, the more time the project manager must spend communicating between them. The basic roles are described in the following sections.

Sponsor

Sponsors were discussed in Chapter 1, but to reiterate, you should look for sponsors from across the company to give your project a cross-functional structure. The best sponsors are those who are in positions of authority, who can make tough decisions, and who can commit resources. They also should be connected around the company, be well liked, and understand the history, politics, and agendas of the business.

Project manager

Data warehousing projects are very user-centric. As such, the project manager must be extremely focused on building a rapport with all levels of the user community as well as gaining a good working knowledge of the business problems the project was designed to solve. The project manager also serves as the interview facilitator during the requirements-gathering phase described later. A working knowledge of the business problems is a prerequisite to successfully conducting the interview process.

The other major task that resides with the project manager is that of expectation management at all levels. Mismanaged expectations are the primary reason that projects fail. It is possible to be technically correct and fail in the users' eyes because of mismanaged expectations. Conversely, I've seen situations where the technical decisions were less correct, but the expectations were managed to coincide with the implementation and the users absolutely loved it. By the way, this project team went on to move the warehouse through two more iterations with smashing success, in part because they left themselves some room with the technology.

Business analyst

This role is responsible for the business requirements activities and definitions. This role can be staffed with IT resources, but is generally more effective if someone from the business side performs this function. In any event, look for candidates who are customer-centric, articulate, have a good grasp of technology, and are well liked across the company.

DBA

The DBA role has a lot to do in any database project, and warehouses are no different. They are responsible for creating the physical instance of the logical model and the many tasks associated with collecting and loading the data. Additionally, they might be responsible for user access and other monitering functions of the data warehouse. You might want to consider having this resource person participate in the data-modeling exercise to give him or her a better understanding of the Red Brick Decision Server technology.

This resource is usually staffed with an existing DBA. Most DBAs find that being a Red Brick Decision Server DBA is a refreshing change because it's fun and they are not overloaded with so much busy work to do like they are with some of the other merchant database systems.

Dimensional data modeler

This is perhaps the most critical member of the project team. This role is responsible for developing and rendering the logical data model. Data modelers are often most effective when they participate in the requirements-gathering activities. Having a solid understanding of the business is critical to building an accurate logical model. The person who fills this role must be able to break away from OLTP modeling practices. Sometimes the data modeler with the most experience is not the best choice. The key is flexible thinking and a willingness to learn something new. Many companies hire an outside consultant to fill this role and subsequently mentor an in-house resource.

Staffing from Within Your Organization

It's natural for most companies to want to staff data warehousing projects from within their own organizations. Often, warehouse projects are highly visible to upper- and mid-management people. In addition, team members are routinely exposed to lots of information that they would not otherwise be in a position to know, and frequently, successful data warehouse projects lead to raises and/or promotions. All of these are positive incentives and opportunities for your in-house resources. In looking for project team members, you want to enlist those who are enthusiastic, are willing to learn, and have the ability to roll with the punches. If this is your first effort, there will be lots of opportunity to test your project skills.

Leverage existing skill sets

Frequently, you can leverage the skill sets of the folks you have in-house. You do this by placing individuals in jobs or giving them tasks that fall within their strongest skills. At the same time, you want to try to challenge them just enough for them to grow, but not so much that they feel frustrated and lost. By leveraging existing skill sets, you can get more out of your project than you otherwise might.

Don't overextend in-house resources

There is one word of caution, however. Occasionally, a critical resource is allocated to a data warehouse project temporarily. This is usually because this person is indispensable to some other project or task the business depends on. There are several problems with this.

First of all, there is the whole business issue of becoming dependent on a single person for a critical process. It's a bad idea and, unfortunately, an all-too-frequent problem. Secondly, when a resource is over-extended, he or she usually has more than one manager – which is unfair to both the project and the resource. This is the type of issue that the project's sponsor should be able to solve. It's not easy, and I wouldn't want to make some of the decisions I've seen others try and navigate, but if you can avoid this, you're much better off.

Be willing to engage consultants if necessary

The obvious solution is to hire the talent you need. Some companies hire it all, while some hire none and do it all with in-house resources. More often, most companies hire the skill sets they need for the duration of the project and pair them with in-house people. This type of technology transfer works very well and is often the best way to grow the resources you already have. It's very important, however, for you to retain ownership of the project if you have outside help.

Often the consultants come in and, because they have the skill sets, end up (either by accident or design) owning the project. This is unadvisable because you now have little or no control over where the project goes. The best course of action is to set yourself up to retain ownership by creating a situation where the hired help is acting in a technology-transfer role in addition to any deliverables they might have. Remember that data warehouse projects are iterative, and at some point, you want to be self-sufficient.

Be somewhat conservative in evaluating the capabilities of in-house staff for a first project in Red Brick Decision Server. The area that causes the most trouble is the modeling phase. Dimensional modeling *is* different, and unless you have someone on staff that has implemented at least four or five truly dimensional models (as defined in Chapters 4 and 5), I encourage you to rent the talent you need. If the model is wrong, you are in for no end of trouble. You still might succeed, but it's unlikely.

Lessons from the Trenches

The lessons from the trenches for this chapter are taken from actual field situations I faced at Red Brick. These were notable because in each case, the oversight made by the project team almost resulted in failure. Fortunately, there were review processes in place that kept the project from going too far afield, but not everyone is so lucky.

Manage expectations

This is the never-ending task for the project manager. Expectations must be managed at all levels – from top management on down. Anyone who is aware or involved will have expectations, and they must be kept in line with the technology, scope, and functionality of the solution. Nothing will guarantee failure more quickly than exceedingly high expectations that were dismally met.

Manage scope creep

This is the other never-ending process for the project manager. This is a little subtler in that it's incremental. It's worth the effort to teach the project team to "just say no" and refer the person making the request to the project manager and the change management process.

Don't wait to ask for help

I'm sure you've heard the old adage about how an ounce of prevention is worth a pound of cure, and this is no different. In today's wired world, there is no reason to work in the dark any more. In the early days, data warehousing, dimensional modeling, and indeed Red Brick Decision Server technology were so new that there were limited places you could go to get help. Now you have Informix technical support, Red Brick Decision Server user groups, and consultants available to show you the way.

Summary

Getting started is sometimes the most difficult part of a data warehouse project because of the many political issues and directional decisions that must be made. Communication is the key to resolving these issues as quickly as possible. You should also rely on the project sponsors to take the lead in many of the issue resolutions.

The scope document is the primary instrument you will generate and use to communicate to the entire project team where the project is headed and exactly what's to be delivered. You will also use this document to evaluate new requests for functionality and data. Remember that the scope of the project is what you are committed to deliver. If it changes, then so must something else.

Be realistic in staffing your team with in-house resources. The project team outlined in this chapter is a bare minimum of roles required. It's unlikely that you can succeed with fewer than these. A single resource can play more than one role, but more than two seems to be problematic. By evaluating your staff this way, you will be able to more accurately determine where you need to supplement the team with outside resources.

Chapter 3

Gathering Requirements

IN THIS CHAPTER

♦ Getting started with requirements gathering

♦ The mechanics of interviewing

♦ Who you should be talking to

♦ What you should learn

♦ Who is your customer

♦ How to ask questions

♦ A word about group dynamics

♦ Tips on how to stay on track

♦ How you know when you're done

♦ The importance of vocabulary

♦ Introduction to the Sample Database

DETERMINING THE GOALS for a data warehouse is the easiest and the hardest activity to do. At a high level, it's fairly easy to identify where you are and where you want to go; it's getting there that's difficult. Many a project has gotten off to a good start only to end up in a ditch because the team didn't have realistic or complete requirements, lost its focus, or was not able to manage the change that naturally accompanies warehouse projects.

There is an element of "art" associated with requirements gathering; however, by following a few simple guidelines, almost anyone can do a very respectable job of identifying who to interview and what the interviewer needs to know to deliver the most valuable warehouse project possible. Most people I've dealt with over the years have little or no trouble with the "who" and "what" — it's the "how" that presents the problem.

The "how" of requirements gathering is a mix of technology skills and what I like to call "soft skills." As a practical matter, not everyone is comfortable in this type of environment, so we'll look at the basics of requirements gathering and provide a simple process to follow that is field tested and should get you where you need to go.

We'll start by discussing the mechanics of doing interviews and why it's important. From there, we'll take a look at how to identify whom you should be talking to and why. Next, we'll discuss what you need to learn through the interview process; finally, we'll examine some tips on how to ask the questions and some tests you can use to determine when you've completed the interview process.

Requirements gathering and logical modeling are very closely related and are often treated as a single process by some of the more experienced Red Brick consultants. Because of this tight relationship, we'll also discuss the logical modeling process as an abstract so we can see how they are related.

We'll wind up with a discussion of the sample database included on the CD: the business problem and related issues. The rest of the book continually refers back to the sample database.

Getting Started With Requirements Gathering

Requirements gathering is the most important step in a data warehouse project. This is where we define *exactly* what we are going to do, who is going to do it, and what the results should be. Along the way, we must also learn a tremendous amount about the business, what makes it work, where it has problems, who owns what, which data is available – the list is almost endless.

This is also a time for relationship building. As the project leader, who will have to bring back issues that need to be solved, this is your opportunity to develop a working relationship with each person you interview. Investing a little extra time to learn more than just the facts will pay huge dividends later in the process. And who knows? You just might end up with a really good friend when it's all over.

If you ever have the opportunity to spend some time with a good analyst, you will notice how quickly he or she gets things done and is able to grasp the business issues and concepts almost from the start. That only comes with practice. If you are a consultant, you might have already had the chance to work with someone of this caliber. You might even be that person. To you, this is so much common sense. However, if you will only work on one or two warehouses in total, to you, this subject may represent a bigger challenge.

In any event, the task is still the same: how do you find out what you need to know to build a data warehouse that delivers the most value possible – on time and on budget? The answer is by interviewing different groups of people and managing expectations as you go.

The Mechanics of Interviewing

The entire process starts with interviews of one sort or another. The process of interviewing is very tightly coupled with the logical modeling process – which is discussed in the next chapter. Interviews are absolutely necessary. They are the basis of *great* data warehouses because interviews define the *real* business rules.

In a transaction system, the data is modeled around data relationships or data rules. The reason for this is to keep an individual transaction as small as possible. This is what the traditional database companies were all about in the 1970s and 1980s. In a data warehouse, everything is modeled along business relationships or *business rules*. It's a much different view of the world.

Therefore, it's not surprising to see several different definitions of a business rule or object based on a person's job responsibility. For example you might ask, "Who is your customer?" or "What is the definition of the product?" and get a finance answer, an MIS answer, a customer service answer, and so forth. All are correct (in the context of their job or department function), yet none are totally correct in the context of the business. The real answer is a combination of all the different views.

Interviews provide the context in which to interpret the data. If it were only as easy as taking the transaction data and plopping it into a warehouse, we wouldn't have the data warehouse marketplace to begin with. This, in fact, is what some folks do, and for the most part, the results speak for themselves — it's hardly worth the effort. The reason for this is actually quite simple: if the users could get the answers they were looking for from the transaction system in the first place, you wouldn't be building a warehouse and reading this book. To put it bluntly, transaction data simply can't answer typical data warehouse questions, which is why the entire data warehousing market segment came into existence.

To really understand the business, you must understand the context in which different business events happen. Data in and of itself is marginally useful in understanding how a business works or determining how a given business rule is applied. Without the context, it's just plain data.

Interviews help identify the existence of supporting data: that is, data that will answer the questions that the warehouse is supposed to provide answers to. This is extremely critical to any data warehouse project because although it's not your first priority, you need to determine if you have the data to support a solution to the business problem. Determining whether you have the necessary data may sound academic, but situations do occur where, after having understood the business process and defined a business problem, the customer does not have the data to support an answer. It wasn't "in there," so to speak.

There are three basic types of interviews: true interviews, facilitated sessions, and what a colleague of mine calls "a day in the life." Each has its purpose, and you'll often use all three to get all the information you need.

True interviews

A *true interview* is perhaps the easiest to do because it requires a limited amount of time and can be used with individuals or small groups. This type of setting usually fosters a lot of participation among the participants, and it often results in a lot of information transferred in a short amount of time.

Facilitated sessions

Facilitated sessions are more useful for larger groups of people. They generally take more time, but they also encourage more creative thinking on the part of the participants. These require a little more preparation up front but are usually productive. Be careful not to let one or two members of the group monopolize all the time. If that's how it's going to go, then you are better off doing individual interviews with these people. It's no good to gather an entire group of people together just to hear one or two people do all the talking – and that goes for you as well. Once the meeting gets started, you should speak enough to effectively facilitate the meeting, but no more. Remember, the goal is to get the other people in the room to talk about the business and their related job functions.

A day in the life

Occasionally, a situation presents itself where you just don't have a good grasp of a particular function or business process, even after several interviews. In cases like this, spending a day in the life of the person whose function or process is causing you problems is the best thing to do. The best way to accomplish this is to move into their cube or office, do what they do, go where they go, and be observant – ask lots of why questions. Spend some time understanding who interacts with the person you're shadowing and why the interaction is necessary. It's valuable for several reasons:

- ◆ It gives you a chance to see and hear information firsthand.

- ◆ You have the opportunity to ask as many questions as it takes until you understand the task at hand.

- ◆ It shows that what this person does is really important to the project (and indeed it is!) and encourages further communication.

Who Should You Be Talking To?

The next step in this process is identifying whom you should talk to and why. The minute details about all of the different scenarios you might encounter are beyond the scope of this book; however, we can break the subject down into several major categories of people that you should strive to interview.

Don't assume that you can (or should) talk to everyone in the company; you must carefully choose a few individuals you want to interview. This decision is greatly aided with an up-to-date organization chart, but remember, organization charts don't tell you the whole story. There is almost always an unofficial organizational structure to take into account. Also remember that like the development of the data warehouse, the interview process is iterative. Taking information learned in interview #5 back to interviewee #2 for confirmation or to resolve a conflict is often part of the iterative process.

Note that although the groups are listed here in a serial fashion, that does not mean that you should interview in that order. You should try to mix and match the individuals so that each session has somewhat of a cross-functional flavor to it.

The project sponsor

The project sponsor is the person to start with. Actually, this could be considered a "pre-interview" interview because this person should be able to provide you with most of the basic information that you will require to conduct further interviews. You accomplish this by identifying individuals within the company who are considered visionaries – or "out of the box" thinkers – and who support the project. You'll also want to identify those who are less than enthusiastic about the project and why they feel that way. Often, you will uncover some very important information about mistakes made by others.

Do not overlook this most important interview. Ideally, the project sponsor is high enough in the organization to make key decisions, resolve issues of conflicting priorities, and make critical resources available when needed. If this is not the case, then you must enlist the sponsor's help in identifying the proper individual(s) who can make those types of decisions.

If you're in the consulting field, identifying a project sponsor without the clout to make things happen might be an indication that the project has not been sold high enough and that the sales team needs to do some more work to make the contacts at the proper level. In any event, a project sponsor with little or no authority will greatly complicate matters and indeed may doom the project's success before it has even begun.

On the up side, it's common to have a sponsor committee made up of several individuals from across the company. This usually happens in organizations that are highly distributed or that have a less rigid reporting structure and more of a dotted-line type of organization. This situation usually works very well, provided the individuals on the committee are in positions of authority.

Data owners

Data "owners" are the folks who are responsible for large sections of the data. For example, the accounting manager owns the receivables/payables data, the HR manager owns the personnel data, and so on. In most situations, you will find that this ownership is aligned along individual business functions.

Data ownership is important to recognize because in the day-to-day operations of the company, there is little or no incentive to share data with any other internal organization; however, a data warehouse, by definition, aligns data along business rules. Just discussing the project will potentially push a number of people outside their comfort zones with regards to their data.

One of the obstacles you may run into when interviewing the data owners is that they are afraid to let anyone know too much about their data. They may feel that their jobs are threatened because they could be replaced by a computer. This fear is usually evident when they don't understand the data warehouse project and what it's supposed to bring to the organization. The data owners must be assured that they are a very important part of the team because they know the data better than anyone else, and that this intangible knowledge can't be replaced by a machine. The data owners may actually be the toughest nuts to crack if they don't want to be interviewed, yet they hold the most critical knowledge about data relationships, where the data originates, and so forth.

End users and analysts

End users and analysts are the people who make the day-to-day decisions – the folks who slice, dice, and otherwise manipulate the data every way they can think of to get their jobs done. This is where all the action is. It's important to get a cross-functional group of people for this group, even though you might be concerned with only one or two subject areas, so that the definitions of common objects (like customer or product) are "directionally correct."

When you select the individuals in this group, keep in mind that you really want to see people from all levels: from managers all the way down the chart to the data-entry people (if necessary). This is really the only way to understand the business. Harking back to the relationship-building concept, although you are the data warehousing expert, these are the people who hold the detailed knowledge or "intellectual capital" about the business, and, as such, you should establish that you appreciate their help and you look forward to any additional information they may like to add in the future.

IT people

Data – the final frontier. Nothing makes or breaks a warehouse project faster or more completely than data. The first point you need to keep in mind is the difference between *knowing* the data and *knowing about* the data.

Business people generally know the data: what it means, how it's used, what decisions are made based on it, and its impact on other parts of the company. The IT people generally know about the data: how/when/where it's stored, where it comes from, how it gets here, where it goes, how/when it's backed up, how clean it is (sometimes), and a laundry list of other characteristics about it. Every so often, you'll get lucky and have an IT resource who has the business understanding of the data in addition to the IS knowledge he or she already possesses. If so, you should definitely take advantage of this resource.

As you progress through the process, you will get to a point where you have to decide if the data you have identified as necessary to solve the business problem is actually available: does the data exist, and, if so, can you have it? Every so often, the data is available, but no, you can't have it. The sidebar gives you some ideas on how to navigate this situation.

Can You Have It?

The "can you have it?" may be a critical point. In general, most people will grant you access to data, but not always. Occasionally, you may run into a system administrator or DBA who does not want to grant access to certain data sets or other sensitive information. I'm not talking about a security issue, as in government clearance, but rather an unwillingness to make data available. These folks must be reassured that you're not going to mess up his or her system. Do not be too harsh with these people, because they usually have prior experience that they feel justifies their holding out on you.

The only way to effectively address this situation is to build team spirit and mutual trust and respect. It's possible to bully them into what you want them to do, but if that's how you play it, be prepared to hit roadblocks along the way. It's easy for someone just starting out as a consultant to assume that everyone will automatically be on board and be extra willing to help out — not necessarily true. Politics and attitudes or personality conflicts can hinder progress from time to time, and you should be prepared to smooth out wrinkles with people skills (not just technical skills).

What You Should Learn

We've identified who to interview; now we have to determine what information you should go after. This may sound overly simple, but a number of informational topics are important in any data warehouse project. In general, the more information you have, the better, but there is a point of diminishing returns – at least as far as the project is concerned.

Chapter 2 discussed scope and *scope creep* – the piecemeal adding of functionality and the process of managing scope. The interview process is an opportunity to validate the scope of the project. Do not assume that the scope of the project as defined prior to the requirement-gathering process is cast in stone. Often, you will find that the scope cannot be accomplished because of previously unknown problems that have come to light only through the requirements process. This is not as dire at it may sound because as Chapter 2 also discussed, you should have a change process in place. The change process exists solely to address these unforeseen changes, and you should use it to your benefit.

Resolving problems with scope can range from a simple modification to the scope to a complete reevaluation of the project feasibility – and in extreme circumstances, dropping the project altogether; it really depends on your situation.

The number of questions you could pose to a group of people regarding their business process is practically endless. However, you can categorize them into eight basic topics that cover the major areas of information required. The categories are presented from general to specific:

1. Group/individual responsibilities
2. Relationship to other parts of the organization
3. Business objectives
4. Obstacles interfering with the objectives
5. How the current process works
6. Critical success factors and key performance indicators
7. Data sources
8. Warehouse expectations

You do not have to follow this order, but there is a more contiguous flow to the information if you do because each successive category builds on the last. In reality, try as you might, the interviewees will take you all over the map — jumping from one category to the next. This is actually okay, and it's worthwhile to become comfortable with the process because, after all, the goal here is to get them to talk.

Group/individual responsibilities

This category is all about what the individual or the group is responsible for on an ongoing basis. Here is where you want to learn as much as possible about any processes that individuals and groups have: both internal to the person (or his or her group) and external to other groups/individuals in the company. Be aware that some individuals/groups interface with customers, vendors, and others, and you want to understand those responsibilities as well.

Relationship to other parts of the organization

This category is designed to help you understand how a given individual or group is related to other parts of the company. Again, there are most likely relationships between internal organizations that do not show up on the organization chart. Be aware of these and try to understand as completely as possible how they work.

Business objectives

This category is obvious — we've talked about it already. I've included it here because each group may have different objectives to be accomplished with the warehouse project. Often, one or more of the objectives from one group will conflict with objectives from another group. You can't have it both ways.

By understanding each group's objectives, you will easily see conflicts as you move from group to group in the interview process. When you do (and you will) encounter conflicts, don't panic. The project manager/sponsor/team should be able to resolve these issues in a reasonable time frame. If not, you have a much bigger problem than conflicting objectives. You will most likely have input into the solution, but don't let it sidetrack you from the rest of the interview process.

Obstacles interfering with the objectives

This category teaches you about the common problems that obstruct employees from performing their job duties smoothly. These are the processes, politics, or in some cases people that continually interfere with employees accomplishing given business goals, such as missing data, a "broken" business process, internal political issues, etc. The list is practically endless; however, be careful to listen for issues that can be changed or otherwise addressed, those that can't, and then set expectations accordingly.

How the current process works

This category is self-explanatory. What you want to know is how the process works today – what's the procedure. You will often hear a lot of conversation about what's wrong with the process, but you really need to focus on how it works. The goal is to submit a document that describes the current process and get a signoff from the process/procedure owner. Often this document does not agree with the common knowledge version of how management thinks the processes are working. As an outside person, you can often communicate tough messages to management that they need to hear but that the regulars don't feel comfortable sending up the flagpole.

Critical success factors and key performance indicators

There are several ways to measure the success of your Red Brick data warehouse project: Return On Investment (ROI), Critical Success Factors (CSF), or Key performance Indicators (KPI). Keep in mind that any success criteria must be measurable. If they are subjective, then you've just developed the never-ending project.

Back when warehousing was just becoming a hot topic, most people measured the success of their project in ROI: how much did I get back on each dollar spent on the project? Unfortunately, it's rather difficult to measure the success of a warehouse strictly in terms of dollars spent/dollars earned. For example, what is the dollar value of increased customer satisfaction? It's hard to measure it in terms of dollars.

CSFs and KPI are a more real-world measure of what is required to declare success. Typically, you will want to listen for things that are measurable, but not necessarily in dollars. There will most likely be a few items that are measured in dollars, but they will not be the *only* measures. For example

- ◆ All queries return in less than one minute.
- ◆ Hold five years of data.
- ◆ Meet target load windows.
- ◆ Extract data from the XYZ system.

Just because a person makes a statement about what he or she needs to succeed does not mean that it is realistic, doable, usable as a measure, or that it does not conflict with something else. Your job is to collect the measures, agree with the project team and sponsor on what's reasonable, and manage expectations accordingly. A data warehousing project is not a cheap undertaking and should not be viewed as such. Building a strong business intelligence foundation takes commitment, time, and resources.

Data sources

This category is also fairly self-explanatory. You want to know which data is available, where it comes from, how and when it's available, and what employees do with it while they have it. You are also interested in what they produce from it and whom those products are distributed to. Pay attention to any decision based on a specific data set, and be sure you understand any timing issues associated with availability. At this early stage, you shouldn't be too concerned with the quality, but you will be later on.

Warehouse expectations

This is an area that will take a fair mount of the project manager's time — managing everyone's expectations. Take a step back and look at what you are doing to this organization by implementing a data warehouse: you are taking the data from across the organization and realigning it along business rules, and in the process, you are placing demands on the different groups to do the following:

- ◆ Play nice with each other because you are adopting a cross-functional view of the business to understand and solve a given business problem.

- ◆ Share their data with the warehouse team. This is often painful for the data owners because now people can look at and see it for what it is, not what it has been represented to be. No one likes others to see their dirty laundry.

- ◆ Be honest about how their processes work. For the warehouse to be successful, you need to know how everything works. If you can't get that, you are wasting your time.

- Be willing to give more that they get. Everyone can't be first on the list of deliverables, and sometimes they have to wait their turn.

- Warehouse projects generally represent a significant amount of work for the customers. And while they are busy doing what you've asked them, they still have a business to run.

It's easy to see how all of this can lead to unrealistic expectations, especially if the project has been oversold in an effort to get sponsors behind the idea. Customers tend to latch on to anything that is going to help them get their job done faster or better. It's out of this desire to get their jobs done faster that their expectations grow. Articles they read and conversations with others also influence their expectations. This is one area where a little knowledge can be extremely dangerous. Be absolutely sure that everyone's expectations are in line with the solutions capabilities. Assume nothing, suspect everything, and above all, don't confuse marketing with reality.

Managing everyone's expectations is vitally important because it's so key to your success. It is possible (and I've seen it happen) to be technically correct and be a dismal failure because the expectations were not in line with the solution. Fortunately, there is a way to be successful in this.

You should start to manage expectations from the minute you get started. Don't wait, because by the time you figure out that you have a problem, it's already too late. It's also a good idea to enlist the help of the project sponsors to help you do this. You will start to sound like a broken record as you progress through the project. That's okay – the more frequently you set the expectations, the sooner it becomes common project knowledge, which is what you are shooting for.

It's also important to understand that you must manage expectations at all levels of the project:

- User

- Group

- Sponsor

- Company

Each of these levels of individuals will have a different view of the project and different expectations. You cannot afford to neglect any of these groups of people; otherwise, you will fail. Success is really made up of two components: perception on the part of the users, and the actual measures used to determine it. It is important to start getting the expectations documented. Meeting notes, memos, etc. are great ways to make sure those who should be interested are paying attention. For some reason, issues, problems, or progress often are not real until it comes across someone's desk as part of a written document.

When all is said and done, and the project is completed, it really doesn't matter what the measures say if the users don't like the warehouse or feel that the functionality doesn't meet their needs. It is very difficult to prove you are successful if they already hate the results, but it's much easier to claim success if they love it.

Understanding Who Your Customer Really Is

Who is your customer(s)? This question is interesting, and, depending on your particular situation, it can have different answers. By customers, I'm referrnig to the person or group of people you are ultimatly responsible to for the project. If you are a consultant, this would be whoever is paying the bill.

Early on in Red Brick's history, management spent a lot of time talking to our field resources about getting to the end users: the people who were going to make or break the project and who held the keys to our success. That was and still is true. However, every once in a while, someone lost sight of who the customer really was and navigateed an organization in an inappropriate manner or otherwise complicated the project unnecessarily.

Complicating your project in this way is not so hard to do either, especially if you are an outside consultant. Politics, internal organizational structures, hidden agendas, and individual personalities all contribute to the confusion that can sometimes occur. As an outsider, you will not be aware of all these issues, which is why you need to rely on the project sponsor to help you navigate effectively.

Figure 3-1 shows an example of such a situation. All the comminications should take place between each of the boxes, not around them. Comminucations, actions, and decisions that take place by skipping boxes (indicated by the outside lines) are what you need to stay away from.

You should remain as neutral as possible in the organization's politics and agendas. This is admittedly harder to do if you are a direct employee, but it is imperative for a consultant. You must also remain accountable to the correct party. Don't persue the users at the expense of your accountability. You may not fail completely (although you've just increased your chances a hundredfold), but you have certainly made your task as difficult as humanly possible.

How to Ask Questions

Asking questions is the artful component of requirements gathering. Many people are intimidated to some degree by speaking to CFOs or by getting up in front of groups of people. This is natural; however, you can't let that get in the way of your project. If you think about it, gathering information and requirements all comes down to how well you can ask questions and solicit answers.

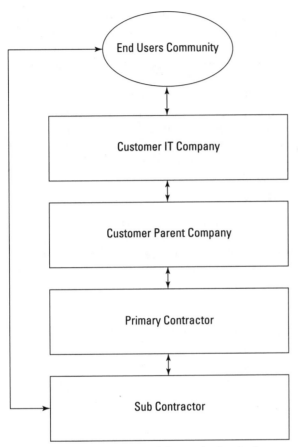

Figure 3-1: The relationships of the parties involved

You have probably seen numerous lists of sample questions to use in the interviewing process. These are helpful as examples, but I believe you will get more benefit out of learning how to ask as opposed to what to ask. Experience is the best teacher in this area; however, you can also learn a tremendous amount about how to ask questions by watching others. What follows is a combination of years of consulting experience from myself and several of my colleagues whom I consider to be excellent at this task.

Ask early and often

Don't overlook the opportunity to gain valuable information as people are introducing themselves. You should ask each person to explain who he or she is, discuss his or her relationship to the project, and outline any department or team goals he or she has. These introductions will most often provide you a starting place for asking questions, and you should take advantage of it. Once the interview process gets started, you have to quickly get at the heart of the matter.

In grade school, we used to play this game called Telephone where everyone stood in a straight line. The person on one end would whisper a phrase to the next person, and so on down the line. Once the last person in line heard the phrase, we would compare the starting phrase and the ending phrase. They were almost *never* the same.

People hear words and sentences differently, so you should ask the same basic question often until you start getting consistent answers. Frequently, the differing answers provide you with sources of other questions to drill into later on. You also want to ask questions as they occur to you. The people in the room may not have an answer, but you should get it on the table for everyone to think about.

Ask open-ended questions

Open-ended questions require multiple sentences to answer. The goal is to get people to talk about what they do and how they do it. You need to get them talking as quickly as possible. A lot of what you will hear in the beginning may be general, and there might be some complaining about how bad the situation is, but these comments provide the roots of what you want to know. If you ask yes/no questions, the interviewee has no incentive to provide any more information than that. Try and ask questions that require a multisentence answer.

Don't forget that your interviewees should do 80 percent of the talking and you should be doing 80 percent of the listening. An example of how to do this might be asking questions about customers and marketing efforts. Instead of asking, "Do you advertise for customers?" and receiving a "yes" answer, you might approach it like this:

- How does your company attract customers?

- What mediums do you advertise in?

- How do you determine which advertisement attracted a specific customer?

- Do your customers identify with your company?

- How do you determine campaign effectiveness?

- What do your customers like most about your company?

- What do they like least about your company?

- How do your customers perceive the changes taking place in your industry?

This is a simplified example, but you get the idea. Each of the preceding questions requires a multisentence answer. Your interviewees are going to have to talk a little while to answer the questions and explain all the new terms used in the process.

You must be very careful when asking leading questions. It is easy to ask questions designed to get the answers you want, not necessarily the answer you need to hear.

Repeat answers

Repeating answers is very important. As you are given an explanation, take the time to repeat it back to the interviewee in your own words. You probably don't want to do this for every single answer you get, but for those longer, more complicated explanations, you should take a second or two and summarize what you've just heard. This has a few very important benefits:

1. It shows the group that you are really listening. Don't be in too much of a rush to complete their thoughts for them (my favorite vice). Let them complete their thoughts, and then repeat them in your own words.

2. It demonstrates the level of understanding you have about the task at hand, and this builds confidence in you as well as them, which usually leads to a higher degree of participation.

3. It provides you with immediate feedback about how you are doing and where you need to spend extra time.

Another helpful idea is to provide a summary of the interview sessions up to that time, highlighting the main points identified so far, paying particular attention to any issues that were difficult to talk over or took a long time to explain and get consensus on. This overall summary provides you a chance to step back from the conversations, articulate a higher view of the session, and evaluate the overall understanding.

Take nothing for granted

I can't stress this point enough. Assume nothing and suspect everything until the information is proven to be true (or false). This is really the only way to keep yourself from making bad decisions. Once the process is underway and you've interviewed a handful of people, you will begin to get a feel for what's reliable and what you need to drill into.

A Word about Group Dynamics

In every group setting, you can count on a number of behaviors. Most people will listen, some will participate, and a few will be totally silent. Don't be upset by this because you can still learn some valuable information from them.

Who talks

Often the person or people who talk the most contribute the least. They are like the color commentary that goes with the sporting event on TV. It's directionally correct information but marginally useful for the task at hand. If this is the case, you want to try to help others get a word in edgewise. You can accomplish this by directing the question to a specific person first, and then solicit input from the rest of the group.

In other instances, the folks who do all the talking actually do contribute a fair amount of information. This can be good so long as those people don't monopolize the whole conversation. Try to give everyone equal time.

Who doesn't talk

Take note of the people who don't talk. Presumably, they were identified as interview candidates either because they have specific knowledge that the project requires or they are in a position of authority or influence to make decisions, etc. In either case, the fact that they have remained silent should not escape your attention.

Frequently, there are very good reasons for this silence – primarily, a superior/subordinate relationship exists between individuals in the room. Rare is the subordinate who speaks up with his or her superior in the room. Approaching these people separately to get their input might be worthwhile.

Aggressive personalities

You probably won't run across aggressive people often, but sometimes you will. Most of us are unprepared when it comes to dealing with these types of people, but you can take a few steps to mitigate the situation. Typically, these people are either afraid for their job after the project is over, they have another (perhaps hidden) agenda, or they are eager to make themselves indispensable to the project. Occasionally, I've run across folks who just want to learn something new and in their zeal, they forget their manners and ride roughshod over the rest of the group.

To effectively handle this situation, you must identify their motivation for such behavior and take appropriate steps to address it. Frequently, you will successfully understand their motivation and use it to your advantage. Occasionally, you won't, and you'll have to seek a solution elsewhere. In three instances in almost 15 years of consulting, I have approached the sponsor or appropriate decision makers and asked for some relief. Most of the time, the situation can be resolved in a reasonable manner. Sometimes all that's required is a side conversation to understand their point of view and all is well. It's hard to give more guidance than this because each situation will be very different from the next, except to say that these people will generally require more expectation management than the others.

Tips on How to Stay on Track

Staying on track during the interview process can be somewhat challenging. With so much information to gather and so many people involved in the process, you often feel like you are going down the road less traveled.

The success of the interview process is really based on your ability to correctly identify rabbit holes and out-of-scope issues. A *rabbit hole* is a topic of conversation that, while perhaps interesting, has minimal if any value to the project. I'll generally let this happen once or twice at the beginning, but once I've established a rapport with the group, I'll call a time-out, identify the topic as a rabbit hole, and move on. This is fair and necessary if you are to get to the end of the process.

Out-of-scope issues are a little harder to identify because, generally, the determination as to whether or not the issue is in or out of scope is unclear when the issues are first identified. I become suspicious of an issue if, after ten minutes or so of conversation, we have gone nowhere or have no more agreement on the issue than when we started. The main point is that you don't want to get sidetracked on a single issue – at least not in this meeting. It may be that a subsequent meeting is necessary to resolve a specific issue, but not at the expense of an unplanned re-direction of the current meeting.

More often than not, some amount of follow-up research must be done to determine the status, but the current interview is not the place. I keep a list of out-of-scope issues and add to it liberally. Scope creep is your biggest enemy. The more groups that are involved, the higher the potential for scope creep.

Publishing the list of identified needs and assigning their delivery to a project phase is a good way to encourage continued participation and prevent creep. In some cases, the project plan may end up having a phase 1, 2, 3, and so forth, with appropriate expectations established for each deliverable.

You can always come back to an item on the list if necessary, but you should record it so you don't forget later. This list is a great starting place for follow-up projects and opportunities to define new functionality once you have completed the current project. The only way you can ensure that all of this information is recorded, processed, and passed around to the project team is by taking good notes, meeting minutes, and interview summaries.

It is *extremely* important to write things down, even if the information doesn't seem significant at the time or if it seems out of scope. Maybe the group is discussing something that is actually very important, but at the moment, your understanding of the subject is not as complete as theirs. Later, when you go back and review your notes, things may catch your eye and make more sense or help trigger you to ask more questions so that you do understand the issue more completely.

The Logical Process Reviewed

Earlier in this chapter, I mentioned that the interview process and the logical modeling process are closely tied together. This is primarily because the logical model phase (discussed in the next chapter) is an iterative process. It's also technology independent.

Technology independent means you should do the business discovery without regard to any of the technology available to you. Why? Because very few businesses are willing to define their business process based on the capabilities or deficiencies of a particular technology product. Only after the business is understood, and the problem clearly defined, do you look at technology solutions to help solve it.

The iterative nature comes from the steps in the logical model process (see Figure 3-2):

1. **Interview** – Conduct the interviews.

2. **Document** – Document the interviews.

3. **Model** – Render/update a model based on what you just learned. This model is then the basis for the next round of interviews.

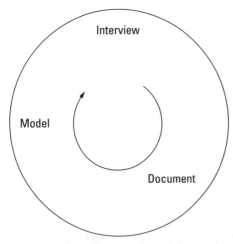

Figure 3-2: The iterative nature of the requirement-gathering process

If you wait until you've completed all the interviews and then start to render the model, you will have lost some valuable context related to the information. Document and update the model while the information is fresh in your mind.

Here are some tips on conducting interviews. These hints will help you get the most out of your interview time:

- Conduct interviews in familiar surroundings for the participants.

- Avoid interruptions – including the telephone.

- Use the interviewees' vocabulary as quickly as you can learn and understand it. Nothing communicates credibility more than using the terms they are familiar with. Don't be afraid to ask for a definition of a term you are not sure about. They will appreciate it.

- Try to keep the interview sessions to a reasonable amount of time – two hours maximum. You should be seeing each group at least twice, so don't try to cram it all into one meeting.

- Give ample notice to the participants so they can schedule effectively. Poor planning on your part does not constitute an emergency on their part. This also gives them an opportunity to collect any materials that might help them explain their job function, etc. Be sure to get copies of everything.

- Listen. Listen some more, and when you're done, don't forget to *listen*.

- For a large project, the interview/logical model process should not last more than two or three weeks.

- Always try to view a problem from different perspectives. Don't stick with the initial line of reasoning because it might be based on invalid assumptions.

- Seek input from a variety of people. This gives you multiple contexts in which to evaluate information and uncover other assumptions to be investigated.

- Try not to influence others by explaining your thoughts first. This often leads to you being told what you want to hear rather than what you need to know. Watch out for the reverse as well: don't tell others what they want to hear; tell them what they need to know.

- Be aware of the status quo. This is the attitude of "We've always done it this way." Review the objectives of the project and see how they will be served by status quo. The status quo is *never* the only alternative, and asking the group if they would choose the status quo if things were different may help to point out other options.

- Avoid exaggerating the effort or cost involved in the project. This is certainly important information, but don't beat everyone over the head about it. More than likely, most participants will be far enough out of their comfort zone that no real benefit is gained by adding to the stress that they already feel.

◆ Build in a fudge factor so that you're likely to finish a day early rather than a day late. So which is it – don't exaggerate, or build in a contingency factor? Actually, the real answer is to add a contingency factor without exaggerating. This is very much a gut feeling type of skill that you learn over time with the more projects you do. It is largely driven by the situation you have and the problems you have to solve. I hesitate to provide numbers here because every situation is so different, but I would reconsider your contingency factors if you've left yourself less than 5 percent or more than 30 percent of the total time. Any higher than this, and I'd suspect you have other issues to deal with that are not fully understood.

◆ If there was a previous data warehouse project (or attempted project), seek out people who were involved in that activity and listen to what they have to say. You will often gather valuable information about why the project succeeded or failed.

◆ Be willing to learn and be open-minded. You are not there to dictate their business to them; it's the reverse. Once you understand the business, and more importantly, once the customer understands that you understand the business, then (and only then) you can proceed to build the warehouse.

How Do You Know When You're Done?

So, you are interviewing, rendering a model, and you've been at it for 10 or 12 days. How do you know if you're finished with this process? It's not as hard as you might think.

The biggest clue is that you are not hearing any new information to your questions. This is an indication that you have the process down and you are about where you should be, as long as the questions you are asking are in scope.

The second clue has more to do with your understanding of the business than the groups. When you are able to make rhetorical statements about business processes that everyone agrees with, then you can say with a fair amount of certainty that you are finished. Often, I'll start making these types of statements as soon as I'm sure I understand the basics. This comes with practice and experience, but once you master the art, it's a powerful tool.

The Importance of Vocabulary

Earlier I mentioned using the business vocabulary in the interview process. The importance of a relevant vocabulary for any given industry is immeasurable. It doesn't take that much time to surf the Web and check out some of the association

Web pages for an industry to find a glossary of terms common to that industry. The hour or two it takes to find this material and read it will pay handsome dividends from day one.

This aspect of requirements gathering does more to communicate your credibility than anything else. Rare are the clients who will turn you loose on a project if you can't hold a 10- or 15-minute conversation about their industry and make sense.

Often, the communications you hear on the first day or so at the client site can sound like a foreign language. Health care and telecommunications tend to fall into this category. I have a functional vocabulary in both of these areas, but every so often, I'll have a conversation with someone and I'll understand the words, but I have no idea what it is he or she just said. Don't be afraid to ask questions – just because you have a vocabulary does not make you an expert in the field. The same is true the other way around. Just because clients have a data warehousing vocabulary doesn't mean they can design the model.

Lessons from the Trenches

There are several lessons to be learned from the trenches. I have seen the results of projects where one or more of these important points were ignored or otherwise compromised. If you don't do the project right the first time, where will you find the time to do it over?

Listen

Listen, listen, and listen some more. I can't stress this enough. In my opinion, most issues arise because someone didn't listen closely enough and understand.

Manage expectations

Almost as important as listening, mismanaged expectations do more to limit project success than anything else. You want to be in a position of meeting or exceeding everyone's expectations. If you are to do that, you *must* manage appropriately. The two situations you want to avoid at all costs are failing and not succeeding – and there is a difference. I *fail* because of specific events or decisions that can be identified and measured. I *succeed* for the same reasons. The toughest one to manage is when I didn't fail and I didn't succeed. I can be technically correct, but if expectations are not in line with the solution and the users are markedly undecided about the results, more often than not, the project slowly fades away.

Document everything

You'd be surprised at how a person's memory changes over time. We all suffer from selective memory, and it's more than nice to be able to refer back to credible, accurate, and detailed documentation. By the way, it's worth the effort to organize this information into a project notebook. It's professional and it can make all the difference when a problem crops up and people start coming to you for answers.

Render a logical model as interviews are conducted

The requirements process is very iterative. It's designed to be. Don't wait until all the interviews are completed to start rendering a logical model. You will already have lost valuable information, both in terms of context and meaning, that will make the logical modeling process stretch out longer than it needs to, and/or you will end up with a less effective model.

Introduction to the Sample Database

Inevitably, people seem to choose some sort of retail example for their sample database — perhaps because a retail example is one of the easier types of schemas to produce and provide data for, and it's something everyone can relate to. I wanted to do something different.

The chapters that follow have a section at the end that deals with the sample database. For example, this chapter discusses how the interview information was used to arrive at the definition and classification of the business case. Note that all of this information is fictitious in that it has been created solely for this book and has been designed more as a teaching aid.

The business problem

The sample database is based on a fictitious regional telephone company — Local-Tel. It serves a four-state area, and, in addition to providing standard local and local/long distance, it also provides ISDN, 800, 900, WATS, and T1 services. It has a base of about 1 million customers and services approximately 10 million telephone lines.

Like many smaller phone companies in the new economy, Local-Tel has difficulty understanding who their customers are, why they are happy, and why they leave. In addition, because it has a hodgepodge of different systems, Local-Tel has a difficult time tracking how much revenue its business generates, making product comparisons, observing customer usage patterns, and understanding how, why, and how often its customers churn. *Churn* is defined as an event where a customer chooses to terminate service with telephone Company A and commence service with telephone Company B. If you have ever switched long-distance services, you have churned. The interview process revealed that the business problem can be broken down into several areas, as described in the following sections.

Customer analysis and profiling

These issues came from the CFO and the marketing people. They want to understand who their customers are, observe how different groups of customers use their services, and see some of the more important characteristics of their most profitable customers as well as those they will lose.

This information is important because if you know why the customers are happy, you can make them happier. If you know why they are unhappy, you can address that as well. The key business questions for this group of people are as follows:

◆ What are the three characteristics of the most profitable customers?

◆ What are the top ten industries you service?

◆ What kinds of customers are you losing to the competition?

◆ What are the top three characteristics of customers you eventually lose?

◆ What is the average active life of a lost customer?

Line type analysis

You are interested in looking at the types of lines being used to determine if you should discontinue certain types of services or expand into others – cable, perhaps. The questions you should ask here are as follows:

◆ Which is the most profitable line type you provide?

◆ Which type of line is most used by your business customers?

◆ What percentage of your residential customers has an ISDN line? Are they a candidate for your expanded child-friendly Internet service?

◆ Do you have enough 800 numbers to meet expected growth based on the last two years?

Calling patterns

This information tells you how your customers use your services. You can use the results of these business questions to help identify customers to cross-sell other products or services to. Key business questions here include these:

◆ What is the most frequently called exchange? Area code?

◆ What are the ten most frequently called businesses?

◆ How many calling card calls are placed by week and by month? (Rank them by time of day – busiest to slowest.)

◆ What are the heaviest call days and time periods for business accounts and for residential accounts?

Billing analysis

The company has several different billing systems because of mergers and acquisitions that have occurred. Although there is a unified billing system, it keeps no history and once the bills are generated for the billing cycle, the data is lost — until now. The company wants to place the data into the warehouse and perform some analysis to better understand its financial picture. Key questions here are the following:

◆ What is your revenue per residential unit? By business unit?

◆ Which geographic area generates the most revenue?

◆ What is the breakdown of revenue by month, taking various customer demographics into account?

◆ What are the characteristics of customers who churn, and how many current customers have those same characteristics?

Summary

Requirements gathering is one of the most basic tasks associated with a data warehouse project, no matter what technology is being employed. The information acquired from this process is critical to your project's success. In general, the whole process lasts from one week for the simpler environments to three weeks for the more complicated environments. Be careful of "analysis paralysis" and constantly evaluate the information you receive in terms of the project goals.

Once you stop hearing anything new, that's a good indication that you may be finished with this process. Don't be in a hurry to complete the process because the allotted time is up. It's much easier to do it right now than after you've loaded all the data. Remember that not everyone possesses the same interviewing skills, so as much as possible, get comfortable with your skill set and follow the guidelines presented here. Experience will sharpen these skills.

The sample database is a fictional telecommunications company that provides local telephone service. I picked this example because it's different from the retail examples most often used in these types of books and because it provides an opportunity to develop some large fact and dimension tables.

Part II

Modeling

Chapter 4

Logical Modeling

IN THIS CHAPTER

◆ A schema design overview

◆ The basics of logical modeling

◆ The mechanics of fact and dimension tables

◆ Fact table and dimension table how to

◆ Advanced dimensional issues

◆ Lesson from the trenches

◆ Sample project logical model

LOGICAL MODELING IS PERHAPS the most difficult part of any Red Brick project. It's not that dimensional modeling is so hard to comprehend; it's more because the concepts and methods of dimensional modeling go against the grain of what's required for OLTP modeling, and it sometimes seems that the longer a person has been practicing OLTP modeling, the harder it is for him or her to master dimensional modeling.

To make the modeling process even more confusing, many authors and technology companies have put forth different versions of the dimensional model. This is understandable in light of the huge amount of money spent by corporations on data warehousing installations; however, these additional views of the world, while beneficial to the authoring individuals and/or organization(s), do not demonstrate dimensional modeling techniques very well to the beginner.

To get you started on the right track, I'll discuss logical modeling (or schema design) from a high level to set some groundwork. From there, I'll review the basics of the dimensional modeling process including fact and dimension tables and the process of determining where each of the columns goes.

Basics are great, but there is more you must know if you are to succeed in implementing a warehouse, so I'll also discuss a number of advanced issues, such as slowly changing dimensions and natural vs. generated keys. Finally, I'll wrap up this chapter with some valuable lessons gathered from actual field experience, and then I'll discuss the sample database logical model.

A Schema Design Overview

Schema design, or logical modeling, is one of the essential components of a data warehouse. It is even more basic to a Red Brick installation because the whole of Red Brick Decision Server technology is based on the dimensional model and is designed to take full advantage of the opportunities the dimensional paradigm offers for solving business problems. For this reason, it's vitally important that you not only understand the concepts of dimensional modeling, but also use them appropriately in developing the model for your project.

A 10,000-foot view

As I noted in Chapter 3, there is a close relationship between requirements gathering and schema design. You are fortunate that in today's IT environments, dimensional modeling is now an accepted method of modeling data warehouses — so much so that many popular data modeling tools support it. This was not the case just a few years ago.

   At one time, Red Brick field resources had to prove everything we were saying about the dimensional model and why it made so much sense to potential customers, because what we were preaching was so "out there." It's gratifying in a way to see the industry grow up and adopt many of the radical ideas we started with years ago. Many years later, the basics remain the same. What follows is a primer on dimensional modeling the way Red Brick has always presented it, but with the added benefit of many years of field experience thrown in for good measure.

Defining terms

Before I get too far, I should define a number of terms so that we are all on the same page.

   To some degree, the *operational data store (ODS)* has been defined and redefined so many times that it's almost useless — however, there is some benefit to be had in this type of data store. The ODS is a long-lasting, generally nonsummarized but queryable form of legacy transaction-level data that exists in a transaction-oriented model.

   The *data staging area* is a place where data can be worked on in between extraction from the source system and loading into the warehouse. In actual practice, data staging is a necessary *function*, not necessarily a required *database* — there's a difference. If your staging requirements are fairly easy to manage (simple calculations, conversions, and such), then you might have nothing more than a set of extraction routines or programs with the appropriate logic in them to address the issues at extraction time (although admittedly, this doesn't happen too often).

   On the other hand, if you have complex requirements (such as generated keys, complex conversion or calculation requirements, or situations where you have to apply a considerable amount of logic to transform data values into meaningful information), you should strongly consider building a data staging area.

You may very well be able to perform most (if not all) of the transformation work in the source database, but remember that everything costs something, and you just might want the extra margin of safety that the data staging area provides by doing all the extra processing outside the production database.

The primary concept that must be adhered to is that no matter where the data is taken from, whatever processing is required to load it into the warehouse has these qualities:

♦ Repeatable — If you run the process today and get a result, you should get the same result over the same data tomorrow.

♦ Scaleable — Developing and testing a conversion program or SQL script over a handful of rows is okay, but be sure the process can handle the expected amount of data necessary.

Figure 4-1 illustrates how these different components are related. It's possible build an ODS, and/or a data staging area, or neither of them. Your specific situation should dictate how you proceed with these types of data sorts.

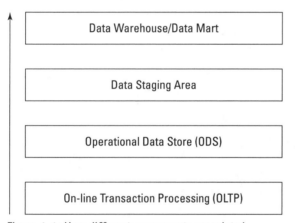

Figure 4-1: How different components are related

The correct way to approach dimensional logical modeling

Logical modeling should be approached in a logical fashion. (Couldn't resist the pun!) This means giving the business requirements first priority, rendering a dimensional model that solves the problem, and then evaluating the technologies available to implement the model. Many times, the technologies are chosen first. I believe that this compromises the results even before you get started.

I realize that often you are not given a choice in the technology components you must use. This is unfortunate but a reality nonetheless. If this is your situation, try your best to develop the logical model without regard to the choices already made. Once the logical model is completed, only then should you consider the technology options or choices.

The truth is, everything's a tradeoff and there is no one right answer. There is no substitute for due diligence. Implementing a data warehouse is an endless list of tradeoffs you must make, and the items and tradeoffs you choose to make will be different from the next person's. The following list should give you some idea of what I'm talking about:

◆ Data acquisition: Includes issues like how and when is the source data available, how much work needs to be done to extract the required information, how much work is required to apply transformations and business rules, and so forth.

◆ Load performance: Refers to load windows available, available bandwidth to actually load the data, post-loading maintenance issues (such as index building), and issues concerning duplicate or missing rows.

◆ Query performance: Addresses issues dealing with user expectations on how queries are being processed, system resources available for queries, average result set sizes, and the like.

◆ Administration costs: Addresses items having to do with the actual physical equipment and personnel required to administer and maintain the data warehouse – backup, recovery, DBA resources, and other necessary items to maintain an installation.

◆ Storage space: Deals with issues related to storage warehouse information, including online query, backup, and recovery, as well as staging-area requirements to load new data. Warehouses can be quite large, and more that one budget has been busted over the amount of hardware necessary to store the required data.

◆ Load windows: Identifies issues relating to how much time you have to load the data and what you must do to ensure that it has been loaded correctly.

◆ User capability: Identifies issues related to the complexity of the users, how technically skilled they are, and how quickly they grasp new tools and concepts.

◆ Technology employed: Often, the technology to be employed for a warehouse has been chosen long before the requirements are known. This can be a very complex issue and often leads to tradeoffs being made that in other circumstances would not be made at all. In my opinion, it's a little shortsighted to choose technology components prior to knowing exactly what the requirements are.

◆ ?: Your list here. In addition to the items listed previously, many other intangible items exist, such as politics and business circumstances, that sometimes end up having an undue influence in the choice of technology. Be careful!

The Basics of Logical Modeling

Now that you have a larger view of the world, how do you approach logical modeling without getting mired up in all the ancillary issues? It's not that complicated, but there is a word of warning:

Just because you can design any type of schema you choose does not mean that it will perform well with a given decision support technology. Don't fall into the OLTP design trap by rendering a model that is close to or identical to the production system. This is truer of Red Brick than any other technology. Red Brick was designed from the ground up to leverage the dimensional model. It's not an afterthought or add-on functionality that was cobbled together over a weekend – it's designed in the database engine itself. It's possible to build any type of model you care to with Red Brick technology, but if you ignore the principals on which the technology was based, well, it would be like buying a Ferrari and driving 10 mph.

 Don't fall into the OLTP design trap. Dimensional models are different for a reason. Do your best to resist these design tendencies.

Dimensional modeling basics

There are some basic differences between transaction systems and Decision Support Systems (DSS) that you should understand before moving forward. These basic differences are why it's so difficult for a transaction system to perform as well as Red Brick in the warehouse environment – they have competing goals.

Transaction databases

Transaction databases are perhaps the type of data model we are the most familiar with. These are the data models that IT has been building since the 1970s. These types of database installations have the following characteristics:

◆ High transaction rates – The TCP benchmark wars of not too many years ago were all about how many transactions second databases can perform. A lot of engineering and marketing dollars were spent in making the database engines perform in this arena.

◆ Constant change – This is the very nature of a transaction database. It's always changing. Some refer to this as a "twinkling" database, but in any event, transactions are always being written to the server.

◆ Changing join paths – This is perhaps the biggest Achilles' heel of a transaction database system. It's possible for you to submit a query today and obtain an answer set. You can then submit the exact query tomorrow, and it may be processed differently. The join paths are not static. They are chosen based on a host of items that the server looks at when the query is processed. Ideally, you'd expect to get the same answer, but often, you don't.

◆ No redundancy – There is little (if any) redundant data. Not a bad idea (for transaction systems) because it helps keep the tables narrow and the transactions small.

◆ Relational integrity issues – I like this one. As you'll discover later, data is the biggest issue you will have to deal with. If you were the wagering sort, you could make a fair living going around placing bets with others about how clean their data is. Nothing will expose this more that putting it into a warehouse. Transaction data is modeled along *data* normalization rules, not *business* rules. Because of this, there are routine instances where data integrity fails due to a lack of validation along the business rules.

◆ Predictable SQL queries – Queries in a transaction system are predictable. You're running data-entry and reporting applications on top of the database. The whole notion of data warehouse came from not being able to get the data out in any reasonable amount of time. Data entry screens, canned or repetitive reports, and so forth all add to the predictability of transaction system queries.

Turning Referential Integrity (RI) Off

From time to time, you will run into someone who proposes that the data does not need to be subjected to the rigors of Red Brick RI checking because "It was checked when it was put into the transaction system." Don't believe it! Pursuing this idea rarely does anything more than waste time you probably don't have in the first place so that you can do it the correct way a second time.

DSS databases

Decision Support databases have a very different set of characteristics that define them:

◆ Understandable – Generally speaking, a data warehouse schema and a transaction schema for the same problem will be significantly different. The warehouse schemas are greatly simplified. There are many fewer tables, and the business users readily understand what tables there are. It's unrealistic to think that a business user can effectively navigate a schema with hundreds of tables.

◆ Mostly static – This means there are not lots of transactions happening every second. Before Query Priority Concurrency (QPC) – the Red brick facility that allows updates to the database while queries are running – there was generally one transaction a day/week or month, depending on your load cycle. Now, with the concurrent facility, it's possible to have updates, but they take a back seat to queries.

◆ Known join paths – Because of how the tables are related to one another, the paths to each fact table are known. This simplifies the optimizer's work in figuring out how to get the data and puts more emphasis on determining which index to use, not which tables to join through.

◆ Referential integrity – Perhaps the biggest asset of Red Brick technology is that RI is *not* optional. Other products market features that allow you to turn RI off or delay the RI checking process, but what for? Faster load times? If you turn it off altogether, the data is no better than the transaction system. If you defer the RI check, you haven't really decreased your load time because it must be performed before the data can be used in the decision-making process. Consistent and enforced RI is the *only* way to know that the data in the warehouse is correct, and nobody does it better or faster than Red Brick.

◆ Unpredictable/complex SQL queries – This is the whole nature of warehouse activity. Generally, it's not the first or second query that I'm interested in as a user; it's where those queries take me for further investigation that's important. Business users want to be able to pose a question, get some results, and out of that, pose another question, and so on. This is often referred to as "drilling down" on a result set. This is often impossible in a transaction system because of the time it takes to get the results.

◆ Large result sets – Generally, query results from a DSS system are much larger than those from a transaction system because you have the ability to look over years of data.

It's All About the Business

I feel it necessary to say a few words about the general subject of schema design. Unfortunately for you, your users, and your customers, the whole topic of the type of data model to render for a data warehouse has become very convoluted, driven by marketing dollars and product affiliations in a desire for market share. When all is said and done, the users don't care how you build your warehouse, or what type of data model you used — as long as it's easy to understand, easy to navigate, and the warehouse performs at or above (appropriately managed) user expectations. As you read through the rest of this chapter, keep in mind that this is a book about Red Brick Decision Server technology and how to implement it, *not* a book about the benefits of one modeling method over another.

The whole of Red Brick Decision Server technology is based on the premise that users must be able to understand and navigate the data they must work with, the data store has to be as easy to manage as possible, and above all, it must provide added value to the business users. These simple but fundamental ideas are where it all started and have evolved into the Red Brick Decision Server you know today. It's still about the business, the users, and providing added value based on proven methods that work, not think-tank discussions and useless debates.

Having said all this, I encourage you to try to operate at a level above the marketing and the hype, and seriously consider the opportunity you have to deliver content and value. You may not agree with the approach; however, if you are using Red Brick Decision Server, it's the way to go.

A word about other schema types

Earlier, I mentioned some myths and misconceptions about dimensional modeling. As it turns out, a few terms are floating around that have from time to time been put forth as options or types of dimensional models. I discuss them here to familiarize you with the terms and to put them in proper perspective.

In my opinion, a dimensional model is a dimensional model, and this whole "type" business only serves to confuse everyone. The ideas below, although more or less directionally correct, are not the place to start in understanding the concepts of dimensional modeling.

Constellation	This is basically a dimensional (or star) schema. Dimension tables are separate from fact tables, and the largest dimension is usually normalized (read: snowflake or outrigger). Although this is directionally correct, I caution you to approach this in a different manner. You may very well end up with this type of model, but let the business rules, data volumes, and query requirements dictate any denormalization of the dimensions.

Federation

A federation schema is simply a dimensional data model with two or more fact tables. The dimensions are denormalized (as they should be), and the facts are normalized (as they should be). You just have more than one fact table in the model, perhaps each representing a subject area. The basic misunderstanding here is that a dimensional model cannot have more than one fact table. Untrue.

Snowflake

A Snowflake schema gets its name from the fact that as the data models are normalized, the picture starts to look like a snowflake. Snowflake schemas (also referred to as outboard tables or outriggers) are really a form of normalization. The larger dimension tables are denormalized, usually in an attempt to save space or provide functionality for a query tool.

 Don't fall into the trap of letting a technology define your business process or influence the logical data model. There is a place and time to consider the technology components of the solution, but not here and now.

Dimensional modeling myths

Common thinking notwithstanding, there are still far too many instances where misconception and myth about the dimensional modeling process complicate warehouse projects. People in these instances tend to make "safe" choices and don't take the time to consider anything new. Out of this selective ignorance arise several common misconceptions about data warehouses and the dimensional modeling process. In my opinion, these issues are either designed to increase the fear, uncertainly, and doubt (FUD) factor (see the sidebar "FUD"), or they are an attempt to force-fit a piece of technology into the dimensional modeling space. In either case, they are of little value.

FUD

FUD is a sales and marketing term that stands for *fear, uncertainty, and doubt*. It is a tactic that is sometimes employed to convince someone to change his or her mind by playing into his or her fears (What if it doesn't work? What will my boss say?) or to take advantage of a perceived lack of knowledge.

STOVEPIPE IMPLEMENTATIONS

Stovepipes and data islands both have the same meaning: you build a warehouse or data mart, and when you're done, it has no connection to the rest of your IT infrastructure, business processes, and so on. While it is *absolutely* possible to build such a system, it is *not* inherent in the dimensional modeling methodology. It's like anything else; if you work in a vacuum, you get what you deserve; if, on the other hand, you work in such a way that you keep yourself aware of the larger picture, there's no reason why you can't succeed.

NO UNDERSTANDING

The premise here is that it's too hard to learn how to do it, and that even if you could, none of your users would understand it. Nonsense. If done correctly, dimensional models are much less complex than their OLTP counterparts, and consider this – how would you ever train a business analyst to navigate a model with hundreds of tables that are interconnected by various relationships? Every dimensional modeler started in the OLTP space, so obviously, it's learnable. The key here is to manage expectations appropriately.

ONLY WORKS WITH RETAIL

I think this idea came about because retail was the first industry to adopt the concept of dimensional modeling. It was the practice baby. As you will discover from the sample database, it works with telecommunications as well. Actually, dimensional modeling will work with any industry or subject area, as long as you pay attention to the rules.

SNOWFLAKING AS AN ALTERNATIVE TO DIMENSIONAL MODELING

This is my favorite pet peeve. In my opinion, indiscriminate snowflaking ruins more warehouse implementations than anything else because if you do it enough and you have the transactional model back, why bother in the first place?

Often, you will hear something to the effect that snowflaking is required for the front-end tool to function properly and be able to be a requirement for distinct lists of values to populate select lists. The reality is that if you set up the metadata correctly and index appropriately in Red Brick, the outrigger is not necessary. Having said all this, on a few occasions it is necessary to model a snowflake or outrigger table. These instances are the exception and most often have to do with loading syndicated data or providing some relief to some particular performance problem. That is the key word – performance. "If it ain't broke, don't fix it!" And more importantly, if you must denormalize, be absolutely sure you understand *why* it's necessary, and the price you are paying for the denormalization.

When all is said and done, my best advice is don't confuse marketing with reality. The goal of a dimensional model is to capture the business rules and issues *first*. Once that's done, you can take a look at the technology you would like to employ. Often, you may be forced to return and rethink sections of the model.

That's okay, as long as you're doing it with a complete understanding of the business and applying a technology to a business problem, not letting a technology *define* your business problem.

Fact and dimension tables

Dimensional models are composed of fact tables and dimension tables. These tables are put together in a way that resembles a star: hence, the name star schemas. Fact tables are usually the largest tables in the database and are the starting point in the modeling process. These fact tables contain a multipart key. Each element in the key is a foreign key reference back to a primary key in a dimension table.

Figure 4-2 illustrates a simple star schema, which contains a single fact table and three dimensions. Notice that the dimension tables are normalized, the fact tables are highly denormalized, and the primary keys to the dimensions are foreign keys to the facts.

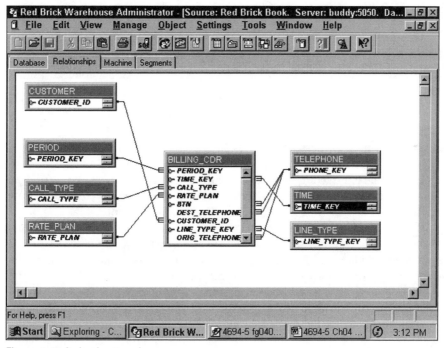

Figure 4-2: A simple star schema

Figure 4-3 is a slightly more complicated model in that it has several fact tables. Notice that all fact tables do not share all the dimensions.

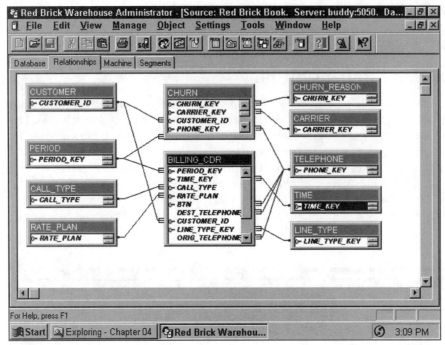

Figure 4-3: A model that has several fact tables

FACT TABLES

Fact tables are usually the largest tables in the warehouse in terms of number of rows. They generally have fewer columns than the dimensions, but not always. Facts exist at the intersection of the dimensions — if you sold three boxes of widgets to John Doe today in Store 5, then the dimensions would be Day, Product, Store, and Customer. The facts would be Quantity, Cost, Total Tax Amount, and so on.

Fact tables contain the *measures* of the business processes. These are the data elements that tell you how many, how much, cost, quantity, and so on. Measures are generally additive, mostly numeric, and are continuously valued, meaning that every row instance has a value for a given measure column. Note that a measure can appear in as many fact tables as necessary.

Fact tables are also highly normalized. This means that the only elements you keep in the fact table are the measures themselves. All other descriptive information is kept in appropriate dimension tables and is connected to the fact table through a foreign key reference. This is a fundamental concept to Red Brick technology.

Because of the foreign key references, fact tables have multipart keys. Each element of the key is itself a foreign key to a dimension table. Take another look at Figure 4-2. Notice how the fact table refers to the dimension tables.

DIMENSIONS

Dimension tables are the descriptive tables in the warehouse and contain the by values. These attributes are the items on report headers, subtotals, and so on. Show me sales by store, by region, and category. Columns that describe a business entity (such as product, customer, or store) would be dimension candidates.

Attributes should appear only in one dimension. For example, you would not place the attribute column product color in any other table except PRODUCT. If your analysis required product color as an element, then you would have to get this information from the PRODUCT table. The key to the dimensional attributes is how descriptive the level of descriptiveness. Typical dimensions might include PERIOD, TIME, STORE, CUSTOMER, and so forth.

One of the most powerful tools in a warehouse is the absence of cryptic codes that mean something only to the few people who created them. In a warehouse, you have the opportunity to expand these codes into something meaningful. For example, if the number 1 stands for Blue in the color code column of the ITEM table in the transaction system, you have an opportunity to place a Color column in the warehouse and populate it with the word blue. It makes much more sense.

Dimension tables serve as the entry point into the facts. This means that, ideally, you would not go after any data in the fact table without accessing it through one or more dimensions. Rarely would you submit a query against a fact table that didn't have some kind of constraint on at least one dimension.

Digging deeper: fact tables

There is actually more to identifying facts than meets the eye. Those of you who have built warehouses before are probably familiar with the different types of facts, but for those who aren't, I'll list them here.

TYPES OF FACTS

There are four basic types of facts: additive, nonadditive, semi-additive, and textual:

- ◆ Additive facts – These are the columns in the fact table that can be added across all dimensions. For example, you can add individual sale amounts for the month of January, for all snack products, in all stores, and get a valid result that makes business sense.

- ◆ Nonadditive facts – These are elements in the fact table that cannot be added along any dimension. It's not that you can't add them; it's just that the result doesn't make any sense when you do. For example, you would not add densities or temperatures; however, if you average these elements, the result can be useful.

- ◆ Semi-additive facts – These are elements that are generally additive across everything except time or, put another way, can be added across some but not all the dimensions. Generally speaking, monthly balances, credit limits, and so on fall into this category.

◆ Textual facts – These are elements in the fact table that are textual in nature. Textual facts do not occur often, but you should be aware of them. You should make every attempt to place textual facts into a dimension table for several reasons: chief among them is table size. The fact table will have many times more rows than the largest dimension table.

BASE FACTS AND DERIVED FACTS   There are two types of facts: base facts and derived facts. This is always an interesting discussion because of where it leads some folks. It's the "Which came first?" question. In general, base facts are those data elements that cannot be broken down into smaller components – quantity, for example. It's impossible to break that into anything else but quantity. It is what it is.

However, consider extended cost. It's the product of quantity multiplied by cost. It can be broken down into two other component (or base) facts. These types of elements are called *derived facts* because they can be calculated (or derived) from other facts in the data.

The question of the day is this: if you are given extended cost in the input stream, is it a derived or a base fact? This question has sparked more than one interesting conversation. The question I would be asking is "Is it correct?" You'd be surprised at how often precalculated data elements are incorrect.

PRECALCULATED VALUES   Often you will get precalculated values in the data you are to load into the data warehouse. If you get the components, as well as the calculation, then I'd be inclined to store the components and ignore the precalculated value. If you have a situation where the calculated value does not match the precalculated amount provided in the input data, then you have a problem. You can either fix the extraction routine (if indeed the problem exists there) or store both the components and the precalculated amount. In either case, you need to identify where the problem exists and address it if possible. The only other time I'd store precalculated results is in instances where the calculations required are complex or require knowledge or information that is unavailable in the warehouse.

TYPES OF FACT TABLES

Finally, two different types of fact tables exist. Most people consider a fact table to contain lots of numeric columns. True enough, but sometimes there are no other facts to measure than the intersection of dimensions. The classic example of this is a table that measures enrollment in a class or attendance at some type of event. These types of fact tables are called "factless" fact tables. They contain nothing but foreign key references.

The PERIOD dimension

Before I get too involved in the details of dimension tables, I want to take some time to discuss the PERIOD table and its importance. The basic premise of the data warehouse is to freeze data at a moment in time to allow consistent querying and reporting against the data. This is accomplished in part by the existence of a

PERIOD table. This dimension is probably the most-used dimension in the database and, as such, must contain information relevant to the business at a level of granularity that will allow for a logical association with the data.

For example, it's common for executives to request information for recent sales broken down by date, while at the same time wanting this very same data "rolled up" into a monthly and yearly snapshot. If the raw incoming data is at a daily level, it isn't logical (or generally practical) to maintain a time dimension based on months or years.

Here, the granularity of the warehouse is defined and the limits to reporting are set. If all you capture is data at a monthly level, there is no way to report at any level lower than monthly. This is the primary reason I recommend that you strive to capture the data at its lowest level.

THE IMPORTANCE OF PERIOD TABLE DESIGN

This dimension must be built correctly at the outset, or you will have the pleasure of explaining to executives why a seemingly logical request cannot be processed.

 I can't stress this enough: the PERIOD dimension must be designed properly from the beginning. Attempts to alter the time dimension after data has been loaded into the warehouse tend to be very expensive.

As you will discover, the PERIOD table is usually the basis for the segmentation (storage) of your warehouse. Given that, any changes to the period table may have far-reaching implications to the rest of the data in the warehouse. I'll have more to say about segmentation and the PERIOD table in Chapter 9.

You can build the PERIOD dimension data using spreadsheet software and then load it into the dimension table itself. This population of data is customarily an event that happens on an infrequent schedule. Chapter 9 has more detail on how you should approach the population of your period table.

There are elements that have become more commonplace than others and can be grouped in three distinct categories:

◆ Calendar values

◆ Fiscal year values

◆ Seasons

Calendar values represent date values and time frames measured in days, months, quarters, years, and possibly centuries. A calendar year is considered to be from January 1 to December 31. Fiscal year values represent time values for a corporation's fiscal year calendar. This fiscal calendar does not necessarily mirror the calendar year.

Seasons are more ambiguous. Seasons can represent the true weather seasons: that is, spring, summer, winter, and fall, or perhaps the large-sale seasons for a retailer, such as Easter, Thanksgiving, Christmas, or back-to-school. Seasons provide you a method to group data that would not otherwise be easily recognized as belonging together. The definition of seasons will vary from client to client based on the business practices of each. Examples of typical season definitions might include the following:

◆ Holiday – A column that indicates a given day or range of days that is considered "more special" than other days. An example of this would be 12/25, Christmas. From the sales perspective, this is an important day.

◆ Season1 – A column that indicates a given range of days that is considered to be associated. For a sports retail chain, March 1 through June 30 could be flagged as "Track & Field." By marking November 23 through December 25, any retail chain can locate sales for the Christmas season.

◆ Season2 – It is conceivable that a holiday can overlap a season, and that several seasons can overlap each other. An example of this could be baseball and football – two distinct and separate start and stop periods that blend together.

CALENDAR LOGIC AND END-USER APPLICATIONS

Because a warehouse is so time-driven, many well-intentioned programmers are tempted to put date and calendar logic into the applications. I caution you against this for several reasons:

◆ As the application is distributed, you now have *n* instances to maintain and make changes to, if, for some reason, there is a fundamental change in the business. If the date definitions and functions exist in the database, then there is only one version of the truth.

◆ By distributing the application, you leave the possibility open that the period functions you envision are open to interpretation.

The answer is to build everything into the PERIOD table and leave no room for confusion. The rest of your warehouse will be governed by the behavior of this single table. Make sure it's right.

The final caution I have for the PERIOD table is about incompatible rollups. As I outlined previously, there are usually calendar components and fiscal components to a PERIOD table. Pay attention to how these different hierarchies roll up:

◆ Days-Weeks-Months-Quarters-Years

◆ Day-Fiscal Week, Fiscal Month, Fiscal Quarter, Fiscal Year

If you're lucky, your company runs on a calendar year. Otherwise, pay attention and make sure the users understand the difference between these hierarchies. Most do, but it doesn't hurt to check. The subject of hierarchies and how they can be used by Red Brick Decision Server is discussed in Chapter 7.

Digging deeper: dimension tables

Just as fact tables have another level of detail, so do dimensions. As it turns out, you'll spend most of your time defining the dimension tables. This is appropriate because the business users will spend most of their time in these tables browsing around, looking at values, and building constraints to their queries. If you skimp on the detail in the dimensions, you will have done yourself (and your users) a great disservice.

Keep in mind that the users are going to need to browse your dimensions to properly build queries. In an ideal world, the users should not know nor care much about the underlying structures of the warehouse. What they will notice is the performance of the warehouse: good, bad, or indifferent. Don't take this for granted. To constrain effectively, the users must be comfortable with the database contents and be able to quickly identify the constraint values they are looking for.

SLOWLY CHANGING DIMENSIONS

Many people consider their tables in the warehouse as static. They don't change. In reality, this is not true. Businesses change over time, and so must the warehouse. New products are introduced, old ones are retired, new customers are acquired, and so on. There are three types of slowly changing dimension tables, and each has its place in the warehouse. You must consider carefully which type to employ to resolve any given slowly changing dimension issue(s), as it is very time consuming to change them afterwards, although it's been done from time to time.

- ◆ Type 1 – This is the easiest to implement. As data for this dimension changes in the transaction system, it's extracted on a regular basis. As it's written to the warehouse, new rows are added and existing rows are overwritten with the new values. Notice that implementing this method means that you can only look at your history by the most current definitions. An example of this would be a STORE dimension with a region column. If Store A belonged to Region 1 all of last year, and this year the regions were redefined so that Store A is now in Region 2, then all of Store A sales for last year would show up under Region 2.

- ◆ Type 2 – This is most useful when you need to keep track of the before and after picture. In this scenario, when a change is recorded, you add a new record to the table. Frequently, appending a version number to the basic key makes the data a little easier to manage. Going back to our STORE example, you would leave the original row with the region value of 1 and add a new row for Store A with a region value of 2. Notice that by adding the second record, we have partitioned our history.

◆ **Type 3** – This is the most complicated solution to the problem, but it allows you to track both old and new values for a column. The first time a value in a column changes, two columns get added: an initial value column and an effective date column. Using the Store/Regions example, you would do the following:

- Add the INITIAL REGION column

- Add the region_ effective_ date

- Update the initial region column with the value in region

- Update the region column with the new region value

- Update the region_effective_date column with the date of the change

Since this solution introduces an effective date column to each row, each query run against this type of dimension must have the concept of time. The additional concept of time can often be difficult for the user community to understand, but it's necessary if they are to use the warehouse effectively.

JUNK DIMENSIONS

Often, you will end up with a number of flags and other indicators that don't really belong in the dimensions you've already identified. These are candidates for a junk dimension. Generally, these extra elements have a limited number of values. What you do is put them all together and build a Cartesian product of all the values for all the columns and assign it a key. You must be able to duplicate the process and assign the correct key to each new fact row you are going to load. Note that junk dimensions require a generic key.

You can also just keep the observed occurrences, meaning that the rows in the junk dimension are only the rows observed in the fact rows loaded to date. This might be a more appropriate approach if the number of rows in the junk dimension starts to climb much over 30,000 or so. Occasionally, you may run into a situation where there is a perceived requirement to store comments. The first question to ask is how much value will the comments have over the duration of the warehouse. In other instances, there might be legal issues that mandate that the comments be available. If you must store them, the best solution might be to sequentially number the comment, place it in a dimension, and attach it to the proper fact row.

DEGENERATE DIMENSIONS

Frequently, you will have a fact table that represents a numbered document like a purchase order or sales order. Rarely will the users ever constrain by this number; however, it's generally required for uniqueness and therefore is included in the primary key. In Red Brick, it isn't necessary to carry the primary key of a dimension table to the fact table if there is a STARindex that uniquely identifies a row (that is, if there is a combination of the other keys in the fact table that can uniquely identify a row).

This means that if you created a dimension table that contained only order numbers, you could then attach it to the fact table via a foreign key reference, and therefore build a STARindex over it. This would then allow you to drop the primary key as long as at least one STAR index uniquely identified a row in the fact table. By pulling the document number out of the fact table, you are able to lose an extra index that you won't use anyway.

MONSTER DIMENSIONS

These are the best! They often cause the most trouble, but they also give you an opportunity to test your DBA skills. In most cases, this is the customer dimension. It's hard to say exactly what the definition of *monster* is. Five or six years ago, a customer table that had 200,000 rows or more was considered big. Today, it's common to see customer dimensions upwards of 5 million to 10 million rows or more.

When you have this kind of situation, you must be somewhat conservative in how you handle the dimension, both in terms of indexes available and how infrequent updates to the table are managed. Fortunately, Red Brick Decision Server is able to handle these larger dimensions without making you pay a penalty just because the dimension is large.

If the dimension is large *and changes rapidly*, you have a different problem on your hands. The solution to this problem is to break the offending table into two tables. The first table would be all the static information (customer name, address, and so on). The other table would be the frequently changing elements. Demographic information falls into this category. This is about the only option you have because the sheer size of the table makes the standard methods of managing changing dimensions unacceptable. If you want to create the ultimate monster table, take a ten-million row customer table and treat it like a Type 3 slowly changing dimension. That truly is a table that is "large and in charge"!

The Mechanics of Fact and Dimension Tables

You should also be aware of some general observations about the modeling process and some definitions that are basic to the understanding of the modeling process. So far, you've reviewed the components of a logical model; now it's time to look at the process itself.

Some definitions and observations

The logical modeling process should not take much more than two or three weeks for a large or complicated project. There is a fine line between a logical process and analysis paralysis, but as I point out later in the chapter, there are a few ways you can determine when to stop. There are exceptions, but the average time frame for the logical modeling is about two weeks, and it generally runs concurrently with the requirements of gathering activities to a certain extent.

Your success is tied to your ability to manage project scope and scope creep. I've mentioned this already, but it warrants repeating. Managing scope is a full-time job, and there is no better place to pay more attention to it than in the modeling phase. Why? On paper, all you're doing is drawing boxes and lines, but in reality, each box and line equates to a fair amount of work.

Don't exclude data elements if they're necessary to solve the business problem, but don't be in a hurry to add elements that, although perhaps "directionally correct," are not contributing to the overall solution. Remember that the modeling phase of the project is iterative by nature. Any attempt to short-circuit that process generally isn't worth the results obtained.

Keeping the following definitions in mind will help you navigate the modeling process. I point them out here because you will move back and forth between a logical and physical model and it's important to know what belongs where.

◆ **Logical model** – A picture representation that shows the objects of the business and their relationships to other objects in the business. It is technology *independent*.

◆ **Physical model** – An implementation of a logical model that is technology *dependent*. This representation includes data types, key definitions, and other technology components.

One last point to keep in mind is that a logical model should be developed without regard for query tools, reports, data sources, database technology, political issues, and so on. These issues do not define the business process; they exist either to support the business process or because of it. Either way, there is no added value if these issues are considered at the logical level, and more often than not, the model ends up being compromised.

These concerns are properly addressed as you implement your logical model and start to make choices and trade-offs involving technology, tools, politics, and other considerations. If addressed here, you now have the opportunity to make a more informed decision and foresee more clearly the impact on the warehouse project.

Logical Model Components

A logical model has just a few components. These read like a fairly simple list, but don't be fooled.

◆ Process to be modeled: To start with, you must identify the process to be modeled. This might be a single process or a set of related processes. An example might be Order Entry, Shipments, and Returns – three separate processes, all related and sharing common dimensions.

◆ Fact table grain: The next item to identify is the grain of the fact table(s). The grain of a fact table is simply a detailed definition of what each row in the fact table represents. You can't be too detailed when it comes to grain definitions.

- ◆ Facts: These are the measurements of the process. As I discussed earlier, they are mostly numeric and additive in nature.

- ◆ Dimensions: Once the grain is declared, then you must identify any supporting dimensions that exist. Detailed grain statements make this task much easier.

- ◆ Dimension attributes: Finally, once the dimensions have been identified, you want to populate them with as many descriptive attributes as you possibly can. Further refinement will naturally take place as you proceed through the rest of the project, but don't eliminate candidate dimension columns without a good reason. I'll have more to say on this shortly.

Fact Table How To

This next discussion is all about the *how* of defining fact and dimension tables. There is not much mystery in this, although at times it can be a challenge. Remember that these steps are a starting point. There may be any number of reasons why you might have to make some compromise decisions. That's okay as long as you know why the compromise is being made and you understand and can articulate the costs, risks, and benefits of the decision.

Identify the process

Generally speaking, there is one fact table per process to start with. As you go through the requirements/modeling cycle, you will often have other fact tables fall out of the discussions based on your understanding of the business. Don't get too excited about the number of fact tables yet; just make sure the processes they zrepresent are in scope.

Identify the grain

As stated earlier, the grain is the detailed definition of the fact table. It tells you *exactly* what a row in the fact table is. In the sample database, BILLING_CDR table, the grain statement reads like this:

```
A billing record of every call charged to each customer's billing
phone number, at all times of the day, every day.
```

Obviously, there are more dimensions than those few mentioned in the grain statement; however, they do not change the grain and are okay. Often, the initial grain statement will indicate some initial dimension definitions, and you should investigate them, but there are usually others.

Be as clear and concise as possible when declaring the fact table grain. You also want to start with as low a grain definition as possible. You may change it to a higher one, but start as low as possible. The less ambiguous the definition, the easier it is to go the next steps.

It is generally better to start with a single source for your first warehouse effort (if you have a choice!). Single source means that there is only one data source system for the data. Multiple source systems tend to have many data issues that need to be resolved, and these data issues generate lots of ancillary problems that a first-time project team could do without. If you don't have a choice, pay very close attention to the data sources and the extraction processes. I'll have more to say about this in Chapter 11.

Identify the dimensions

As I just pointed out, the more detailed the grain definition, the easier it is to identify the dimensions. You should select dimensions without regard to user queries, reports, or other user criteria. You should select them because they support the grain of the fact table.

Correct dimension choices are those that have a single value for each instance of a fact row. You also want to make sure the grain of the dimension matches the grain of the fact table. For example, if the grain of the facts is daily, a period dimension with a grain of month is not correct. If the dimension grain doesn't match the fact grain, you can eliminate it from consideration or change the grain of the fact table.

Identify the facts

Here is where you identify those elements that are going to be measured. Not everything you identify in this step ends up in the warehouse, but record them anyway. As you move through the business requirements, you will start to get a feel for what's necessary. If you do run across a text fact, I encourage you to try very hard to place it in a dimension if possible.

Dimension Table How-to

The "how-to" of dimension tables is similar to fact tables. The goal is to identify the attributes that describe each dimension as fully and completely as possible, once all the dimensions have been identified. Take as much information as possible and then consider carefully.

Attribute definition

Dimension table attributes have a number of characteristics that define them. If you are considering an attribute that does not meet the following criteria, then you either have a data problem or the element isn't really an attribute. Be sure of what you put into your tables:

- Verbose — All codes and indicators have been expanded into words to make their definitions and meanings absolutely clear. The product color example earlier illustrates this point. You may elect to keep the codes or indicators, but they should not be the only way to get at the data.

- Descriptive — All descriptions and definitions are written for mere mortals to read and understand.

- Complete — All codes and indicators are accounted for (that is, every available color, size, and so forth).

- Quality Assured — This is a step that many companies pay little attention to, but each attribute should be put through some type of quality assurance process so that the integrity of the data is validated.

- Documented — Each element is documented as to what it means, where it came from, and what information is necessary to use and understand it.

Advanced Dimensional Issues

While this book is more of a primer, you should be aware of a couple of more advanced issues when modeling your warehouse. These will come up frequently, and you should be conversant with them.

The level column

The level column stems from the idea that you will keep several levels of data in one set of tables. I think this is an extraordinarily poor idea because it ends up being too confusing for the users. Leveling is most often encountered with front-end tools that require this type of schema to exist. It functions like this.

Every row has a level column, and that column is populated with a description of the level (hierarchy) or granularity of that row: for example, DAILY, WEEKLY, MONTHLY, or YEARLY values. Every query you submit must supply a predicate on the level column or you will get wrong results.

As long as you stay inside the tool, everything is great — but what happens if you later decide to use some other tool that doesn't have that idea built into it? There are other issues as well: for example, keeping the summary rows updated as you load detail rows. What happens if you decide to change or build different summaries?

The concept of roles

A dimension table can play several roles in a warehouse because of its multiple connections to the fact table. A simple example is order date/ship date. The sample database also has an instance of a dimension playing several roles as well. In the sample database, three connections made the TELEPHONE table: BTN, Originating Phone Number, and Destination Phone Number. Each is connected to the TELEPHONE table for data integrity and query purposes.

A situation where a single dimension table plays multiple roles is a frequent occurrence. Earlier versions of Red Brick Decision Server would have considered multiple connections to the same logical entity as having equal values in each of the respective columns. In the later 5.1.x and hire versions, the server is generally able to keep the connections straight. Although not a technical requirement any longer, you might want to consider two other approaches to represent a dimension with multiple connections to a single fact table: synonyms or separate tables. By creating a synonym for the table, the server evaluates it as a separate object, even though physically, it's the same table. Creating separate tables eliminates the issue altogether, but it's more administrative work. In either case, it's clearly understood what the relationships between the dimension and fact tables are, and in what capacity the dimension is functioning.

Lessons from the Trenches

There are a host of lessons that I've learned in the trenches; however, there are a few that I run into over and over, which I'll describe in the following sections.

Strive for (relative) simplicity

I say *relative* here because a simple retail model will have many fewer tables than a "simple" healthcare model. Not every model will have a few dimensions and one fact table. Not any more. Determining how many tables are appropriate is a little difficult; it depends on the business problem. However, if you feel like there are too many tables, then there probably are. After you've done half a dozen models or so, it will begin to "feel right." I realize that that's a tremendously technical term, but it's the best I can do. Be comfortable with simplicity, but do not sacrifice business rules or issues to avoid adding another table. Business issues must come first, simplicity second, and normalization third (if necessary).

Do not duplicate the OLTP model

Whatever you do, don't do this – especially in Red Brick Decision Server. Red Brick Decision Server will let you build the model and connect the tables sure enough, but there would be no performance guarantees. Remember that you've got other tools in your toolbox besides a hammer, so everything doesn't have to be a nail. This is by far the most serious mistake that people new to Red Brick Decision Server make. It's understandable, but resist it at all costs.

Carefully consider slowly changing issues

Carefully! Most often, changing dimension issues will resolve themselves as a result of the business rules and the process of drilling into the business issues. However, from time to time, there really isn't a good choice, just a bunch of bad ones. The best you can do in these situations is hedge a bit and choose the one with the least (perceived?) pain.

Today, large dimensions are becoming more the norm, so pay careful attention to those tables that present slowly changing issues. A conservative approach here will perhaps be the least painful until you figure it all out. It may take a few iterations to understand the nuances of its behavior, so set expectations and work at it until it becomes acceptable.

Let the model evolve

Another mistake that is frequently made is not letting the model evolve. Remember that the requirements and logical modeling process are tied together and are iterative by nature. Don't wait until all the requirements gathering is completed to start rendering your model, or you will lose some valuable insight and context. Be willing to rethink those parts of the model that are "done." More than one project has had trouble because of some oversight in this area.

Don't denormalize unnecessarily

My views on denormalization or snowflaking should be clear enough at this point, but in case you missed it: *don't do it*! Seriously, do not be in too much of a rush to denormalize your dimensions. Build the model in true dimensional form, and let performance be your guide. There are situations where denormalization is necessary, and it usually revolves around including syndicated data in your warehouse.

Above all, as with any other compromise decision, be sure you understand *why* you are making it and what the benefits of the compromise are costing you. If you can't answer these questions, or the answers do not agree with the business goals, then why are you doing it?

Sample Project: Logical Model

The sample database is a simplified telecommunications data model. This is driven in part by my desire to provide an example that has enough data to actually *do* something with, and partly because retail examples are all too frequent. In the previous chapter, I discussed the types of analyses that were required and some of the business questions that you need to provide answers to. You may find it helpful to refer to Appendix B for a definition of the tables and columns defined in the logical model.

The model is centered on two fact tables: BILLING_CDR and CHURN. Telephone companies collect call information from hardware components called *switches*. As each call is processed by the switch, it generates a call data record (CDR), which contains information relating to the call including date, time, and telephone numbers. The billing CDR as modeled in the sample database is a very small subset of an actual CDR that has been enhanced with the appropriate billing information. This enhancement process is quite complicated in most instances, but we'll ignore it for this model.

The other fact table is the CHURN table. In the telecommunications industry, *churn* is defined as losing a customer to a competitor. If you have ever switched your long-distance carrier, you have churned. Customers churn for a variety of reasons: service availability (or lack thereof), cost, or customer service issues. Telecommunications is a very competitive environment, and information about customer habits and why they left is extremely valuable.

The rest of the tables are dimensions that support one or both of the fact tables. Most are self-explanatory, and descriptions can be found in Appendix B. However, a few of the dimension tables require a comment or two on their designs and why they were chosen.

Customer

You may recall from the requirements section that there are two types of customers — residential and business customers. In the sample model, there is only one table because there is no significant reason to have more than that. In reality, the relationship between telephone numbers, the concept of account, and the concept of customers can be modeled a number of ways, all of which are more complicated than necessary for this exercise.

I also referred to some customer analysis. This usually implies some demographics, and indeed, there are a few demographics columns; however, note that some only apply to residential customers and others to only business customers.

Because there are relatively few columns, the demographics columns are not denormalized. Why? First, it's *not* a space issue. If you were keeping upwards of 30 or more demographic elements, perhaps it might be something to look at, but with only a handful, denormalization is not worth the effort. Secondly, denormalization will only complicate the browsing, and as I've pointed out earlier, that's something you should only undertake when necessary.

Telephone

One of the basic assumptions of the sample database is the idea of point-to-point calling. I have chosen to ignore certain types of calls (international, out of network, and so on). Every telephone number that can place or receive a call (in our example) is contained in the Telephone table. I did this for simplicity and to avoid a lengthy discussion on the inner workings of the telecommunications industry.

Summary

The logical modeling phase of any data warehouse project is one of the most important components of a successful implementation. It is worth every bit of attention you give it, because if it's wrong, it will cost you several times as much to correct it because so much of Red Brick's technology is tied to the logical model.

Logical modeling is a technology-independent activity. Notice that nowhere did we discuss data types, key definitions (other than the concept of primary and foreign keys), or other physical aspects of the design. These issues are addressed in the next chapter. You will uncover physical information during the whole process, but don't let it influence the physical implementation (yet!).

Much of the trouble in dimensional modeling comes from slowly changing dimensions. I've outlined the three basic methods for addressing these issues and have added a couple more for you to think about. Often, it will be very difficult to choose the right solution to a slowly changing dimension problem. Choose carefully. Keep in mind that it's an iterative process; be willing to rethink "completed" parts of the model, and let it evolve as you learn new information — this is the best advice I can give you.

Chapter 5

Physical Modeling

IN THIS CHAPTER

◆ Turning a logical model into a physical model

◆ Choosing a query tool

◆ Developing a load strategy

◆ Creating a data definition language

◆ Developing an aggregation strategy

◆ Implementing key definitions

◆ Learning lessons from the trenches

◆ Looking at a case study schema review

ONCE YOU HAVE THE LOGICAL model to a point where it captures the business rules and addresses the scope of the project, the next step is to turn it into a physical instance – something you can build, load data into, and query. Up until now, all your modeling efforts have been centered on the business, with no real thought to the physical aspects of implementation, although you probably have a short list of specific physical implementation issues that must be addressed.

Changing the model has been relatively easy, especially if you have been rendering the model in conjunction with the interview process – it's been a "paper-based" exercise. However, from now on, changes will not be so simple. This is why you must carefully consider all your options as you move from a logical design to a physical instance. This chapter takes you through the process of committing to a physical implementation by evaluating the most frequently encountered issues when building a Red Brick Decision Server data warehouse.

In this chapter, we'll begin by reviewing the historical duration of your warehouse and its affect on the physical model, load processes, and population of the period table. Next, we'll evaluate the requirements and impact of slowly changing dimensions and outrigger tables and review any denormalization that may be necessary. We'll make data-type decisions for the columns in the tables that provide the most efficient storage of the data. We'll also look at any Extraction, Transformation, and Load (ETL) issues and assess their impact on the planned physical implementation. Next, we'll evaluate index definitions and choices, sizing issues, and segmentation decisions. All of these are necessary to create the database instance.

From here, this chapter goes into two other major discussions: summary tables and generated keys. These two issues are separated out because they are the source of much conversation and differing viewpoints, so they are explained in some detail. We'll consider some "Lessons from the Trenches" and wind up with a discussion of the physical model for the sample database in the "Case Study Schema Review section. Be prepared to consider some model changes based on the results of some of these evaluations, especially when considering slowly changing dimensions and outrigger tables. Model changes are commonly driven by ETL issues or other performance considerations.

Turning a Logical Model into a Physical Model

The physical model establishes the structure of the data warehouse and includes strategies for data storage and backup, segmentation, indexing, data loading, and aggregation. The process of turning a logical model into a physical model has a number of components as follows:

- Detailed physical data model

- Data volume analysis and load frequencies

- Indexing strategy

- Segmentation strategy

- Data source to target mapping

- File name and location strategy

- Backup and recovery strategy

- Aggregation strategy

- Data definition language to create the database objects

The major issues of segmentation, indexing, and aggregation are discussed in subsequent chapters, so we won't spend a lot of time on them here other than to point out that these items are part of the physical implementation of your database.

You must consider a number of necessary review points because they may impact performance, database size, load windows, and ETL efforts, to name a few. This is the time and place to consider issues such as query tools, data quality, extraction and transformation issues, and any other issues that you put aside during the logical modeling phase that may impact the physical implementation of your warehouse. You should examine these issues in the order presented because some of the early issues affect the later ones. In actual practice, many of these issues are related (sizing and data types, for example), and you will move between them as you resolve any issues.

The physical model

In many ways, the physical model is the result of a number of the other steps reviewed in this chapter. To properly render a physical model, you must review the following items and be sure you understand their impact on the project and any steps that you must take to mitigate them:

- Historical duration

- Changing dimension issues

- Outriggers (Snowflakes) and their implications

- Data typing the model

- ETL issues

- Data conversion issues

- Missing data

- Relational integrity

HISTORICAL DURATION

As discussed in the last chapter, the *historical duration* is the amount of time a given fact row will exist in the database, and it is defined at the beginning of the logical modeling stage. Now you must evaluate the duration and how it affects three major components of your warehouse – the total size of the database, the size and configuration of the period table, and the segmentation plan – and decide how to represent the PERIOD table:

1. The total size of the database – This is obvious:: the longer the historical duration, the more data. You must be sure you have enough disk space to store all the data necessary for that amount of time. A rough sizing will help you determine if you have an issue here or not. Additionally, this is an opportunity for you to ask some questions relating to how valuable the information will be over the historical duration and make any decisions necessary to either change the duration or buy more storage.

2. Size and configuration of the PERIOD table – As briefly discussed in Chapter 4, the number of rows in the PERIOD table and how they are stored in the database are the subject of many design and performance conversations. Chapter 9 discusses two basic approaches to resolving this issue: have a segmenting PERIOD table that holds only those period rows for the current duration, or load 50 years (or 100 years, or all time) into the PERIOD table.

The larger your warehouse will be (the more data), or the greater your need to store date references that are far outside the historical duration, the more inclined you should be to have a segmenting PERIOD table along with a standard PERIOD table.

3. The segmentation plan – Segmentation is the process by which the fact table data is broken up into "logical" chunks, usually by period (date). Each of these chunks of data might represent a week, month, quarter, or year, for example. At this point, you should understand that any decisions made on how to represent the PERIOD table may affect the segmentation plan. Once you've read Chapter 9, you'll more fully grasp the implication here.

CHANGING DIMENSION ISSUES

If you haven't done so already, you should thoroughly examine each of the dimensions identified in your logical model and decide how to handle any that are identified as "slowly changing." You may have to review interview notes and have follow-up conversations to determine how best to manage each instance.

Much of the answer may depend on how and when the data is available, and what ETL procedures are required for the table, so be sure to consider the impact of those elements on your decision. In general, it's difficult and time consuming to change the way a slowly changing dimension is handled once it's been built and loaded with data, but it can be done. It might help to create a grid of pros and cons for each table, listing the issues associated with each to help you articulate the problem and make a more informed decision.

Frequently, decisions made to address changing dimension issues will necessitate changing the model. This is normal, and for the most part, the changes should be relatively minor. It might also be a good idea to review the proposed changes in light of the scope document to be sure that your plan is in scope and hasn't modified the goals or business rules. Often, decisions made here will affect the ETL procedures, so be sure you include the necessary people in the discussions.

OUTRIGGERS (SNOWFLAKES) AND THEIR IMPLICATIONS

As you know, *outriggers* or *snowflake tables* are denormalizations of dimension tables. As indicated in Chapter 4, you should undertake these with great care and for deliberate reasons relating to either query performance or data-loading issues. In other words, "I want to save space" is not a reason, and neither are "I think I need to" or "That's how I design things." Remember that Red Brick Decision Server was developed from the ground up to take maximum advantage of the dimensional or star schema, and denormalized dimensions tend to defeat that purpose, not to mention that outriggers generally complicate the "browseability" of the model from the user's point of view.

The issue of outrigger tables will come up frequently when evaluating query tools as a requirement for the tool to be able to provide pick lists of distinct values to the user. Generally speaking, the tool vendors want to see a denormalized table that has distinct values for columns that the users will constrain on: state or color, for example. Resist the urge to denormalize the dimensions until you have investigated the possibility of satisfying the request another way. I know from experience that by indexing properly to support the request and/or by leveraging the metadata layer of the tool, providing pick lists can be done very effectively, without compromising the underlying design.

Outriggers can also complicate the education process for the end users. If you are using a tool that hides the complexity, then the training issue isn't a problem. However, the moment you want to employ a different tool or train someone to write RISQL scripts for batch reporting, you now have an education issue to address. You *must* make any decision to denormalize dimensions for specific reasons, and be able to articulate the benefits as well as the costs. Doing this in any other way or for any other reason is inviting trouble that you may not be able to undo without a significant amount of pain.

DATA TYPING THE MODEL

Next, you must make decisions about data types and storage considerations. At this point, the logical model has no data type information in it (at least it shouldn't). This is the step where you go through the exercise to assign a data type to each column in the warehouse. This is necessary to both create the tables and other database objects as well as to calculate an accurate sizing for the database objects.

Every column in a Red Brick Decision Server database must have a data type associated with it. Data types determine columns' relevant properties and are declared when a table is created. For example, you can't "add" character columns (in the numerical sense) – the data type doesn't support that operation. In addition to doing all sorts of RI checking, Red Brick Decision Server also does extensive data type checking, thereby ensuring that only good data is populated to the warehouse.

You should also carefully consider the costs and benefits of the NOT NULL option when data typing your columns. As you know, if a column is defined as being NOT NULL, it will not allow blank or missing values to be placed in the table. If you are working with dirty data, the NOT NULL declaration can result in large numbers of rows being discarded because of missing values. There have been arguments on each side, and only you and your project team can make the final decision; however, you should strive for a warehouse implementation devoid of null columns.

 If you plan on using VISTA hierarchies, you must declare any columns used in the hierarchy definition as not null, or the hierarchy validation will fail. Chapter 7 discusses Vista and aggregations in more detail.

Red Brick Decision Server supports all the ANSI SQL-89 data types along with tinyint and a subset of the ANSI SQL-92 date data types. The following data types are supported:

CHARACTER (CHAR)	Character columns
DATE	Date values
TIME	Time values
TIMESTAMP	Timestamp values
DECIMAL (NUMERIC or NUM)	Decimal values
TINYINT	Tint integers
SMALLINT	Small integers
INTEGER	Integers
REAL	Floating-point – single precision
DOUBLE PERCISION (FLOAT)	Floating-point – double precision

Chapter 2 of the SQL Reference Guide has a more in-depth discussion of the data types and their ranges.

In assigning data types, you want to strive to assign a data type large enough to hold all the possible values but small enough to not waste space. This may sound a little academic; there have been instances where every numeric column was declared either an integer or float, regardless of the data. The model was easy to build, but a lot of space was wasted, and once it was loaded with data, the project team uncovered an unexpected performance problem or two that they eventually had to ask us to help solve.

Wasting space in this manor is especially true of fact tables. Dimension tables are supposed to be big and wide but not very deep (not so many rows). That's their nature. In comparison to the fact tables, dimension tables are usually quite small. Fact tables, on the other hand, are large and in charge! They tend to be more narrow (fewer columns), but they have many times more rows than the dimensions. For example, declaring a column in the fact table to be an integer data type when the values would easily fit into a tinyint data type is potentially a colossal waste of space. It also robs you of query performance out of the gate because of the work required to manage the space and read the data. Because the fact table will have many millions of rows, you have to consider whether the extra allocated and unused (read *wasted*) space is not more valuable. In the end, it all comes down to physics, so choose wisely.

ETL ISSUES

Herein lies the single biggest threat to successful data warehouse projects the world over: data, data quality, and data availability. That's a bold statement, but I have yet to see it *not* be a major source of issues to be resolved. The quality, accessibility, and availability of the source data are three potential issues that can send your data warehouse project into the data dumpster by turning it into a data cleansing project with the warehouse effort a mere afterthought.

Don't let that happen. This is another reason for recommending that you start with a single data source for your first project. The number of data issues encountered is usually greatly reduced in this instance. As the number of sources goes up, the number of data issues also increases exponentially.

You can use any number of ways to extract the data from the source systems: everything from SQL queries to high-powered ETL tools to basic COBOL and C programs. The most important point to keep in mind when developing the extraction routines is that they must be flexible, maintainable, consistent, and above all, documented, so that the next person to manage the process has some clue about what's going on and why.

DATA CONVERSION ISSUES

Data conversion can consume large amounts of your load window. It's impossible to list all the issues you might encounter; however, be prepared to spend some time in this area. In general, the more conversion activities that are required, the easier it is with one of the ETL tools. Data conversion can cover everything from data type conversion, to date validation, to converting codes into descriptive values and assigning generic key values. Above all, these processes must be repeatable, consistent, documented, and extensible so that as the requirements change, the extraction routines can change as well.

MISSING DATA

The other big issue is missing data. You usually discover this while loading the fact table data for the first time. The other instance where you discover missing data is where there are columns that contain null values. Depending on how the columns were defined concerning nulls, the rows in question may or may not have been loaded. In either case, a fair amount of time and effort is usually required to resolve the issues surrounding missing key values or missing column values. Often, the missing rows point to some business process, rule, or function that has a loophole in it, which must be addressed at some other level. Fixing an up-stream process is one of the main reasons that a warehouse project can turn into a data-cleansing project. Not only is this type of maintenance out of scope for the warehouse, it's really a separate project. Be vigilant, and keep the warehouse project moving as best you can.

RELATIONAL INTEGRITY

The final major issue in the ETL space is that of relational integrity. Whatever you do to extract the data, you must make sure to keep the relational integrity intact. Again, this is somewhat of a no-brainer; however, it's not too difficult for issues to creep in, especially if generating generic keys or doing other large-scale data conversions. Any routines or programs employed must be tested thoroughly or the whole process will be suspect.

File-naming and location conventions

Before you start the actual physical implementation, you should take some time to develop a file-naming and location procedure. Many customers already have standards in place, and, if so, you should feel comfortable in using them. This is important because once the system moves into production, there will be more hands in the pot — loading data, validating and fixing discarded rows, and performing other routine maintenance. If standards are in place that dictate the location of source file logs and other elements, then routine maintenance and use will be much easier.

In any event, the following recommendations may help you establish a directory and file-naming structure that you can then implement to help manage your environment:

/tmu	tmu load scripts
/ddl	database ddl
/discards	loading discard files
/data	source data files
/scripts	load and ddl scripts
/query	miscellaneous sql queries
/logs	loader output message files

These directories can exist as subdirectories of a common parent directory. You usually set this is up underneath the directory where the database has been created. In any case, you should consider creating aliases (if your OS supports them) to make moving between them easier.

In addition to the naming conventions just outlined, you should also create naming conventions for the following TMU file types:

- Discard files
- Loader output files of logs
- Source data files

Obviously, these naming conventions depend on application and client requirements; however, the following example is a good place to start. As you can see, separate directories have been created for each type of file, with a date subdirectory to further separate them by date created. This assumes a nightly load and allows you maximum flexibility in moving into a production-loading environment, as this naming scheme can be easily scripted to be automatic.

Discard Files:

```
/discards/{TYPE}/{YYYYMMDD}/{table_name}.dis
/rbdwdirectory/discards/DIM/20000101/cust.dis
/rbdwdirectory/discards/FACT/20000101/sales.dis
```

TMU Loader Output Messages:

```
/logs/{TYPE}/{table_name}_{YYYYYMMDD}.ldo
/rbdwdirectory/logs/DIM/cust_20000101.ldo
/rbdwdirectory/logs/FACT/sales_20000101.ldo
```

Source Data:

```
/data/{TYPE}/{YYYYMMDD}/{srce_data_filename}
/rbdwdirectory/data/DIM/20000101/cust_dim.Z
/rbdwdirectory/data/FACT/20000101/sales_fact.Z
```

A backup and recovery strategy

Backup and recovery is not something you think about too often in the initial phases of a project. Most often, the team is preoccupied with getting, cleaning, and loading the data. Once it's "in there," they turn their attention to the question of backup. What makes this such an interesting topic is that the amount of data can be extremely large. To further complicate matters, you have all the bells and whistles of today's redundant disk platforms with all the variants of RAID to the advanced capabilities of disk subsystems from EMC Corporation and others. Additionally, Red Brick Decision Server is also capable of accessing data written to near online storage or CD technology, which gives you even more flexibility in how you back up your database.

You can approach backup and recovery for a Red Brick Decision Server database in several standard ways. Each has its strong points, and each comes at a price. You must decide which one best suits your specific environment.

The basic choices are the following:

◆ **Back up the actual operating system files.** This option uses operating system utilities to back up and restore files. You have all the flexibility the system utilities provide (which in some cases is quite extensive). However, you may have some trouble determining exactly what must be restored in the event of disk failure or another limited exposure event.

◆ **Back up the source data that was loaded.** This option is designed around keeping the source files that were initially loaded. In this scenario, assume that in most cases, if a problem occurs that requires data to be restored, it will affect only a limited number of tables and/or segments, and therefore, it's fairly easy to re-create the damaged segments and reload them. The major drawback of this idea is that if a lot of work is necessary to manage discards or other loading issues, then you might want to look for a better choice or be sure the load files you save are clean and complete.

◆ **Unload the segments in external format.** This is perhaps the easiest option to implement. The idea is that as a segment is being populated (say a monthly segment loaded on a daily basis), after each load cycle, the segment is unloaded in external format, and a copy of the DDL is placed on the tape for good measure. When the segment is completely populated, it's unloaded one last time, along with the DDL, and archived.

An indexing strategy

The next challenge is in determining how to index your brand new model appropriately. This is a rather complicated subject that will be discussed in more detail in Chapter 6; however, this is where you must decide on what indexes to build initially and how to segment them. Note that all primary indexes must be defined before you can create the model in the warehouse.

The primary point here is that like the warehouse itself, indexes are not static. They tend to change as the analysis changes, the data volumes grow, and the users become more and more able to not only use the warehouse but also to begin to leverage it.

You should resist the urge to index everything for several reasons: it's expensive both in terms of space and load time, and you don't really get the chance to see how the system is being used. A better approach is to start with the minimum number you think you need and move on from there. Vista (which will be discussed in Chapter 7) will help you identify the correct indexes to build and those you can delete because they are no longer used. Keep in mind that indexes must be maintained during the load cycle. You should also segment any STAR indexes created on a fact table to facilitate moving data in and out of the warehouse.

Data object sizing

Another step in preparing the physical model is calculating an accurate sizing for each of the database objects. This includes tables and indexes. There are three ways to size database objects: with the dbsize utility, with the sizing wizard in the Warehouse Administrator, or with custom-made spreadsheets. I like using the Administrator because it's much less tedious; however, you can't use it until you create the database, the tables, and the indexes. You sometimes end up re-creating tables or indexes, but once it's done, it's just a matter of plugging in the row counts and, voila – instant sizing.

The dbsize utility is a command-line program that asks questions about each table, the number of rows, and data type, and sizes each table. It works, but it's a bit tedious. The third method is to build a spreadsheet with the sizing formulas found in the documentation and manage it that way. For those of you who are longtime Red Brick Decision Server customers, you may have been given one of several sizing spreadsheets that were developed by the Red Brick field resources. These work; however, they tend to become obsolete as the product evolves and the sizing calculations change slightly. An accurate sizing is a must-have item to proceed with loading and segmenting data, so don't ignore it.

One of the most common mistakes people make in sizing their data warehouse is forgetting to allow for growth over the historical duration. In other words, they size the objects for the amount of data they can identify today and give no thought to tomorrow. This is one reason why a review of the duration is necessary so that it's fresh in your mind when you size the database.

Often, customers will not know how much the data will grow over the entire duration, so in these situations, you may have to extrapolate it out. In any case, be sure you allow for some reasonable growth over the historical duration. If you don't, you may find yourself in a position of having used all the allocated space just to load the initial data.

That brings up another point about loading history. Many customers have several years of historical data that they want to load into the warehouse. If so, you must account for this data as well when calculating the object sizes. Often, the load will be broken up into current date and historical data just to make the initial process more manageable. This idea of planning for growth isn't new, but if done correctly, it can help you avoid unplanned downtime and avoid make-you-instantly-famous scenarios that tend to occur in less well-considered situations.

Segmentation

Segmentation is a subject for Chapter 9, but it is definitely a part of the physical model implementation. Segmentation is primarily a data management tool. As such, you need to understand how the data will be rotated in and out of the database.

Segmentation is perhaps the primary physical issue connected with a Red Brick Decision Server implementation and can affect many parts of the implementation. Because it is such an important part of the warehouse, segmentation will be discussed in detail in Chapter 9. For now, you need to know that it's one of the primary physical issues associated with a Red Brick Decision Server data warehouse and that it can impact many areas of your implementation, including query performance and data loading, and backup and restore operations.

Data source to target mapping

A data source mapping is one of the most necessary exercises required in building a warehouse. The purpose is to map a data source for every column in every table. This is a task that has varying degrees of complexity, based on the level of source system documentation and what type of system it is.

This is your first real look at what you have to work with, and don't be too surprised at what you find. As you go through the exercise, you will want to record the source system, table/column of the data, and any pertinent facts about the data that might be useful, such as transformation rules, data type, and any dependencies the data might have.

Query Tool Considerations

Choosing a query tool can be a Pandora's box of issues, depending on the tools chosen, the level of sophistication of the users, and the complexity of the reporting requirements. Add to that the need to perhaps provide batch reporting capability and accommodate a number of different tools, and you have a situation in which it's difficult (if not impossible) to please everyone.

In many circumstances, you have no choices because of corporate standards or special tool capabilities that are critical to the project's success. Remember, the users' view of the warehouse will be through the tool and may not accurately represent all the warehouse is capable of doing. You must strive to build in as much functionality as possible to any mechanism you develop (such as views, macros, and so on) so that the users can take maximum advantage of the tools they have to work with.

When considering query tool integration with Red Brick Decision Server, you should think about the following:

- ◆ Integration level – Many tools do not integrate well with Red Brick Decision Server. That's unfortunate, but a reality nonetheless. Almost any tool will connect to Red Brick Decision Server via ODBC, but the majority do not take advantage of the RISQL functions. However, a few tools integrate very well with Red Brick Decision Server and should be given some consideration.

- ◆ RISQL-aware – Many tools do not take advantage of the RISQL functions. Some try to implement similar functions on the client, but from a performance standpoint, these functions should be performed on the server where all the resource and horsepower are. One tool in particular that is very RISQL-aware is BRIO, and it might be worth a look if RISQL is important.

◆ Temp table requirements — Many tools require the creation of temporary tables while running their queries. This is okay as long as you are aware of it. Red Brick Decision Server does support user temp tables, but you must allocate resources to accommodate them. The use of temporary tables does impact system performance to some degree. Note that some query tools submit what amounts to very small queries that build all sorts of temporary tables, and do the joins themselves. What the user sees as a single query may actually be a series of many actual queries processed by Red Brick Decision Server.

◆ Dependence on aggregate tables — Still other tools depend on aggregates to deliver the performance their marketing literature talks about. It's no secret that aggregate tables are the single most effective tools to increase query performance; however, you should take a balanced approach to aggregates. In addition, for those tools that implement some type of aggregate functionality of their own, you must decide whose aggregate technology you are going to use: Red Brick Decision Server's or the tools' — you almost never have it both ways. I'm partial to Vista because it's invisible, it's smart, and it actually helps manage the aggregates. In other circumstances, you're on your own.

◆ Views required to "hide" RISQL from a tool — If you happen to be using a tool that is not RB-aware, you still have an opportunity to "hide" some of the cool stuff so that your tool won't choke on the syntax of keywords it doesn't recognize. Many tools perform a syntax check on any query submitted to the server. So when it would see the RANK keyword, well — it isn't ANSI, it isn't a table name, it isn't a view name or macro, and it isn't a column name, so it must be an error. This can be remedied by creating views that take advantage of the cool stuff but still pass the syntax check the query tool will do. This is actually quite powerful, as Red Brick Decision Server allows anything inside a view that you can submit on the command line.

◆ Connections to Red Brick Decision Server per instance — Some tools make a single connection to the server per instance. So for a single user with tool A, there would be one connection. Other tools, however, use more than one. Usually, one is for metadata (table and column names); the others are for the actual query connection. It depends on the tool. This multiple-connection-per-tool-instance can be quite a problem when trying to configure for multiple concurrent users, and it definitely makes managing UNIX processes a challenge.

◆ Concurrent users capability — All tools are not created equal. Concurrent users and the number of concurrent sessions depend on the system resources on hand, the query load, the Red Brick Decision Server configuration, *and* the query tool.

Developing a Load Strategy

This subject is rather broad, and it varies substantially from one situation to the next. A number of issues need to be addressed here, and although they are not mission-critical (yet), they will become necessary as you move into a production environment. Note that the assumption with these items is a nightly data load. The basic issues you should address are the following:

- Defining load window times – This defines how much time you have to get the data loaded. Frequently, the load window is defined for you because of business or environmental issues you have little or no control over. If that is your case, be sure to communicate and set expectations frequently as to how fresh the warehouse data will be – that is, current as of yesterday, last night, or last week.

- Approximate data volumes – How much data do you have to load? Ideally, you have a load window large enough to load it all. But sometimes you don't, and you have to look at other strategies to accommodate the requirements. Red Brick Decision Server versioning (which allow loads to occur while queries are being processed) is one option, or perhaps a mirror database that you load all day and switch with its counterpart might be the answer.

- Recovery strategies – This is the plan that determines what happens when a load fails, a disk drive dies, or some other major failure occurs.

- Define night batch processing (unloads and loads) – This is the process of "lights out" operations, and automating the loading process of getting the data, loading, validating, and so forth.

- Exception processing, error checking, and notification – This is the process of the server handling certain error conditions and notifying via e-mail or pager that a process has completed or experienced an unexpected error condition.

- Automating rolling on/off of storage segments – This is the process of having the server manage the rolling on and off of the data and index segments. This is a more advanced issue, but you should start to think about it now.

Most of the items in the previous list are not so much Red Brick specific as they are the application of UNIX shell scripting and other UNIX facilities. Windows NT has much of the same functionality, and you can accomplish almost anything you have the ability to write a UNIX script for. You don't need to address all of these issues – in fact, some may take a while to implement. However, you should introduce them now and start the team thinking about how to address them.

Creating the Data Definition Language

These are the scripts that generate the database objects. Usually, they are generated out of the data-modeling tool; however, they can also be created by hand.

The DDL for the sample database is included on the CD and provides good examples of what DDL scripts look like.

Many customers have some type of revision control in place. If not, you will have to manage it yourself. If you are on UNIX, Source Code Control System (SCCS) is a good alternative. It's imperative that the scripts accurately reflect the current configuration and definition of the database. A few people have been caught unprepared and, because the scripts were not up-to-date, ended up making a bad situation worse. You've been warned!

It's also a good idea to add comments to the top of the scripts, as illustrated in the following example for the sample database:

```
#--Billing_cdr.sql
#-- Robert J. Hocutt
#-- Created: 6/23/00
#
# Revision History:
#

create table BILLING_CDR
(
PERIOD_KEY INTEGER not null,
TIME_KEY INTEGER not null,
CALL_TYPE TINYINT not null,
RATE_PLAN TINYINT not null,
BTN INTEGER not null,
DEST_TELEPHONE_NUMBER INTEGER not null,
CUSTOMER_ID INTEGER not null,
LINE_TYPE_KEY INTEGER not null,
ORIG_TELEPHONE_NUMBER INTEGER not null,
REVENUE_AMOUNT DECIMAL( 9, 2 ),
```

```
CALL_DURATION SMALLINT,
TAX_AMOUNT DECIMAL( 5, 2 ),
constraint  BILLING_CDR_PKEY_CONSTRAINT primary key ( PERIOD_KEY,
TIME_KEY, CALL_TYPE, RATE_PLAN, BTN, CUSTOMER_ID, LINE_TYPE_KEY ) ,
constraint  BILLING_CDR_FKEY9_CONSTRAINT foreign key ( BTN )
references  TELEPHONE ,
constraint  BILLING_CDR_FKEY8_CONSTRAINT foreign key (
DEST_TELEPHONE_NUMBER ) references  TELEPHONE ,
constraint  BILLING_CDR_FKEY7_CONSTRAINT foreign key ( PERIOD_KEY )
references  PERIOD ,
constraint  BILLING_CDR_FKEY6_CONSTRAINT foreign key ( RATE_PLAN )
references  RATE_PLAN ,
constraint  BILLING_CDR_FKEY5_CONSTRAINT foreign key ( CALL_TYPE )
references  CALL_TYPE ,
constraint  BILLING_CDR_FKEY4_CONSTRAINT foreign key ( TIME_KEY )
references  TIME ,
constraint  BILLING_CDR_FKEY3_CONSTRAINT foreign key (
ORIG_TELEPHONE_NUMBER ) references  TELEPHONE ,
constraint  BILLING_CDR_FKEY2_CONSTRAINT foreign key ( CUSTOMER_ID )
references  CUSTOMER ,
constraint  BILLING_CDR_FKEY1_CONSTRAINT foreign key ( LINE_TYPE_KEY
) references  LINE_TYPE
 )
maxsegments 4
maxrows per segment 6250000;
```

As you can see, the ddl scripts can get a little long, and the comments at the top can help make them more readable, as well as track revision history and any other pertinent information you need to know when working with the ddl.

Developing an Aggregation Strategy

Red Brick Decision Server has always maintained that summary tables are *not* always required to get the performance the users are expecting. This message is still true; however, it has gotten somewhat diluted recently. This measured approach to aggregates may seem odd to some of you, especially if you've been exposed to the "aggregate everything" model sometimes employed to build a warehouse.

Aggregates are not a replacement for missing base technology. The basic underlying technology must be capable of working with the lowest grain data efficiently and effectively. As the performance characteristics change, only then should aggregates be built. Aggregates are expensive. They cost time, space, and maintenance. Creating aggregates on a whim makes no sense.

It is not necessary to build aggregates because the project team thinks they are required. Aggregates should be built only when the performance of the offending query is unacceptable and all reasonable efforts at tuning the query have not produced the desired result. This implies that a review of the indexes, segmentation, and configuration has been completed. The proper message to convey is this: Yes! Red Brick Decision Server absolutely supports summary tables, and it has great technology to help build and maintain them.

Do not build them right out of the box; let the performance characteristics of the queries dictate which summaries to build.

Key Definitions

This is one of the most debated issues of all when it comes to building a warehouse. When the data warehouse "movement" began, everybody built their tables with "natural" keys — keys that held some significance: actual dates, item numbers, UPC codes, and so on. It wasn't long until someone realized that all these keys were introducing some confusion and creating some education issues as well.

Current thinking holds that surrogate (or generated) keys are the answer to the entire question, and I agree — to a point. There are numerous books and magazine articles on the subject that represent the argument very well. However, I believe the "Surrogate keys at all costs" message is just a little off target. Don't misunderstand that last statement. Surrogate keys are extremely useful, and they solve a number of problems in the warehouse, but I believe that you must make the decision to use them with a little more caution and realistic evaluation of their costs and benefits than the current popular thinking seems to indicate.

The question that I'm always asked is, "Natural key or generated — which is better?" To me the answer is, "It depends. . . ."

Let me be clear: all things being equal, I believe that surrogate keys are the way to go, provided you have the mechanisms, procedures, and resources in place to implement them correctly. I also believe that in most instances, surrogate keys are well worth whatever effort is required to be able to use them, but above all, the process must be consistent and repeatable.

Generated keys are the preferred method for implementing a data warehouse, *provided* you have the mechanisms, procedures, and resources to implement them correctly. If not implemented correctly and consistently, then at the very least, the database is suspect, and in extreme cases, totally unusable.

Natural keys have the following characteristics:

- **Easiest to implement.** Generally, you don't have to do any work at all: the key values are what they are in the production system and are passed right through to the warehouse. This was the default method when warehousing was young and we didn't know any better.

- **Less tolerant of change.** This is very true, especially if you have dimensions that are changed frequently.

- **Can complicate user understanding.** Perhaps this is the biggest issue because there are multiple places to constrain on a given data element. Therefore, you end up with either an education issue in trying to educate the users about a dimensional model, trying to decide how to express predicates and/or how queries are processed (which most people don't care about anyway). Or you have chronic performance problems because constraints are routinely placed on the fact table (which is wrong).

- **Little or no overhead to identify key value.** The keys are already defined: you just use them.

Generated keys have these characteristics:

- **Can be very complicated to implement.** This is because there has to be a process or procedure in place to convert the existing production keys into generated keys for both dimensions and facts on a consistent and repeatable basis.

- **Very tolerant of change.** As you know, any time you must change a primary key value, it spells *pain* for the DBA. Generated keys allow you to replace or otherwise modify data as necessary without (or greatly reducing) the usual amount of work generally associated with this type of activity.

- **Meaningless to users.** This has a significant value because now the education issues go away. Users see only a meaningless number (if they see anything at all), and they are forced to place the constraints in the proper places. You are happy, the DBA is happy, the server is happy, and the user ends up being happy because the query runs fast.

- **Generally, a fair amount of overhead is required to identify key value.** In most instances, the method to identify and manage surrogate or generated keys ends up being a complete development project in itself. It's a lot more complicated than a simple cross-reference table for the dimensions. You also have to consider identifying the facts, allowing for possible exceptions, disk failures, and recoverability. In addition, generating surrogate keys adds time to the load window and data transfer requirements. Generated keys generally push a fair amount of work back into the extraction process so that the load and query processes are as fast as possible.

Fair enough, but the minute you decide to implement generated keys, you are also making the following assumptions:

◆ **You can identify dimension rows you've seen before.** This is relatively easy and is the part that comes to most people's minds when talking about surrogate keys. You must be able to identify dimension rows you've previously loaded into the database before so that you don't end up duplicating an existing row. This also implies that since you can identify previously loaded rows, you can also identify new rows as well. This process can become quite complicated if you are also dealing with a type 2 or 3 slowly changing dimension.

◆ **You have the ability to accurately attach the correct surrogate dimension key to a fact row.** This is much trickier. Most folks don't think about this until you mention it to them. It's not enough just to identify the dimension rows; you also have to be able to accurately attach the new dimension key to the appropriate fact rows as well. If you can't do this, then there is no use in using surrogate keys in the first place.

◆ **The process is repeatable and consistent.** The process *must*, without a doubt, be consistent and repeatable. It is possible to build the process, but it doesn't come free. It takes time and resources, and it must be maintained and managed just as closely as the warehouse.

 If the process employed to manage surrogate keys is not foolproof, then the entire warehouse is suspect. Really!

It's hard to make a general statement about how you should implement your key structures, because it really is a tradeoff. Overall, you would be best served by implementing surrogate keys with the idea that the cost to implement them would be recouped in the flexability they offer, but as we all know, rarely are all things equal in business today.

Lessons from the Trenches

The lessons from the trenches in this chapter are fairly simple and straightforward. The details of implementing a physical model are the subjects of the next several chapters; however, as you move towards performing the tasks contained in subsequent chapters, keep these lessons in mind.

Be reasonable

If there was an alternate title to this book, it might be *Exercises in Reasonable Decision Making*. The physical implementation process of your warehouse is where you actually get committed to a number of decisions that have ramifications to other parts of the project, including performance, maintenance, and so on. While it's fine to have someone tell you how to implement your warehouse, you still have to operate within the constraints of your organization. That doesn't mean you have to compromise everything, but rather you have to choose your battles wisely and clearly articulate the pros and cons of your decision points.

Denormalize carefully

You will see more commentary on this issue in other chapters; however, this is the place to pay the most attention to it. Denormalization of dimension tables is not wrong. Rather, it must be justified for a few very specific reasons: performance or some particular data-loading anomaly that can't be accommodated any other way. There is a lot of hype on this issue, especially from some of the tool vendors. However, I can tell you from experience that it is possible to employ one of these tools against a Red Brick Decision Server database without the denormalization of the dimensions and get as good a performance (or in most cases, better) than if you would have gotten if you had denormalized the model.

Consider natural/generated key issues carefully

The potential of generic or surrogate keys is quite large, but it comes at a price. You must be willing to commit the appropriate number and amount of resources to implementing this type of key structure, or the entire database will be suspect and of little or no value to anyone. You must understand the pros and cons of each key and be sure that you can justify your decisions. Frequently, you will find a mix of natural/generated keys, which is okay. It's all a tradeoff that only you can manage.

A Case Study Schema Review

The sample database schema, from a physical point of view, is fairly straightforward. The basic design has nine dimension tables and two fact tables in it. Most of the physical decisions have been made fairly simple to accommodate the building of the sample database. There are two aggregate tables that will be added as discussed in Chapter 7 to illustrate aggregate and the VISTA technology.

Subsequent chapters provide the basic conservative approaches to segmentation, indexing, and aggregates that I typically employ. This approach actually does very well in that I don't hamper my performance initially, but I haven't wasted lots of time tuning. That comes later, once the performance and other characteristics of the database are known.

Please keep in mind that the sample database has been designed as a teaching tool, rather than a true-to-life example of a telecommunications company. To that end, I have oversimplified some issues to either better illustrate an aspect of Red Brick Decision Server technology or to avoid a lengthy discussion of the telecommunication industry, which although useful, only serves to complicate the model.

Summary

You've now seen the issues related to taking a logical model and creating a physical instance from it. The process of turning a logical model into a physical model has a number of components, and even though many of these issues are subjects of later chapters, they all come into play here.

This is the time and place to consider query tools, data quality, extraction issues, and anything else that you put aside during the logical modeling phase that may impact your warehouse implementation. In actual practice, many of these issues are related (sizing and data types, for example), and you will move between them as you resolve any issues.

Query tool consideration also plays a large part in how the physical model is rendered and drives how you index the database to some extent. There are several things to consider when selecting query tools:

- Ease of use

- Integration level with Red Brick

- User capability

Finally, we discussed surrogate versus natural keys. Only you and the project team can accurately decide which is the best for your situation; however, all things being equal, surrogate keys are your best bet because they offer so much flexibility and performance.

Part III

Planning the Implementation

Chapter 6

Red Brick Indexing

IN THIS CHAPTER

- ◆ Why indexes are important
- ◆ Types of Red Brick indexes
- ◆ Uniqueness and referential integrity checking
- ◆ Aggregate query index optimizations
- ◆ Maintenance versus performance
- ◆ Mechanics and DDL
- ◆ Indexing strategies
- ◆ Lessons from the trenches

THIS CHAPTER EXPLAINS how to create and use indexes on database tables. Indexes are used primarily to optimize query performance, but they are also essential in the referential integrity-checking phase of a TMU load operation. The Red Brick Decision Server supports three different types of indexes that are used to optimize different types of queries and different phases of query execution. This chapter explains how to implement each type of index, with examples of where and why an index would be useful.

Why Are Indexes Important?

An index on a database table behaves just like an index at the back of a book: it contains quick-reference pointers to information that would otherwise take a long time to find. If the book you are reading lacks an index, you have to sift through every page manually until you stumble onto the right topic. The same operation happens with large amounts of data stored in a table that has no index: the whole table has to be scanned. The tables in decision-support applications – especially the detail fact tables – contain millions or even billions of rows; consequently, anything that you can do to prevent the database engine from having to read every row to resolve a query is a substantial savings in terms of both query performance and the effort involved.

In database terminology, an index is a physical object that can be built on one or more columns of a table. A single table can have multiple indexes created on different columns for different purposes. The index entries either can be created after the data is loaded into the table (via a `create index` SQL statement) or are compiled when the data is loaded into the table and the indexed column is adjusted as required (via a TMU process). The end user is not aware of the index, but you are. In other words, an index is *dynamic* but *transparent* to users. These characteristics allow you to adjust the portfolio of indexes without changing the application from the user's point of view. As query performance improves or degrades and as users request new reports, indexes can be dropped or added to support the evolving application.

The structure of an index and its actual contents (called *entries*) depend on the type of index in question; in general, however, all Red Brick Decision Server indexes are balanced-tree or *b-tree* structures. This includes STARindexes as well as TARGETindexes. All the index information is kept in a b-tree-like structure. The structure of an index is like a tree with root nodes that branch out into leaf nodes that contain entries. The term *balanced tree* refers to the fact that the index entries are spread evenly across the leaves. The more balanced the structure, the more efficient the index, in terms of both query performance and storage requirements. All Red Brick indexes are stored on disk, so efficient storage is an important issue for you to consider as new indexes are added and existing ones are maintained.

An index entry contains two parts — an actual value from the table, known as a *key* (whether a primary or foreign key) and a *pointer* to the location of that value in the table, usually a row pointer. In some cases, these pointers are stored in binary form; in others, they are stored as ASCII values. In either case, the goal of the entry is to provide a compact reference to a row in a table that qualifies for some constraint or join condition. In this sense, an index behaves very much like a small version of the table on which it is built.

The storage and structure of Red Brick indexes is initially of less consequence to you than the issue of which indexes to build. However, you should understand the costs associated with maintaining indexes on large tables and ways in which to ensure efficient building and maintenance of indexes during loads These issues are discussed in more detail in Chapter 8; however, as you may already have guessed, the larger the index object, the more you have to think about how you manage it.

The main focus of the next few sections is the query performance that can be obtained by building the optimal portfolio of indexes over the tables in your dimensional model. There are three types of query operations that can be optimized with indexes: joins, scans, and simple aggregations. Indexes are also used to enforce uniqueness on columns and to speed up the process of checking referential integrity during loads. Before discussing how these query and load optimizations work, you need to understand the types of Red Brick indexes that are available.

Types of Red Brick Indexes

Different database engines support different types of indexes with their own peculiarities of storage and query execution. You must learn how and where to build and maintain the indexes available to the Red Brick Decision Server and understand that their performance characteristics are ultimately going to be different from those of indexes supported by other database vendors. It is not reasonable to compare performance across database engines by building the "same" indexes on equivalent schemas. Moreover, the set of indexes that optimizes performance for one type of schema is not likely to fit every other application you can build. Nonetheless, there are several best practices that apply to Red Brick indexing, which are explained later in this chapter

Do not make the mistake of comparing performance of "identical" index types across different database engines. Each engine implements its respective technology in different ways; therefore, point comparisons are often useless.

The first step toward creating a successful portfolio of indexes is to understand the three different types of indexes supported in Red Brick databases.

B-tree indexes

When you create a table in a Red Brick Decision Server database (either a base table or a temporary table), a default b-tree index is automatically created on the primary key of the table if one has been defined. The primary key and its resulting index can be single column or multicolumn – meaning that one or more columns can participate in the primary key. The primary key declaration implies that uniqueness will be enforced on the primary key column(s); however, the declaration does not enforce the uniqueness constraint, but rather the index itself. As new rows are being added, the primary index is probed for the new value we'd like to add. If it's already there, then the row is not unique and is discarded. So, for example, in a single-column primary key, every value must be unique. In a multicolumn primary index, the combination of the columns must be unique.

It's possible to create tables without any primary key definition; however, we are concerned here only with keys, indexes, uniqueness, and referential integrity.

The primary key index is also essential to the process of preserving *referential integrity*, which is fundamental to the integrity and usability of the database itself. At a high level, as rows are added to the fact tables, each foreign key value is checked via a reference back to the appropriate dimension table. The primary index is probed to see if the value we want to add to the table already exists. If so, then great!

If not, then the row is discarded because of a missing value. An example of this behavior would be adding rows to the sales fact table for the sale of product XYZ when all you sell are products ABC and DEF.

I've talked about RI in earlier chapters, but it bears repeating here. Referential integrity is not optional, nor should it be. It is a necessity for the integrity of the database.

Like all Red Brick indexes, the primary key index is a dynamic database object that automatically changes as its underlying data changes in response to load operations performed through the TMU or SQL operations performed by the server (inserts, updates, and deletes).

COMPOSITE VERSUS CONCATENATED KEYS

We also have to take a look at *composite keys* (keys made up of multiple parts) and *concatenated keys* (all the parts mashed together into a single column). There are a few performance issues to be aware of when using concatenated keys. For starters, when joining tables with composite keys, you should have all components of the key in the join – otherwise, the performance can be downright hideous.

If you are constraining on a composite key and you are constraining on the trailing columns of the key (meaning not the first column), then the server tries to use the b-tree index in reverse order, which is very inefficient. In other words, instead of traversing the index from the root (or top) down to the leaves (bottom), it tries to read the leaves (bottom) and work its way back to root (top).

NAMED CONSTRAINTS

One other point worth mentioning with regard to multipart b-tree keys is named constraints. When you create a table, you also define constraints that reference table relationships and index definitions. The server automatically names the primary key constraint as follows:

```
<TABLENAME>_PKEY_COINSTRAINT
```

For example, the TELEPHONE table in the sample database has a primary key constraint name of:

```
TELEPHONE_PKEY_CONSTRAINT
```

For tables that have foreign key references, if you don't name the constraints, the server names them for you as follows:

```
<TABLENAME>_FKEYn_CONSTRAINT
```

Again, looking at sample database, we can see this behavior with the BILLING_ CDR fact table. It has foreign key constraint names as follows:

```
BILLING_CDR_FKEY1_CONSTRAINT
BILLING_CDR_FKEY2_CONSTRAINT
BILLING_CDR_FKEY3_CONSTRAINT
BILLING_CDR_FKEY4_CONSTRAINT
BILLING_CDR_FKEY5_CONSTRAINT
BILLING_CDR_FKEY6_CONSTRAINT
BILLING_CDR_FKEY7_CONSTRAINT
BILLING_CDR_FKEY8_CONSTRAINT
BILLING_CDR_FKEY9_CONSTRAINT
```

Each constraint name refers to a foreign key reference. Named constraints are required if you're making a foreign key reference back to a dimension table with a multipart primary key. Otherwise, the server would not know which column in the multipart b-tree it should use. It needs to use them all, and the constraint name is the mechanism that allows that to happen.

 You must use named constraints if you are making foreign key references back to a dimension with a multipart primary key.

In general, named constraints are just good practice, and they help make the DDL more readable. If you do not specify specific names, the server names them for you as just outlined.

One last point to note is that STARindexes can be created by using either actual column names or constraint names. The following `create index` statements are syntactically correct:

```
create star index churn_star1
 on churn (
    period_key
   ,churn_key
   ,carrier_key
   ,rate_plan
   ,customer_id
   ,phone_key
);

create star index billing_cdr_star1 on billing_cdr
(
billing_cdr_fkey7_constraint,
```

```
billing_cdr_fkey5_constraint,
billing_cdr_fkey6_constraint,
billing_cdr_fkey9_constraint,
billing_cdr_fkey4_constraint,
billing_cdr_fkey2_constraint,
billing_cdr_fkey1_constraint
 );
```

TARGETindex

A TARGETindex is the Red Brick Decision Server equivalent of a bitmap or bit-vector index. These types of indexes have two uses:

♦ Weakly selective dimension columns

♦ TARGETjoin processing on fact tables

In the first instance, you have frequently constrained dimension columns that are weakly selective. For example, in a customer table of 5 million individuals, constraining the GENDER column to MALE won't limit the results significantly. Without a TARGETindex, the entire table would either have to be scanned or a b-tree would have to be built – neither is a great option. TARGETindexes really shine when used in conjunction with each other. For example, constraining on GENDER along with characteristics like AGE, INCOME RANGE, and HOME_OWNER together quickly narrows down the results you are looking for.

In the second instance, you want to allow TARGETjoin processing on your fact tables. At first glance, you might question why this might be good, but consider these situations:

♦ You are carrying a large number of STARindexes. This poses a maintenance issue when loading and can also present some issues when the server is trying to select among several valid STARindexes to process a query. Remember that once the server has identified the candidate STARindexes that could be used to satisfy the query, it will choose the first one listed in the RBW_INDEXES table. Entries in the rbw_index table are reused, and as such, the index you think it should use might not be the one it selects.

 After the server has identified the candidate STARindexes that can be used to process the query, it will use the first one it finds in the rbw_indexes system table that is on the candidates list. This may *not necessarily* be the most appropriate STARindex to use.

◆ All dimensions are equally likely to be constrained. This is usually found in situations where there are a large number of STARindexes, and no one dimension is constrained any more than any other.

 Do not be in a big rush to abandon STARjoin processing for TARGETjoin opportunities. You should make every reasonable effort to make use of the STARjoin technology.

TARGETINDEX STORAGE FORMATS

TARGETindexes have several storage formats depending on the *domain* – the number of distinct values – the column in question contains. For example, a STATE column in a domestic U.S. Customer table might contain a domain of 50 distinct values while an AGE_BRACKET column might contain as few as 10 distinct values (0–10 yrs, 11–20 yrs, and so on).

The idea of domain size is fundamental to TARGETindex creation. You can use three domain specifications: small, medium, and large. The domain size you specify dictates the internal composition if the index entries.

SMALL DOMAIN

Specifying a small domain size for the index on creation results in bitmap storage. This format works well for indexes with very small domains of up to 100 distinct values. Each value in the domain is evaluated as either true or false in a given row. A bit represents a row and is set according to whether the row contains the value. The expected size of the index becomes a simple calculation of the number of rows multiplied by the domain size.

MEDIUM AND LARGE DOMAINS

Specifying a medium or large domain size for the index results in compressed or uncompressed list format. The list of row IDs is composed for each distinct value, compressed in the case of medium domain indexes. The compression conserves index storage space, and the low I/O cost associated with the compression outweighs the CPU cost associated with uncompressing the index during query execution. The performance of compressed and uncompressed lists is comparable; both formats provide fast performance for the evaluation of constraints at query time.

You should use the medium domain when there are between 100 and 1,000 distinct values and use the large domain for those instances where there are between 1,000 and 10,000 distinct values.

HYBRID FORMAT

There is actually a fourth format available to you called the hybrid format. Sometimes referred to as "continually adaptive" indexes, these TARGETindexes use all three of the previously described formats according to the best fit for each value in the domain. The system dynamically determines which representation is best for each indexed value given its cardinality. This format is very useful for columns that contain "skewed data" – for example, very few instances of one value but hundreds of instances of another value.

Many customers absolve themselves from the whole issue of TARGETindex storage by creating TARGETindexes with no declared domain size, thereby creating hybrid indexes. This approach is recommended whenever the domain size is known not to fall in the 0 to 100 range and the data is skewed. Keep in mind that as the ratio of distinct row values to the number of rows that share that value becomes 2.5 or less, then a b-tree index is more appropriate.

STARindexes

The STARindex is a unique multicolumn index structure built on the foreign keys of a fact table. A STARindex entry contains the concatenation of dimension table segment and row IDs for each set of foreign keys in the index key. These concatenated row IDs are sorted and stored in binary form to produce a very compact, perfectly ordered index that can be probed quickly and efficiently to qualify the rows for a join of several tables.

The composition of entries and the combination of STARindexes and STARjoin (a unique Red Brick Decision Server join technology) are discussed in detail later in this chapter. The next section concentrates on how indexes are used to enforce uniqueness and optimize referential integrity checking.

Uniqueness and Referential Integrity Checking

To enforce uniqueness on a column in a Red Brick Decision Server database table, you must first declare that the column is intended to be unique as part of the Create Table statement and then define an index on that column. Unique columns do not have to be primary key columns, but primary key columns are unique by definition.

If you declare a column as "unique" but fail to build an index on it, you will not be prevented from inserting duplicate values into the column – the *index* is the mechanism for enforcing the unique constraint.

Although primary key columns *must* by nature be unique, you might require other table data to be enforced as unique as well. For example, your application might depend on precise references to individual product codes that can be used only once. The only way to enforce their uniqueness is to build an index on the product code column.

It used to be a fairly common exercise when implementing Red Brick Decision Server to "cube" the tables by removing the primary key index. This was back when the idea of generated keys was rather novel, and for the most part, the b-trees were large and, more often than not, multipart. As the concept of generated keys has become accepted practice, the cubing of fact tables is much less frequent than it used to be.

Having said that, cubing a fact table is possible only if a STARindex uniquely identifies a row in the fact table. If so, then you can safely remove the primary key index. If you decide not to cube the table, then you should make the primary key as small as possible and make it still be unique. There is no sense in carrying the extra columns around in a multipart tree if they are going to show up as parts of a STARindex.

Unique primary key indexes on referenced tables are used to optimize *referential integrity checking* (RI checking) during TMU load operations and SQL inserts, updates, and deletes. When a fact table is loaded, its foreign key values are checked against the corresponding primary key values in the referenced tables (the dimensions). If a fact table row contains a foreign key value that does not exist in the dimension table, that row breaks the condition of referential integrity and must be discarded, or a row with that value must be inserted in the dimension table by the load process.

A fact table load, which usually occurs on a regular schedule (nightly or weekly, for example), typically involves hundreds of thousands or millions of new rows, and each row might contain five or more foreign key values. If all of these values were checked directly against the dimension table data without the benefit of indexes, the load would take a very long time to complete. To optimize the RI checking phase, the values for each foreign key column are instead looked up in the index built on the dimension table's primary key. To further optimize the lookups, as many of these indexes as possible are mapped into memory during the load. B-tree indexes serve not only as quick reference points for referential integrity checking, but during query execution they may be critical to the fast evaluation of constraints on dimension tables and to the matching of key values over two tables in a join. There will be more on these query optimizations later in this chapter.

Aggregate Query Index Optimizations

Aside from joins and scans, there is a class of simple aggregate queries that benefits from index-assisted optimization. The concept behind this optimization is that certain queries can be evaluated directly against the indexed values; no table data has to be involved. The data in the index itself is sufficient to compute the aggregate values and display the required result set.

These queries involve simple aggregations on single tables, such as a select count(*) against a large dimension table. The optimizations are very useful in ad hoc query environments with users running "browse" or "pick list" queries that require some sort of aggregate calculation.

Under the right conditions, the following types of queries are optimized:

◆ MIN(indexed column)

◆ MAX(indexed column)

◆ COUNT(indexed column)

◆ COUNT(*)

◆ COUNT(DISTINCT column)

◆ Simple GROUP BY queries *without* aggregate functions

The conditions are as follows:

◆ One b-tree or TARGET_indexed column is referenced in the query.

◆ Predicates reference only the indexed column and not the aggregated values; no HAVING clause is allowed.

◆ A GROUP BY clause is allowed.

The following query qualifies for the optimization as long as the product_name column is indexed:

```
select product_name, count(product_name)
from product
where product_name like '%tea%'
group by product_name;
```

In this case, the primary key index is used for the optimization:

```
select count(*) from product;
```

In this case, the discount_dollars column must be indexed:

```
select max(discount_dollars) from promotion
```

In most cases, you can detect that this kind of optimization on aggregate queries has taken place by looking for the "general purpose" operator in the query plan chosen at run time.

We'll discuss the EXPLAIN functions in detail in Chapter 12, but from a graphical point of view, this it what you would look for to determine if your query took advantage of the index optimizations.

Maintenance versus Performance

Indexes, although technically virtual objects like tables, are composed of PSUs just like tables. As such, the portfolio of indexes for a set of tables can represent a significant portion of the database in terms of its size and maintenance requirements. As a general rule, index overhead for Red Brick Decision Server databases is much less than the merchant database overhead running anywhere from 30 percent for the "simpler" implementations like retail to perhaps 50 percent or more for very complex models like health care and telecommunications.

You must also take the indexes into account when the database is initially sized and the administration overhead is scoped out. The cost of the disk space and the administration and backup requirements must be weighed against the expected performance boost the indexes will provide. In a Red Brick database, there is no doubt that indexes will not only improve performance, but in many cases will make the difference between performance that is unacceptable and performance that surpasses expectations.

It's possible to reach the point where the time and disk space required to maintain indexes becomes counterproductive and the cost outweighs the gain. At the other end of the spectrum, the DBA who builds too few indexes will waste significant opportunities to optimize query performance for a large number of join-intensive queries. A Red Brick Decision Server database without the "right" indexes cannot be expected to perform well, and no amount of hardware or software tuning can overcome this deficiency. We'll look at how to determine initial indexes shortly – read on.

When you create any Red Brick index, you can set a "fill factor" that represents the percentage to which index nodes are filled when they are first created. In other words, setting the fill factor to anything less than 100 percent is a means of reserving space for future index entries. The density of a Red Brick index node rarely falls below 50 percent. When a node becomes 100 percent full, it splits into two 50 percent full nodes that can then grow to 100 percent until they also split. Reserving space in nodes by setting a "low" fill factor is a way of preventing nodes from splitting too frequently, which in turn increases the performance of incremental data loads.

Also keep in mind that high-density nodes are generally better than low-density nodes when it comes to the work of traversing the index during query execution. The deeper and sparser the nodes, the longer it takes to do the lookups. Finally, the additional space allocated in a sparse node may not get used if subsequent loads to the table do not need that space for new index entries.

Keep in mind that the indexes you build will have to be sized initially. For this exercise, I generally recommend that a modest fill factor be used (around 50 to 60 percent) depending on the sort order of the data. For dimension tables, it is possible to sort the data by the primary key and end up with a very compact index that will perform very fast.

For fact tables, it's a little different. You can sort the data only one way to load it. Once it's loaded, then the index that most closely matches the sort order will be the smallest in terms of splits. Data sort order is discussed in Chapter 11.

Once the data has been loaded, you will most likely perform a series of incremental loads. I'm referring primarily to fact tables; however, this discussion applies equally well to dimensions. In setting the fill factor, consider how much of the data will eventually be loaded. If you expect to add a large number of data rows that will be out of sequence in terms of their index entries, set the fill factor relatively low (60 percent). This is most likely to be the case with STARindexes. If, on the other hand, few updates to the table are expected or few will be out of sequence with the index, set the fill factor fairly high (80 percent). For TARGETindexes with small domains, the best setting is the default (100 percent).

Mechanics and DDL

Detailed descriptions of the syntax for creating and managing indexes are covered in the *Red Brick Decision Server SQL Reference Guide.* The system tables that contain the metadata for all database objects, including tables, indexes, and segments, are documented in the *Red Brick Decision Server Administrator's Guide.* The following information is a brief overview of the detailed information found in those documents.

A CREATE INDEX statement consists of three main components:

- Index name and type

- Table and column names

- Segmentation scheme, if any

Some examples:

```
create index btree1 on product(product_name) in btree1seg;
create star index star1 on sales(daykey, productkey, storekey);
create target index tgt1on demographics(age_bracket);
```

The mechanism for specifying the fill factor for an index is the optional WITH FILLFACTOR clause:

```
create index btree_city
on demographics(city)
with fillfactor 80;
```

The mechanism for explicitly specifying the storage representation of a TARGETindex is the optional DOMAIN clause:

```
create TARGETindex tgt_age
on demographics(age_bracket)
domain small;
```

Indexes can be dropped with a standard DROP INDEX command and modified with an ALTER INDEX command. (You can alter the fill factor setting or the domain of a TARGETindex.)

When you create an index, you can either build the index entries from the table data at that moment or defer the index build until later. The deferred building option is useful when you want to put some database structures in place without taking the time to populate the indexes. To create a deferred index, just add the DEFERRED keyword to the end of the CREATE INDEX statement.

```
create TARGETindex tgt_age
on demographics(age_bracket)
deferred;
```

To populate a deferred index, use the PTMU REORG command, as documented in the *Table Management Utility Reference Guide.*

System catalog information

The following system tables contain useful metadata about indexes and related objects:

- ◆ RBW_INDEXES and RBW_INDEXCOLUMNS – These tables contain information about the indexes built on tables and the columns that form each index key.

- ◆ RBW_SEGMENTS and RBW_STORAGE – These tables contain information about the storage (segments and PSUs) for both tables and indexes.

Configuration file information

The configuration file (rbw.config) contains several parameters that pertain to indexes. In particular, the TUNE INDEX_TEMPSPACE parameters give you some control over the space allocated for index builds. There are also some OPTION parameters that apply to the segmentation of indexes. In many cases, session-level SET commands exist that correspond with these configuration parameters. For details, refer to the *Red Brick Decision Server Administrator's Guide* and the *SQL Reference Guide.*

Indexing Strategies

Initially, a Red Brick database should have a lean set of indexes – all of the obvious ones and few others. Over time, you should analyze performance carefully to pinpoint operations that would benefit from additional indexes. The following factors will affect your decision to add or drop indexes:

- ◆ What are the types of queries and their frequencies?

- ◆ What are the users needs? (What level of performance is acceptable?)

- ◆ What are the demands of the schema? (Are multifact STARjoins required? Is the schema snowflaked to some degree?)

- ◆ To what extent can aggregate tables be built to offset the burden on joins over detail tables?

- ◆ How much time is available to load the database, and how much of that time is absorbed by index builds?

Best practices for fact tables

There are as many approaches to indexing fact tables as there are people reading this book. The bottom line is that most folks will end up in the same place; it's just a matter of how long it takes to get there. Having said that, I've tried to condense the experiences of my colleagues and me into a few simple but straightforward rules of thumb to help get you started. You may not agree with the approach; however, most Red Brick Decision Server installations I'm aware of started with indexes developed by these methods.

Note that your indexes will not stay static – they will change over time to accommodate new functionality, new data, and eventually, more complicated user requests. Do not look at the indexes as static. They won't be.

PRIMARY KEYS

Primary keys on fact tables can get quite large, so it's worth looking at a couple of issues concerning them.

Dropping the primary key index is possible if one of the STARindexes contains the columns required to uniquely identify each fact row. Consider this carefully, especially if you will need to do outer joins to the fact table in question. Primary keys are required in order to perform outer joins on the fact tables. If you decide *not* to drop the primary key index, then make it as small as possible. There is no sense in carrying those extra columns in both the primary key and one or more STARindexes.

Remember that primary key indexes are used for RI checking. If there is no primary key index, then you *will* load duplicate records.

Primary key indexes are automatically created for you when the table is created if you have defined a Primary Key constraint in the DDL.

TARGETINDEX AND TREE INDEXES

TARGETindex and tree indexes are the indexes created over each of the foreign key columns in the fact table.

Consider creating TARGETindexes or b-tree indexes over the foreign keys of a fact table when you have a large number of dimensions and all dimensions are equally likely to be constrained. If you didn't create any STARindexes, this would give you TARGETjoin performance.

STARINDEXES

These are the "bread-and-butter indexes" of Red Brick Decision Server. If done correctly, they will provide the overall best performance for your database.

Create STARindexes with the segmenting dimension first and then the other dimensions in cardinality order—lowest to highest. This will result in a good general purpose STARindex to get you started. If you have identified one or more dimensions that will be heavily constrained on a regular basis and those dimensions appear further to the right in the general purpose STARindex just discussed (meaning they have a higher cardinality), then you may want to consider creating another STARindex with the dimension in question closer to the start of the index.

For example, consider this example from the sample database:

```
create star index billing_cdr_star1
 on billing_cdr (
    period_key
   ,call_type
   ,rate_plan
   ,line_type_key
,time_key
   ,customer_id
,btn);
```

This is a good general purpose STARindex because the columns participating in the index appear in cardinality order, following the `period_key`, which is the segmentation column. (More on this in Chapter 9.) If you knew that the users were going to perform a lot of analysis on the BILLING_CDR fact table by billing telephone number and customer, you might consider creating an index as follows:

```
create star index billing_cdr_star2
 on billing_cdr (
    period_key
   ,customer_id
,btn);
```

The point is that you can create STARindexes in any order you wish, but that you should pay some attention to how frequently they are going to be used and what it will cost to maintain them.

There are a few guidelines you can follow when building STARindexes that will result in better performing virtual stars for fact-to-fact joins:

- ◆ Keep all the common dimensions in the same *absolute* order.

- ◆ If the constraints on the shared dimensions are tight, put the shared dimensions at the beginning of all STARindexes participating in a query.

◆ If the constraints on the shared dimensions are loose (the dimensions are only used for the purpose of the join), put the shared dimensions at the end of the first STARindex and at the beginning of the other index (or indexes).

◆ The first STARindex should have its leading dimensions as tightly constrained as possible; however, the server will analyze the expected performance of alternative fact table join orders at run time and potentially reorder their evaluation.

Best practices for dimension tables

There are also a few ideas to keep in mind when considering the indexes to build on your dimension tables.

◆ Do not drop the primary key b-tree index.

◆ Create a b-tree index on every foreign key column. This speaks to outrigger tables in that you want to index the column in the dimension that is the foreign key to the outrigger.

◆ Create a b-tree or TARGETindex on any column that is routinely constrained in queries. (Determine the domain of the column before choosing the index type.)

Sample database example

The sample database has been designed more as a teaching tool than as a complete business problem to solve. As you will notice in Chapter 12 on queries, each of the first five queries are designed to produce a specific type of join and corresponding explain plan so that you can see firsthand how the different options work. To achieve this baseline, I have defined a minimal set of indexes to be built. Once these are built and you have run baseline numbers, you can then experiment with other indexes and index types and see for yourself how they perform.

The indexes defined for the sample database are as follows:

All dimensions have a primary b-tree index as defined in the DDL for each dimension table.

The BILLING_CDR fact table has a Primary key index with the following definition:

```
PERIOD_KEY, CALL_TYPE, RATE_PLAN, LINE_TYPE_KEY, TIME_KEY, CUSTOMER_ID,BTN
```

It also has the following STARindex defined:

```
PERIOD_KEY, CALL_TYPE, RATE_PLAN, LINE_TYPE_KEY, TIME_KEY, CUSTOMER_ID,BTN
```

The CURN fact table has the following indexes defined:

- A Primary Key of:

  CHURN_DATE, CHURN_KEY, CARRIER_KEY, CUSTOMER_ID, PHONE_KEY

- A STARindex defined as:

  CHURN_DATE, CHURN_KEY, CARRIER_KEY, RATE_PLAN, CUSTOMER_ID,
  PHONE_KEY

The TELEPHONE dimension has TARGETindexes on both the AREA_CODE and STARE columns.

The CUSTOMER table has TARGET indexes on the following columns:

- MARITAL_STATUS

- CUSTOMER_TYPE

- HOME_OWNER

- CUSTOMER_STATE

We will define additional indexes in Chapter 9 as part of the discussion on query plans and execution.

Lessons from the Trenches

The process of indexing a Red Brick Decision Server data warehouse is not so much a destination as it is a journey. This is primarily because the users will continually find new ways in which to use, and ultimately leverage, the warehouse in their daily quest to get their work done faster with better results.

Therefore, you must approach the task of indexing as being more of an evolving task based on user requirements. Having said that, experience has shown that taking a more conservative approach to which indexes to build often allows you to reach the optimum set of definitions more quickly than indexing everything. Yes, there will be some pain associated with this approach the first time you run a query that can't find an appropriate index to use, but if the proper amount of analysis is done while deciding which indexes to build, you should not have this experience.

Index appropriately

Based on the previous discussions, you might be tempted to index everything in an attempt to hedge your bets and get the best performance. However, I caution you against such a strategy. The server tries its best to process the query with as little I/O as possible. To that end, it does its best to determine up front the best set of indexes to use. Additionally, If you index everything, you are adding a potentially significant amount of overhead to the load process that is most likely unnecessary. Start with as few indexes as seems reasonable, given the expected query behavior, and improve from there.

Follow best practices

Take care to build your first set of indexes using the previous guidelines. This will get you started in the right direction with a minimum amount of fuss and also allow you to evaluate the performance of each index built and make appropriate adjustments.

Use hybrid TARGETindexes

Unless you know for certain that the domain of a column falls into a DOMAIN SMALL TARGETindex, use the hybrid form when creating TARGETindexes. This is the easiest and most efficient way to implement them because although the domain may be known, the data skew is a lot harder to determine.

Summary

Indexes on Red Brick Decision Server tables optimize the following operations:

- ◆ Joins of three or more tables in a star schema
- ◆ Scans of dimension tables
- ◆ Queries that request certain aggregations over one table
- ◆ Referential integrity checking during fact table loads

Red Brick databases support three different types of indexes:

- ◆ B-tree indexes for scans and b-tree 1-1 Match joins
- ◆ TARGETindexes for scans and TARGETjoins
- ◆ STARindexes for STARjoins

The storage and creation of each type of index is somewhat different, but in terms of the underlying technology, all of these indexes are b-tree structures. Index entries can be built either when the index structure itself is built or when you run a TMU REORG against the table (deferred index building). As a rule, index building is part of a single-pass load activity performed with the TMU. Once a load has completed, the tables are completely ready for queries, with the indexes fully up-to-date and online. No statistics need be run.

You must decide which additional indexes to build based on the schema design and the typical query activity. Before adding to the portfolio of indexes in a database, weigh the maintenance and storage costs the new indexes will incur against the query performance gains they will return. You must have a good working knowledge of the EXPLAIN and SET STATS commands to evaluate the performance gains actually brought about by index-assisted joins and scans. This is discussed in detail in Chapter 9.

At a minimum, you should build at least one STARindex on each fact table's set of foreign keys (usually with the time dimension as the leading key); b-tree or TARGETindexes on individual primary keys on the dimensions; and TARGETindexes or b-tree indexes on the most frequently constrained columns of the dimensions. TARGETindexes are preferred over b-tree indexes when the domain of the column is small (less than 1,000 distinct values).

Chapter 7

Aggregates

IN THIS CHAPTER

◆ Why aggregates are important

◆ The Vista solution

◆ Rewritten queries

◆ Advisor analysis

◆ Automatic aggregate maintenance

◆ Mechanics and DDL

◆ Sample database example

◆ Lessons from the trenches

CHAPTER 6 EXPLAINED the different types of indexes available to the DBA as a means of optimizing performance for different types of queries and query operations. This chapter concentrates on another standard means of optimizing queries – aggregate tables. The Red Brick Decision Server handles aggregates in a unique way: the Vista subsystem rewrites queries containing aggregate functions automatically and transparently, giving you "another type of index" to use as a means of improving ad hoc query performance in a decision-support environment. The Vista tools also include an Advisor, which is a system that provides cost/benefit analysis on existing and potential new aggregates, giving you an efficient and sophisticated means of monitoring aggregate query activity to determine the optimal set of aggregate tables to build and maintain.

Why Are Aggregates Important?

One of the most frequent operations performed in decision-support queries is the calculation of aggregate totals such as monthly and quarterly totals, revenue by product or customers, or other types of grouping analysis. In the absence of aggregates, these queries must read hundreds of thousands or million of rows in order to calculate and group the results. While the query is running, you are waiting for the results.

For example, if you asked for a total of sales by customer by year, you might have to read several hundred million detail rows in order to get the answer. The quickest way to run a query that reads large number of detail rows is not to run it at all. What you really want to do is run that same query over a much smaller table that has the information (aggregations like SUM, AVG, MIN, and MAX) you need but that reads a significantly fewer number of rows. You want to run the query over an aggregate table. Once you build this aggregate, you would then notify the users and developers that the aggregate tables are available; such processes will run much faster.

Building aggregate tables as just described may sound like a simple solution to aggregate query performance; however, it comes at the price of creating, loading, and maintaining a large number of aggregate tables. Additionally, all the queries and applications must be rewritten to take advantage of the newly created aggregate tables. As if that were not enough, these queries and applications will also require constant maintenance as aggregate tables are created or deleted from the database.

From the database perspective, you also have to address the time and overhead to build and maintain the aggregate tables, which can get even more complicated if the aggregate can't be built within the normal load window and so is now a day, week, or month behind. Altogether, you've added quite a bit of work to your average day at the office just by building a few aggregates. If you aggregate everything, then you also have add the issue of disk space to store the aggregates and the overhead to build and maintain them.

To manage all the overhead associated with aggregates and to be able to guarantee good query performance while at the same time minimizing the maintenance workload, you need an integrated solution that is more than just a mechanism for precomputing the aggregate rows. The Red Brick Decision Server approach to aggregates known as *Vista,* introduced in version 5.1, provides a systematic approach to precomputing aggregate values for decision-support queries.

Your project team will (eventually) develop a strategy for aggregation to improve query performance. In developing this strategy, remember that for many queries Red Brick performance precludes the necessity of developing summary tables. Two main messages I want to convey concerning Red Brick and aggregations are these:

- ◆ Red Brick absolutely supports aggregation tables and the technology to help build and manage them.

- ◆ Do not build them right out of the box but let the performance characteristics of the queries dictate which summaries are required.

Building aggregates implies all reasonable efforts at tuning the query have not produced the desired result. This means that a review of the indexes, segmentation, and configuration has been completed before aggregation is considered. The primary reason I hold to this position is that even with the technology components of Vista aggregates are expensive, and who wants to pay more than necessary for anything?

The Vista Solution

Vista is based on the idea that the users always query the same set of database tables. This fundamental concept goes a long way toward simplifying your educational and development requirements because users and application developers have only one set of tables to learn to navigate. The complexity introduced by building aggregates is hidden.

The process from the user's point of view is as follows: I run a query today, and it's slow; I call the DBA, run my query tomorrow, and now it's fast. Nothing changes. No new tables, no new query instructions, no list of exceptions – nothing but faster queries.

This is all possible because before the query is executed, a cost-based analysis is done to determine whether the query can be intercepted and rewritten to improve its performance or not. This capability to intercept the queries and possibly rewrite them, unbeknownst to the users, is one of the most compelling reasons to use Red Brick and Vista.

In addition, Vista keeps statistics about query execution so you can find out how your aggregation strategy is working, as well as how to improve it. Vista provides the following four functional components:

◆ A way for you to define and create aggregates.

◆ A query rewrite system that intercepts and rewrites queries to use aggregate tables. This process is completely transparent to the query, whether issued by a user or an application.

◆ An advisory subsystem that tracks aggregate usage and recommends new aggregates or a query-logging and analysis facility that can be queried for advice on the size and relative benefits of both existing aggregate tables and new tables that would be useful to create.

◆ A maintenance facility that updates and maintains the aggregate tables as the base tables are loaded.

The maintenance facility is new in version 6.1.

Implementing Vista

Implementing Vista requires an understanding of several concepts in order to get the most out it. In a dimensional model, I can aggregate different types of tables in different ways. This may be a little fundamental; however, it's necessary to have a working knowledge of these aggregate fundamentals in order to understand the other components of Vista, specifically the Query Rewrite system and the Advisor.

The Query Rewrite System evaluates all of the aggregate tables defined to it (by the database administrator) and decides whether a query is better suited to run against an aggregate table than against the original target. If so, it will rewrite the query to run against the aggregate table. The aggregate table does not have to be at the same level of aggregation as the query for Vista to use it. This is enabled by defining data hierarchies.

The aggregate table is defined to Vista via a precomputed view. The precomputed view looks much like the standard definition of a view in Red Brick and defines the aggregate and its relationship to the underlying detail table. Vista uses this, along with the defined hierarchies, to determine whether it will rewrite a query to use the aggregate table.

Vista uses defined hierarchies to enable it to use aggregate tables where the aggregation of the table is not at exactly the level the query requires. For example, if a query requires an aggregation by year by store and an aggregate table exists with an aggregation by month by store that has been defined to Vista, it can be utilized to satisfy the query.

Follow these steps to use the Vista Query rewrite system:

1. **Create the appropriate aggregate tables.** The appropriate aggregates can be chosen with the advice of the Vista Advisor or may be based on knowledge gathered by the database administrator. The aggregates can be created using an Insert/Select or the TMU, or they can be created on another platform; however, they must be defined to Vista as if they were created using an Insert/Select.

2. **Tune the aggregate.** Create required dimensions, derived dimensions foreign key relationships, and indexes.

3. **Define the aggregates to Vista using a precomputed view.**

4. **Validate the precomputed view.** When a precomputed view is created, it defaults to an invalid state and will not be used by Vista until it is validated. Note that the precomputed view is invalidated when the underlying detail table is changed.

A query rewritten by the Aggregate Navigator will run in the same way and will appear the same to the Red Brick Database Management System as a query written specifically to go against that aggregate table. Therefore, these tables must be tuned in the same way that any other fact table must be tuned. Dimension tables must be related to the aggregate fact tables through foreign keys. STARindexes must be created. Other indexes (B-TREE, TARGET) must be created as appropriate.

In some cases a dimension table with a foreign key relationship to the detail fact table can have a foreign key relationship to the aggregate table, whereas in others the dimension table will have no direct relationship to the aggregate table. In some cases, there is a relationship between the dimension table and the aggregate table but with the dimension table in a modified form. This is known as a *derived dimension.*

A derived dimension is required when a dimension table related to the underlying detail table is not suitable in exactly the same form for the aggregate table. An example of this is the case where the underlying detail table has a time granularity of day. It is likely to have a foreign key relationship with a date table whose key is date (possibly in the format CCYYMMDD). If an aggregate table is created where the rollup is done by month, the date table used by the detail table will not be suitable for the aggregate table. Instead, a date table with the key CCYYMM will have to be created and related to the aggregate table.

Derived dimensions can be useful for any aggregate table, not just those associated with the Aggregate Navigator.

The following warnings and hints should be considered in implementing Vista:

1. The aggregate navigator is assuming that the information you give it is correct. This includes the definition of the aggregate tables and the indication that the detail and aggregate tables are in synch. If these assumptions are not true, Vista will give no warnings, and users will probably get incorrect results.

2. If the underlying detail table is changed, the precomputed views for all aggregates associated with it are invalidated (unless this feature is turned off). Again, when the precomputed view is validated, Vista assumes that the data are correct and synchronized. No error or warning will be issued if it is not.

3. The Aggregate Navigator does not create any indexes on the aggregate table. Indexes and dimension tables required by the aggregate table must be created as with any other fact table.

4. The definition of an aggregate table is not limited to using only the underlying fact table. Often, aggregate tables can be created by using a fact table and one or more of its dimension tables.

5. Third-party front end tools often give end users a list of all the tables available to users. Because it is often desirable to hide the existence of aggregate tables from users, they must be hidden from the front end tool. A slight modification is required to the precomputed view definition to do this.

Red Brick Decision Server allows you to aggregate both fact table data and dimension table data. This first fundamental idea is the basis of hierarchies and precomputed views, which form the basis of the query rewrite system.

AGGREGATE FACTS

An aggregate fact table is simply a table that contains data that have been summarized at a given level. Aggregate fact tables are often referred to as *summary tables.* The possible levels of summarization really depend on the layout of the dimension tables, whereas the specific facts to be summarized are driven largely by the query requirements and the SQL functionality available to support the computations. Figure 7-1 illustrates the relationship between detail facts and aggregate facts.

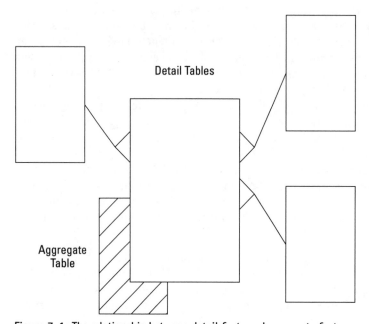

Figure 7-1: The relationship between detail facts and aggregate facts

LEVELS OF SUMMARIZATION   Dimension tables reflect the natural hierarchies of the businesses they support. Geographical regions and districts, time periods, customer demographics, and product categorizations are typical examples. For example, most every production data warehouse environment has a time dimension, often with a detail grain that represents a day. An aggregate level is simply a step up from the detail level. If the detail level is daily, aggregate rows could be stored at weekly, monthly, or quarterly levels. If the detail level is a timestamp, hourly aggregates might be stored, and so on.

SQL FUNCTIONALITY   The ANSI standard offers a somewhat limited group of functions, often referred to as "set functions," for computing aggregates (SUM, MIN, MAX, AVG, and COUNT). The Red Brick server supports all of these functions. You can use complex expressions based on these functions in the select list of a query and use the standard HAVING clause to constrain on the grouped rows. In Red Brick Decision Server 6.1, you can specify multiple DISTINCT aggregate expressions in the same select list.

Versions prior to 6.1 allowed you to have only one distinct expression on a SELECT list. In version 6.1 and forward, you can have multiple distinct expression on the same SELECT list.

In addition, the Red Brick Decision Server supports various "RISQL display functions," which are useful in precomputing aggregate facts. For example, you can use the RANK function over a SUM to store ranked totals for a given column. The combination of aggregate functions and RISQL display functions is efficient and flexible, allowing a variety of standard business metrics to be computed. Some third-party query tools provide integrated support for these RISQL functions in their drop-down menus, allowing users to specify the functions through a graphical interface.

AGGREGATE DIMENSIONS

You can also aggregate dimension table rows to precompute a subset of the rows in a detail dimension. For example, you can issue a simple query with a SELECT DISTINCT in the select list and a set of corresponding grouping columns to populate a Period dimension:

```
insert into week
(select distinct week, month, qtr, year
from date
group by week, month, year);
```

This kind of dimension, known as a "derived dimension" or "shrunken dimension," provides an efficient join path to a table grouped at the same level; in the preceding example, either the week value itself (if unique) or a surrogate key at the same grain would become the primary key of the table and a foreign key in the aggregate fact table. In general, the surrogate key approach is more efficient:

```
Week values as primary key
WK01-99
WK02-99
...
WK52-99
WK01-00
...
Surrogate keys as primary key
1 = week 1 of 1999
2 = week 2 of 1999
...
52 = week 52 of 1999
53 = week 1 of 2000
...
```

The other characteristic of a derived dimension is that its rows contain information about all the coarser (higher aggregate) levels beyond its own grain – in this case, month, quarter, and year are the coarser levels included in the table. This characteristic is important because it allows the derived dimension to be used for queries that require additional rollups (beyond the level of the precomputed aggregate facts). Any other columns that are meaningful at those levels can be retained in the derived dimension, while the rest of the columns cannot. For example, a Season column that identifies different holiday periods in each year could be added to the derived Week dimension, but a Holiday flag for specific days would not make sense at this level. Figure 7-2 shows how a derived dimension would be attached to an aggregate table.

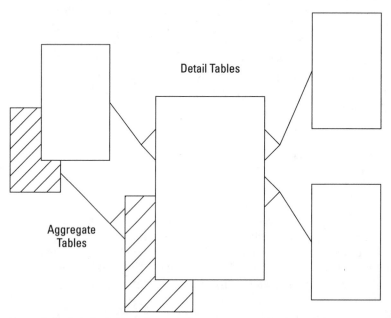

Figure 7–2: A derived dimension and the aggregate table share the same type of relationship as the detail facts and dimensions.

It is important to distinguish derived dimensions from "outboard dimensions" or "mini-dimensions" that are normalized versions of very large dimension tables. You create derived dimensions specifically to provide an efficient join path to an aggregate fact table; they are by definition derived from the data in the detail dimension.

Outboard tables and mini-dimensions are snowflaked dimensions that are built to remove redundancy from and reduce the size of a frequently constrained large dimension. They are twice removed from the fact table and may contain rows that are not derived from the referencing dimension. For example, a very large Customer dimension might have an outboard Demographics table. This approach eliminates large amounts of repetitive character data from the Customer table and improves query performance for those queries that do not constrain on the demographic data. See the Chapter 4 for more detail on outboard tables.

AGGREGATE SCHEMAS

As you build aggregate fact tables from the detail fact tables and derived dimensions from the detail dimensions, you start to build a complete aggregate schema — a higher-level view of the detail schema that optimizes a subset of the business questions asked each day. Figure 7-3 illustrates a case where the same fact table has two aggregates at different levels. Each aggregate fact table has its own derived dimension.

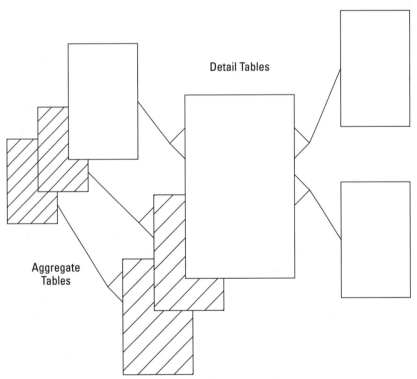

Figure 7-3: The detail fact table has two aggregate tables with corresponding derived dimensions.

The collection of aggregate tables built around a single fact table is sometimes referred to as a "family" of aggregates. Figure 7-4 illustrates a case where a single aggregate table is derived from the detail fact table. This aggregate table joins to a complete set of derived dimensions, one for each detail dimension.

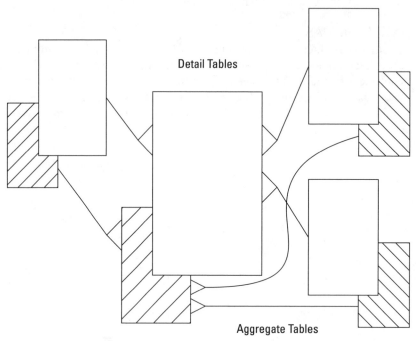

Figure 7–4: A single aggregate fact table and its derived dimensions.

As with indexing, the effort required to build and maintain these aggregate schemas at some point outweighs the gain in query performance. As the query profile changes, the usefulness of certain aggregate tables might decline, and as the detail table changes, the aggregates must be maintained and refreshed. This maintenance overhead puts further strain on the push to meet the nightly or weekly load window.

The Informix Red Brick Decision Server's Vista system is very attractive for various reasons. The following sections describe the ways in which Vista features solve various problems in applications that benefit from aggregate tables. Although it is true that any warehouse database engine can create and maintain aggregate tables, the Vista features make the maintenance and use of aggregates much more manageable and efficient from the point of view of both the DBA and the user.

Aggregate tables are physical objects that store row data in exactly the same manner as the tables they are derived from. If all you did was build aggregates, then you would have a significant amount of space allocated to their storage and indexing.

Building new aggregates is perhaps not the most challenging problem to solve, but determining which aggregates are no longer useful is.

To address this issue, the Advisor can help you to discover the optimal set of aggregates to build in the light of the query history. The Advisor analysis helps you cut back on the number of aggregates by showing you exactly what rollups are useful and how many queries could be rewritten if those aggregates were available. It also tracks the utilization of aggregates that have already been built, giving you a valuable information on which aggregates are no longer useful.

But there is a bigger issue. Unlike indexes, which are transparent to the user community, *traditional* aggregate tables are just like other tables — they have to be named in queries in order to be used. In other words, users have to know they exist, and they have to know when to use them. Every time you build (or drop) an aggregate, the application that the users see changes, and they have to be trained to use the new version.

The Vista approach to building aggregates solves this problem in a very elegant way. The Vista query rewrite system, introduced in Red Brick Warehouse 5.1, treats aggregate tables like another kind of index. Instead of expecting the user to name the aggregate tables that best fit the query, the rewrite system chooses the best aggregate table and then rewrites the query to select rows from the aggregate rather than the detail fact table. The rewrite occurs transparently. The user always queries the same detail table, but the rewritten SQL runs much faster than the user's SQL (or the SQL generated by the client tool).

The rewrite system contains unique technology that is fully integrated into the database server engine. Unlike several other "aggregate navigation" systems, Vista is built into the server and gets the server's metadata. Optimal rewrites are based on precomputed view definitions, and hierarchy definitions are stored as metadata in the system tables.

Hierarchies

A Vista hierarchy is a logical database object — metadata that the server uses to optimize query rewrites. A hierarchy defines a functional dependency from one column to another coarser-grained column, either in the same table or in another related table. The purpose of the hierarchy definition is to facilitate rollups to higher levels than the grouping columns in the Vista precomputed view.

The Administrator tool window (shown in Figure 7-5) illustrates the definition of a hierarchy from the City column to the State column in a Store table.

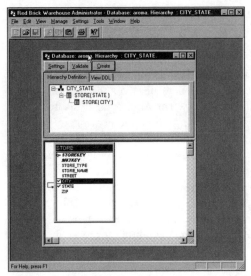

Figure 7–5: A graphical view of the hierarchy between city
and state as shown in the Warehouse Administrator tool.

The Administrator tool validates the hierarchy on creation – in other words, it
runs a query to verify that the two columns are functionally dependent. The two
columns must have a many-to-one relationship. Every city has a unique state
(required by definition of functional dependency), but every state need not have
just one city.

City	State
Philadelphia	PA
Philadelphia	PA
Philadelphia	PA
Atlanta	GA
Atlanta	GA
Atlanta	GA
Tampa	FL
Tampa	FL
Tampa	FL
Orlando	FL
Orlando	FL

If you were to add a row to the Store table that contains these values:

Atlanta   CA

the hierarchy would become invalid because Atlanta can appear in two states, not one. Although the hierarchy definition is logical, it must be valid in terms of the physical data in the tables. If it is not, rewritten queries might produce incorrect results. The City_State hierarchy would enable additional rollups from precomputed data grouped by the State column. For example, consider the following precomputed view:

```
create view annual_product_city_sales_view (col1, col2, col3, col4) as
select prod_name, year, city, sum(dollars)
from product, day, store, sales
where product.prodkey = sales.prodkey
and day.daykey = sales.daykey
and store.storekey = sales.storekey
group by prod_name, year, city
using annual_product_city_sales (prod_name, year, city, sum_dollars);
```

This view adds the City column to the previous example. Given the hierarchy illustrated above, the following query qualifies for a rewrite:

```
select prod_name, state, year, sum(dollars)
from product, day, store, sales
where product.prodkey = sales.prodkey
and day.daykey = sales.daykey
and store.storekey = sales.storekey
and year = 2000
and prod_name like '%Wheat%'
and state in ('PA', 'NY', 'OH')
group by prod_name, state, year;
```

The hierarchy makes the view more flexible because the rewrite system can now resolve queries at both the City and State levels, even though State is not a physical grouping column in the view.

Aside from the general need for an efficient join path between aggregate facts and dimensions, the use of hierarchies in rewritten queries is optimized when derived dimensions are available. For example, when the City_State hierarchy is used, the distinct groups of city and state rows have to be found by running a subquery within the rewritten SQL. If a derived dimension exists, the results of this subquery already exist, precomputed, in the table. In turn, the rewritten SQL is more efficient and much faster.

Validity of precomputed views

One of the key benefits of Vista is that it keeps track of the validity of the precomputed views. The concept of validity has to be understood not so much in terms of a flag set to Yes/No, but rather in terms of what it denotes with regard to the detail data being in sync with the aggregate data. When a view is initially created, it is marked invalid and must be explicitly marked valid. After the aggregate has been populated and the view explicitly marked valid, the system automatically keeps track of changes to the detail tables that might affect the validity of the aggregate table. As the underlying data change, the system propagates these changes to the aggregates, if maintenance is enabled and possible.

Key-based rollups

Another approach to rolling up precomputed data is inherent in the structure of every table that has a primary key. When a view defines keys as grouping columns, it is implied that rollups are feasible at every point in the dimension. The primary key functionally determines the contents of the entire row in the same way that the first column in a hierarchy determines the contents of the second column.

Consider another modification to the previous example:

```
create view annual_product_city_sales_view (col1, col2, col3, col4) as
select prodkey, year, city, sum(dollars)
from product, day, store, sales
where product.prodkey = sales.prodkey
and day.daykey = sales.daykey
and store.storekey = sales.storekey
group by prodkey, year, city
using annual_product_city_sales (prodkey, year, city, sum_dollars);
```

This view broadens the range of query rewrites quite significantly – to include rollups throughout the Product table. If Prod_Name, Prod_Category, and Prod_Subcategory are columns in the Product table, the following query can be rewritten using key-based rollups throughout the Product table and hierarchy-based rollups from City to State:

```
select prod_name, state, year, sum(dollars)
from product, day, store, sales
where product.prodkey = sales.prodkey
and day.daykey = sales.daykey
and store.storekey = sales.storekey
and year = 2000
and prod_name like '%Wheat%'
and prod_category = 'Dry Goods'
and prod_subcategory = 'Breakfast Cereals'
```

```
and state in ('PA', 'NY', 'OH')
group by prod_name, state, year;
```

As the flexibility of the view increases, so does the size of its aggregate table. The more grouping columns in the view, the bigger the table. Likewise, the more grouping columns that are keys, the bigger the table. As you build aggregate tables, remember that the fundamental goal is to reduce the number of rows that have to be processed during an aggregate query. In terms of finding the optimal set of aggregates to build, the Advisor is a very useful tool, as is discussed later in this chapter.

Rewritten Queries

The Vista query rewrite system, hereafter referred to as the rewrite system, is a unique query technology that transforms each block of each SQL SELECT statement it executes into an aggregate-aware query expression. When a query is compiled, a cost-based analysis determines whether aggregate tables can replace the tables referenced in the FROM clause. If a rewrite is feasible, it takes place transparently, and the results are returned to the client in the usual way. No end user interaction is required — only the foresight of the DBA who must build the aggregate tables and supply the metadata that makes them visible to the rewrite system. The rewriter can even rewrite subqueries with correlation references and sum-case expressions.

That metadata comes in the form of a SQL view defined over the physical aggregate table. One such precomputed view must exist for each aggregate table (including each derived dimension). These view definitions are implemented with a standard CREATE VIEW statement, which defines the content of the aggregate table in terms of a query against the detail schema:

```
create view annual_product_sales_view (col1, col2, col3) as
select prod_name, year, sum(dollars)
from product, day, sales
where product.prodkey = sales.prodkey
and day.daykey = sales.daykey
group by prod_name, year
using annual_product_sales (prod_name, year, sum_dollars);
```

As long as the aggregate table "annual_product_sales" specified in the USING clause is derived from the product, day, and sales detail tables as stated here and its data are in synch with those tables, the rewrite system can safely rewrite queries like this one:

```
select prod_name, year, sum(dollars)
from product, day, sales
where product.prodkey = sales.prodkey
and day.daykey = sales.daykey
```

```
and year = 2000
and prod_name like '%Wheat%'
group by prod_name, year;
```

Note that the constraints, grouping columns, and aggregate function requested by the query all fall within the scope of the Vista view definition. In other words, this query qualifies for a rewrite against data that are precomputed (physically in the aggregate table, logically in the view).

Conversely, the following query would *not* qualify for a rewrite:

```
select prod_name, qtr, year, sum(dollars)
from product, day, sales
where product.prodkey = sales.prodkey
and day.daykey = sales.daykey
and year = 2000
and prod_name like '%Wheat%'
group by prod_name, qtr, year;
```

The addition of the Qtr column makes it impossible to resolve the query against the view. The aggregate table cannot "roll down" to the quarter level; it contains only data grouped at the product and year levels.

This is an important point. You want to try to define your hierarchies in such a way that they can be rolled up. So in the previous example, if the view definition were defined at the month level and carried the quarter and year attributes as well, like this:

```
create view annual_product_sales_view (col1, col2, col3) as
select prod_name, month, quarter, year, sum(dollars)
from product, day, sales
where product.prodkey = sales.prodkey
and day.daykey = sales.daykey
group by prod_name, month, quarter, year
using annual_product_sales (prod_name, month, quarter, year, sum_dollars);
```

then the previous query could be rewritten as well. Notice that in the first definition of the view (by year only), you would have 1 row for every product year combination — that is, if you had 30,000 products and 5 years of history, the aggregate table would have 150,000 rows in the table, 5 rows for each product (1 per year).

In the second definition of the view, the aggregate table would have 60 rows per product — that is, 1 row for every month for every year. The resulting aggregate table would now have 1,800,000 rows in it, but consider the performance gains to be had be being able to rewrite month and quarter queries, especially in light of the fact that the table the view is derived from has many, many times more rows than the aggregate.

The rules for creating precomputed views can be summarized as follows:

♦ One physical detail fact table and aggregate table must exist per view.

♦ The aggregate table should be in synch with the detail tables from which it is derived; however, Vista can continue to rewrite queries when the detail and fact are out of sync if you want it to work that way.

♦ The logical view definition must describe the exact contents of the detail and aggregate physical tables.

Cost-based analysis

When the query rewrite system is turned on in the rbw.config file (as it is by default), a cost-based analysis takes place when each query is compiled. If a view qualifies, its aggregate table is used in favor of the table named in the query. If more than one view qualifies, the view whose aggregate table is the smallest and the most efficient (in terms of joins) is chosen. If you are not sure whether a rewrite is feasible, use the EXPLAIN command and study the contents of the query plans. To verify that a rewrite occurred, precede the SQL statement with the SET STATS INFO command and look for the sequence of messages as shown in Figure 7-6.

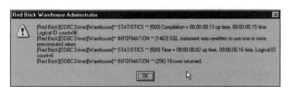

Figure 7-6: This window from the Warehouse Administrator
tool indicates the query was rewritten to use an aggregate table.

Aggregate tables can become large in their own right — smaller than the tables they are derived from, but large enough to require you to think about indexing and segmentation. Remember that once the query is rewritten to use the aggregate tables, it's processed just like any other query and is subject to all the rules and behaviors the optimizer tries to impose when processing a query.

For this reason, it is important to index your aggregate tables following the guidelines in Chapter 6. Indexes are not factored into the cost-based analysis, and therefore, it's possible to end up with a nonindexed rewrite when an index-assisted join over the detail schema might have been faster had the appropriate indexes existed on the aggregate table.

Flexible rewrites

As the preceding example shows, the rewrite system qualifies queries in accordance with the following components:

- Aggregate functions (select list)
- Tables to be joined (FROM clause)
- Grouping columns (GROUP BY clause)
- Constraints (WHERE clause, HAVING clause)

The qualification applies to each block of each query, so a subquery might be rewritten while its parent query is not (or both blocks could be rewritten). Furthermore, some additional constraints, computations, and aggregations can be applied to the precomputed data. Going back to the previous example, the following query also qualifies for a rewrite:

```
select prod_name, year, sum(dollars), rank(sum(dollars))
from product, day, sales
where product.prodkey = sales.prodkey
and day.daykey = sales.daykey
and year = 2000
and prod_name like '%Wheat%'
group by prod_name, year
having sum(dollars) > 10000
order by 4 desc;
```

The additional RANK function can be computed from the aggregate table data; the HAVING clause constrains on the precomputed groups; and the ORDER BY simply sorts the precomputed rows. There is no need to go back to the detail tables to resolve this request.

The extent to which additional *aggregation* is possible in a rewritten query depends on the availability of functional dependencies between precomputed grouping columns and higher-level columns in the same dimensions. There are two ways to exploit this "rollup" capability:

- Declare functional dependencies as Vista "hierarchies."
- Create precomputed views with key columns as grouping columns.

Advisor Analysis

The Vista Advisor uses an intelligent scheme to define the subset of the aggregation space that needs to be analyzed. In other words, if you have several dimensions with many different points along these dimensions, the Vista Advisor does not perform cost/benefit analysis on every possible aggregate (that is, using all combinations of groupings). Instead it analyzes a subset of the set of all possible aggregates that can be created. It uses user query history to define this subset — so the "advice" given by the Advisor isn't static. It changes with query patterns.

The Advisor has two components:

◆ A logging utility that logs information from queries that either were rewritten to use existing aggregates or could have been rewritten to use aggregates had they been created.

◆ An interface in the form of two system tables that can be queried to obtain cost/benefit analysis on existing and potential new aggregates.

The Advisor maintains a log file that you query for advice on aggregation strategies; it performs a lot of computations based on information in the log when it (the Advisor) is queried. You can initialize the log and start logging aggregate queries by using the Administrator tool. In general, the graphical tool makes the Advisor features easier to use; however, if you prefer, you can use SQL commands equivalent to the graphical features. The most important thing to remember about Advisor logging is that the query history must be representative in order for the advice to be meaningful. You must capture the "difficult" queries in the log if you want advice on how to optimize them with aggregates.

The Advisor logs the number and nature of aggregate queries issued against the database and keeps track of whether they qualified for rewrite. When you query the Advisor, it offers two kinds of advice — utilization information and "candidate" information. The interface to the log is a pair of system tables that provide a means of constraining the time period you wish to analyze as well as the specific detail fact table you are interested in:

◆ RBW_PRECOMPVIEW_UTILIZATION

◆ RBW_PRECOMPVIEW_CANDIDATES

Utilization analysis

Utilization analysis provides information for existing aggregates only. A utilization analysis returns information relevant to a single detail fact table that you specify. The Advisor returns the number of rows in each aggregate table (Size), the extent to which the aggregate table is smaller than the detail table (Reduction Factor), the number of times the aggregate was used in a rewritten query (Reference Count), and a calculated overall Benefit value for that table.

The Benefit simply means the number of rows saved by using the aggregate table rather than the detail table or some other less efficient aggregate. Figure 7-7 indicates that 907,777 rows did not have to be processed because this aggregate table was used 13 times. Each time it was used, 69,829 rows were "saved."

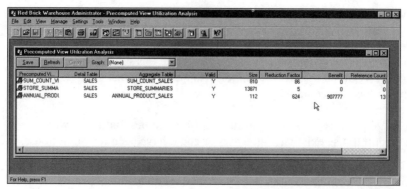

Figure 7-7: The utilization analysis screen from the Warehouse Administrator.

Obviously, these numbers are raw row counts that do not necessarily map to query performance gains, but they do give a very clear picture of the relative usefulness of each aggregate table you have built. In particular, the reference counts are decisive indicators as to whether an aggregate is worth maintaining. As long as the log history is representative and the analysis is applied to a reasonably long period of time, the utilization report provides valuable insight into aggregate query activity.

Candidate view analysis

Candidate analysis provides information for both existing and potential new/candidate views. A candidate analysis returns information relevant to a single fact table; however, the information now comes in two forms: useful metrics like those returned in the utilization report and the SQL text for "candidate views."

A candidate view is a precomputed view definition that the Advisor suggests you consider implementing. The Advisor presents the SQL text for the view, but it does not create it (or its aggregate table). Existing views are also featured in the analysis, allowing you to compare the expected utilization of the candidates to the utilization of the views already in use.

Candidate view analyses can take a long time to run, but you can speed up the process by either applying the analysis to a sample of the fact table rows or omitting benefit, size, and reduction factor in the select list of the candidates query. For example, you could issue

```
select text, name, reference_count from
rbw_precompview_candidates
```

to get the text and `reference_count` for candidate views. A NULL in the name field indicates that the view is a candidate view and not an existing one.

You can use the new sampling function in Red Brick Decision Server 6.1 to do this. In earlier versions, you can manually build a sample view and constrain on it as part of the Advisor query. In either case, the analysis will reflect the size of the sample in its calculations, rather than the true size of the detail table. You have to evaluate the report with this distortion in mind.

IMPLEMENTING A CANDIDATE VIEW

To see the SQL text for a candidate view, click the name of the Candidate inside the report window.

Alternatively, you can run a SQL query against the Advisor system table to return the view text. In both cases, the generated SQL reflects an internal convention: table and column names are always aliased. To find out which tables are which, look at the FROM clause. (The generated SQL takes this form, too, when queries are rewritten.)

The view text can be pasted as is into a CREATE VIEW . . . USING statement. Remember, however, that the view is useless without an aggregate table that contains the physical data described by the view. The Advisor does not produce SQL for the CREATE TABLE statement or a load script. However, you can click the Create button in the report window to go to the Create Precomputed View Wizard, which does incorporate a CREATE TABLE step and an INSERT step to load the aggregate. If you intend to use the PTMU to load the aggregate table, you can leave the table empty when you run the wizard.

ADVISOR GRAPHS

The Administrator tool offers one other feature that the RISQL command line cannot give you – graphs that illustrate the relative usefulness of existing views and candidate views. After running either a utilization or a candidate analysis, select a graph type and click the Graph button. In the following example, the relative benefits of three existing views and three candidate views are presented in a pie chart, as shown in Figure 7-8.

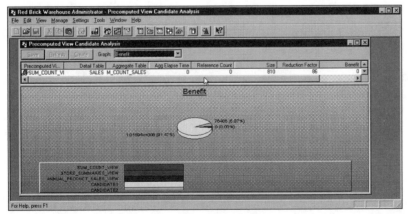

Figure 7-8: The graphic analysis of precomputed and candidate views in Warehouse Administrator.

The following graph shows the relative reduction factors of the same set of views. These graphs are helpful because they help you isolate the metrics returned in the Advisor reports so that you can analyze them relative to each other. The graph shown in Figure 7-9, for example, emphasizes the fact that although Candidate1 has the highest benefit, one of the existing views has a much higher reduction.

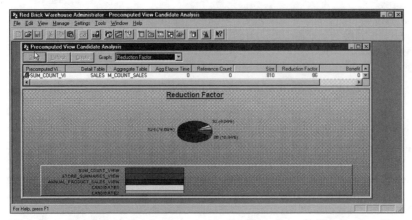

Figure 7-9: Warehouse administrator graphic representation of the reduction factor for precomputed and candidate views.

If you intend to use the Advisor routinely for candidate view analysis, it is a good idea to declare all the hierarchies that exist in your schema. If you do not do this, the candidate view analysis will be skewed in favor of key columns as grouping columns. The Advisor needs to know what hierarchies are available in order to recommend candidate views that can make use of them.

Automatic Aggregate Maintenance

The fourth component of the Vista technology, which is new in Version 6.1, is aggregate maintenance, or ColorTV as it's known internally. This is the facility that provides transparent maintenance of precomputed aggregates by providing an automatic maintenance feature to keep aggregates in synch with the detail tables when the detail data are modified.

How it works

In the current Vista system prior to version 6.1 when the detail data are modified (either through server-based inserts/deletes/updates or through the TMU loader) any aggregates derived from these detail tables get invalidated because the changes are not propagated to the aggregates. Once the aggregate is flagged as invalid, it normally cannot be used in rewriting queries, because such rewrites could result in wrong answers (although users do have the option of enabling invalid aggregates for rewrites).

In order to bring the aggregates in synch with detail data, you are forced to use scripts to maintain aggregates. Such scripts typically contain SQL statements for computing the changes to the aggregates and then applying them.

Disadvantages

This approach has several disadvantages:

- Complexity of scripts – Figuring out the SQL for change propagation is not always easy or straightforward.

- Maintaining scripts – The scripts have to be changed whenever new aggregates are created (or existing aggregates are dropped).

- Inefficiency of scripts – Embedding maintenance logic in SQL is inefficient.

- Delayed maintenance – Aggregates are not maintained in the same transaction as the one that modifies detail data; hence, aggregates are often a load cycle behind.

By providing an automatic maintenance feature, the process of maintaining aggregates becomes much less cumbersome and a lot more efficient; this feature thus increases the availability and usage of aggregates.

Key maintenance points

Several key points about aggregate maintenance describe its functionality. It is

- Transparent
- Efficient
- Comprehensive
- Robust

TRANSPARENT

Aggregate maintenance can be done in either *immediate mode* or *deferred mode*. In immediate mode, aggregates are maintained in the same transaction as the one that modifies the detail data. In deferred mode, aggregates are maintained at a later point in time, much like deferred index building. Aggregate maintenance performed in immediate mode increases the availability of aggregates, although it does affect load windows.

EFFICIENT

The efficiency of the maintenance algorithms comes from minimizing the amount of detail data access necessary (if any) and leveraging the STARjoin, TARGETjoin, and other efficient query processing techniques of the Red Brick Decision Server. An aggregate can be maintained either incrementally by using the changes to the detail data (deltas) or by recomputing the aggregate from scratch from the detail data.

Incremental maintenance can be extremely fast for some types of aggregates, though in other cases it may be better to recompute the aggregate from a parent table. (A parent table is either the detail table that the aggregate is derived from or an aggregate of a finer granularity that it could be derived from.) The determination of incremental versus rebuild is done dynamically in accordance with the actual changes to the detail data.

COMPREHENSIVE

Automatic maintenance can be performed when detail data are modified either through server-based inserts/deletes/updates or through the loader and when all types of aggregates (including those with MIN/ MAX and DISTINCT aggregate functions) are supported.

ROBUST

Maintenance will be done according to only those detail data changes that are successful. For example, inserts that fail referential integrity checks will not be propagated to the aggregates.

Mechanics and DDL

As shown throughout this chapter, the Vista features are well represented in the Administrator tool, making it possible to fully implement aggregate tables, precomputed views, and hierarchies without using SQL.

Administrator wizards

The Administrator tool provides wizards to automate and simplify (graphically) the creation of various database objects, including tables, views, and hierarchies. The Manage Precomputed Views Wizard offers a means of building, populating, and validating an aggregate table and its precomputed view in one sequence of screens. The dialog box (shown in Figure 7-10) is the starting point for this sequence. The only thing you cannot do is load the aggregate table via the TMU; in this context, the load step must be an INSERT INTO . . . SELECT statement, which the wizard generates for you, along with all the other SQL it needs to create objects.

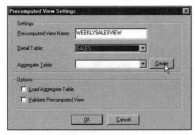

Figure 7-10: The Warehouse Administrator window
that shows the detail and aggregate tables used in
a precomputed view.

SQL statements

If you prefer to use the RISQL Entry Tool to pass Vista-related SQL to the server, you must familiarize yourself with the syntax for the following commands:

◆ CREATE TABLE for creating aggregate tables

◆ CREATE VIEW . . . USING for creating precomputed views

◆ ALTER VIEW to manage the state of precomputed views (validity and aggregate maintenance settings)

◆ CREATE HIERARCHY to declare functional dependencies as Vista hierarchies

◆ A number of SET commands and their equivalent rbw.config file parameters, used to control various aspects of the rewrite system, Advisor logging, and aggregate maintenance

All of these commands are documented in the *SQL Reference Guide.*

System tables

The following system tables contain information pertinent to Vista features:

◆ RBW_TABLES

◆ RBW_VIEWS, in which a *Y* or an *N* in the Valid column indicates that a view is precomputed (and whether it is currently valid or invalid). Regular views are marked NULL in this column.

◆ RBW_HIERARCHIES

◆ RBW_PRECOMPVIEWCOLUMNS

◆ RBW_PRECOMPVIEW_UTILIZATION (Advisor)

◆ RBW_PRECOMPVIEW_CANDIDATES (Advisor)

Sample Database Example

Perhaps the best way to illustrate Vista, hierarchies, and precomputed views is to walk through an example based on the sample database. To properly illustrate how to implement Vista, we'll look at two different aggregate table examples: one with a derived dimension and another using an explicit hierarchy. In order to understand how Vista rewrites the queries, you need to be familiar with the outputof the EXPLAIN command. The EXPLAIN command is covered in Chapter 11.

The AGG_CDR example

The first aggregate example rolls up the BILLING_CDR table by day, area code, and customer, along with all the smaller dimensions. We'll keep it at the daily level (so we can still use the PERIOD table as a foreign key) and we'll also drop some of the other dimensions that don't make any sense at this level. This is the easier of the two examples because it implements an aggregate the same way detail fact tables are implemented in Red Brick: a central fact table with dimension tables related to it by foreign keys.

There are several steps to implementing this aggregate scenario:

1. Creating the derived dimension table (AREACODE_STATE)

2. Loading the AREACODE_STATE table with data

3. Creating an explicit hierarchy

4. Creating a precomputed view

CREATING THE DERIVED DIMENSION

This requires a derived dimension. As you know, a derived dimension is created by collapsing an existing dimension into a smaller table. In this example, we collapse the telephone dimension onto an AREACODE_STATE table as follows:

```
drop table areacode_state dropping segments;

create table AREACODE_STATE(
AREA_CODE SMALLINT not null unique,
STATE char(2) not null,
constraint AREACODE_STATE_PKEY_CONSTRAINT primary key ( AREA_CODE ))
maxsegments 1
maxrows per segment 10;
```

POPULATING THE DERIVED DIMENSION

The code above creates the derived dimension of AREACODE_STATE. The SQL that follows populates the AREACODE_STATE table with the distinct combinations of both AREA_CODE and STATE.

```
insert into areacode_state
(select area_code, state from telephone
group by area_code, state)
order by area_code, state;
```

CREATING THE DERIVED DIMENSION PRECOMPUTED VIEW

Creating the derived dimension is only the start. In order for Vista to be able to use it, we have to build a view that explains or defines to Vista via SQL the data contained in the areacode_state table. The view is created by issuing the following SQL:

```
create view AREACODE_STATE_VIEW( AREA_CODE,STATE ) as
select TELEPHONE.AREA_CODE as AREA_CODE,TELEPHONE.STATE as STATE
from TELEPHONE
group by TELEPHONE.AREA_CODE,TELEPHONE.STATE
using AREACODE_STATE( AREA_CODE,STATE ) ;
```

Notice that the `select` statement in the view definition is exactly the same one we used to populate the preceding table. This is a necessity. If the results of the SQL contained in the hierarchy definition do not match the content of the table it refers to, then you will get wrong answers.

CREATING THE EXPLICIT HIERARCHY

The next step is creating the explicit hierarchy that explains how the state and area_code columns are related. This allows Vista to rewrite queries that reference either state or area_code. Creating the explicit hierarchy is done as follows:

```
create hierarchy AREACODE_STATE( from TELEPHONE( AREA_CODE ) to
TELEPHONE( STATE ) ) ;
```

CREATING THE AGGREGATE TABLE

Now that the derived dimension is created, we focus on the aggregate table itself. We'll create the aggregate table AGG_CDR, along with a STARindex, with the following SQL:

```
drop table agg_cdr dropping segments;
create table AGG_CDR (
PERIOD_KEY INTEGER not null,
AREA_CODE SMALLINT not null,
```

```
CALL_TYPE TINYINT not null,
RATE_PLAN TINYINT not null,
LINE_TYPE_KEY INTEGER not null,
CUSTOMER_ID INTEGER not null,
REVENUE_AMOUNT DECIMAL( 15, 2 ) not null,
COUNT_REVENUE INTEGER,
CALL_DURATION DECIMAL( 11, 0 ) not null,
COUNT_DURATION INTEGER,
TAX_AMOUNT DECIMAL( 11, 2 ) not null,
COUNT_TAX INTEGER,
constraint AGG_CDR_PKEY_CONSTRAINT primary key (PERIOD_KEY, CALL_TYPE, RATE_PLAN,
CUSTOMER_ID, LINE_TYPE_KEY, AREA_CODE ),
constraint AGG_CDR_FKEY2_CONSTRAINT foreign key (CUSTOMER_ID) references CUSTOMER ,
constraint AGG_CDR_FKEY3_CONSTRAINT foreign key (CALL_TYPE) references CALL_TYPE ,
constraint AGG_CDR_FKEY6_CONSTRAINT foreign key (AREA_CODE) references
AREACODE_STATE ,
constraint AGG_CDR_FKEY5_CONSTRAINT foreign key (PERIOD_KEY) references PERIOD ,
constraint AGG_CDR_FKEY1_CONSTRAINT foreign key (LINE_TYPE_KEY) references
LINE_TYPE ,
constraint AGG_CDR_FKEY4_CONSTRAINT foreign key (RATE_PLAN) references RATE_PLAN);

create STAR index AGG_CDR_STAR1 on AGG_CDR(
AGG_CDR_FKEY5_CONSTRAINT,
AGG_CDR_FKEY6_CONSTRAINT,
AGG_CDR_FKEY3_CONSTRAINT,
AGG_CDR_FKEY4_CONSTRAINT,
AGG_CDR_FKEY1_CONSTRAINT,
AGG_CDR_FKEY2_CONSTRAINT);
```

Notice several things about the code. First, the data types for the columns are much larger than their detail table counterparts. Second, we've included counts of each of the fact columns (revenue, duration, and tax). This is to allow the calculation of averages through the precomputed view. This point will be explained in a moment. The third thing to notice is that we've created a STARindex on the aggregate table. This means that the aggregate table will behave just like any other fact table when queries are run against it.

CREATING THE PRECOMPUTED AGGREGATE TABLE VIEW

The next step is to create a precomputed view that relates the detail tables with the aggregate table using the following SQL:

```
drop view day_cdr_agg_view;
create view DAY_CDR_AGG_VIEW( PERIOD_KEY,CALL_TYPE,AREA_CODE,
RATE_PLAN,LINE_TYPE_KEY,CUSTOMER_ID,REVENUE_AMOUNT,
CALL_DURATION,TAX_AMOUNT,COUNT_REVENUE,COUNT_DURATION,
```

```
COUNT_TAX ) as
select PERIOD.PERIOD_KEY as PERIOD_KEY,
CALL_TYPE.CALL_TYPE as CALL_TYPE,
TELEPHONE.AREA_CODE as AREA_CODE,
RATE_PLAN.RATE_PLAN as RATE_PLAN,
LINE_TYPE.LINE_TYPE_KEY as LINE_TYPE_KEY,
CUSTOMER.CUSTOMER_ID as CUSTOMER_ID,
SUM ( REVENUE_AMOUNT ) as REVENUE_AMOUNT,
SUM ( CALL_DURATION ) as CALL_DURATION,
SUM ( BILLING_CDR.TAX_AMOUNT ) as TAX_AMOUNT,
COUNT ( BILLING_CDR.REVENUE_AMOUNT ) as COUNT_REVENUE,
COUNT ( BILLING_CDR.CALL_DURATION ) as COUNT_DURATION,
COUNT ( BILLING_CDR.TAX_AMOUNT ) as COUNT_TAX
from BILLING_CDR,PERIOD,CALL_TYPE,TELEPHONE,
RATE_PLAN,LINE_TYPE,CUSTOMER
where PERIOD.PERIOD_KEY = BILLING_CDR.PERIOD_KEY
and CALL_TYPE.CALL_TYPE = BILLING_CDR.CALL_TYPE
and TELEPHONE.PHONE_KEY = BILLING_CDR.BTN
and RATE_PLAN.RATE_PLAN = BILLING_CDR.RATE_PLAN
and LINE_TYPE.LINE_TYPE_KEY = BILLING_CDR.LINE_TYPE_KEY
and CUSTOMER.CUSTOMER_ID = BILLING_CDR.CUSTOMER_ID
group by
PERIOD.PERIOD_KEY,CALL_TYPE.CALL_TYPE,TELEPHONE.AREA_CODE,RATE_PLAN.
RATE_PLAN,LINE_TYPE.LINE_TYPE_KEY,CUSTOMER.CUSTOMER_ID
using AGG_CDR(
PERIOD_KEY,CALL_TYPE,AREA_CODE,RATE_PLAN,LINE_TYPE_KEY,CUSTOMERID,RE
VENUE_AMOUNT,CALL_DURATION,TAX_AMOUNT,COUNT_REVENUE,COUNT_DURATION,C
OUNT_TAX ) ;
```

RUNNING A QUERY

Let's take a look at the following query and accompanying explain output. This query was submitted with the precomputed view in the aggregate table marked invalid.

```
Select quarter, state, area_code, anual_income_band, sum(revenue_amount),
avg(revenue_amount)
From period natural join customer natural join billing_cdr, telephone
Where telephone.phone_key=billing_cdr.btn
And year_number=1999
and customer_type='Residential'
Group by quarter, state, area_code, anual_income_band;

[
-  EXECUTE (ID: 0) 8 Table locks (table, type):
-  (PERIOD, Read_Only),
```

```
-  (CUSTOMER,Read_Only),
-  (TELEPHONE, Read_Only),
-  (BILLING_CDR, Read_Only),
-  (CALL_TYPE, Read_Only),
-  (RATE_PLAN, Read_Only),
-  (LINE_TYPE, Read_Only),
-  (TIME, Read_Only)
--- HASH AVL AGGR (ID: 1) Log Advisor Info: TRUE, Grouping: TRUE, Distinct: FAL
SE;
----- CHOOSE PLAN (ID: 2) Num prelims: 2; Num choices: 2; Type: StarJoin;

Prelim: 1; Choose Plan [id : 2] {
BIT VECTOR SORT (ID: 3)
-- TARGET SCAN (ID: 4) Table: PERIOD, Predicate: (PERIOD.YEAR_NUMBER) = (1
999) ; Num indexes: 1 Index(s): Index: PERIOD_TARGET_4
}

Prelim: 2; Choose Plan [id : 2] {
BIT VECTOR SORT (ID: 5)
-- TARGET SCAN (ID: 6) Table: CUSTOMER, Predicate: (CUSTOMER.CUSTOMER_TYPE
) = ('Residential') ; Num indexes: 1 Index(s): Index: CUSTOMER_TARGET4
}

Choice: 1; Choose Plan [id : 2] {
FUNCTIONAL JOIN (ID: 7) 1 tables: PERIOD
-- FUNCTIONAL JOIN (ID: 8) 1 tables: CUSTOMER
---- FUNCTIONAL JOIN (ID: 9) 1 tables: TELEPHONE
------ FUNCTIONAL JOIN (ID: 10) 1 tables: BILLING_CDR
-------- STARJOIN (ID: 11) Join type: InnerJoin, Num facts: 1, Num potential
dimensions: 7, Fact Table: BILLING_CDR, Potential Indexes: BILOING_CDR_STAR1
;
Dimension Table(s): PERIOD, CALL_TYPE, RATE_PLAN, LINE_TYPE, TIME, CUSTOMER, TE
LEPHONE
}

Choice: 2; Choose Plan [id : 2] {
FUNCTIONAL JOIN (ID: 12) 1 tables: PERIOD
-- BTREE 1-1 MATCH (ID: 13) Join type: InnerJoin; Index(s): [Table: PERIOD
, Index: PERIOD_PK_IDX]
---- FUNCTIONAL JOIN (ID: 14) 1 tables: CUSTOMER
------ BTREE 1-1 MATCH (ID: 15) Join type: InnerJoin; Index(s): [Table: CU
STOMER, Index: CUSTOMER_PK_IDX]
-------- FUNCTIONAL JOIN (ID: 16) 1 tables: TELEPHONE
---------- BTREE 1-1 MATCH (ID: 17) Join type: InnerJoin; Index(s): [Table
: TELEPHONE, Index: TELEPHONE_PK_IDX]
```

```
------------ TABLE SCAN (ID: 18) Table: BILLING_CDR, Predicate: <none>
}


]
```

Notice several things about how this query is being run:

◆ The query is being run over the detail table. That's because the view is marked invalid and has no other choice.

◆ It contains a STARjoin plan and will most likely use it to process the query, just like any other detail query you would expect to see in Red Brick.

◆ The server is using the Target index in PERIOD to resolve the YEAR=1999 predicate. This will become important in the next aggregate example.

If we set the precomputed view to valid and rerun the above query, we get the following explain output:

```
[
-   EXECUTE (ID: 0) 7 Table locks (table, type):
-   (PERIOD, Read_Only),
-   (CUSTOMER,Read_Only),
-   AREACODE_STATE, Read_Only),
-   (AGG_CDR, Read_Only),
-   (CALL_TYPE, Read_Only),
-   (RATE_PLAN, Read_Only),
-   (LINE_TYPE, Read_Only)
--- HASH AVL AGGR (ID: 1) Log Advisor Info: TRUE, Grouping: TRUE, Distinct: FAL
SE;
----- CHOOSE PLAN (ID: 2) Num prelims: 2; Num choices: 2; Type: StarJoin;

Prelim: 1; Choose Plan [id : 2] {
BIT VECTOR SORT (ID: 3)
-- TARGET SCAN (ID: 4) Table: TABLE_3, Predicate: (TABLE_3.YEAR_NUMBER) =
(1999) ; Num indexes: 1 Index(s): Index: PERIOD_TARGET_4
}

Prelim: 2; Choose Plan [id : 2] {
BIT VECTOR SORT (ID: 5)
-- TARGET SCAN (ID: 6) Table: TABLE_2, Predicate: (TABLE_2.CUSTOMER_TYPE)
= ('Residential') ; Num indexes: 1 Index(s): Index: CUSTOMER_TARGET4
}

Choice: 1; Choose Plan [id : 2] {
```

```
FUNCTIONAL JOIN (ID: 7) 1 tables: TABLE_3
-- FUNCTIONAL JOIN (ID: 8) 1 tables: TABLE_1
---- FUNCTIONAL JOIN (ID: 9) 1 tables: TABLE_2
------ FUNCTIONAL JOIN (ID: 10) 1 tables: TABLE_0
-------- STARJOIN (ID: 11) Join type: InnerJoin, Num facts: 1, Num potenti
al dimensions: 6, Fact Table: TABLE_0, Potential Indexes: AGG_CDR_STAR1;
Dimension Table(s): TABLE_3, TABLE_1, CALL_TYPE, RATE_PLAN, LINE_TYPE, TABLE_2
}

Choice: 2; Choose Plan [id : 2] {
FUNCTIONAL JOIN (ID: 12) 1 tables: TABLE_3
-- BTREE 1-1 MATCH (ID: 13) Join type: InnerJoin; Index(s): [Table: PERIOD
, Index: PERIOD_PK_IDX]
---- FUNCTIONAL JOIN (ID: 14) 1 tables: TABLE_1
------ BTREE 1-1 MATCH (ID: 15) Join type: InnerJoin; Index(s): [Table: AR
EACODE_STATE, Index: AREACODE_STATE_PK_IDX]
-------- FUNCTIONAL JOIN (ID: 16) 1 tables: TABLE_2
---------- BTREE 1-1 MATCH (ID: 17) Join type: InnerJoin; Index(s): [Table
: CUSTOMER, Index: CUSTOMER_PK_IDX]
------------ TABLE SCAN (ID: 18) Table: TABLE_0, Predicate: <none>
}

]
```

Notice several things about this query:

◆ It's using both the AREACODE_STATE table and the AGG_CDR table
   we created.

◆ It is able to calculate the average function because we included the sum
   and count values for the facts in the precomputed view definition.

◆ The table references have been changed. You now see references to
   TABLE_0, TABLE_1, and so on. This is because the SQL the server is
   processing is not the SQL you submitted.

The WEEKLY_CDR example

The second example illustrates an aggregate table that employs an explicit hierarchy in a dimension table (the PERIOD table in this example) and how to relate it to
an aggregate fact table. In this example, there is no foreign key relationship
between the PERIOD table and the aggregate table. This situation tends to confuse
longtime Red Brick users because it goes against everything they have learned to
do in terms of making foreign key references back to dimension tables and building
STARindexes.

That said, keep these two issues in mind:

◆ Aggregates are all about reading fewer rows — the fewer data I have to read to get the answer, the faster the query will be.

◆ In an aggregate environment, it may be possible to get performance gains using an explicit hierarchy and reading the aggregate rows using traditional join methods.

These two points are critical to understanding how to implement an aggregate with an explicit hierarchy. The second point does indeed seem to go against traditional Red Brick thinking; however, if I can answer the question faster by reading fewer data, do you really care how the server resolved the query?

THE WEEK_TO_YEAR HIERARCHY

In the PERIOD table, several column have a one-to-many relationship, expressly to show how explicit hierarchies work. As you know, there are two types of hierarchies: explicit and implicit. *Implicit hierarchies* are those relationships defined by the primary/foreign key relationships between fact and dimension tables.

Explicit hierarchies are those relationships that exist in the data that the server is otherwise unaware of, unless explicitly told about them. In our example, the PERIOD table is at a daily grain — 1 row for every day for every year. In the PERIOD table, you will also find week, month, quarter, and year_number columns. You can see how the data were generated by taking a look at the period.xls spreadsheet included on the CD.

To create the hierarchy that explains to the server how these columns are related, we must issue the following command:

```
create hierarchy WK_TO_YEAR( from PERIOD( QUARTER ) to PERIOD( YEAR_NUMBER ) ,
 from PERIOD( MONTH ) to PERIOD( QUARTER ) ,
 from PERIOD( WEEK ) to PERIOD( MONTH ) ) ;
```

This explains to Vista how the columns are related and is the mechanism that allows Vista to recognize that it can read weekly or monthly data to arrive at a quarter rollup.

CREATING THE AGGREGATE TABLE

This example summarizes the BILLING_CDR data up to a week level. Everything else stays the same as the previous example, including the derived dimension for area code and state. The only difference is that in this example, there is no direct foreign key relationship between the aggregate table and the period table.

The table is created with the following statement:

```
create table WEEKLY_CDR
(
WEEK CHAR( 15 ) not null,
```

```
AREA_CODE SMALLINT not null,
CALL_TYPE TINYINT not null,
RATE_PLAN TINYINT not null,
LINE_TYPE_KEY INTEGER not null,
CUSTOMER_ID INTEGER not null,
REVENUE_AMOUNT DECIMAL( 15, 2 ) not null,
COUNT_REVENUE INTEGER,
CALL_DURATION DECIMAL( 11, 0 ) not null,
COUNT_DURATION INTEGER,
TAX_AMOUNT DECIMAL( 11, 2 ) not null,
COUNT_TAX INTEGER,
constraint WEEKLY_CDR_PKEY_CONSTRAINT primary key ( WEEK, CALL_TYPE, RATE_PLAN,
CUSTOMER_ID, LINE_TYPE_KEY ) ,
constraint WEEKLY_CDR_FKEY1_CONSTRAINT foreign key ( LINE_TYPE_KEY ) references
LINE_TYPE ,
constraint WEEKLY_CDR_FKEY2_CONSTRAINT foreign key ( AREA_CODE ) references
AREACODE_STATE ,
constraint WEEKLY_CDR_FKEY5_CONSTRAINT foreign key ( RATE_PLAN ) references
RATE_PLAN ,
constraint WEEKLY_CDR_FKEY4_CONSTRAINT foreign key ( CALL_TYPE ) references
CALL_TYPE ,
constraint WEEKLY_CDR_FKEY3_CONSTRAINT foreign key ( CUSTOMER_ID ) references
CUSTOMER
  )
maxrows per segment 1;

create STAR index WEEKLY_CDR_STAR1 on WEEKLY_CDR
(
WEEKLY_CDR_FKEY2_CONSTRAINT,
WEEKLY_CDR_FKEY4_CONSTRAINT,
WEEKLY_CDR_FKEY5_CONSTRAINT,
WEEKLY_CDR_FKEY1_CONSTRAINT,
WEEKLY_CDR_FKEY3_CONSTRAINT
  )
with fillfactor 100 ;
```

Notice that there is a week column that is part of the primary key but is not included in the STARindex definition. That's because there is no table to refer back to. We created a STARindex definition because as predicates are placed on the dimension tables connected to this aggregate table (customer for example) that part of the query can be resolved using the STARindex, so it rightly belongs there. Resolving the predicate on the PERIOD table is handled a little differently, as you'll see shortly.

CREATING THE PRECOMPUTED VIEW

The next step is to create the precomputed view to use the newly created aggregate table. Notice that we are selecting the week column from the period table – this will become important in a moment. To create the weekly aggregate view, we issue the following SQL command:

```
create view CDR_WEEK_AGG_VIEW(
WEEK,AREA_CODE,CALL_TYPE,RATE_PLAN,LINE_TYPE_KEY,CUSTOMER_ID,REVENUE_AMOUNT,CALL
_DURATION,TAX_AMOUNT,COUNT_REVENUE,COUNT_DURATION,COUNT_TAX ) as
select PERIOD.WEEK as WEEK,TELEPHONE.AREA_CODE as AREA_CODE,CALL_TYPE.CALL_TYPE
as CALL_TYPE,RATE_PLAN.RATE_PLAN as RATE_PLAN,LINE_TYPE.LINE_TYPE_KEY as
LINE_TYPE_KEY,CUSTOMER.CUSTOMER_ID as CUSTOMER_ID,SUM ( REVENUE_AMOUNT ) as
REVENUE_AMOUNT,SUM ( CALL_DURATION ) as CALL_DURATION,SUM ( TAX_AMOUNT ) as
TAX_AMOUNT,COUNT ( BILLING_CDR.REVENUE_AMOUNT ) as COUNT_REVENUE,COUNT (
BILLING_CDR.CALL_DURATION ) as COUNT_DURATION,COUNT ( BILLING_CDR.TAX_AMOUNT )
as COUNT_TAX
from BILLING_CDR,PERIOD,TELEPHONE,CALL_TYPE,RATE_PLAN,LINE_TYPE,CUSTOMER
 where PERIOD.PERIOD_KEY = BILLING_CDR. PERIOD_KEY
 and TELEPHONE.PHONE_KEY = BILLING_CDR.BTN
 and CALL_TYPE.CALL_TYPE = BILLING_CDR.CALL_TYPE
 and RATE_PLAN.RATE_PLAN = BILLING_CDR.RATE_PLAN
 and LINE_TYPE.LINE_TYPE_KEY = BILLING_CDR.LINE_TYPE_KEY
 and CUSTOMER.CUSTOMER_ID = BILLING_CDR.CUSTOMER_ID
 group by
PERIOD.WEEK,TELEPHONE.AREA_CODE,CALL_TYPE.CALL_TYPE,RATE_PLAN.RATE_PLAN,LINE_TYP
E.LINE_TYPE_KEY,CUSTOMER.CUSTOMER_ID
using WEEKLY_CDR(
WEEK,AREA_CODE,CALL_TYPE,RATE_PLAN,LINE_TYPE_KEY,CUSTOMER_ID,REVENUE_AMOUNT,CALL
_DURATION,TAX_AMOUNT,COUNT_REVENUE,COUNT_DURATION,COUNT_TAX ) ;
```

RUNNING THE QUERY

Once we load the table with data and set the view to be valid, we can now run the query we ran in the first example. With this view marked valid, we get the following EXPLAIN output:

```
[
- EXECUTE (ID: 0) 7 Table locks (table, type): (CUSTOMER, Read_Only), (AREACODE
_STATE, Read_Only), (WEEKLY_CDR, Read_Only), (CALL_TYPE, Read_Only), (RATE_PLAN
, Read_Only), (LINE_TYPE, Read_Only), (PERIOD, Read_Only)
--- HASH AVL AGGR (ID: 1) Log Advisor Info: TRUE, Grouping: TRUE, Distinct: FAL
SE;
----- HASH 1-1 MATCH (ID: 2) Join type: InnerJoin;
------- CHOOSE PLAN (ID: 3) Num prelims: 1; Num choices: 2; Type: StarJoin;
```

```
Prelim: 1; Choose Plan [id : 3] {
BIT VECTOR SORT (ID: 4)
-- TARGET SCAN (ID: 5) Table: TABLE_4, Predicate: (TABLE_4.CUSTOMER_TYPE)
= ('Residential') ; Num indexes: 1 Index(s): Index: CUSTOMER_TARGET4
}


Choice: 1; Choose Plan [id : 3] {
FUNCTIONAL JOIN (ID: 6) 1 tables: TABLE_3
-- FUNCTIONAL JOIN (ID: 7) 1 tables: TABLE_4
---- FUNCTIONAL JOIN (ID: 8) 1 tables: TABLE_2
------ STARJOIN (ID: 9) Join type: InnerJoin, Num facts: 1, Num potential
dimensions: 5, Fact Table: TABLE_2, Potential Indexes: WEEKLY_CDR_STAR1;
Dimension Table(s): TABLE_3, CALL_TYPE, RATE_PLAN, LINE_TYPE, TABLE_4
}


Choice: 2; Choose Plan [id : 3] {
FUNCTIONAL JOIN (ID: 10) 1 tables: TABLE_3
-- BTREE 1-1 MATCH (ID: 11) Join type: InnerJoin; Index(s): [Table: AREACO
DE_STATE, Index: AREACODE_STATE_PK_IDX]
---- FUNCTIONAL JOIN (ID: 12) 1 tables: TABLE_4
------ BTREE 1-1 MATCH (ID: 13) Join type: InnerJoin; Index(s): [Table: CU
STOMER, Index: CUSTOMER_PK_IDX]
-------- TABLE SCAN (ID: 14) Table: TABLE_2, Predicate: <none>
}


------- HASH AVL AGGR (ID: 15) Log Advisor Info: FALSE, Grouping: TRUE,
Distinct: FALSE;
--------- FUNCTIONAL JOIN (ID: 16) 1 tables: TABLE_0
----------- TARGET SCAN (ID: 17) Table: TABLE_0, Predicate: ( TABLE_0.YEAR_N
UMBER) = (1999) ; Num indexes: 1 Index(s): Index: PERIOD_TARGET_4
]
```

Notice the section at the bottom. This is how Vista uses explicit hierarchies and aggregate tables where no foreign key reference exists: it joins them with one of the pairwise join operators. If you look at the graphical explain for this query, you will notice that the HASH_AVL_AGGR (ID: 15) operator is at the same level as the CHOOSE_PLAN (ID: 3) operator. This fact tells you that no matter how the server processes the main part of the query, it will process this step to join back to the PERIOD table in order to get the results.

Earlier in this example, I mentioned that it is possible to get performance gains by using methods we usually think of as slower. True, it's not the nice multitable STARjoin we strive so hard to achieve, but as I said earlier, if I can answer their query by reading fewer rows, do you really care how it's joined?

Explicit hierarchies are a good choice so long as this structure does not take a lot of time to process the dimension in question and there are not a large number of hierarchies involved in the query. For example, the hierarchy presented here runs on a small table and has a result set of a handful of rows.

Creating a hierarchy of area code and state over the telephone table would be a bad choice because even though the result is small (10 rows), it takes a long time to process the table (even when there are target indexes on the columns in question) to get the result.

Herein lies the difference between the two methods. Using explicit hierarchy definitions yields the performance of running a query over a table with fewer rows, even though it might not use the fastest join method Red Brick Decision Server can use. Implementing aggregates in this way provides the flexibility to leverage the existing aggregate tables to answer as many queries as possible, drawing on explicit relationships inherent in the data.

When more performance is required, you can get the benefit of reading a table with a smaller number of rows combined with the benefits of STARindex/STARjoin processing by creating derived dimensions and attaching them directly to the aggregate tables (via a foreign key) as in the AREACODE_STATE table.

Lessons from the Trenches

As with indexes, the choice of aggregates is driven by the specifics of the schema design and the profile of the queries that must be optimized. Nonetheless, a few useful guidelines apply to most data warehouse applications.

Don't be in a rush to aggregate

Red Brick Decision Server is fully capable of managing aggregate tables and, with the addition of Vista, does so in a very neat and straightforward way. However, remember that aggregates cost something to build and maintain. Let the performance of the system and the user queries dictate what aggregates to build. Aggregate tables are not necessary for *acceptable* performance in Red Brick Decision Server; you generally get that over the detail data. Rather, aggregate tables are optional and, if implemented correctly, get you superior performance.

Define as many hierarchies as possible

When building your schema, define as many hierarchies as possible to Vista. The existence of these hierarchies will assist the Advisor in making better recommendations in building aggregates. These hierarchies often serve as the basis for any derived dimensions you may end up building.

When a query is run against the Vista system tables, all the tables referenced by the queries that have been logged during the period being surveyed are read dynamically by Vista in order to calculate the savings associated with an existing aggregate or the potential savings associated with a potential aggregate table. Running these types of queries against the advisor in a large and busy database could take days, so it's advisable to run the report during a weekend or other low usage time.

General guidelines

Keep the following general points in mind when building aggregate tables or analyzing the benefits and performance of existing summary tables:

♦ Large fact tables usually benefit from one or more time-based aggregates in just the same way that a good STARindex often has the time dimension as its leading key.

♦ Aggregate fact tables need not represent all of their referenced dimensions. Again, in the same way that a STARindex can represent a subset of the fact table foreign keys, an aggregate table can group by columns from a few of the most frequently constrained dimensions.

♦ In general, try to build aggregate star-schemas, rather than floating tables that lack primary-key/foreign-key relationships with the rest of the database. An efficient join path must exist from an aggregate fact table to all of its dimensions; in many cases, these tables should be derived dimensions. What is gained in query performance because of a table's smaller size can easily be lost because of inefficient joins.

♦ Index your aggregate tables as you would any other tables in Red Brick Decision Server. Create STARindexes over aggregate fact tables and their dimensions. Index derived dimensions the same way you index the detail dimensions.

♦ If you are building a new database, run the expected queries with Advisor logging turned on. Then, query the advisor log, see what candidates it suggests, and try them out. For databases with existing aggregates, build precomputed views over them and monitor the rewrite performance. Then use the Advisor to verify utilization and evaluate alternatives (candidates).

Some design approaches suggest that databases store facts at different levels in the same fact table, for example, storing weekly and monthly data in the same table as the daily data. This approach (common with some front-end tools) introduces a lot of redundancy and maintenance overhead and is usually not practical for large data warehouse applications.

Summary

When a Red Brick Decision Server has a portfolio of indexes, as described in Chapter 6, *and* a set of Vista aggregate tables, the DSS production environment can provide the expected OLAP performance. Indexes and aggregates are a very powerful combination for optimizing ad hoc decision-support queries for large numbers of concurrent users querying hundreds of gigabytes or terabytes of data; these optimization techniques rely on good physical and logical schema design, rather than on competition for system resources.

In addition, the Vista Advisor and automatic aggregate maintenance features allow DBAs to manage the aggregate workload and continuously monitor the effectiveness of the strategy. All of this can be done without troubling the user community — all the users see is the improvement in query performance; the workings of the system are otherwise transparent.

Chapter 8

Sizing the Database

IN THIS CHAPTER

- ◆ The importance of sizing

- ◆ Estimation techniques

- ◆ dbsize command-line program

- ◆ Red Brick Decision Server Administrator

- ◆ Other space requirements

- ◆ Lessons from the trenches

- ◆ Sample database sizing

THIS CHAPTER DISCUSSES THE importance of sizing your database objects. This topic is not usually overlooked or assumed to be a simple process. However, a little information and some planning at this stage of the project can help you alleviate or avoid a number of issues that may not crop up until after the database has been loaded and you are in production.

One of the realities of warehouse projects is that often, you will be asked "How big will it be?" long before you have all the necessary data to determine an accurate figure. Being able to provide ballpark estimates is a valuable skill, so we'll discuss an estimation method that results in reasonably accurate numbers.

There are two methods to size your database tables and indexes: use the dbsize utility or the Warehouse Administrator. Note that the dbsize utility results are in kilobytes, and the Administrator results are in bytes. If you do the math, you will discover that the results are equal.

You must account for several server-specific types of space when determining the total amount of disk space required to implement the warehouse. This chapter describes each of these in detail and provides some hints on how to "share" space in those situations where extra disk space is limited. These are only suggestions and may not be applicable to your situation.

The Importance of Sizing

Sizing the warehouse installation used to be a tedious task until the Administrator came along. If you made a mistake, you had to start over. But even with the Administrator, you must have a complete set of DDL to work from. Otherwise, you will only be able to size part of the database. An accurate sizing is a necessary component of your implementation because a number of other components depend on it:

- ◆ Segmentation
- ◆ Machine capacity
- ◆ Index choices
- ◆ Data staging
- ◆ Machine configuration
- ◆ Performance characteristics

A complete sizing of a data warehouse in Red Brick Decision Server includes the following elements:

- ◆ User table size
- ◆ Temporary tables
- ◆ Index size
- ◆ System table size
- ◆ Index build area
- ◆ Query temporary space
- ◆ Log file size
- ◆ Data staging area

Some of these items are shared by all the databases that are managed by the server instance. An example is Query Temporary space. This area is defined in the rbw.config configuration file that points to one or more directories used when running queries. Because it applies to the server, all databases defined on (or attached to) this server share that space. Because this is a shared space, the size must be calculated to account for query activity across *all* databases on that server. I'll discuss this in more detail shortly.

As you begin to size your database, you should strive to allow for anticipated growth. Considering this growth now actually buys you some breathing room up front to concentrate on other issues centered around data acquisition, cleansing, and loading, without having to worry about running out of space at the start. Some people have failed to consider this, and I can tell you from experience, having space issues right up front really complicates maters.

To decide on your disk space requirements, you need to estimate the size of each table and index in the database. You also need to estimate the total disk space requirements for the database, which is the sum of the space required for each permanent and temporary user table, each automatic and optional index, and the system tables.

As previously mentioned, calculating these numbers requires a complete set of DDL that identify the following:

◆ The specific permanent user tables to be included in the database.

◆ The maximum number of temporary user tables that might exist within the database.

◆ For every permanent and temporary table, the initial number of rows to be loaded or inserted into the table.

◆ For every table, the data types and sizes of every column.

◆ For every table, the columns to be indexed and the types of indexes to be used. Consider automatic indexes (primary key b-tree indexes) and optional indexes (additional b-tree indexes, STARindexes, and TARGETindexes).

◆ Anticipated growth patterns for all tables, including growth rate and maximum expected number of rows, within your planning horizon.

Once you collect this information, sizing is very straightforward. If you have been using Red Brick Decision Server for a number of years, you may have several different sizing spreadsheets. Red Brick developed these spreadsheets as field resources to make the sizing task less tedious. At this point, however, I recommend using either the dbsize utility or the Administrator because as the product evolves, the sizing algorithms may change, making the spreadsheet obsolete. I prefer the Administrator because it's less tedious and allows you to experiment.

Red Brick Decision Server data types have the following sizes. These are included here to give you an idea how important it is to choose data types wisely, especially for your largest tables.

Char	The actual length you defined for the column (max is 1,024)
Date	3 bytes
Time	3 bytes without the fractional seconds; 5 bytes with the fractional seconds
Timestamp	6 bytes without the fractional seconds; 8 bytes with the fractional seconds

Integer	4 bytes
Smallint	2 bytes
Tinyint	1 byte
Float or double	8 bytes (-1.e-308 to 1.e308)
Real	- 4 bytes (1.e-38 to 1.e38)

Decimal or numeric

Precision	Bytes
1–2	1
3–4	2
5–9	4
10–11	5
12–14	6
15–16	7
17–18	8
19–21	9
22–23	10
24–26	11
27–28	12
29–31	13
32–33	14
34–35	15
36–38	16

Estimation Techniques

In almost every project I've been involved with, the question of how big the warehouse will be comes up long before I have the information necessary to provide an accurate answer. Usually, the question is being asked to help in the acquisition of hardware to put the warehouse on. It is possible to provide a reasonably accurate estimate on the size of your warehouse by using the following simple calculations.

Estimates are nice and they allow you to proceed with certain parts of the project, but they are not a replacement for detail sizing. Occasionally, someone will use the estimates to implement the warehouse but then have to rework all or parts of the segmentation plan because the estimate wasn't accurate. Be careful, and don't skip the sizing step. That being said, here is the formula for estimating the overall size of the database:

```
(Total Raw Data Size(G) * 1.(3 to 5) + 2G +2G ) * 1.1 =
Expected Size
```

The total raw data size is just that — the amount of raw data you expect to put into the warehouse. You can estimate this from the data sources. Use the 1.3 to 1.5 multiplier to indicate the complexity of the design. The simpler instances (like retail schemas) would have about 30 percent overhead (for indexes and temporary space) and move up to 50 percent for the more complicated instances like telecommunications, healthcare, and insurance. Next, add 2GB for index build area and query temp space, for a total of 4GB, and finally, add 10 percent to account for anything you missed.

This is an estimation technique — nothing more. Normally, the total size of your warehouse should be something less than the number just calculated; however, there is no replacement for an accurate sizing.

A Word About Index and Query Temporary Space

Notice that we used a plug value of 2GB for INDEX BUILD AREA and QUERY TEMP SPACE. The INDEX BUILD AREA is disk space used to build index entries while data is being loaded. The server uses QUERY TEMP SPACE to process queries and store intermediate result sets.

Unfortunately, there is not much guidance in the documentation on how to estimate the sizes of these two areas. I have always used a value of 2GB to start with and increased it if necessary. The bottom line is that you want to have enough space defined for these areas so that in a multiuser environment, you can run your largest queries concurrently, and from a loading perspective, you can load the table with the most indexes on it without running out of space. You can sometimes cheat and use the same space for both functions as long as you don't routinely have loads going on while users are running queries.

Don't forget to include any other space required for data staging and other large disk requirements in your final estimation. In general, once you have the user objects sized, identified the data staging area size, and gotten a reasonable lead on the temporary space requirements, the extra 10 percent added at the end should take care of other components that are a little difficult to size such as logs, discards, DDL files, and other miscellaneous items.

Using Dbsize

Dbsize is a command-line program that allows you to size tables, indexes, and system tables. You must supply a data type for each column, making this process a little tedious. Once you've answered all the questions on data type and supplied a target number of rows, it returns the size of the object in kilobytes.

The best way to illustrate this is with an example. The following set of figures shows the progression through the process of sizing a table from the sample database.

Notice the command-line interface that provides options to size user tables, indexes, and system tables, as shown in Figure 8-1.

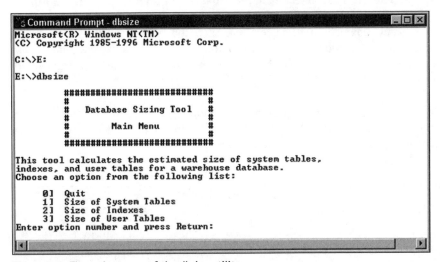

Figure 8-1: The main screen of the dbsize utility

Selecting Option 3, User Tables, you are presented with the text shown in Figure 8-2. Notice the elements you must know to size you user tables. For this example, we'll use the TELEPHONE Table.

After entering the number of columns in the table, you are asked if you want to see some examples of how to size tables and whether you want dbsize to calculate the row length, as shown in Figure 8-3.

Once you've answered the previous two questions, you are presented with a list of supported data types, as shown in Figure 8-4. You will see this list for as many columns as you said are in the table — entering the appropriate data type each time.

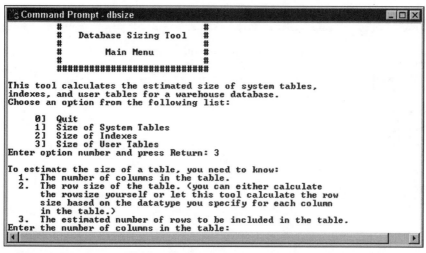

Figure 8-2: The dbsize utility indicating information required to size database objects

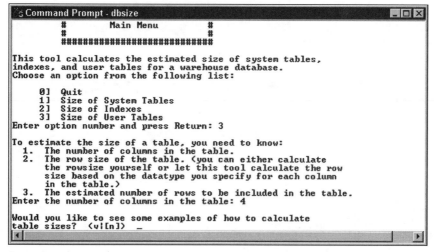

Figure 8-3: There are four columns in the table being sized.

```
Command Prompt - dbsize                                          _ □ ×
Would you like to see some examples of how to calculate
table sizes? (y![n])  n

Do you want this tool to calculate the row length based on
the datatypes you will specify?  ([y]!n)

Enter the number of one of the following options to indicate
the datatype of the column:

  0] DONE
  1] character
  2] varchar
  3] integer
  4] smallint
  5] tinyint
  6] date
  7] time        (without fractional seconds)
  8] time        (with fractional seconds)
  9] timestamp   (without fractional seconds)
 10] timestamp   (with fractional seconds)
 11] float       (or double)
 12] real
 13] decimal

Enter: _
```

Figure 8–4: For each column, you must supply a datatype.

After supplying the data types for all columns, you are asked to provide the estimated number of rows the table will contain. In our example, the TELEPHONE tables will have approximately 10 million, as shown in Figure 8-5.

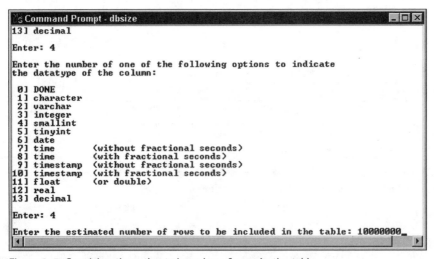

```
Command Prompt - dbsize                                          _ □ ×
 13] decimal

Enter: 4

Enter the number of one of the following options to indicate
the datatype of the column:

  0] DONE
  1] character
  2] varchar
  3] integer
  4] smallint
  5] tinyint
  6] date
  7] time        (without fractional seconds)
  8] time        (with fractional seconds)
  9] timestamp   (without fractional seconds)
 10] timestamp   (with fractional seconds)
 11] float       (or double)
 12] real
 13] decimal

Enter: 4

Enter the estimated number of rows to be included in the table: 10000000_
```

Figure 8-5: Supplying the estimated number of rows in the table

Finally, dbsize returns the size of the resulting table in kilobytes, as shown in Figure 8-6.

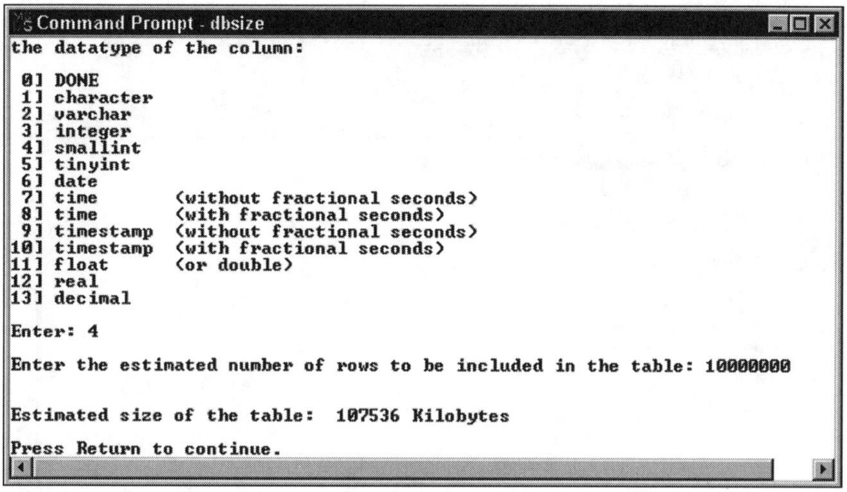

```
 ;Command Prompt - dbsize                                    _□×
the datatype of the column:

 0] DONE
 1] character
 2] varchar
 3] integer
 4] smallint
 5] tinyint
 6] date
 7] time        (without fractional seconds)
 8] time        (with fractional seconds)
 9] timestamp   (without fractional seconds)
10] timestamp   (with fractional seconds)
11] float       (or double)
12] real
13] decimal

Enter: 4

Enter the estimated number of rows to be included in the table: 10000000


Estimated size of the table:  107536 Kilobytes

Press Return to continue.
```

Figure 8-6: The total size of the table is returned.

Using Red Brick Decision Server Administrator

The Red Brick Decision Server Administrator tool is an easy-to-use, point-and-click sizing tool that takes much of the drudgery out of the sizing process. The Sizing Wizard displays size information about tables, indexes, and TARGET indexes. You can navigate between the different types of objects by using the tabs in the wizard.

To use the wizard, you must have the database created and the user tables and index built. This should not be too much trouble because you had to have the DDL to use dbsize anyway. What's nice about the Administrator environment is that you can experiment with datatypes and index definitions, as well as check the resulting impact on the size of the objects, all within a few minutes.

You can access the Size Wizard from either the View menu shown in Figure 8-7 or the Size Wizard icon shown in Figure 8-8.

Once you select the Size Wizard, you are presented with the list of tables in your database. The example shown in Figure 8-9 shows the tables for the sample database. It would be nice if you could navigate the list with a scroll bar, but since there isn't one, you are forced to use the arrow keys to move up and down. Notice the Indexes tab and the TARGET Indexes tab.

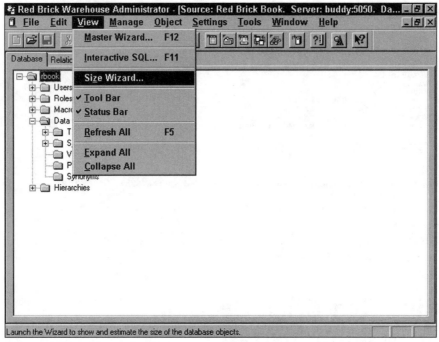

Figure 8-7: The View menu, where you can access the Size Wizard

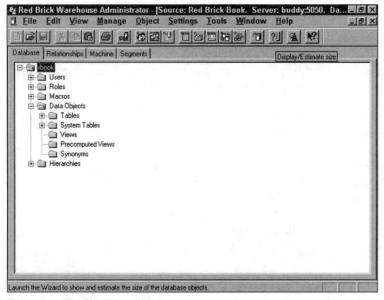

Figure 8-8: The Size Wizard icon

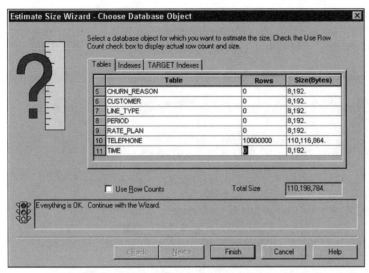

Figure 8-9: The initial window of the Size Wizard displays the tables in the database.

Notice the check box that allows you to use actual row counts in the tables to calculate the sizes. This is a handy feature for checking actual size versus estimated size and growth patterns.

The Index tab allows you to size b-tree and STAR indexes already defined in the database, as shown in Figure 8-10.

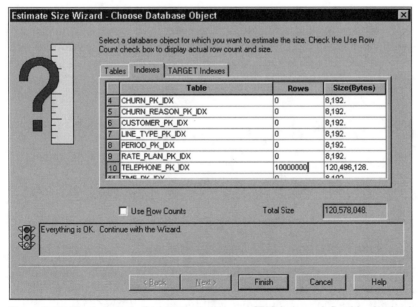

Figure 8-10: The Index tab displays the b-tree and STAR indexes defined in the database.

The Use Row Counts check box is available here as well.

The TARGET index tab displays the estimated domain size (the number of possible unique values) for the indexed column and the estimated percentage of NULL rows in the indexed table, as shown in Figure 8-11.

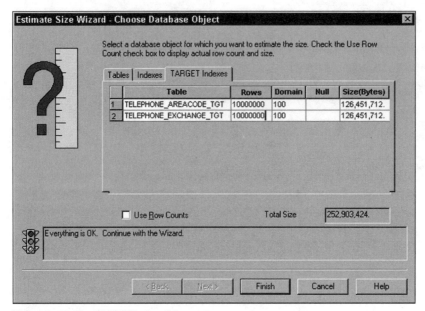

Figure 8-11: The TARGET index sizing page

By default, the Size Wizard displays maximum size. You can display actual size by selecting the Use Row Counts check box at the bottom of the Wizard window. If you want to set the default to display actual size, you can use the File menu's Properties - Size Mode dialog box to change the default.

Other Space Requirements

As mentioned earlier, you must account for several other types of space when sizing your database. Although these other types of space are not directly related to database objects, they still impact the overall system, and you should make every effort to size appropriately.

INDEX_TEMPSPACE

This is the space used by the TMU to build and maintain sections of indexes while loading data into tables. These sections of intermediate index entries are written to the specified directories in what are called spill files. Initially, the index entries are kept in memory and are written to disk once the memory threshold is reached. You must take care to allocate enough disk space to load the table with the most indexes on it so that you don't run out of room. If you do, the load operation stops at the point you ran out of room, and you must restart it from that position.

QUERY_TEMPSPACE

This is much like INDEX TEMPSPACE in that as each user runs a query, the results are initially stored in memory until the memory threshold value is met. Once this happens, the intermediate results are spilled to disk in spill files. This space is shared by all users connecting to the specific instance of the server, so you should take care to allocate enough space to accommodate multiple users running the biggest queries.

Data staging space

This is the area generally set aside for the data ready to be loaded into the warehouse. You can get creative in how and where this space resides – the point is that the data you want to load has to exist somewhere for Red Brick Decision Server to load it.

System

You don't necessarily need to size the system tables unless there is a compelling reason to do so. Generally, when you are estimating the other data/disk areas, you allow enough slack in the estimate that the system tables don't make any difference, but if you feel the need to size them, then do so.

Lessons from the Trenches

There are just a few lessons from the trenches, but they are no less important. An accurate sizing is important to a well-thought-out and well-implemented data warehouse. You will size the database objects correctly: either before you load the data or while you are attempting to load the data. The difference is that if you take the time to calculate database object sizes early, the load process will be a much smoother operation.

Be accurate

Although I cheated a little in the sizing of the last few items, I cannot stress enough the importance of an up-to-date and accurate sizing of the user database objects (tables and indexes). The segmentation plan is the primary component that depends on the sizing. Improperly sized objects wreak havoc on the best-intentioned segmentation schemes. Do yourself a favor and take the time to do this right – you will end up doing it in the end anyway.

Build in a "pad"

Once the sizing has been done, build some extra space into the numbers so that you have some breathing room. One of the nice advantages about Red Brick Decision Server is that you don't necessarily have to allocate the space up front; you can wait until it's required.

Don't be intimidated

A warehouse's total data size can be intimidating at first, especially if you've never dealt with something that big before. It brings to mind all sorts of questions and fear of failure, which is natural. On the other hand, it's also exciting when you get the final size and realize what a beastie it will really be. Be comfortable with the size of the warehouse. As your installation grows, the data volumes will require that you think carefully about tasks that are considered routine in smaller environments. Dropping and re-creating an 800GB index is not always an option, so think before you act and you should be okay.

Sample Database Sizing

In sizing the sample database, I wanted to give you enough of a start to get the data loaded, but leave a complete and detailed sizing as an exercise for you to pursue. Sizing the database is one of the key components in building a warehouse, and there is much to be learned in going through the sizing process.

Sizing also directly affects your segmentation plan in terms of the number and size of the PSUs. Chapter 9 walks you through the process of generating the appropriate segmentation, but you should size the sample database before you get there.

To give you some measurements to start with, Table 8-1 shows the number of rows, and the data size of the sample database, as created with the DDL scripts included on the CD. If you create other objects, then your total database size will change. Table 8-2 shows the indexes.

I have not sized the aggregate tables – that's left up to you to complete. You have knowledge to size them appropriately; you just need to figure out how many rows are in the tables.

TABLE 8-1 SIZING AGGREGATE TABLES

Table Name	Number of Rows	Size (Bytes)
AREACODE_STATE	10	16384
BILLING_CDR	32084904	1347903488
CALL_TYPE	7	16384

Table Name	Number of Rows	Size (Bytes)
CARRIER	9	16384
CHURN	91280	2572288
CHURN_REASON	5	16384
CUSTOMER	1000000	126042112
LINE_TYPE	5	16384
PERIOD	1000	172032
RATE_PLAN	9	16384
TELEPHONE	10000000	130048000
TIME	86400	2260992

TABLE 8-2 INDEXES

Index Name	Size (Bytes)
BILLING_CDR_PK_IDX	969916416
BILLING_CDR_STAR1	773103616
CALL_TYPE_PK_IDX	16384
CARRIER_PK_IDX	16384
CHURN_REASON_PK_IDX	16384
CHURN_STAR1	2236416
CUSTOMER_PK_IDX	12075008
CUSTOMER_TARGET1	172032
CUSTOMER_TARGET2	172032
CUSTOMER_TARGET3	172032
CUSTOMER_TARGET4	172032
LINE_TYPE_PK_IDX	16384
PERIOD_BTREE1	40960
PERIOD_PK_IDX	32768

Continued

TABLE 8-2 INDEXES *(Continued)*

Index Name	Size (Bytes)
PERIOD_TARGET2	49152
PERIOD_TARGET3	49152
PERIOD_TARGET4	49152
RATE_PLAN_PK_IDX	16384
TELEPHONE_PK_IDX	120496128
TELEPHONE_TARGET1	1302528
TELEPHONE_TARGET2	1302528
TIME_PK_IDX	1056768
TIME_TARGET1	57344
TIME_TARGET2	57344

These are the sizes as reported from the warehouse administrator sizing wizard, using the row counts provided. There, the total space requirements are yours to complete, because they are dependent on the environment you are running the sample database on.

Summary

This chapter discussed the importance of sizing your database objects. Database sizing can affect a number of other choices such as relating indexes and data staging. Sizing estimates can get you started and allow you to acquire the hardware components; however, it's necessary to accurately size the user objects and consider the requirements for queries, the loader, and data staging.

There are two ways to accurately size your database objects: by using the dbsize utility or the Warehouse Administrator. Dbsize is command-line oriented; the Administrator is a point-and-click application. I prefer the Administrator because it's easier, faster, and more open to experimentation.

Chapter 9

Segmentation

IN THIS CHAPTER

- ◆ The basics of segmented storage
- ◆ The Period Table revisited
- ◆ Choosing a segmenting time period
- ◆ Coordinated segmentation plans
- ◆ Implementing a segmentation plan
- ◆ PSUs and their functions
- ◆ Basic segmentation guidelines and considerations
- ◆ Lessons from the trenches
- ◆ Sample database segmentation

DATA WAREHOUSES ARE STORING more and more data every year, and managing it all would become quite a challenge if it weren't for segmentation. Segmented storage, or *segmentation,* is fundamental to understanding and implementing a Red Brick warehouse, and we will discuss a number of basic concepts to be mastered, including the following: what segmentation is, how segmentation works, and why segmentation is so important in any warehouse implementation of any size.

Understanding segmentation is only half the battle, so we will also take a look at how to use it, present some guidelines to follow in determining how best to segment your data, and discuss some lessons learned from actual experience. Finally, we will review the segmentation plan for the sample database and then discuss its design decisions and why they were made.

The Basics of Segmented Storage

Data warehouses today store larger and larger amounts of data than they did three or four years ago. On the surface, that doesn't seem like a big deal, until you reach the point of having to archive the oldest year — and you realize a year's worth of data is 100+ GB. Not something you're going to back up without some planning because you just might want to bring that data back some day.

Additionally, you must consider performance issues when building your warehouse because these issues have a huge impact on load times, query response times, and routine administration tasks. Very often, people either skip this step entirely or pay token attention to it – only to later find themselves with lots of other problems they hadn't counted on. It's much easier to spend the time working out your segmentation plan on paper now than after you've loaded all 500+ GB of data.

Wouldn't it be great if you could store a year's worth of data in a way that made it easy to load, query, back up, restore, and maintain? This is precisely what segmentation is built to do. As with almost everything else in Red Brick, you have a number of choices regarding how you implement a segmentation plan, and fortunately (or not), there are few "wrong" answers.

Segmentation and data management

Segmentation is, first and foremost, a data management tool that just happens to have some very interesting performance benefits thrown in for good measure. The larger your database, the more benefits segmentation offers. In general, segmentation offers the following benefits:

- ◆ **Simplifies the loading and management of time-cyclic data or data that is replaced in some sort of time schedule.** For example, if you keep a rolling 36 months of data in your warehouse, then when month 37 comes around, you will roll off the data for month 1 and replace it with data for month 37. In month 38, you will roll off the data for month 2 and replace it with the data for month 38. At any given time (after the first 36 months of data have been loaded), you will always have 36 months of data in the warehouse, and none of it will be more than three years old.

- ◆ **Improves data recovery by breaking large tables/indexes into smaller units.** Warehouse tables tend to get large. There are Red Brick customers who have single indexes that exceed 500GB. Segmentation allows you to manage large objects in more reasonable sizes. As far as the users are concerned, it's all one table, but really, it's a collection of more manageable units.

- ◆ **Separates the data to allow for parallel query processing.** As you will see in Chapter 13, the number of segments helps define the upper limit of the number of processes that could ever be applied to a given query. Parallel processing is a side benefit to segmentation; it is not segmentation's primary function. Generally speaking, the fewer CPUs you have available to you, the less parallelism you will be able to take advantage of.

- ◆ **Provides a dynamic storage capability that allocates storage as it's required.** As you will see later in this chapter, segments can be very dynamic in how they manage the space you have allocated to them. It is possible to allocate it all up front when the segment is created, or allocate it as required by the data-loading processing. Of course, there are infinite options in between as well.

◆ **Allows queries to be run even when some segments of data are not available.** If a particular segment of a table is unavailable (perhaps there was a disk failure), the server is able to continue satisfying query requests that don't require the offline data. If a query is submitted that needs the missing data, it will either process the query with a warning message that all the required data was not available, or not process the query at all, based on the status of a configuration parameter.

Most people tend to think of the tables in a warehouse as just that: a physical table. In fact, that is not true. A table (or index) in Red Brick is actually a virtual object, made up of one or more segments. There are two types of segments: *default segments* and *named segments.*

Figure 9-1 illustrates the relationship between tables and segments. The table is indicated by a dotted line to indicate that it is a virtual object.

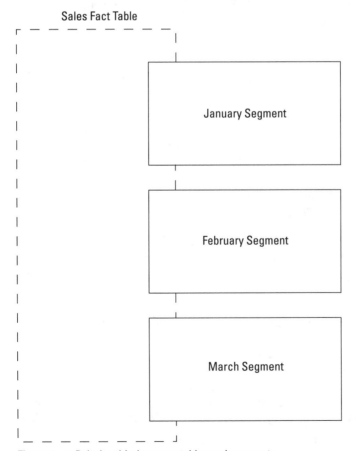

Figure 9-1: Relationship between tables and segments

DEFAULT SEGMENTS

Default segments are the easiest to understand and employ because they are created by the system for tables and indexes that are not explicitly placed in named segments. As a practical matter, default segments are invisible to everyone and are generally satisfactory for static or very small tables. They are created when a CREATE TABLE or CREATE INDEX statement is executed without any explicit segment assignments. There is nothing to do, no sizes to calculate; the server does it all. The sample database has a few of the small tables in default segments.

Note that all default segments exist on the same file system and do not offer much flexibility. Should circumstances change, these segments can be altered and manipulated just like named segments, but it's much easier to plan ahead and put everything into named segments if you think you might do it later.

NAMED SEGMENTS

Named segments are much more flexible but require a good deal more effort and planning to implement. The benefit of all this planning is complete control over all the physical aspects of your data storage, placement, space allocation, and growth rate and file sizes. Named segments are explicitly created with a CREATE SEGMENT statement and must be associated with a table or index before they will be loaded with data.

Query considerations

Segmentation also contributes to improved query performance. From the server's perspective, if it can quickly determine which segments the requested data is in, then it can concentrate on returning the rows in question and not bother with the rest of the segments in the table. This is accomplished by pointer information that is maintained in the STARIndex, which tells the server which segment contains the row pointed to by the index entry.

HOW THE QUERY ENGINE PROCESSES A SEGMENT

After the server identifies which segments contain the data it needs, only those segments are opened and the query proceeds. The ability to quickly determine which segments to look at and then process only those it needs drastically reduce the amount of I/O required to process a query. As you will learn in later chapters, data sort order and data locality can also contribute to further reductions in I/O.

PARALLEL QUERY PROCESSING

If you have a multiple CPU environment and have configured the server to allow it, you can process queries in parallel. This is discussed in more detail in the Chapter 10 and 13, which deal with configuration and parallel processing respectively; however, at a high level, if the query is going parallel, then the server will look at multiple segments concurrently.

Segmenting by Something Other Than Time

It is possible to segment your data warehouse by the primary key column in any of the valid dimension tables in your warehouse; however, most warehouse installations segment by some sort of time definition, be it a day, week, month, quarter, or year (or a fiscal variation of one of these). Therefore, I'll focus on segmenting by time; however, the concepts of the segmentation discussion apply equally well to other segmentation column choices.

The PERIOD Table Revisited

In Chapter 4, I discussed the PERIOD table and its importance to a warehouse from the standpoint that you will keep multiple years of data at a time. The PERIOD table has one other important role to play, and that has to do with segmentation.

For the record, a PERIOD table is not something that most customers have around. They don't have any real need for one in the transactional systems. The warehouse, on the other hand, is built around the concept of time, hence the PERIOD table.

Time-cyclic data

Data warehouses are time-cyclic by nature. As I indicated earlier, you will keep a specific number of time periods in your warehouse and rotate the oldest one regularly (generally monthly or quarterly).

Figure 9-2 illustrates the concept of time-cyclic data. It starts out with 12 months of data, in 12 monthly segments.

As data is added to the warehouse, you will eventually reach a point where the first data you loaded is older than the historical duration, at which point you roll it off in order to replace it with current information. The steps are as follows:

1. Data in the oldest segment is backed up to long-term storage (tape, CD, and so on).

2. Segment is cleared of old data, renamed, and resized to fit the new data coming on. You could also drop the segment altogether, and re-create new segments. Either approach is fine.

3. New data is loaded into the resized (or newly created) segment.

4. Freshly loaded segment is attached to the table.

Sales Fact Table

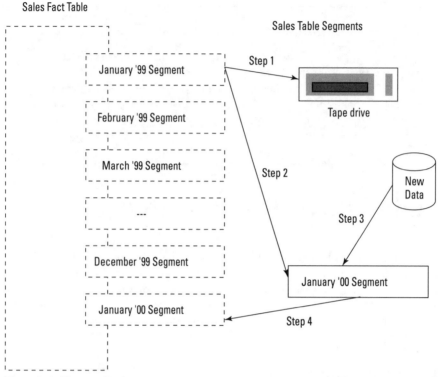

Figure 9-2: Time-cyclic data

ROLLING OFF

The rotation, or rolling, of data can be greatly simplified by an intelligently planned segmentation scheme that takes into account how you want to manage your data. You would not want to define your segments to run from midmonth to midmonth, for example. In this case, a calendar month of information is spread across two segments, and it would be much more difficult to manage because the data is mixed between segments. If you wanted to remove the data for March, for example, you'd also be taking away the last half of February and the first half of April.

Don't forget that you may want to bring some archived data back into the warehouse at some point for special analysis or other projects, so it also makes sense to simplify that process as much as possible. It's also a good idea to archive a copy of the fact table definition with the data to aid in bringing the data back.

BRINGING BACK ARCHIVED DATA

Frequently, archived data is required for analysis or some sort of special project. I mention this here because the data will be brought back in the segment of time in which it was archived. Segmentation allows you to "patch in" a slice of older data into a fact table, as long as the fact table definition today is identical to the fact table definition of the archived data. If this is true, then you're in great shape.

Sometimes this is not true. Warehouses change over time, and it's possible that columns have been added or deleted, or key definitions have changed. In these cases, you have to place the data into its own table – which is where the archived table definition comes in – you know what it looked like and can re-create it. Some folks take the extra time to unload a segment that is going to be archived so that they can reload the data in any way they want to. This is a good idea, and I'll discuss this more in Chapter 11.

Fiscal calendar considerations

Many businesses run on a fiscal calendar instead of a calendar year. For example, your company's fiscal year might run from July 1 to June 30. In addition, many retail businesses have a 53-week year. These are important issues to account for in your PERIOD table because it's natural that the users will want to perform analysis by those periods.

Be sure you include these columns in your PERIOD table. Often, the first question I am asked is, "Where do I get a PERIOD table?" The answer is Microsoft Excel. This is relatively easy to build.

A sample Excel PERIOD table on the CD-ROM accounts for fiscal periods.

Considering a segmenting period table

The data in your warehouse will most certainly have other dates in the data that you will not segment by. For example, in a Sales database, you might have order data, ship date, return date, and payment date. All are valid dates; however, only one will be used for segmentation.

These other date columns, however, may be attached to the PERIOD table as foreign keys for referential integrity purposes. This is all well and good, but what happens if, for referential integrity reasons, you have to have dates going back to the 1800s? How realistic is it to place all those dates into a single PERIOD table when you're interested in keeping the fact data only for a few years?

There are two ways to address this issue:

1. Place all necessary date rows in a single PERIOD table.

or

2. Consider having a PERIOD table and a SEGMENTATION PERIOD table.

In the first instance, the PERIOD table now has lots of other rows that you don't normally care about from a segmentation point of view. Additionally, the table is larger than it needs to be for segmentation purposes, which, as you'll discover in the indexing chapter, can actually work against you. On the plus side, it's fairly easy to educate end users about where to go when they are looking for date constraints.

The second instance is, in my opinion, much more reasonable for segmentation purposes; however, it sometimes requires slightly more effort in end-user training. The idea here is to place the rows required for the segmentation plan into the SEGMENTATION PERIOD table and have all the necessary date rows in the PERIOD table.

I tend to choose the two-table method when I'm faced with really large warehouse installations, instances where I'm overly concerned about data management, or situations where I have references to dates that routinely fall far outside the historical duration of my warehouse.

Above all else, try to be reasonable in deciding which column to segment by, and if segmenting by time, whether you use one PERIOD table or a PERIOD table and a SEGMENTING PERIOD table. It's not just a matter of size: it's a combination of size, date ranges, and how the data must be managed.

Choosing a Segmenting Time Period

In keeping with the time-cyclic nature of a data warehouse, queries sent to the server will almost always reference some type of time frame: for example, CURRENT QUARTER, YEAR TO DATE, or the month of FEBRUARY. Therefore, the challenge is in deciding by which time period to segment your data and indexes. How do you decide and how do you know if it's right? There are many right answers. It's more a question of what's reasonable.

The answer to the preceding question is not as simple as it may sound. Many issues need to be considered before making a decision, and most of the time, you won't have as much information as you'd like when you're ready to move ahead with this issue.

Generally, you will find that as you go through the modeling process, the segmentation period will start to work itself out. You will start to hear recurring ideas about specific processing or data availability windows that govern access to the data in some way. These make very natural choices to start with as candidates.

However, you will often encounter situations where it's not so easy to make the correct decision. These instances usually come about when there are data anomalies, some sort of administration requirement that can't be changed, or some vagueness about the query workload expected.

In any case, you should carefully consider the following elements and how they might affect your segmentation plan.

Business requirements

Often, there will be a set of business reporting requirements that necessitate a certain amount of data be kept in the warehouse. These requirements are hard to overlook and must be accounted for. For example, suppose a sales report covers 13 weeks. If you segment by month, you'll have to carry an extra month to accommodate the 13th week.

Many times, you will have business requirements that prevent you from selecting the "ideal" segmenting time period. It is worth investigating to see if there is some room to maneuver; sometimes you win, sometimes you don't.

Historical duration

I've touched on this a few times already – the historical duration is how long you plan to keep a specific set of data in the warehouse. Data that is older than the duration would be archived and removed from the warehouse. Sometimes, I'll hear a comment to the effect, "I'll keep it forever." This is both impractical and unrealistic, especially from a hardware perspective. Last time I looked, disk farms weren't free (unless, of course, you manufacture them, in which case it's all monopoly money . . . sort of).

Deciding on the historical duration isn't all that difficult. By the time you get involved with the project, the duration may have already been tentatively identified. It doesn't hurt to have someone justify the decision and explain to you the logic behind it. If it hasn't been chosen, you may want to ask some questions during the interview process to help you understand how valid the data would be after different lengths of time – one year, two, three, and so on.

Unfortunately, many times the answer to this question of how long to keep the data in the warehouse is governed by available disk space. On average, the historical duration is between two and five years, although I am aware of several very effective installations with durations of just a year. It all depends on your specific requirements.

Planning horizon

Once you've defined the duration, it's sometimes necessary to define a *planning horizon*: a period of time for which you can accurately estimate data growth. With this information, you are able to develop a segmentation plan that has some growth built into it and buy yourself some maintenance time until after the initial activity of going live has settled down and everyone is comfortable with the system. While we are on the subject of planning, I'd also encourage you to incorporate routine, scheduled downtime in your warehouse maintenance cycle at least once a year. See the "Planning for Routine Downtime" sidebar for more information.

Planning for Routine Downtime

I encourage you to plan for routine system downtime at specific intervals. This is a time for performing some of the more major maintenance tasks that, while not mission critical, still take more time than is generally available on a daily basis. It might be over the holidays, a long weekend, or some other convenient time where you have the system for a period of three days to a week, once a year or so.

Set appropriate expectations going in so that this downtime is not a surprise. If you must maintain 24 x 7 availability, being granted this type of downtime can be somewhat of a challenge, but you should try to carve out maintenance time if possible. In any case, you will most likely experience at least one period of unscheduled maintenance downtime for some reason, so you should give some thought to contingency planning.

Determining a planning horizon can be a double-edged sword. If you don't consider data growth, and size your segments for the data you know about today, then you will spend lots of time expanding segments and adding space. The time you take to do this expansion and maintenance could be spent doing something more productive.

On the other hand, it's very hard to estimate growth for more than a year or two at the outside. That's okay! What you are looking for is a best guess on the growth rate so you can build it in now for a specific period of time. You will not only save time, but you will have a chance to settle into the warehouse without having major space issues right from the start. Be reasonable and you should do okay. A planning horizon of at least a year, but not larger than half the historical duration, is most common.

 The most often used planning horizon is at least a year but not more than half the historical duration.

Data-loading criteria

Often you'll see a decision to segment by the load frequency. This is not necessarily a bad decision: just be aware that this thinking makes more sense as the loads represent longer periods of time — say weeks or months or perhaps quarters — and makes less sense at a day or year level. However, there are exceptions. In situations where the daily load represents a large amount of data (15GB or more a day), then a daily segmentation strategy is appropriate.

Query Considerations

In addition to the subjects just discussed, you should also take the time to investigate the query environment. A preliminary evaluation of the query patterns expected will be a good indication of how directionally correct your segmentation plan is. If you test the plan against the following criteria and nothing seems to break, then you can feel reasonably sure you are headed in the right direction.

NUMBER OF CONCURRENT USERS

Number of concurrent users is your first view into how many people may want the same segment of data, and more importantly, of the workload you might expect to see on the system. Often, you will have no real idea of how many concurrent users you will have. All you may know is total user count. In this situation, assuming a 10 to 20 percent concurrency rate is a safe guess. From here, you can start looking at the segmentation plan from the standpoint of how queries might process if a number of people all wanted the same segment.

QUERY WORKLOAD

This is sometimes tough to estimate, but it is perhaps the most helpful of all. The answer is almost always a guess because of the ad-hoc nature of a data warehouse. Experience will make you more adept at figuring this out, but look at it this way: what are the users going to do 80 percent of the time? If you can answer this, you're in the ballpark.

You can (almost) answer this question by looking at the types of queries the users are going to run. It would be terribly easy if someone actually knew the answer to this question, but, you guessed it, no one really does. Remember that data warehouses are characterized by unpredictable queries, so you arrive at the "answer" by looking back at the business rules and understanding the problems being addressed. Don't ignore any queries or reports you may know about, but they are not the whole answer. Be sure to account for any batch or overnight query processing that generates large reports or data extracts.

System configuration

The system you are running on also impacts a segmentation plan. This includes looking at the number of CPUs and the number of file systems or disks. In general, the more CPUs, the more performance. With one processor, all you really get out of segmentation (for all practical purposes) is the data management functionality. The more CPUs you have, the more you can take advantage of parallel processing for both queries and loads.

The number of disks is also important because it limits your ability to spread data out. Situations where there are a small number of disks (say five or less) tend to suffer from I/O bottlenecks more often than systems with a larger number of disks.

Notice I used the word *disk* instead of file system. This is intentional to point out the fact that it is possible to have multiple file systems reside on the same disk. Having two or more file systems share the same physical device in a non-redundant environment may not reduce the I/O associated with loading and retrieving data because they share the same device, and the operating system talks to the device.

In today's system environments, we have the advantage of redundant array of inexpensive disks (RAID) technology. There are many flavors of RAID technology, from RAID 0 to RAID 5 to RAID S on high-end disk arrays such as EMC[2].

The impact of RAID file systems is generally a smaller number of very large file systems. Because they are redundant, each file system is able to support more than one process when accessing data. I'll discuss this in more detail shortly.

All of this disk/file system discussion might sound a little intimidating, but it really is fairly simple. The best way to illustrate how all this information is combined to formulate a segmentation plan is by looking at an example.

Consider a retail customer with the following parameters for their warehouse:

◆ A daily load of 1GB.

◆ Fifty-two weekly periods in their accounting year.

◆ Fiscal year runs from July to June.

◆ Keep a rolling two years of history.

◆ Want to do "this period vs. same period last year" and "this period vs. prior period" types of analysis.

◆ Seventy percent of their analysis is done by calendar week.

◆ Twenty percent of the analysis is by month, quarter, or year. This 20 percent is what the senior staff sees and is generally run once a month.

◆ Ten percent of the analysis is a mixed bag of user-defined periods.

◆ The hardware platform has six CPUs and 30 file systems.

◆ The data growth rate is between 3 and 5 percent per year.

What would your answers be to the following questions?

1. How would you segment this data: by week, month, year, or something else?

2. How many physical storage units (PSUs) per segment would you have?

3. How big would each PSU be?

4. How many segments would have to be online to accommodate the "period this year vs. period last year" analysis?

The answers might surprise you. Table 9-1 might help:

TABLE 9-1 SEGMENTATION EXAMPLE

Segment Period	Total Segment Size	Total Number of Segments	Total Table Size
Weekly	7.01GB	104	730GB
Monthly	30.41GB	24	730GB
Quarterly	91.25GB	8	730GB
Yearly	365GB	2	730GB

Each of these options represents a possible scenario that you could use to segment the data. The solution you choose depends on numerous factors, including the query load. We'll come back to this shortly and see how to make a choice.

Coordinated Segmentation Plans

A *coordinated segmentation plan* is one in which all of the STARindexes are segmented exactly like the data. This means that if the data is segmented by month on the ORDER_DATE column, then every STARindex for that fact table is segmented by month and has ORDER_DATE as its first column. There are some pros and cons to this approach, however, and you should consider them carefully. Everything costs something, and segmentation is no different than anything else.

The benefits

In my opinion, the benefits of a coordinated segmentation plan generally outweigh the costs — in *most* situations. Sometimes it doesn't work out as planned, but those are the exceptions. The biggest benefit is data management. When you take a segment out of a table, the server must go and find all the index entries and take them out too. When the index segments agree with the data segments, this is a quick and painless operation because the server can go directly to the index segment and perform the operation on the entire segment. If done a different way, the server has to interrogate each index entry to see if its corresponding data is valid or not, and this interrogation process takes time. This is why a coordinated segmentation plan greatly enhances rolling data off and on.

The costs

The costs are a little more difficult to articulate, and it's even harder still to say if or exactly when you might actually experience some of the downsides to a coordinated segmentation plan. The first cost may be some amount of reduced query performance — maybe. I say *maybe* because it really is hard to say. Red Brick has traditionally taught customers to build STARindexes in a way that only had the columns necessary for top performance.

If push came to shove, however, I'd say in most cases it's less than 1 or 2 percent, especially if you have a small PERIOD or a SEGMENTING PERIOD table.

The next cost to consider is that your STARindexes will be slightly larger due to the extra column. This extra column tends to be noise in the overall scheme of things, but you should be aware that the index has one more column, and does take up slightly more space.

The last cost is some TMU overhead in loading the larger indexes, but I'm of the opinion that the extra load overhead is generally worth the increased data management capabilities.

Implementing a Segmentation Plan

A segment is also a virtual object just like tables and indexes. It is a collection of one or more PSUs: a single file native to the operating system on which you are running. PSUs have several parameters that govern their behavior, and we'll discuss them shortly, but first, there are several items to be aware of when using named segments:

- A named segment can contain data for one table *or* one index *or* nothing at all. The data for a table can reside in multiple segments, but you cannot have data from multiple tables reside in the same single segment. The same is true for indexes. In addition, it is possible to have empty segments attached to a table. Segments are a database object just like a table or index.

- A segment can contain up to 250 PSUs. This implies that there is a maximum size for your segments, *not* your tables. A PSU can be up to 2GB.

- Segments of multi-segment tables/indexes can be taken offline for maintenance operations while still providing limited query access.

PSUs and Their Function

The discussion so far has been all about how segmentation can help with data management, and we've alluded to a performance benefit or two, but we haven't yet talked about how it all works behind the scenes. PSUs do all the work, and they are where you will spend most of your time in segmentation management.

As I pointed out earlier, a segment is a virtual object made up of one or more physical storage units or PSUs. These operating system files are what get spread across the file systems and provide for parallel processing. There are some general points to keep in mind when planning for segmented storage:

♦ Red Brick uses disk space in 8KB blocks. This is true for data, indexes, everything – so when you define sizes for PSUs, the system rounds up to the nearest 8K boundary.

♦ The first PSU in a segment is always allocated a minimum of 2 blocks or 16KB.

♦ The number of PSUs per segment and their location is totally up to you. I'll discuss this in more detail shortly.

♦ As the server processes a segment, all the PSUs are opened.

♦ The number of PSUs per segment is the upper limit for any parallel processing of that segment. In other words, if a query can be processed in parallel, the server can allocate an absolute maximum number of processes equal to the number of PSUs it has determined it has to read. This is covered in more detail in Chapter 13, but know that you will almost never get this number of processes because of the other items that affect parallel query process allocation.

♦ PSUs are written to in the order in which they are defined in a segment. This means that the server starts at the first one and writes data into PSU 1 until it is full. It then goes on to PSU 2, 3, and so on. Astute readers will note that the sort order of the data now becomes important. I'll talk about data locality in Chapter 11.

♦ A specific named PSU can belong to only one segment.

Figure 9-3 shows the relationships between tables, segments, PSUs, and disks. Notice that a segment is a virtual object. Also notice how the PSUs are allocated among the disks.

PSUs have a number of parameters that you can set when creating a segment. These parameters are expressed in bytes.

Initial size	This space is always reserved at the time of creation. This is an optimal parameter, and if not specified, the system will use 16KB.
Maximum size	Defines how big the file can grow (rounded up to the nearest 8KB block). This is the only mandatory parameter.
Extend size	The amount of space in kilobytes that the file can grow from Initial size up to Maximum size. This is also an optional parameter with 16KB as the default.

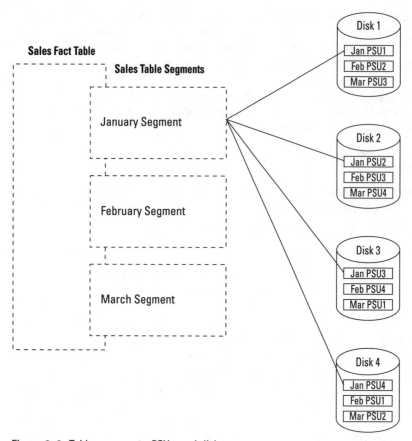

Figure 9-3: Tables, segments, PSUs, and disks

We now know enough to take a look at a sample CREATE SEGMENT script:

```
create segment [segment name]
storage 'psu name1'  maxsize 100 initsize 16 extendsize 8
storage 'psu name 2' maxsize 100
storage 'psu name 3' maxsize 100;
```

The [segment name] is the name of the segment you are creating. The psu1, 2, and 3 designations are the names of the PSUs that belong to this segment. The location of the disk files is explicitly defined by the PSU name. Notice also that the MAXSIZE parameter is required on every PSU defined.

To give you an idea of what a segmentation script looks like, I've included an excerpt from an actual customer script:

```
create segment    finance_199501
   storage '/redbrick_4/finance_199501.psu1' maxsize 500000,
```

```
    storage '/redbrick_1/finance_199501.psu2' maxsize 500000,
    storage '/redbrick_2/finance_199501.psu3' maxsize 500000,
    storage '/redbrick_3/finance_199501.psu4' maxsize 500000;

create segment     finance_199502
    storage '/redbrick_1/finance_199502.psu1' maxsize 500000,
    storage '/redbrick_2/finance_199502.psu2' maxsize 500000,
    storage '/redbrick_3/finance_199502.psu3' maxsize 500000,
    storage '/redbrick_4/finance_199502.psu4' maxsize 500000;

create segment     finance_199503
    storage '/redbrick_2/finance_199503.psu1' maxsize 500000,
    storage '/redbrick_3/finance_199503.psu2' maxsize 500000,
    storage '/redbrick_4/finance_199503.psu3' maxsize 500000,
    storage '/redbrick_1/finance_199503.psu4' maxsize 500000;
```

Notice several points about this previous example:

◆ While naming conventions are not necessary in Red Brick, consider for
   a moment your DBA or system administrator who will spend lots of time
   working with files and file systems outside of Red Brick. With a naming
   convention in place that makes sense, it's easy to identify which database
   object any given PSU belongs to. What the DBA sees as PSUs, the system
   administrator sees as plain old native operating system files.

◆ There are four file systems. This customer had a large IBM RISC 6000
   with lots of disk space carved up into four large RAID5 file systems:
   redbrick_1, redbrick_2, redbrick_3, and redbrick_4.

◆ The PSUs are 500MB in size.

◆ For each of the segments created, the PSUs were rotated to each start on a
   different file system. If all the PSUs for all the segments start in the same
   disk or file system, we haven't really spread out our I/O. Remember, one
   of the goals is to spread the I/O out as much as it makes sense. Because
   we had only four file systems, it made no sense to have more than that
   many PSUs per segment.

◆ Notice the absence of the initsize and extend size parameters. These
   are optional and have generated more than a few conversations about
   specifying values for these parameters or not. To me, it's a relatively
   moot point. I have seen instances where no initialization was done at
   all, other situations where the first few PSUs were initialized and the rest
   left uninitialized, and still other implementations where all the PSUs were
   initialized. In every circumstance, the system performed well. Take a look
   at the amount of the data you expect to place in a segment, and the load
   frequency for the table, and then go from there.

PSU guidelines

As you might guess, there are a few guidelines that you can follow in creating your segments and PSUs. These are field derived and tested by the Red Brick Professional Services Organization. These are by no means the last word, but they are reasonable places to start, and there are a fair number of Red Brick installations running today with segmentation schemes built under these guidelines.

◆ Keep PSUs to between 300 and 500MB or so. This is a reasonable starting place because you've allowed a reasonable amount of parallel processing. If you actually do have to scan the segment, 500MB is not that bad a file to scan on today's hardware. For most instances, this nets out to a very reasonable number of PSUs per segment. It's okay to go smaller or larger, but be sure you understand *why* you are doing it.

◆ Generally, you don't want more PSUs than you have file systems. If you do wrap them around the disks within a segment, you can actually add to the I/O problem that you're trying to solve. For systems with few file systems, say less than five, you have to make a tradeoff or two to get the most out of segmentation. In general, it doesn't make sense to have more PSUs than you have file systems because of how the servers access the segments. Unless you are running on some type of redundant file system such as RAIDx, the best performance occurs when there is one read process per file system.

◆ Do not preallocate the initial space under normal circumstances. This tends to be a "comfort" issue for most folks. I haven't felt it necessary to preallocate, in all but a few cases dealing with very large amounts of data, or issues where the amount of data swings wildly between load cycles. An example of the latter is a customer who collects 25GB a day during the week and 50GB during the weekends. Frequently, you'll have someone make a comment about UNIX and fragmentation or ask about the performance at load time. If you don't preallocate the space when you create the segment, the server will have to go and find it as it fills up the blocks already allocated. If you get to the point that you have pinpointed your performance problems to UNIX fragmentation, I'd argue that you've missed the real problem all together.

Determining the number and size of segments

This is the one area of segmentation that confuses people the most and sends them off into all of sorts of directions in managing their segmentation plan. There is no substitute for common sense when it comes to this task. If this step is done correctly, once the initial segments are created, planning and verifying your segmentation should not take more than an hour or two per load cycle. Period.

To illustrate how tedious some folks have made segmentation management, I had a customer who had a 200-300GB database that was loaded daily. After setting up the initial segmentation plan and loading the first set of data, the DBA decided that the space needed to be managed more closely. To make a rather long story short, what could have been done in a couple of hours a week was now his entire job – all day, everyday, looking for *bytes* of space for the next day's data. Folks, this is too extreme.

Another common mistake people make is that the number of segments and/or PSUs intimidates them. Generally, a warehouse of any size will have a fair number of segments and an even higher number of PSUs. What they fail to realize is that from a maintenance point of view, they will only be working with a few segments at a time at most. Even if a segment has 50 PSUs, that's still a manageable number.

 Don't micromanage your disk space. Segmentation is designed to be flexible. Take advantage of it.

Determining the number and size of your PSUs is another one of those tasks in Red Brick that has many "right" answers. In general, if you approach it with some common sense, the system will allow a reasonable amount of leeway and tolerate an even greater amount of change should it become necessary to adjust either the size or number of PSUs for a given segment.

SEGMENTING TABLES

There are two basic objects that can be segmented in Red Brick: tables and indexes. For tables, the number of segments is generally defined by the historical duration and the segmenting time period selection: for example, three years of data segmented by month. If you follow the PSU guidelines previously outlined, you would try to have a maximum of as many PSUs as file systems and you would let the PSUs be whatever size the math works them out to be.

If you end up in a situation where the PSU size approaches 2GB and you have one PSU per file system, then you should rethink the size and number of PSUs. None of these rules are hard and fast, but I like large (2GB) PSUs less than I like rotating the PSUs around the file systems.

Table 9-2 shows how the example outlined earlier in the chapter for the retail customer might look when we consider the size and number of PSUs.

TABLE 9-2 SEGMENTATION EXAMPLES

Segment Period	# PSUs Per Segment	PSU Size	Total Segment Size	Total Number of Segments	Total Table Size
Weekly	14	500MB	7.01GB	104	730GB
Monthly	30	1.1GB	30.41GB	24	730GB
Quarterly	46	1.98GB	91.25GB	8	730GB
Yearly	184	1.98GB	365GB	2	730GB

Notice how the size of the table stays the same and the size and number of segments changes, based on the choice of the segmenting period. When you start to consider the number and size of the PSUs, you can see how these decisions can impact everything from loading and querying to data management. This is the point where you need to know something about how the data will be queried (at a high level) and balance those requirements with the physical aspects of collecting and loading the data.

Let's analyze the how and why of the results presented in Table 9-2. Showing you the results is fine, but it's the explanation that is most helpful. For this purpose, review the example outlined earlier in the chapter of a customer with the specific implementation characteristics.

SEGMENT BY WEEK ANALYSIS   A weekly segment solution is a very good choice. Seventy percent of the analysis in the example is done by calendar week. This is the lion's share of the processing, and because I'll have to do a lot of "this period vs. last period" and "this period vs. same period last year" analysis, at most, I'm looking at two weeks (or two segments), tops.

In all likelihood, most of the processing would not be parallelized unless you were looking over more than perhaps four weeks or so. This leaves you with enough system resources to handle the other 20 percent of the month-end processing and still be able to handle the other 10 percent effectively.

Size and number of PSUs are manageable, especially on this size platform, and you should see very reasonable performance over the largest part of the queries. In addition, since there are only 14 PSUs per segment, you have the opportunity to spread the I/O over the available file systems. You can probably spread the data in such a way that for all but the biggest queries, no data being looked at shares a file system with any other data being looked at (given that, in general, you're only looking at two weeks).

SEGMENT BY MONTH   The segment by month solution is a little trickier because of some tradeoff being made between administrations (larger segments for keeping data longer), but it's still very manageable. When doing the "this week vs. last week" analysis, about half the analysis will be done in one segment and the other half over two segments – still not too bad. However, you'll have to push a lot more data around to get the answer. You might consider allowing more parallel processing (lowering the thresholds) so when comparing between larger weeks, you have an opportunity to go parallel. You still have an opportunity to spread the data across the file systems, but the PSUs for each month will span all the file systems, so you need to pay a little more attention to data placement for this choice.

SEGMENT BY QUARTER   This choice starts to become unwieldy for the daily level data because the PSUs have reached the 2GB limit, forcing you to have more PSUs, and because you have more PSUs than file systems, you will have to pay close attention to data placement. Because 70 percent of the analysis is looking at only two weeks out of 12 (a quarter's worth), you would spend a lot of system resources just getting the data. Under these criteria, this would not be a good choice. In addition, segmenting by year only makes the problem worse.

SEGMENTING INDEXES
Segmenting indexes works just like it does for tables. The only difference is that the PSUs are smaller and you generally have fewer of them to contend with. Very often, someone will struggle with sizing the index PSUs. Because the indexes are a lot smaller than the data, you have a couple of choices: you can either keep the same number of PSUs but make them a small percentage of the data (10 or 12 percent is a good place to start, if you want to guess), or you can reduce the number of PSUs (or both.) It's not rocket science, and common sense helps a lot.

Guard segments

Guard segments are very small segments with one 16KB PSU. There is one at the low end of the data and index range, and another at the top end of the range. They serve two purposes:

1. They provide a quick check during the load process that all is well. Since these segments are designed to be empty, if one of them fills up during a load, you know you have a problem with your segmentation range definitions (or the data that is being loaded).

2. They aid in rolling data on. When a segment of data is added to a table, the server must check the segments on either side on the segment being added. With the guard segment, when new data is added, it's always inserted between the last real segment and the guard segment. In this way, the check for overlapping data is instantaneous because the guard segment is empty.

The guard segments exist "before" the oldest data and "after" the newest data. Subsequent segments are attached between the last segment and the guard segment, as shown by an insertion of the April data segment in Figure 9-4.

Sales Fact Table

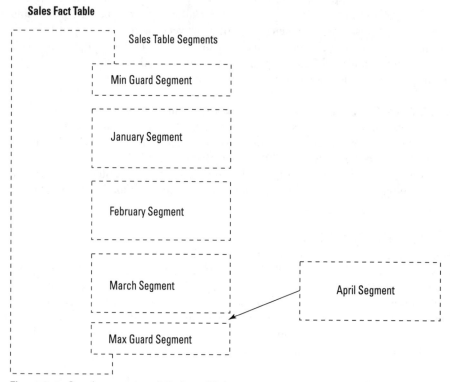

Figure 9–4: Guard segments and their positions

Placing the segments on disk

PSU placement is often the subject of debate as to how best to accomplish the task. There are two basic approaches: segregate your data into index-only and data-only space, or integrate the data and have indexes and data share all the space available.

You may run into the situation where well-meaning DBAs have partitioned their available disk space into data space and index space – the idea being that they can't exist together. This is an idea that had been carried forward from 30 years of OLTP thinking.

Old habits are hard to break, and data placement is not that important to argue about as long as you observe a couple recommendations.

I'd strongly advise you against carving up your space into data-only and index-only space. Carving up your disk farm in this manner just complicates the management issues later on when, for some reason, you are forced to place data or index elements where they don't belong.

Do consider *all* your disk space as available for data *or* indexes. Put the data in one place and its corresponding index in another. For the next table, place the data in the same place as the index for table 1, and the index for table 2 in the same space as the data for table 1.

Another useful tool to have is a spreadsheet that contains the pertinent information of all your file systems and PSUs so that you can manage your disk space and play some "'What if?" games. The Warehouse Administrator has simplified the management of PSUs a great deal, but being able to manipulate the information outside the system can be useful at times.

Creating segments

At this point, we've looked at the benefits of segmentation and how it works, and we've discussed a number of issues that impact your segmentation plan. Now let's take a look at the more practical side of segmentation and how you actually interact with it. Creating the segments themselves is one thing, but they must be attached to a table or index before they can be used.

ATTACHING SEGMENTS TO TABLES/INDEXES

As a practical matter, the segments required to hold a table's row or index data must exist before the table is created. The process of creating a table is what actually associates segments to a given table. The following example presents a complete CREATE TABLE statement with the segmentation for the data and the primary key:

```
create table orders (
invoice integer not null,
line_item integer not null,
perkey date not null,
prodkey integer not null,
classkey integer not null,
custkey integer not null,
promokey integer not null,
dollars integer,
weight integer,
constraint orders_pkc primary key (invoice, line_item),
constraint orders_fkc1 foreign key (perkey) references period
(perkey),
constraint orders_fkc2 foreign key (prodkey, classkey) references
product
prodkey, classkey),
constraint orders_fkc3 foreign key (custkey) references customer
(custkey),
constraint orders_fkc4 foreign key (promokey) references promotion
(promokey) )
data in (orders_data1, orders_data2, orders_data3)
```

```
segment by values of (perkey)
ranges (min:'04-01-1995',
'04-01-1995':'07-01-1995',
'07-01-1995':max)
primary index in (orders_ix1, orders_ix2, orders_ix3)
segment by values of (invoice)
ranges (min:1000, 1000:3000, 3000:max)
maxsegments 3
maxrows per segment 50000
```

We're interested in the last ten lines because in it, we've made a number of important declarations concerning where our row and primary index data are going to go. We've also made some other choices that affect our offline operations.

PLACING THE DATA

Segmentation can apply to row data, primary key information, and STARindexes. In the previous example, we can see there are declarations for the data and the primary key information for the ORDERS table. There are two basic ways to place your data:

- ◆ By a hashing algorithm

- ◆ By range definitions

Segmenting by hash writes rows to the segments in a round-robin fashion. I've seen it done a few times by others, and they ended up changing from segmenting by hash to segmenting by range. This is mostly due to how STARindexes work. The hash was increasing the number of disk reads so much that almost every key entry resulted in a physical disk read.

Segmenting by range, on the other hand, provides the advantage of knowing exactly where the data and its associated index are. This allows offline operations to be performed quite easily. The only thing to keep in mind when segmenting by range is that the data will not be distributed evenly.

This is generally not too much of a problem, but it can cause you some headaches if there are wild swings in your data distribution. If your data distribution does have significant swings, it's common to have to resize one or two segments to accommodate the deviation from the norm. For example, you might have 50GB a month of data, but have 150GB in December because of the holidays. It really does pay to know your data.

Segmentation starts with the data and is declared by the DATA IN clause of the create table statement. From the previous example, we have:

```
data in (orders_data1, orders_data2, orders_data3)
```

This line of code tells us the data for this table will be kept in three segments. If a single segment is named (or created by default), all the data will be placed in that segment. If multiple segments are identified, the data is allocated between them based either on range specification or on a hashing function. Notice that multiple names are separated by commas. If no segment name is specified, the server will create a default segment and place all the data in it.

The next part of the declaration is the segment range specification:

```
segment by values of (perkey)
ranges (min:'04-01-1995',
'04-01-1995':'07-01-1995',
'07-01-1995':max)
```

The segment range specification tells the server exactly how we want to allocate the data to the segments. In our example, it's by period key as identified by the column (perkey) in the SEGMENT BY VALUES phrase. The RANGES statement defines which actual rows of data go to which segment, based on the value of perkey. The min and max values are based on the data type of the segmenting column and do just what they imply. These are the guard segments mentioned earlier.

There must be a one-to-one correspondence between segments declared in the DATA IN clause and the RANGES clause. For every segment specified, there must be a corresponding range statement. Range statements are read as follows:

```
'Place all data rows with a value from min up to but not including
'04-01-1995' into segment Orders_data1.
Place rows with a value of perkey from '04-01-1995' and up to but not
including '07-01-1995' into segment orders_data2.
Place all rows with a value of perkey from '07-01-1995' up to max into
segment Orders_data3.'
```

There can be no gaps or overlap between the end of one range definition and the start of another.

PRIMARY KEY CONSIDERATIONS
The next set of phrases deals with the primary key to our table. This is how we segment the index. From the previous example, we have the following:

```
primary index in (orders_ix1, orders_ix2, orders_ix3)
segment by values of (invoice)
ranges (min:1000, 1000:3000, 3000:max)
maxsegments 3
maxrows per segment 50000
```

The `primary index in` phrase performs the same function for the index entries as the `data in` phrase does for data. It identifies the segments the index entries will be placed in. In our example, the primary key is segmented by values of (invoice)—meaning that we want to break up the index entries by groups of invoice numbers—hence the range declarations as shown.

The next two statements refer to the maximum number of segments that will be attached to the table and the maximum number of rows per segment. Both of these items are important for calculating the size of a STARindex when the foreign key of another table references this table.

In other words, if this table acts like a dimension to another table, the server needs to know these two values to properly calculate the size of the STARindex on the other table. If they are not specified when the table is created, you will be unable to create a STARindex on any fact table the dimension in question is attached to.

Note that the max rows per segment applies to all segments in the table, so you need to be sure it's large enough to cover the largest segment you expect to have. If you have to make changes to it later, it's very costly and time consuming because the table may need to be unloaded, dropped, and re-created, and — depending on what it is related to through foreign key references — could be very messy.

It is also possible to segment STAR and target indexes using the CREATE INDEX statement. Mechanically, it's very much the same as it is for the data and primary index phrases; however, there are a few items of interest that should be examined.

Recall that a STARindex is a multitable b-tree-like structure that contains all, or a subset of, the foreign keys of a given table. Each STARindex must use a different order or subset of the foreign keys — you can't have duplicate index definitions.

For example:

```
Create STARindex orders_star_index1
On orders (
perkey,
prodkey,
classkey,
custkey,
promokey,
invoice,
line_item)
in ( order_star1_seg1,
     order_star1_seg2,
     order_star1_seg3)
segment by references of (perkey)
ranges (    min:300,
         300:600,
         600:max    );
```

You know what the in phrase does — it identifies the segments the index entries are to be placed in. What's new here is the segment by references of phrase and the associated range statements.

STARindexes contain the row IDs (or reference numbers) from the dimension tables, and the row ID is assigned to a row in the order in which it is written to the table, *not* by order of the primary key. If the data for a dimension is unsorted when it is loaded, record 1 might be 02-02-1995, and record 12 might be 01-01-1995. The `range` statement above reads:

```
Place all those rows whose period key row value is less than 300 into
order_star1_seg1; place all rows whose period key row value is => 300
but less than 60 into order_star1_seg2; and place all rows whose
period key row value is 600 or greater into order_star_seg3.
```

When the data is being loaded, the server looks at the period key VALUE ('01-01-1995') and gets the corresponding row ID for that key value. This is the data element placed in the STARindex index. The concept of references applies only to STARindexes. B-tree and target indexes are based on values. If the data in the segmenting dimension was written in an unsorted manner, then there is almost no way to accurately segment your STARindexes and have the index segments line up with the data segments. This can lead to lots of follow-up issues when moving data in/out of tables, as outlined earlier in this chapter in the section on Coordinated Segmentation plans.

QUERY CONSIDERATIONS

Segmentation is what allows the relevant data to be accessed quickly when running queries. For example, assume that you have two years' (or 24 months) worth of data in a fact table that is segmented by month.

The query performance on a single month of data will be identical to the performance you'll get by querying the same data placed into a fact table with only one month of data. This is possible because Red Brick knows to look only at the PSUs that apply to a given month of data even though there are 23 additional months of data available, thereby reducing the amount of work to be done by a factor of 23.

If this same 24 months of data were kept in an unsegmented fact table, every time you query that table, each PSU that is attached to the table may hold some data for your query and therefore has to be interrogated. In a table segmented by time, a query on a month's worth of data has the possibility of being located *only* in a single monthly segment.

Generally, one read process will work through all the PSUs on a segment. From a parallel query perspective, based on system load, available processes, and parallel query configuration parameters, the possibility exists that you may get more than one read process per segment, which reduces the time to answer the query. This is a simplified explanation of parallel query processing and will be covered in more detail in Chapter 12.

There is one other query consideration to be aware of. From time to time, based on the query, the correct way to get the data is to scan a table or index. You've probably heard that table scans are "bad" and, indeed, they often are. SmartScan is a compile-time optimization that replaces certain kinds of full table or index scans with a table scan restricted to just the segments that contain the data in which you're interested. Again, this is a simplified explanation and will be covered more in Chapter 12, but you should be aware of it.

Basic Segmentation Guidelines and Considerations

I've covered a lot of information in this chapter and felt it necessary to reduce it into a set of guidelines that will help you get started. As I indicated earlier, there are a number of Red Brick installations running today with these guidelines.

1. Red Brick block size — Red Brick reads and writes 8KB blocks. Sizes are expressed in bytes and are rounded up to the nearest 8KB boundary.

2. PSU size — To start, PSU sizes should be kept to something less than 500 or 600MB. As you work through the segmentation plan, this size may change, but it is a good place to start. If your total data for a segment is less than 500MB, consider at least two PSUs to provide some parallel processing potential later on. Anything less than 50 to 100MB should be put into one PSU. If you have a large amount of data per day, you can increase the size of the PSUs as appropriate.

3. PSUs and file systems — In general, try to have one PSU per file system per segment. Don't forget to rotate the starting file system for each successive segment definition. See the example in the text. If you must wrap the PSUs, do it in a round-robin fashion within each segment.

4. Initial space allocation considerations — It's totally up to you whether you initialize your segments or not. I don't, but not everyone is comfortable doing this. A decent compromise might be to initialize the first one or two PSUs in a segment and leave the rest alone.

5. PSU growth considerations — Your data will grow. You will undersize a segment. PSUs grow from their init size to their max size in extend size increments. If you do run out of space in a segment, you can either add space to the PSUs already in the segment or add new PSUs to the segment. It's up to you.

6. Data sort order — This is very important. For fact tables that have only one STARindex, sort the data in the order of the columns of that index. In situations where there are multiple STARindexes for a given fact table, sort the data in the order of the index you will use most frequently. In either case, don't forget to put the PERIOD column first. For dimension tables, you should sort the input data in primary key order. Dimensions should always be sorted before you load. Facts should be sorted if you can. There are real performance gains to be had if you do.

7. Data locality — This is directly related to sorting your data. As the server reads through a segment, it keeps track of where it is in the segment. For each successive index entry for that segment, what you want is for that row to be either where the pointer is or where it's going to be next, not someplace it's already been.

Lessons from the Trenches

Segmentation is a data management tool. As such, it provides you with some capabilities that are now a necessity when building data warehouses. However, it is not rocket science, and all too often, folks can get carried away with implementing and managing a segmentation plan.

Be reasonable

If I had only one point to make about segmentation, it would be this: segmentation is not applied rocket science. It is flexible, and with a little forethought, it can be a powerful tool for both data management and query processing. The most important data point in creating a segmentation plan is how the users intend to use the data. You will not know everything they will ever want to do, but you should have a reasonable grasp of the driving issues behind what they want to do.

It is very easy to get caught up in the details of segmentation planning, and I caution you to take a conservative approach.

Don't micromanage your disk space

This is the other issue I strongly advise against. The work required to maintain a segmentation scheme is largely what you make it. Don't make it harder for your DBA than it has to be. He or she will thank you for it.

Change the question

What if the analysis percentages were different in the working example earlier in the chapter? What if 70 percent of the analysis were at a month level? Could I get away with storing a quarter's worth of weeks, and storing the two years of monthly information? I put this in the "Lessons from the Trenches" section because very often, we get so focused on building something that we don't always remember to take a step back and see the forest for the trees.

If the answers to the previous questions were "yes," then I would have a significantly different segmentation plan and be able to get much better performance – all by asking the "What if?" questions. Every so often, take a mental step back and see if there are some significant opportunities staring you in the face just waiting for you to take advantage of them.

Sample Database Segmentation

As with any sample database, the challenge is to implement it in such a way that the majority of the readers will be able to accommodate it as well. The CD contains a large amount of data spread over a single month. Chapter 11 has instructions on how to generate more data if you want to. For purposes of the book, I'm more interested in having multiple segments than a full two years of data, so I'll talk mostly about that data and provide insight on what could be done if the database were fully loaded.

I have provided complete segmentation examples for three of the tables in the sample database: the BILLING_CDR fact table, the TELEPHONE dimension table, and the CUSTOMER dimension table. I've left the other tables up to you to segment for several reasons:

◆ You should have some experience in segmenting a table.

◆ You will have to edit the segmentation provided to change the file system (or drive letter) designation to match your platform.

BILLING_CDR

This is by far the biggest table in the database. It contains a call data record for every call made from every phone in the system. A daily load represents between 7 and 8 million rows. This represents about 300 to 400MB of raw data per week, based on the data generation script. The table is created as segmented as follows:

```
/* billing_cdr.sql
The Official Guide to Informix Red Brick Data Warehousing
Robert J. Hocutt
ISBN 0-7645-4694-5

This SQL script creates the billing_cdr fact table - including the
segmentation scheme
and indexes. You will have to change the file system names to match
your environment
*/

drop table billing_cdr dropping segments;

create segment BILLING_CDR_4
storage 'f:\rbook\billing_cdr_4_billcdr_psu_4' maxsize 89016
initsize 16 extendsize 8,
storage 'e:\rbook\billing_cdr_4_billcdr_psu_3' maxsize 89016
initsize 16 extendsize 8,
storage 'g:\rbook\billing_cdr_4_billcdr_psu_1' maxsize 89016
initsize 16 extendsize 16,
storage 'd:\rbook\billing_cdr_4_billcdr_psu_2' maxsize 89016
initsize 16 extendsize 8;

create segment BILLING_CDR_3
storage 'e:\rbook\billing_cdr_3_billcdr_psu_4' maxsize 89016
```

```
initsize 16 extendsize 8,
storage 'd:\rbook\billing_cdr_3_billcdr_psu_3' maxsize 89016
initsize 16 extendsize 8,
storage 'f:\rbook\billing_cdr_3_billcdr_psu_1' maxsize 89016
initsize 16 extendsize 16,
storage 'g:\rbook\billing_cdr_3_billcdr_psu_2' maxsize 89016
initsize 16 extendsize 8;

create segment BILLING_CDR_2
storage 'f:\rbook\billing_cdr_2_billcdr_psu_2' maxsize 89016
initsize 16 extendsize 8,
storage 'd:\rbook\billing_cdr_2_billcdr_psu_4' maxsize 89016
initsize 16 extendsize 8,
storage 'g:\rbook\billing_cdr_2_billcdr_psu_3' maxsize 89016
initsize 16 extendsize 8,
storage 'e:\rbook\billing_cdr_2_billcdr_psu_1' maxsize 89016
initsize 16 extendsize 16;

create segment BILLING_CDR_1
storage 'g:\rbook\billing_cdr_1_billcdr_psu_4' maxsize 89016
initsize 16 extendsize 8,
storage 'd:\rbook\billing_cdr_1_billcdr_psu_1' maxsize 89016
initsize 16 extendsize 16,
storage 'e:\rbook\billing_cdr_1_billcdr_psu_2' maxsize 89016
initsize 16 extendsize 8,
storage 'f:\rbook\billing_cdr_1_billcdr_psu_3' maxsize 89016
initsize 16 extendsize 8;

create segment BILLING_CDR_PK_1
storage 'e:\rbook\billing_cdr_PK_1_billcdr_PK_psu_2' maxsize 48512
initsize 16 extendsize 8,
storage 'd:\rbook\billing_cdr_PK_1_billcdr_PK_psu_1' maxsize 48512
initsize 16 extendsize 16,
storage 'g:\rbook\billing_cdr_PK_1_billcdr_PK_psu_4' maxsize 48512
initsize 16 extendsize 8,
storage 'f:\rbook\billing_cdr_PK_1_billcdr_PK_psu_3' maxsize 48512
initsize 16 extendsize 8;

create segment BILLING_CDR_PK_2
storage 'f:\rbook\billing_cdr_PK_2_billcdr_PK_psu_2' maxsize 48512
initsize 16 extendsize 8,
storage 'e:\rbook\billing_cdr_PK_2_billcdr_PK_psu_1' maxsize 48512
initsize 16 extendsize 16,
storage 'd:\rbook\billing_cdr_PK_2_billcdr_PK_psu_4' maxsize 48512
initsize 16 extendsize 8,
```

```
storage 'g:\rbook\billing_cdr_PK_2_billcdr_PK_psu_3' maxsize 48512
initsize 16 extendsize 8;

create segment BILLING_CDR_PK_4
storage 'g:\rbook\billing_cdr_PK_4_billcdr_PK_psu_1' maxsize 48512
initsize 16 extendsize 16,
storage 'd:\rbook\billing_cdr_PK_4_billcdr_PK_psu_2' maxsize 48512
initsize 16 extendsize 8,
storage 'e:\rbook\billing_cdr_PK_4_billcdr_PK_psu_3' maxsize 48512
initsize 16 extendsize 8,
storage 'f:\rbook\rbookbilling_cdr_PK_4_billcdr_PK_psu_4' maxsize
48512 initsize 16 extendsize 8;

create segment BILLING_CDR_PK_3
storage 'g:\rbook\billing_cdr_PK_3_billcdr_PK_psu_2' maxsize 48512
initsize 16 extendsize 8,
storage 'f:\rbook\billing_cdr_PK_3_billcdr_PK_psu_1' maxsize 48512
initsize 16 extendsize 16,
storage 'e:\rbook\billing_cdr_PK_3_billcdr_PK_psu_4' maxsize 48512
initsize 16 extendsize 8,
storage 'd:\rbook\billing_cdr_PK_3_billcdr_PK_psu_3' maxsize 48512
initsize 16 extendsize 8;

create table BILLING_CDR
(
PERIOD_KEY INTEGER not null,
TIME_KEY INTEGER not null,
CALL_TYPE TINYINT not null,
RATE_PLAN TINYINT not null,
BTN INTEGER not null,
DEST_TELEPHONE_NUMBER INTEGER not null,
CUSTOMER_ID INTEGER not null,
LINE_TYPE_KEY INTEGER not null,
ORIG_TELEPHONE_NUMBER INTEGER not null,
REVENUE_AMOUNT DECIMAL( 9, 2 )  not null,
CALL_DURATION SMALLINT not null,
TAX_AMOUNT DECIMAL( 5, 2 )  not null,
constraint  BILLING_CDR_PKEY_CONSTRAINT primary key ( PERIOD_KEY,
CALL_TYPE, RATE_PLAN, LINE_TYPE_KEY, TIME_KEY, CUSTOMER_ID,BTN ) ,
constraint  BILLING_CDR_FKEY1_CONSTRAINT foreign key ( PERIOD_KEY )
references  PERIOD ,
constraint  BILLING_CDR_FKEY2_CONSTRAINT foreign key ( CALL_TYPE )
references  CALL_TYPE ,
constraint  BILLING_CDR_FKEY3_CONSTRAINT foreign key ( RATE_PLAN )
references  RATE_PLAN ,
```

```
constraint  BILLING_CDR_FKEY4_CONSTRAINT foreign key ( LINE_TYPE_KEY
) references  LINE_TYPE ,
constraint  BILLING_CDR_FKEY5_CONSTRAINT foreign key ( TIME_KEY )
references  TIME ,
constraint  BILLING_CDR_FKEY6_CONSTRAINT foreign key ( CUSTOMER_ID )
references  CUSTOMER ,
constraint  BILLING_CDR_FKEY7_CONSTRAINT foreign key ( BTN )
references  TELEPHONE ,
constraint  BILLING_CDR_FKEY8_CONSTRAINT foreign key (
ORIG_TELEPHONE_NUMBER ) references  TELEPHONE ,
constraint  BILLING_CDR_FKEY9_CONSTRAINT foreign key (
DEST_TELEPHONE_NUMBER ) references  TELEPHONE
)
data in ( BILLING_CDR_1, BILLING_CDR_2, BILLING_CDR_3, BILLING_CDR_4
)


primary index in ( BILLING_CDR_PK_1, BILLING_CDR_PK_2,
BILLING_CDR_PK_3, BILLING_CDR_PK_4 )
segment by values of ( PERIOD_KEY )
ranges( MIN:8, 8:15, 15:22, 22:MAX )
maxsegments 4
maxrows per segment 6250000;

create segment billing_cdr_star1_1
storage 'd:\rbook\billing_cdr_star1_1_psu1' maxsize 33000,
storage 'e:\rbook\billing_cdr_star1_1_psu2' maxsize 200000;

create segment billing_cdr_star1_2
storage 'f:\rbook\billing_cdr_star1_2_psu1' maxsize 116000,
storage 'g:\rbook\billing_cdr_star1_2_psu2' maxsize 409600;

create segment billing_cdr_star1_3
storage 'd:\rbook\billing_cdr_star1_3_psu1' maxsize 116000,
storage 'e:\rbook\billing_cdr_star1_3_psu2' maxsize 409600;

create segment billing_cdr_star1_4
storage 'f:\rbook\billing_cdr_star1_4_psu1' maxsize 116000,
storage 'g:\rbook\billing_cdr_star1_4_psu2' maxsize 409600;

create segment billing_cdr_star1_5
storage 'd:\rbook\billing_cdr_star1_5_psu1' maxsize 82000,
storage 'e:\rbook\billing_cdr_star1_5_psu2' maxsize 204800;
```

```
CREATE STAR INDEX BILLING_CDR_STAR1
 ON BILLING_CDR (
    PERIOD_KEY
    ,TIME_KEY
    ,CUSTOMER_ID
    ,CALL_TYPE
    ,RATE_PLAN
    ,LINE_TYPE_KEY
    ,BTN
) IN (
  billing_cdr_star1_1, billing_cdr_star1_2, billing_cdr_star1_3,
  billing_cdr_star1_4, billing_cdr_star1_5)
 segment by references of (PERIOD_KEY)
 ranges (MIN:2, 2:9, 9:16, 16:23, 23:MAX)



create STAR index BILLING_CDR_STAR1 on BILLING_CDR
(
BILLING_CDR_FKEY1_CONSTRAINT,
BILLING_CDR_FKEY2_CONSTRAINT,
BILLING_CDR_FKEY3_CONSTRAINT,
BILLING_CDR_FKEY4_CONSTRAINT,
BILLING_CDR_FKEY5_CONSTRAINT,
BILLING_CDR_FKEY6_CONSTRAINT,
BILLING_CDR_FKEY7_CONSTRAINT
 ) IN (
  billing_cdr_star1_1, billing_cdr_star1_2, billing_cdr_star1_3,
  billing_cdr_star1_4, billing_cdr_star1_5)
 segment by references of (PERIOD_KEY)
 ranges (MIN:2, 2:9, 9:16, 16:23, 23:MAX)

with fillfactor 100 ;
```

CUSTOMER

The CUSTOMER table has about one million rows in it. Based on the table
definition, this is about 126MB. I have placed this into a single named segment so
we can work with the table. It is a slowly changing dimension, and we will want to
manage it. Notice the segmentation for the TARGETindexes on the demographic
columns.

```
/* customer.sql
The Official Guide to Informix Red Brick Data Warehousing
```

```
Robert J. Hocutt
ISBN 0-7645-4694-5

This SQL script creates the customer dimension including
segmentation and target indexes
*/
create segment CUSTOMER_DATA
storage 'f:\rbook\customer_data_psu1' maxsize 50000 initsize 16
extendsize 8,
storage 'e:\rbook\customer_data_psu4' maxsize 50000 initsize 16
extendsize 8,
storage 'd:\rbook\customer_data_psu3' maxsize 50000 initsize 16
extendsize 8,
storage 'g:\rbook\customer_data_psu2' maxsize 50000 initsize 16
extendsize 8;

create segment CUSTOMER_PK
storage 'f:\rbook\customer_PK_psu1' maxsize 20000 initsize 16
extendsize 8;

create table CUSTOMER
(
CUSTOMER_ID INTEGER not null unique,
CUSTOMER_NAME CHAR( 25 ),
CUSTOMER_CITY CHAR( 15 ),
CUSTOMER_STATE CHAR( 2 ),
CUSTOMER_POSTAL_CODE CHAR( 5 ),
CREDIT_LIMIT DECIMAL( 7, 0 ),
CUSTOMER_TYPE CHAR( 11 ),
AGE_BAND CHAR( 5 ),
HOUSEHOLD_COUNT_BAND CHAR( 2 ),
HOME_OWNER CHAR( 3 ),
MARITAL_STATUS CHAR( 8 ),
ANNUAL_INCOME_BAND CHAR( 12 ),
NUMBER_EMPLOYEES_BAND CHAR( 9 ),
ANNUAL_REVENUE_BAND CHAR( 14 ),
SIC_CODE CHAR( 5 ),
constraint  CUSTOMER_PKEY_CONSTRAINT primary key ( CUSTOMER_ID )
 )
data in ( CUSTOMER_DATA )


primary index in ( CUSTOMER_PK )
```

```
maxrows per segment 1000000;

create segment CUSTOMER_TARGET1_IDX
storage 'd:\rbook\customer_target1_idx' maxsize 200000 initsize 16
extendsize 8;

create TARGET index CUSTOMER_TARGET1 on CUSTOMER
(
MARITAL_STATUS
 )
in CUSTOMER_TARGET1_IDX
segment by values of ( MARITAL_STATUS )
ranges( MIN:MAX )
with fillfactor 100 ;




create segment CUSTOMER_TARGET2_IDX
storage 'e:\rbook\customer_target2_idx' maxsize 200000 initsize 16
extendsize 8;

create TARGET index CUSTOMER_TARGET2 on CUSTOMER
(
HOME_OWNER
 )
in CUSTOMER_TARGET2_IDX
segment by values of ( HOME_OWNER )
ranges( MIN:MAX )
with fillfactor 100 ;




create segment CUSTOMER_TARGET3_IDX
storage 'f:\rbook\customer_target3_idx' maxsize 200000 initsize 16
extendsize 8;

create TARGET index CUSTOMER_TARGET3 on CUSTOMER
(
CUSTOMER_STATE
 )
in CUSTOMER_TARGET3_IDX
segment by values of ( CUSTOMER_STATE )
ranges( MIN:MAX )
with fillfactor 100 ;
```

```
create segment CUSTOMER_TARGET4_IDX
storage 'g:\rbook\customer_target4_idx' maxsize 200000 initsize 16
extendsize 8;

create TARGET index CUSTOMER_TARGET4 on CUSTOMER
(
CUSTOMER_TYPE
 )
in CUSTOMER_TARGET4_IDX
segment by values of ( CUSTOMER_TYPE )
ranges( MIN:MAX )
with fillfactor 100 ;
```

TELEPHONE

This dimension has ten million rows in it. I have placed it in a named segment for all the same reasons I cited for Customer.

```
/* telephone.sql
The Official Guide to Informix Red Brick Data Warehousing
Robert J. Hocutt
ISBN 0-7645-4694-5

This SQL script creates the telephone dimension table
and target indexes on the area_code and state columns
*/
drop table telephone dropping segments;

drop segment telephone_data;
create segment telephone_data
storage 'd:\rbook\telephone_data_psu1' maxsize 120000,
storage 'e:\rbook\telephone_data_psu2' maxsize 120000,
storage 'f:\rbook\telephone_data_psu3' maxsize 120000,
storage 'g:\rbook\telephone_data_psu4' maxsize 120000;

drop segment telephone_PK;
create segment telephone_PK
storage 'e:\rbook\telephone_PK_psu1' maxsize 40000,
storage 'f:\rbook\telephone_PK_psu2' maxsize 40000,
storage 'g:\rbook\telephone_PK_psu3' maxsize 40000,
storage 'd:\rbook\telephone_PK_psu4' maxsize 40000;
```

```
create table TELEPHONE
(
PHONE_KEY INTEGER not null unique,
AREA_CODE SMALLINT not null,
EXCHANGE SMALLINT not null,
NUMBER SMALLINT not null,
STATE char(2) not null,
constraint  TELEPHONE_PKEY_CONSTRAINT primary key ( PHONE_KEY )
 )
data in (telephone_data)
primary index in (telephone_PK)
maxsegments 1
maxrows per segment 10000000;

create segment telephone_target1_idx
storage 'd:\rbook\telephone_target1_idx' maxsize 204800;

CREATE TARGET INDEX telephone_target1 ON telephone (state)
 in (telephone_target1_idx);

create segment telephone_target2_idx
storage 'f:\rbook\telephone_target2_idx' maxsize 204800;

CREATE TARGET INDEX telephone_target2 ON telephone (area_code)
 in (telephone_target2_idx);
```

The rest of the tables

The rest of the tables in the sample database are left up to you. The other dimensions are so small that you could leave them in default segments. The aggregate tables are also left to you to size, as the results will be directly dependent on how much detail data you have loaded.

Summary

Segmentation is a data management tool that provides query performance enhancements. The larger your database, the more benefit segmentation offers. There are two types of segments – default segments and named segments – and each has its function.

It is possible to segment your data warehouse by the primary key of any dimension attached to a given fact table. Most warehouse installations segment by some sort of time definition, be it a day, week, month, quarter, or year (or a fiscal variation of one of these). Often, you will see a coordinated segmentation where all of the STARindexes are segmented exactly like the data. There are some pros and cons to this approach, however, which you should consider carefully. Everything costs something, and segmentation is no different than anything else.

Segmentation is not applied rocket science. The work required to maintain a segmentation scheme is largely what you make of it. It is fairly flexible, and with a little forethought, can be a powerful tool both for data management and query processing. Above all, be reasonable, and strive to keep it simple.

Part IV

Building and Maintaining the Data Warehouse

Chapter 10

Installing and Configuring

IN THIS CHAPTER

◆ Red Brick PreInstallation

◆ Hardware environments

◆ Kernel parameter calculations

◆ Selected configuration parameters and initial settings

◆ Creating a database instance

◆ Overview of users, roles, and connectivity

◆ Lessons from the trenches

INSTALLING RED BRICK, the topic of this chapter, has always been an easy task to perform. I recall an instance where the sales person was explaining to a customer how easy it was to install Red Brick and how it just wasn't complicated. Of course, the customer said to prove it, so with installation guide in hand, the sales rep had a Red Brick instance installed, up, and running the AROMA sample database in less than half an hour. It really is that simple.

Red Brick PreInstallation

You must complete a few tasks prior to installing Red Brick. These are explained in detail in the *Installation and Configuration Guide* for your specific hardware plat-form, and it is a good idea to read it completely before installing the software. These steps gather the information required to answer the installation questions and are generic across operating systems and hardware platforms. Some of this information is used as initial parameter settings in the configuration file. As you read through the *Installation and Configuration Guide*, you will find places to record your answers for easy referral during the installation.

Some of the information you provide during the installation is used as values for configuration settings. Take the time to verify your choices and settings with the *Installation and Configuration Guide*.

Briefly, the preinstallation steps you must perform are as follows:

1. Determine the operating-system shell (UNIX only).

2. Verify that your operating-system version and available disk space meet Red Brick requirements.

3. Configure the operating-system kernel (UNIX only).

4. Determine the locale.

5. Select a warehouse logical name.

6. Select an interprocess communication (IPC) key for the Red Brick Server daemon.

7. Determine the TCP/IP ports for the daemon.

8. Create the redbrick account for administration.

9. Create the *redbrick* directory for the Red Brick Server software. This directory can be called anything you like – however, the redbrick user must have read, write, and execute access to the directory. This is where the software will be installed.

10. Once the steps above have been completed, you can then install the software. Note that some of the installation steps require superuser or root access for UNIX environments or Administrator access for NT environments. In addition, the installation procedure assumes you have the following:

   ■ A CD-ROM drive.

   ■ The minimum amount of disk space recommended for your platform of choice to hold the Red Brick software itself.

   ■ A minimum of 32MB of RAM, with at least 128MB preferred for large-system configurations supporting 20 or more concurrent users. When in doubt, more is better.

   ■ Enough disk space to store the databases to be managed by the Red Brick software.

The next step is starting the server processes or daemons. These steps are discussed in detail in the installation guide. There are different instructions for UNIX and NT; however, once the daemons (or services in NT) have been started successfully, you will receive a message reflecting your specific installation parameters. Most of the issues surrounding the starting of the server are related to paths or permissions. Be sure you follow the instructions carefully. If you have trouble, call Informix technical support.

Most of the issues associated with the servers (UNIX) or services (NT) not starting correctly are directly related to path and permission problems.

Hardware Environments

Red Brick runs on a variety of UNIX platforms as well as NT. This discussion is primarily centered on the UNIX environments, so if you are using NT, you can skim this section. As you know, each flavor of UNIX comes with its own unique set of kernel parameters. HP is different from IBM, which is different from SUN, and so on. Each UNIX installation of Red Brick requires that a handful of kernel parameters be set. Setting the kernel parameters is somewhat dependent on several hardware environment issues.

The key factors for a Red Brick environment are the number of CPUs, the amount of available memory, the amount and configuration of the persistent storage, and any other software that might be competing for system resources. These are all equally important issues that to some extent are codependent. These few parameters are related. They impact some of the kernel settings, and you should be careful in making a judgment on the appropriateness of an environment unless you know the values of each of the parameters.

Often, I have been asked to validate a Red Brick installation only to find that the kernel parameters were calculated incorrectly. The Installation Guide for your platform has the necessary calculations for each parameter. Check your math. Don't forget the order of operations — it does matter. If nothing else, enter the calculations into a spreadsheet.

Determining an appropriate environment

I've frequently been asked whether or not a given hardware environment is appropriate for running Red Brick. It's very hard to answer this question if asked with little or no other information about the size, scope, number of users, and other characteristics of your warehouse. On one hand, if you have the executable for the platform in question, sure, Red Brick will run on that platform. Whether or not it will meet the requirements of the warehouse you intend to build is a different question altogether.

Be careful in making assumptions about platform suitability. You should consider a number of factors in choosing and configuring hardware for your warehouse application. These factors are discussed below.

NUMBER OF CPUS

Determining an appropriate number of CPUs for the environment you are planning requires some thought. While it is true that pound for pound Red Brick Decision Server will run better on less hardware than other database engines, it is still possible to shortchange yourself by not sizing the hardware platform correctly. When determining whether the number of CPUs is sufficient for the environment, you must consider several points:

◆ The capacity of the CPUs

◆ Estimated process load for the system

◆ Desired system throughput

CPU CAPACITY

For our purposes, we measure CPU capacity in terms of *context switches*, or, simply put, the number of tasks a CPU can perform at one time before it has to swap one of them out to memory. While this may not be a completely technically accurate description, it serves our primary need of measuring the relative strength of a CPU in terms of processes. Red Brick Decision Server is process based; therefore, evaluating CPUs in terms of processes has value in sizing the environment.

Most CPUs can handle between four and six contexts before they have to do a context switch or switch one process out and another process in. If there is substantial system overhead, then a value of 4 might be more appropriate. In the case of the larger 64-bit systems, a value of 6 or even 8 is often used with good results. Evaluating the hardware in these terms is not a measurement of good versus bad, but rather, is an approach to using the hardware to optimal advantage. Hardware platforms, like operating systems, are built based on assumptions and tradeoffs. All perform the same functions but are built differently. It's like cars — each functions on the same general principles, but a sports car operates a little differently than the family station wagon.

ESTIMATED PROCESS LOAD

Estimated process load is a factor of the number of concurrent users and the number of processes that will be spawned to satisfy their requests. For example, if the number of *concurrent* users is estimated to be 20, then the process load will never be less than 20. If these 20 concurrent users are normally asking for information spanning several months or years of data, then their requests will probably spawn multiple processes. If these users ask for 3 months of information (on average), then the process load could get as high as 60. (Usually segmentation will result in each month receiving its own process.)

DESIRED THROUGHPUT

If we intend for the hardware to handle those 60 processes without degrading the performance (desired throughput) of the CPUs, you could safely expect to need the number of CPUs specified in Table 10-1.

TABLE 10-1 DETERMINING NUMBER OF CPUS

Estimated Process Load	Context Switch Capability	Recommended Number of CPUs
60 concurrent	6	10
60 concurrent	5	12
60 concurrent	4	15 or 16

In other words:

```
Est_Process_Load / Context_Switch_Capability =
Recommended_Number_CPUs
```

Notice that this discussion is based on concurrent users, not the total number of users.

AMOUNT OF MEMORY

The amount of memory is also tied to the estimated process load, but in reference to the Red Brick Decision Server, it is also somewhat tied to the number of CPUs. Red Brick Decision Server allocates memory in increments as needed up to a specified limit for each process. This limit is an adjustable parameter, either set in the configuration file or at the start of a particular session or query. The default is 50MB. Not all Red Brick Decision Server SQL operators are memory-intensive; however, large intermediate result sets, large indexes or hash tables, and big grouping or sorting operations can all use a lot of memory. If the process needs more than the limit, it will "spill" to disk and thus free up the memory for another's use.

Therefore, in our example of the estimated process load of 60, assuming they will need the full extent of memory (50MB), we would need at least 3GB of available memory for query processing alone. This number should seldom be allowed to be more than 50 percent of the available memory on the system. This allows for enough memory to serve the operationg system and any other software that may compete for the resource. The more competing resources in the environment, the less available memory Red Brick Decision Server will have at its disposal.

Another method, and perhaps a better one when trying to determine total system memory, is to allow for one-half to a full gigabyte of memory for each CPU. When the Red Brick Decision Server product was first introduced, it required at least 512MB of memory to run smoothly. Most systems at that time housed only one CPU. As queries became more complex and/or used more data, the initial recommendation no longer met the need. Recommendations of 1GB or more of memory were becoming normal for adequate performance. As multiple CPU systems became common, this recommendation was extended to 1GB per CPU. This estimate seems to allow for enough memory so that memory isn't normally the performance problem — should performance problems arise. In our example, the 12 CPUs would need 12GB of memory. This allows for the queries to have plenty of memory and certain queries to get more than the minimum when needed.

 This memory recommendation is significantly different than the information found in the *Installation and Configuration Guide* and is based on actual field experience. This is not to say that Red Brick Decision Server will not work with less memory, but that it works better with more.

AMOUNT AND CONFIGURATION OF PERSISTENT STORAGE

Estimating the appropriate amount of persistent storage is important. Configuring that storage so that I/O contention can be minimized is crucial to successful performance. Red Brick Decision Server is file-based; hence, its performance is often linked to the way the files are presented on the devices. Physical storage units (PSUs) are the foundation of all objects stored in Red Brick Decision Server. Red Brick Decision Server was initially designed to leverage placement of files in small file systems with many controllers in order to minimize I/O. The extent to which that could be minimized was impacted by the tradeoffs between the number of controllers, the size of file systems, the relationship between devices and file systems, and the actual placement of files. It still is.

The more the relationship between the physical devices and the file systems (both logical and physical) moves away from one device equals one file system, the more you shift the control and responsibility for tuning away from the Red Brick Decision Server software. In other words, as the device-file system relationship becomes more complicated, Red Brick Decision Server can make fewer and fewer assumptions about how the file systems it sees are implemented on the hardware.

"Logical devices" made up of parts or complete physical devices and RAID strategies that further group "devices" are disk strategies that aid I/O performance in ways that Red Brick Decision Server has no control over. The more extensively these disk technologies are implemented, the less you can be sure that the placement of the PSUs is actually being done in a way that minimizes contention. At that point, you must rely on the performance of the disk strategy.

Simply relying on the performance of the disk subsystem doesn't always provide as much performance as can be achieved by a more informed compromise between the strengths of the disk strategy and the knowledge of how the data will be accessed. Also coming into play is the question of RAID versus mirroring. Something to consider when assessing these two is whether load or query performance is more critical. Mirroring provides the queries with more than one source for the data and often improves query performance. The loading of the data to redundant sources uses more disk space and takes more time during loading. This load performance impact can be somewhat minimized by caching strategies, but it will always take more time and space to write data twice. RAID may not yield as good a query performance as mirroring, but it doesn't use as much disk and doesn't impact load performance.

OTHER SOFTWARE INSTALLED AND RUNNING ON THE ENVIRONMENT

Red Brick Decision Server may not be running in the environment alone. End-user tool products often have a server component; data extraction and transformation products are sometimes targeted for the same system; and other database server products may also be sharing the system resources. These products all require system resources and may require kernel settings to be modified. Information about other products being run in the same platform is important to know when calculating the kernel setting and configuration parameters because the needs of all products that will coexist will all have resource requirements driven by kernel parameters. In this situation, it is imperative that any overlapping parameters be calculated to accommodate the needs of all the software incrementally. Additionally, some software allows "pinning" of CPUs and "reservation" of memory. If this is done, those dedicated resources should not be considered when calculating the Red Brick Decision Server parameters.

General system parameters

Every operating system is different—they all have different kernel parameters and configuration options. To that end, Red Brick Decision Server has an Installation Guide for each hardware platform it runs on, with appropriate discussions on settings for each parameter necessary for that platform. However, a number of Red Brick Decision Server–specific configuration parameters are hardware-independent, meaning that they function the same way across all platforms. They are the following:

- ◆ load_processes
- ◆ max_active_databases
- ◆ max_active_revision
- ◆ max_rbw_users
- ◆ max_nuniq_idx
- ◆ num_cpus

- ◆ max_query_tasks

- ◆ max_parallel_tasks

- ◆ max_PSUs

- ◆ size_of_version_log

Before you can calculate kernel parameters, you must determine values for several basic components of your Red Brick installation. These values are components of the kernel calculations.

load_processes

This is an estimation of the maximum number of processes any data load or reorganization process will fork. If the parallel loader (PTMU) or the Parallel REORG operation is not to be used, this variable is ignored (use 0). In the case of PTMU or the Parallel REORG, multiple processes will be forked to accomplish the loading of data and the simultaneous updating of the related indexes. In determining how many processes to fork, the TMU uses the number of CPUs available and the number of nonunique indexes for the table.

This doesn't consider the primary key index (because it is unique) or any index on a column/constraint that has been designated unique. This variable is used to determine the appropriate settings for the kernel parameters related to number of processes and the message task parameters (msg_mni, msg_tql).

The recommended equation is

```
3 + (3 * number_of CPUs) + number_of_non-unique_indexes
```

The first 3 is a reference to the three overhead tasks of all load processes (coordinating task, cleanup task, and conversion task).

The number_of_non-unique_indexes is the maximum number of indexes on any one table not including the primary index or any index on a column or constraint specified as unique, as it can launch a process to build each one of these indexes.

The (3 * number_of_CPUs) is actually related to how the parallel REORG decides how many tasks to use, because it is greater than the equation used by parallel loading. The parallel REORG will allocate 1.5*number_of_CPUs for scanner and index-building processes. It will also bind a conversion process to every scanner process.

Since we are interested in calculating the maximum number of load processes, if we assume that the entire 1.5*num_CPUs are assigned to scanner processes, there could also be 1.5*num_CPUs conversion processes. So, the maximum for scanner, conversion, and index-building processes for a parallel REORG would be 3 * number_of_CPUs. For parallel loading, it allocates half as many scanner processes as CPUs (or 1, whichever is greater), and the index-build processes are estimated by the `number_of_non-unique_indexes` portion. Again, in the interest of estimating the maximum, the recommended equation has used the "largest" parts of both equations. This estimation should be large enough to calculate kernel parameters.

max_active_databases

This variable identifies the number of active databases being supported by this instance of Red Brick Decision Server. (Every instance of RBDS should be treated individually as separate software needing the resources of the system). `Max-active_databases` is used to allow for the number of sets of system tables that will reside in memory at any one time.

Active database means a database with active connections. (Active connections will require a copy of the system tables to be memory-resident.) The ADMIN database, if started, is active even if there is no one querying it. AROMA (the sample database shipped with the Red Brick Decision Server product) should be counted if it is actively used for testing, training, and so forth, and therefore, can have active connections. All user databases should be included.

The variable is used to define the shared memory parameter `shm_mni` and the number of processes parameters (`max_procs`, `maxuprcs`, `nprocs`, and so on).

max_active_revision

This variable is used only if versioned loading is enabled and is set to the maximum number of revisions between last merged revision and current revision. The default is 500 revisions, and it can be altered with the `MAXREVISIONS` clause of the `ALTER DATABASE` command. It is used in defining the shared memory parameter `shm_max` since the pointers that allow queries to map into the version log quickly are held in shared memory.

max_nuniq_idxs

This variable identifies the maximum number of nonunique indexes other than the primary index or indexes on columns and constraints specified as unique on any single table. If PTMU or the Parallel REORG is not to be used, this variable is not used. In the case of PTMU, a process can be forked for each nonunique index defined for the table. This will allow the indexes to be maintained simultaneously without slowing the load process. Again, a nonunique index is any index other than the primary index on a column and constraint not specified as unique. This variable is used to determine the appropriate settings for the variable `load_processes` previously defined.

max_query_tasks

This variable defines the maximum number of process that can be forked for any one query. It applies only to queries that are eligible for *parallel processing* (that is, have at least one EXCHANGE operator in the plan). Setting it to 0 or 1 effectively turns parallelism off. This will be the value of the parameter QUERYPROCS in the rbw.config file and is closely related to the value of the variable max_parallel_tasks, which controls the total number of processes to be spawned for queries eligible for parallelism. If you have calculated the max_parallel_tasks and know approximately how many queries you hope to process at one time, you can calculate max_query_tasks by dividing max_parallel_tasks by the number of queries you hope to run at one time.

The QUERYPROCS parameter can be altered for a particular query, but this variable should consider the largest value you hope to use, since any value specified that is greater to the one in the rbw.config file is ignored. Only one operating system (DEC Alpha) actually requires you to know this variable to set a kernel parameter (shm_seg), which governs the size of the segment of shared memory for any one parent and all corresponding child processes.

max_parallel_tasks

This is the variable related to the maximum number of processes that can be spawned for all queries that are eligible for parallelism and is used to determine the appropriate settings for most kernel parameters. It also becomes the TOTALQUERYPROCS value in the rbw.config file. Setting this variable to a value of 0 or 1 effectively turns parallel query off so that query plans with EXCHANGE operators will run in a serial fashion.

Only queries that show an EXCHANGE operator in the query plan are eligible to run in parallel.

To calculate this variable:

1. Multiply the number of CPUs by CPU strength (as defined earlier) and add 50 percent. This formula allows for the gradual scaling back of parallel processing as the system resources become scarce.

2. Round to a multiple of the CPUs. The resulting number is your optimum value based only on CPU handling.

To verify the number, multiply it by the memory allocated to each process. (The default is 50MB and is found in the QUERY_MEM_LIMIT parameter in the rbw.config file.) If the result is greater than 50 percent of available memory, then either the memory allocated for each query or the max_parallel_tasks must be adjusted down until the verification calculation yields a number that doesn't exceed 50 percent of available memory or more system memory is needed.

This 50 percent threshold allows for memory needed for the operating system, additional software, and queries not eligible for parallel processing. If the memory required to serve these additional needs exceeds 50 percent, then adjust the comparison value accordingly. Of course, you could always add more memory and calculate it again.

In environments that share with other applications or situations in which there are large volumes of concurrent users, you're better off to reduce the max_parallel_tasks and keep the query_memory_limit. This generally accommodates a higher number of concurrent users at the expense of parallel queries. If you have simple queries and the data volume and user load are low, reducing the query_memory_limit may be a better option. Many kernel parameters depend on this value, as it is critical to determining system load on all resource fronts.

max_PSUs

This is the variable related to the maximum number of files associated with the database and is used to determine the appropriate settings for related parameters (max_files, nfiles, and so on for the HP). max_PSUs is related to the total estimated storage needed for the database, the segmentation strategy you plan to implement, and the number of file handles you will need for a process.

The best you can do is make an educated guess in determining the number of PSUs because usually at the time you configure the system you have little or no information on what the physical implementation is going to look like. Once the database is built, you can compare the kernel value to the actual instance, and if there is a large discrepancy, you may wish to reset the value and have your system administrator create a new kernel.

To make an estimate, you have to have some idea of what the schema will look like once it's built. At a minimum, each table you create will have one default data segment that will create one PSU. You'll likely have a b-tree primary key index on each table (minimum), and if it's created in a default segment, that's another one PSU. So typically, smaller dimension tables will have at least two PSUs (one data segment and one pkey index segment). But then again, if you pile a bunch of b-tree and Target indexes on the attribute columns, they each add more PSUs.

Then there are fact tables. Now you need to figure how many segments each fact table will be created with and how many PSUs each segment will contain. Then do the math to calculate the number of data PSUs for that table. But wait! There's more! You likely have a primary key index on that whopper of a fact table that is also segmented – and maybe even a STARindex or two. Again, figure out the number of segments and the number of PSUs per segment and add them up.

Although this sounds a little like a late night TV infomercial, it's not that bad. The place to start is to know ahead of time how many tables are planned to be built; how many of those are expected to be simple one-segment dimension tables; and how many big, segmented, multiple-STARindexed fact tables are planned.

For example, say you are expecting 60 tables in your finished schema, with 5 large fact tables that will be segmented by month and carry 5 years of data online.

You have half the battle won. If those 55 (60 – 5) tables are all one data-segment, one pkey-index-segment affairs, that's 110 PSUs. Now you just have to dig into your five fact tables. If each data segment has three PSUs and each index segment has one PSU with each fact table having two indexes:

5 years = 60 months, or 60 segments, plus a MIN and MAX segment.

Data segments = 60 x 3 = 180 + 2 (for min & max segments) = 182 PSUs

Index segments = 60 x 1 = 60 + 2 (for min & max segments) = 62 PSUs x 2 indexes = 124 PSUs

So each fact table, in this case, will add 182 + 124 = 306 PSUs to the total.

5 fact tables x 306 PSUs = 1530 PSUs for the fact tables.

1530 fact table PSUs + 110 dim table PSUs = 1640.

Next, add an additional 20+ percent or so to accommodate other database objects like temp tables that get created and dropped, adding extra PSUs for heavy months – like November/December sales – which brings the number to 1968 PSUs (1640*1.2). In this case, I might even round up to a value of 2000 PSUs, just to give me a little room towards the end of my planning horizon.

You can always change the kernel later when you've built your database to get the maximum number of PSUs closer to the actual value. Sometimes it's hard to estimate if you haven't already worked out what your schema is going to look like. That's why adjustments to the kernel may be needed as the database grows or more databases are added to your Red Brick Warehouse system.

max_rbw_users

This variable is related to the number of *concurrent* users on the database. This is a change in definition. In versions prior to (VERSION_NUMBER), this represented the total number for users defined to the database. This is used to determine appropriate settings for most of the kernel parameters.

Frequently, you may not know the concurrent user count at the time you're reconfiguring the system. This is a common problem; however, because this value is tied in some way to most of the kernel parameters, you have to make an estimate. Most often, it's fairly simple to determine the total user count. I've found that using a value of 20 percent of the total user count is a reasonable place to start. Once the process gets further along, you can adjust it.

num_cpus

Simply put, this is the number of CPUs on the system, as defined earlier.

size_of_version_log

If versioned loading is not enabled, this variable is not needed. If versioning is turned on, this parameter is used to determine appropriate settings for shared memory because the pointers that allow queries to map into the version load are held in shared memory.

Kernel Parameter Calculations

Once the all the values described in the previous section are known, it is then possible to calculate the kernel parameters for your hardware platform (if it requires any at all). AIX and NT do not require kernel settings, but all other platforms do. Not all hardware platforms have every one of the kernel parameters, and the calculations may be different from one platform to another – so be sure to check your installation guide.

One other word of warning: be sure you do the math correctly. Very often the kernel parameters are pushed to extreme values because the calculations were incorrect. Each parameter has a formula, and the parentheses do mean something. Be sure of your calculations.

Red Brick Decision Server behavior is governed by a configuration file called rbw.config. Each Red Brick Decision Server instance has its own rbw.config file. This file contains the following:

- ◆ Site-specific configuration information based on answers to questions asked during the installation procedure

- ◆ Option parameters that affect server behavior (including RBWAPI and NLS_LOCALE parameters)

- ◆ License keys for server options

- ◆ Tuning parameters that affect server performance

- ◆ Logging parameters that affect logging activities

- ◆ Password parameters that set rules for user passwords

- ◆ Logical database names and database locations

The configuration file is located in the directory defined in the $RB_CONFIG environmental variable, which is usually the home directory for the redbrick user. The parameters are used by the RBDS instance when handling the databases defined with the DB clauses at the bottom of the file. Many of these parameters can also be set with SQL SET statements or with TMU control statements. Some parameters require the daemon to be restarted. Others take effect for the next process that would use them.The configuration file is initially built by the installation script, but it can be modified by the database administrator. When initially installed, most options are commented out with the default value shown as the first choice on the commented line. To change any value, either copy the line you wish to change and uncomment, or uncomment the original line and alter the value accordingly. For more information on modifying the configuration file, refer to "Modifying the Configuration File" in the *Warehouse Administration Guide*.

The file is made up of sections of parameters that serve similar functions. These functions are grouped into the following sections:

◆ General configuration information

◆ RBWAPI parameters

◆ NLS_LOCALE parameters

◆ LICENSE KEYS section

◆ TUNE section

◆ DEFAULT section

◆ SEGMENT section

◆ ADMIN section

◆ PASSWORD section

◆ DATABASE entries

Selected Configuration Parameters and Initial Settings

There is also a facility to override many of these parameters via SQL or TMU commands as well as personal configuration scripts for each user. As previously indicated, the file is made up of sections of parameters that serve similar functions. All the parameters are discussed in detail in the installation guide. What follows is a discussion of the selected parameters that you need to pay most attention to. This is not an inclusive list, and I encourage you to read through the *Warehouse Administrator's Guide* for the discussion of the others.

General parameters

The following parameters are defined in the General Configuration section of the rbw.config file:

<RB_HOST_NAME> SHMEM (UNIX)

This parameter defines the base number for the IPC key range. IPC key values range from SHMEM to SHMEM plus MAX_SERVERS, with a default base 16 integer of 100. This parameter is not present on all platforms. This range of numbers must be unique and should be assigned to Red Brick Decision Server by the system administrator or person in charge of maintaining IPC key numbers. It is only set within the rbw.config file and, thus, takes a restart of the database server to take effect. This parameter is referenced by the rbwapid daemon and is used by both server and TMU processes.

<RB_HOST_NAME> MAPFILE (UNIX)

This parameter specifies the file used as a shared memory map file and has a default value of ./.RB_HOST.mapfile. It is set only within the rbw.config file and, thus, takes a restart of the database server to take effect. This parameter is referenced by the rbwapid deamon and is used by both server and TMU processes.

<RB_HOST_NAME> SERVER

This parameter defines the host name and port number for all connections made to Red Brick Decision Server. The default value is the host name and port number used for the database installation. It is set only in the rbw.config file and, therefore, requires a server database server restart to take effect. This parameter is used by the rbwapid daemon.

<RB_HOST_NAME> SERVER

This parameter defines the host name and port number for all connections made to Red Brick Decision Server. This is a logical name, and it identifies an individual instance of a Red Brick server. It is possible to run multiple instances of Red Brick on a single machine. This often happens while upgrading to a newer version. The production server will be maintained while the new version is tested and validated.

RBWAPI MAX_SERVERS

The parameter defines the maximum concurrent connections (users) supported by the warehouse daemon on UNIX or warehouse service on Windows NT. The number of connections includes one for the Web user connection option if it is enabled. The default value is a base 10 integer of 50, and because it's set only in the rbw.config file, it requires you to restart the Red Brick Decision Server.

RBWAPI CLEANUP_SCRIPT

This parameter defines a spill file cleanup script to be executed upon startup of the daemon on UNIX or the warehouse service on Windows NT. A sample script is shipped with the server in the bin subdirectory of the redbrick directory. This script is named rb_sample.cleanup on UNIX and rbclean.bat on Windows NT.

RBWAPI UNIFIED_LOGON (WIN NT)

When set to ON, the operating system must authenticate each database user, requiring that each user has a corresponding operating system account with privileges to read and write files in the database directories. The default value is OFF.

RBWAPI MAX_ACTIVE DATABASES

This is the maximum number of active databases defined to the server. This parameter is referenced and used by the rbwapid daemon and set only within the rbw.config file and, thus, takes a restart of the database to take effect.

TUNE section

The TUNE section contains parameters that can be set with a TUNE command in the configuration file, or by using a SET command from a RISQL script, or TMU control file.

TUNE TMU_BUFFERS

This parameter specifies the buffer cache size in 8KB blocks for the TMU; values range from 128 blocks to 8208 blocks. Unless you are running in a very lean memory environment (less that 100MB), this value can be set to 1024 as a starting place. Field experience has shown that this is acceptable for most situations. You still may need to change it after you've had a chance to experiment with the loader, but frequently, this is the most appropriate value. Field observation has also shown that for most situations, there is little benefit with a value over 2048. These are general observations—your specific situation may require something different, and in very low memory situations, you will have to experiment to find the best setting.

TUNE ROWS_PER_SCAN_TASK

As you will learn in later chapters, the TUNE_ROWS parameters are key components in the application of parallel query processing. This parameter indicates the number of rows that must be scanned while running a query before another query process is assigned to assist. Out of the box, these are set to a gigantic number that almost no one will hit. A good starting place is 125,000 or so. This will absolutely be changed as you start to understand the behavior of your queries, but this value will let you see how it works and give you an opportunity to experiment and determine where best to set the value. You will have to make the appropriate adjustments from there, based on the user concurrency, query workload, frequency, and so on. This will be covered a little more in later chapters.

TUNE ROWS_PER_FETCH_TASK

Like the SCAN_TASK parameter just discussed, this parameter also contributes to parallel query processing. The FETCH_TASK parameter specifies the minimum estimated number of data rows to be returned during the fetch portion of a STARjoin before another process(es) is allocated to assist. My favorite starting value for this is 125,000 rows, again from field experience. You will change this value based on your specific situation, but this is a good place to start.

TUNE ROWS_PER_JOIN_TASK

As you might have guessed, JOIN_TASK specifies the minimum estimated number of index entries returned during the join processing (index-probing) portion of a STARjoin before another task(s) is allocated. Like the other ROWS_PER parameters, I like to set a value of 125,000 for this one as well—again, based on lots of field experience. You will want to read the discussion of these values and how they are related in the *Warehouse Administrator's Guide* before you experiment with them.

TUNE QUERYPROCS

This parameter is used to limit the number of processes that will be allocated to a single parallel query. A query is eligible (in part) to be run in parallel if one or more of the previous ROWS_PER thresholds is met. This can result in multiple processes being allocated to a single parallel query. The QUERYPROCS parameter is a mechanism that is used to limit the number of extra processes allocated to a query. For example, if a query qualifies for six processes based on the ROWS_PER_SCAN_TASK setting, and the QUERYPROCS is set to 4, then the query will not get more than four processes. The actual process is somewhat complicated and will be discussed in a little more detail in a later chapter, but the gory details are beyond the scope of this book. A good starting place for this parameter is half the number of CPUs available, based again on lots of field experience. For those with single CPU machines, it doesn't matter.

TUNE TOTALQUERYPROCS

This big switch controls parallel query processing. This parameter represents the total number of parallel tasks that you want to be allocated across all parallel queries for this warehouse server. A value of 0 (zero) forces all queries to be run with one task, regardless of any other parallel settings. Once all these tasks have been allocated to the current running parallel queries, the server will not allow another query to run in parallel until one of the existing parallel queries completes and those tasks become available. Note that this parameter has nothing to do with queries that are not eligible to be run in parallel. Again, the details of how parallel queries are processed will be discussed in a little more detail in later chapters but is largely beyond the scope of this book. You will want to read the sections of the *Warehouse Administrator's Guide* that deal with parallel queries when you address this issue in your project.

TUNE FORCE_JOIN_TASKS

This parameter specifies the number of parallel processes to use when processing joins for a single query. The default is OFF. This parameter does not affect the server; however, if changed, current server processes will ignore the change and new processes will use the adjusted value.

TUNE FILE_GROUP

This facility allows you to group file systems that share the same physical file system. This is used in conjunction with the next parameter to reduce the disk contention when reading data.

TUNE GROUP

This parameter determines how many processes per query will access a given file group. In redundant disk situations (RAID or mirror), it is possible for the disk subsystem to support multiple readers.

TUNE FORCE_HASHJOIN_TASKS

This parameter specifies the number of parallel processes to use when processing hybrid hash joins. The default is OFF. It can be set either within the rbw.config file or within a SQL statement. Current server processes will ignore the change, and new processes will use the adjusted value.

TUNE PARALLEL_HASHJOIN

This parameter specifies whether parallel processes are used to process hybrid hash joins. The default is on and can be set from within the rbw.config file or a SQL statement. Current server processes do not recognize the changed value, but new processes will use the adjusted value.

TUNE FORCE_AGGREGATION_TASKS

This parameter specifies the number of parallel processes to use when processing aggregation functions. The default is off. It can be set with either with the rbw.config file or within a SQL statement. Current server processes do not recognize it, but new processes will.

TUNE PARTITIONED_PARALLEL_AGGREGATION

This parameter determines whether parallel processes are used to process aggregation functions. The value is off and can be set either with the rbw.config file or within a SQL statement. Current server processes do not recognize the changed value, but new processes will.

FILLFACTOR VARCHAR

This parameter specifies the user-estimated size of a column with the VARCHAR data type. The default value is 10 and can be set only with the rbw.config file. The VARCHAR data type is relatively new to Red Brick Decision Server.

OPTION TMU_OPTIMIZE

This parameter turns optimized index building on or off for the TMU. When OPTOMIZE is on, the server builds the leaf nodes while reading data from the input stream and builds the root nodes last. This is possible only with an empty table and sorted data.

TUNE INDEX_TEMPSPACE_THRESHOLD

This parameter specifies the file size (in kilobytes or megabytes) at which spill files for index building are created. For UNIX, the guideline is one-fourth of the maximum data space size for the system. This can be obtained from the maxdsize kernel parameter if your system has it. This value will automatically be rounded up to the next 8K block. For NT, the guideline is one-fourth of the physical memory rounded up to the next 8K block.

TUNE INDEX_TEMPSPACE_MAXSPILLSIZE

This parameter specifies maximum size in kilobytes, megabytes, or gigabytes to which a temporary file used for index building can grow. The default is 1GB.

TUNE INDEX_TEMPSPACE_DIRECTORY

This parameter specifies the directory in which spill files for index building are created. You can specify multiple entries for multiple directories with one directory per

TUNE INDEX_TEMPSPACE_DIRECTORY parameter. If you have multiple directories, the server will use them in a random round-robin order for each query. The default is \tmp on UNIX or c:\tmp on Windows NT.

TUNE QUERY_MEMORY_LIMIT

This parameter specifies the maximum amount of memory used for query processing in kilobytes, megabytes, or gigabytes, at which spill files for query processing are created. The default value is 50MB and can be set either in the rbw.config file or with an SQL SET command. When set via SQL, existing processes will not recognize the new value, but new processes will.

TUNE QUERY_TEMPSPACE_MAXSPILLSIZE

This parameter specifies maximum size in kilobytes, megabytes, or gigabytes to which a file for query processing can grow.

Overriding configuration parameters

Most of the parameters in the rbw.config file can be set to values specific to a particular database or user. The file that will contain these specific parameters is .rbwrc. This file should contain only parameters that need to differ from the values set in the configuration file In the .rbwrc file, parameter values are set using SET statements. The syntax of these statements can be found in the administration guide.

To override configuration settings at the database level, create a .rbwrc file in the directory identified in the location specification of the DB <database logical name> <location>. These entries are at the very bottom of the rbw.config file.

To override configuration settings at the user level, create the .rbwrc file in the user's home directory. The Red Brick Decision Server software evaluates multiple .rbwrc files in order when establishing which parameter to use for a particular load or query process. It will look for parameter values in the user-level file first, then the database level, then will default to the rbw.config in the $RB_CONFIG directory.

Creating a Database Instance

Creating a database instance is a very straightforward affair, although the UNIX environment has a few more items to check than NT does. The steps required to initialize a database instance are as follows:

1. Create the database directory.

2. Initialize the database directory.

3. Verify the creation by listing the system tables.

The following sections discuss each step in detail.

Creating a database directory

In an NT environment, you must be logged on as the Administrator or to the Red Brick account. Creating the directory can be done either at the command line with the DOS mkdir command or with Windows Explorer (File Manager).

In the UNIX environment, you must be logged on as the goldmine user. This is the only account that should be able to read/write to the file systems and directories associated with Red Brick. This prevents database corruption. To create the directory, use the `mkdir` command like this:

```
mkdir /home/redbrick/sample_database
```

You should also set the permissions for this directory using the `chmod` command so that the goldmine user is the only account that can read, write, and execute files in this directory.

Initializing the directory

The next step is to create the database and initialize the directory. For UNIX environments, you must use the `rb_creator` utility. To successfully use this utility, you must be the goldmine user and the directory must be empty. For NT environments, you use the `db_create` utility. You must be logged on as the Administrator or to the Red Brick account, and the directory must be empty.

Verifying the database

Once you have created the database, you can verify that all is well in several ways. The first thing you can do is a directory listing of the files that have been created. You should see the system tables. You can also start a RISQL session to connect to the database and query the `rbw_tables` system table to see what's there.

TIP

Note that when Red Brick creates a database, it also creates a default user system with a password of *manager*. If you've never changed the system password, now is a good time to do it.

To connect via RISQL, issue the following command from the command line:

```
RISQL -d sample_database system manager
```

Once you connect to the database, issue the following SQL statement:

```
Select name from rbw_tables;
```

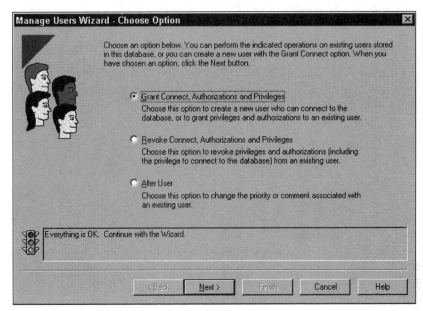

Figure 10-1: The Manage Users Wizard dialog box

Roles can also belong to other roles, and they can have authorizations and privileges associated with them, which give you a tremendous amount of flexibility in managing your user community. This allows the creation of everything from very simple to very complex user access plans.

A wizard also manages roles in Red Brick. The Manage Roles Wizard allows you to perform the various operations pertaining to roles. Figure 10-2 shows the main screen for the Manage Roles Wizard.

Roles can be created, removed, or modified. In addition, roles can have privileges and authorizations associated with them as well. An example is perhaps the best way to illustrate how to take advantage of the functionality. Assume the following situation:

A total of 100 users with the following breakdown:

◆ Finance – 10 users

◆ Marketing – 50 users

◆ Sales – 30 users

◆ IT – 10 users

There are two ways you could manage this group of users: manage hundreds of users or create roles for each group and assign individuals to the correct role. Managing hundreds of users with all the different authorizations and permissions can be quite a hassle, but with database roles, it's easy.

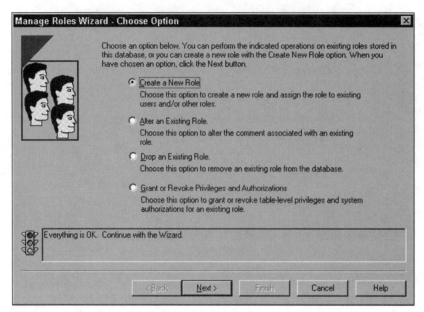

Figure 10-2: The Manage Roles Wizard dialog box

You first create the roles necessary for each group, and then as you create the individual user accounts, assign each user to the appropriate role(s). Users can belong to more than one role. This gives you the power to manage a large number of users with a handful of roles. At the role changes, you don't have to change hundreds of accounts – all that's necessary is a change to the role and you're done.

Database object privileges

All database objects have five basic privileges associated with them. These privileges control how users access tables and other database objects and must be GRANTed to individual user either through a role the user is assigned to or directly by using the SQL `GRANT (OBJECT PROVLEDGE) ON (object name) TO (username)` command. The privileges are as follows:

- ◆ SELECT
- ◆ INSERT
- ◆ UPDATE
- ◆ DELETE
- ◆ ALL PRIVILEGES

Lessons from the Trenches

There are just two lessons from the trenches for this chapter. Most issues that people have with installing and configuring Red Brick are directly related to lack of carefully planning the installation and/or incorrectly calculating the kernel parameters.

Carefully calculate configuration and kernel parameters

Before you can calculate the kernel parameters, you must accurately estimate a number of basic variables for your Red Brick Decision Server installation. Each of these parameters can have a large impact on the performance of your system if it is inaccurate. Take the time to evaluate each of the variables before you look at the kernel parameters.

Each hardware platform is different from the others. Consequently, each has its own flavor of UNIX, and therefore, its own kernel parameters. IBM, for example, has many fewer parameters than does HP. You must take the time to accurately calculate the necessary parameters for your platform. Do the math – correctly!

You also cannot overlook other software that will be running on the same platform. The requirements for system resources and kernel values called out in the installation guides are only for Red Brick. They assume there is nothing else on the machine. If you have other software on the machine, the kernel requirements are cumulative. If you end up with a kernel value over the stated maximum for the platform you are on, leave it at the maximum unless the hardware vendor advises otherwise. If you end up with a value that is lower than the current setting, in most cases you want to leave it where it is and not adjust it downward. There may be some exceptions, but again, seek guidance from your hardware vendor.

Be absolutely sure you do your math correctly. Many, many times folks fail to do the calculations in a given formula in the correct order. This always yields a wrong (sometimes drastically wrong) result. When in doubt, enter the formulas into a spreadsheet.

Don't overlook user security

Implementing a user security plan in Red Brick is not all that terrible a task. Some folks do that first, as soon as the database is available; others wait until it's loaded and ready to go. In any event, be sure you test your roles and access rights. It's very easy to add/remove access rights and privileges from users and roles alike using the Warehouse Administrator tool.

You should think twice about creating a single user account to be used by all the users. A single account that everyone uses makes it impossible to tell who is running which query. Isolating a particular user session is extremely difficult if necessary. You should create an individual user account for each user. You can (and should) place each user into one or more roles to simplify managing the access rights.

Summary

Installing Red Brick is a fairly routine task if you pay attention to a few key areas. The *Installation and Configuration Guide* is a well-written and very useful document and you should read it thoroughly before you install Red Brick for the first time. The installation process makes a few assumptions about the platform you are installing on, so be sure to read the release notes and other related documentation prior to the installation.

Calculating the values of the kernel parameters requires the most effort. If you are on a UNIX platform, this must be done and done correctly. This is not necessary for NT, but it's critical for the UNIX environments. In most instances, you will need the assistance of your system administrator or another UNIX resource capable of cooking a new kernel.

I can't stress enough how important it is to do the kernel math correctly. You'd be surprised at how many problems are created because of calculation mistakes. If you have any doubt, put the formulas into a spreadsheet.

Additionally, you will want to spend some time planning the access and security requirements for your installation. Try to leverage the roles capability as much as possible. This greatly simplifies the management of large groups of users.

Chapter 11

Loading the Data

THIS CHAPTER DISCUSSES DATA and how to go about loading it into the warehouse. Data issues will consume most of the total time the project takes to complete. Problems with data are often hard to identify until you are in the middle of loading data for the first time, and sometimes, you won't find them until you start running validation queries. The number and type of data issues you might face may seem endless; however, there are four major issues you can address that will eliminate or otherwise mitigate a significant number of other related issues.

Following the discussion on data, we'll look at the TMU, the control files that make it work, and some hints and tips on making the TMU work for you as much as possible.

Data: The Final Frontier

I've said much in previous chapters about data and the issues surrounding it as relates to building a data warehouse. Most of what I've said so far is based on personal experience, and I can't stress enough the amount of time that data issues can soak up. For what it's worth, I have yet to be involved in a project that didn't have at least one significant data issue. You should expect this. Unfortunately, it's hard to estimate how long it will take to address these issues, and they will impact your timelines, so be prepared.

I'm not just talking about bad data or missing data. I'm also referring to extraction, transformation, and load (ETL) issues as well. These can take many forms, but the best known are the self-inflicted surrogate (or generic) keys. There are a host of potential ETL issues, ranging from simple code replacements to the complex logic required to match rows over multiple data sources or resolve codes with multiple meanings.

Outlined in the next sections are four basic data issues you should investigate and ask questions about so you understand what you are up against.

Availability

One of the most frequent issues is availability. As you are doing the interviewing, you have been asking questions about how data flows, where it comes from, and where it goes.

You also get to learn firsthand about the load window you have to work with. Very often, it's not physically possible to load the amount of data necessary in the time allotted, especially if you run a 24x7 shop. The versioning feature of the TMU loads data into a database while queries are running and is a way of eliminating the data window problem. However, data can often be unavailable for the load cycle for a number of reasons:

◆ **Time zones** – Sources that come from other parts of the country or from overseas can make all the difference.

◆ **Upstream processing** – Perhaps the day-end processing for all the remote stores must be completed before the data is transmitted.

◆ **Physical environment** – Problems with network or hardware that prevent access.

◆ **ETL** – A large or complex transformation job must complete before the data can be loaded.

The list can be quite extensive. In many cases, the decision is made to run one or two days behind to allow time to address any problems that may occur. That may not be an option for everyone, but for those who have the luxury, it sure does make life a little less stressful when something goes wrong.

In other instances, depending on how mission critical the application is, a complete copy is kept, updated, and switched with its counterpart. In this scenario, each update is run twice. This requires "bulletproof" error handling and good record keeping. Still others use versioning to update the database while queries are going on.

Back in Chapter 2, I mentioned a data-mapping document. This document can help you identify some of these issues prior to getting ready to load the data.

Cleanliness

Next on the hit parade is data cleanliness. By cleanliness, I'm referring to several points:

◆ **Completeness** – This refers to all columns that have values in them that mean something. No missing values.

◆ **Accurate values** – All the values are accurate and validated.

◆ **Intact RI** – The referential integrity is intact for every row in the warehouse.

In practice, you will have all of these issues. This problem is multiplied many times as the number of data sources goes up. You might spend much time and effort on resolving these issues. It is sometimes a good idea to dedicate one or two resources to doing nothing more than following up on the issues found here so that the rest of the team can keep moving.

Data preparation

The next issue is data preparation. This actually refers to the ETL process and what must happen to the data before it's loaded. Data preparation is the "golden egg" of loading the data. This includes the following issues.

DUPLICATES

Duplicates can use up large amounts of processing time while loading the data. As rows are read for the input stream and the necessary operations performed on the input data, the TMU checks to see if the row already exists (meaning the primary key exists). If so, the row is flagged as a duplicate and either written to the discard file or just dumped into the bit bucket. In any case, it took time and resources to identify the duplicate row that could have been spent loading real rows.

In optimized on mode loading, a large amount of duplicates would slow down the loading significantly because all the rows would be inserted first and then the duplicates would be removed. Duplicate removal incurs random I/O and is very slow. The TMU keeps all duplicate row IDs in memory, which could sometimes make a TMU process run out of virtual memory if there are too many duplicates. The consequence of that would be either reorganizing the table or dropping and recreating the table.

In optimized off mode, the TMU basically directly inserts the input row by row. Thus, it can detect and remove duplicates pretty fast. In this mode, special efforts to remove duplicates from the data prior to loading may not be as important because the rows are thrown out as they are loaded; however, anytime you can remove duplicate data prior to loading will result in better performance.

 For input data with a large percentage of duplicates (greater than 5 percent), the rule of thumb is to use optimized off plus sorted data. For input with a low percentage of duplicates, use optimized on.

If at all possible, eliminate as many duplicate rows as you can prior to loading. Do not interpret this as an inability of Red Brick Decision Server to process duplicates;

rather, you should see it as an effort to eliminate duplicate rows as early in the process as possible. Duplicate elimination will happen one way or the other, and Red Brick Decision Server has a facility for doing so; it's just generally easier to eliminate duplicates earlier rather than later.

Duplicates can also have a potentially large impact on the index-building phases of your load cycle. For optimized on mode, only the index build areas hold the index entries for the load job currently in process. For large data loads, these entries must occasionally be merged with the existing index(es) for the table being loaded, and if the number of duplicates is high, this process can take some time.

 The process of duplicate removal in an optimized on load is very time-consuming. If you suspect that the number of duplicate rows is more than 5,000, you should not use optimize on, but rather, use optimize off instead.

DATA SORT ORDER

The sort order of the input data directly affects the performance of both loads and queries. From a loading perspective, the sort order affects the size of the resulting indexes being built, and remember that the data rows are written to the PSUs in the order in which they are read from the input stream. This means that if the data is unsorted, it is possible for the server to have to reread blocks to retrieve necessary rows.

The reason may not be very obvious. Usually, the query would fetch clusters of values, such as values within a key range, if the table data is sorted by that key. Then naturally, there would be fewer blocks fetched. From a loading point of view, sorting data in the leading key columns of the primary star would also significantly reduce random I/O in optimized off load and speed it up significantly.

Sorted data has another benefit: it can speed up large update or delete operations. Such operations could be a TMU load in modify/update mode or a SQL insert. Recent internal tests show that, using default TMU buffer settings, a random order input stream updates a table with random row order over 20 times slower than a sorted input stream updates a table with the sorted row ordering.

Often the question of sort order comes up. In situations where there is only one index, it's easy. But in those instances where you have two STARindexes, a b-tree primary index, and several TARGETindexes, for example, which is the right order? Where STARindexes are concerned, you want to sort the data in the order of the most used star. Normally, b-tree primary indexes on fact tables will not be used for much more than outer joins, so unless you have lots of them in your future, don't worry about it.

Often, it is not possible to completely sort your data (by all elements of the index), but it may be possible to have partially sorted data – meaning by the first two or three elements of the index. Any sorting you can do is better than none, so it is worth the effort if you have the capacity to do so. Even partially sorted data will improve optimized off loading and query performance for those queries fetching data in sorted nature.

DATA FORMAT

There are two basic data formats that Red Brick can read: fixed and delimited. Input data in fixed format generally takes more space than input data in delimited, and there is a slight difference in how each is processed. Fixed length input rows are read into a buffer and each column's value is picked up from the appropriate spot. With delimited input data, the rows are read in line by line and get parsed for column values in the conversion stage, not in input stage. Technically speaking, fixed is faster because it doesn't have to perform the parse step; however, in most cases, it's not that significant for the U.S. ASCII locale.

However, for international locales, to parse the delimiter the server relies on internationalization routines that tend to be more CPU-intensive. To handle the international locales, you might want to consider using fixed format input or increasing the number of conversion tasks.

INPUT FORMAT

There are two ways to keep your input data: compressed or uncompressed. If you happen to be on a UNIX platform, you can zcat your data and then at load time pipe it to the loader like this:

```
zcat file.Z | rb_ptmu ......
```

In an NT environment, there are third-party tools like MKS Tool Kit and free software like gunzip, which has the same functionality as UNIX tools.

Suitability

One last major data issue is whether the data is suitable for the problem at hand. Every so often, you'll run into a situation where the data just won't support the business problem and you are forced to make some decisions. You either have to find other data sources or have to solve the problems the data will support. Any attempt to manufacture data to fill the gaps is (in my opinion) courting disaster. This has been tried more than once, and although the data generation process is neat, complex, and challenging, it rarely results in anything useable. Generated data has its place, is very useful for technology validation and training, and is the basis for the sample database; however I'd be a little leery of making business decisions on data generated to fill gaps in my real data.

Data validation

It's not enough to load the data; you must also take steps to validate it once loaded. This is an important step and one that will occur with or without you. Aside from being good practice, it's necessary because of the way the source data have been realigned along the business rules and dimensions, as opposed to data normalization rules.

Frequently, queries or reports run from the newly loaded warehouse will not match operational reports. This is more normal that you might think. The first (and perhaps most natural) thought that crosses your mind when this happens is that something is wrong with the warehouse. Perhaps, but perhaps not!

The single most important point to remember in this situation is to focus on finding the explanation as to why the reports and values don't match and to not waste time on trying to generate a specific value. This may seem a little odd to some, but there are good reasons for thinking this way:

1. First, as I just mentioned, you introduce a significant amount of change into the data by realigning it along business rules and issues. The source data was never designed to function in this manner. Add to that the necessary denormalization of the source data into the dimensions, through the transformation rules, and through the collection of the measures from multiple tables into single fact tables and you have the data equivalent of culture shock.

2. Second, many of the source systems have been around for so long that they have attained a system of record status — not because they are correct, but because they have been in place for a long time and the folks who implemented them have most likely moved on. Notice I said nothing about their actually being correct. These system are just perceived as being correct due to their age and longevity.

3. Third, the types of data validation you are embarking on have either never been performed on the source systems or have not been performed to the level necessary to ensure accurate data. You'd be surprised at how often the question of how the data was validated goes unanswered. Do not look on this as a failing of the TI staff — all of us have inherited, worked with, or been responsible for in some way systems that, while they meet the operational requirements, are not able to meet the requirements of a warehouse.

Now that you know why data validation is important, you need to know how to address it. Unfortunately, there is not much you can do other than roll up your sleeves and dig in. Occasionally, I've seen customers who have built a table in the database that contains check sums, row counts, and other types of validation information so they can easily double check that the right amount of data was loaded each time. Data validation becomes are a little more difficult when the values in the columns are missing or incorrect. It's common to have go back to the source systems and understand how the data flows to validate the results you have. Frequently, other, more appropriate data sources are the answer. In other situations, the warehouse is correct, but the source system has a flaw in it somewhere.

Don't assume the operational report is valid either. The base data might be right, but the report could still be wrong. It happens. I recall a large financial customer where the warehouse reports were really off – so far off, in fact, that even I thought we missed something. We checked everything we could think of (all with the assumption that the operational report was right), but found absolutely nothing we couldn't account for. In desperation, we started to look into the report and how it as being generated – and bingo! We found the answer. As it turned out, the report, which had existed for years and was an accepted working document for a large number of departments, was wrong from the day it was written. It happens – and more often that you might think.

The interesting (and fun) parts were the looks on individual faces when they were told of the findings and seeing that deer-in-the-headlights look as the implications of what they just learned slowly dawned on them. I say this in part because it really is interesting to watch, but more importantly, for you to understand that what you find often has very serious implications and consequences for the individuals involved and the business in general. You must be extremely sensitive and professional in communicating the information, with whom you communicate it, and under which circumstances you discuss it.

How to Load Red Brick Databases

Red Brick Decision Server databases must be loaded from the outside, meaning that outrigger tables (if any) are loaded first, dimension tables are loaded next, and finally, the fact tables can be loaded. In Figure 11-1, to load the BILLING_CDR fact table, you will have to load all the other tables first. Once that is done, you can add rows to the BILLING_CDR table. As you do, each row's foreign key values will be checked against the appropriate dimension table. Those that fail will be discarded.

If you don't really want to discard those rows, you could also use AUTOROWGEN to create the necessary primary key in the associated dimension to allow the fact table to load completely without any discards. You could then go back and update the newly added dimension rows with the specific details.

Throughout this chapter, the term TMU is used to refer to both the serial version of the loader (TMU) and the parallel version of the loader (PTMU). Unless otherwise indicated, everything discussed about the loader applies equally to both.

To load the BILLING_CDR table from the sample database, you must first load all the other tables pictured. As rows are added to the BILLING_CDR table, RI, as defined by the foreign keys in the BILLING_CDR table, is checked. Rows that fail are discarded. Figure 11-1 shows the BILLING_CDR schema.

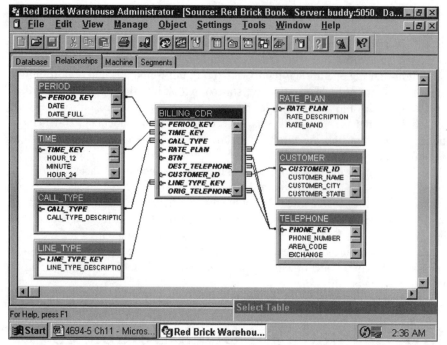

Figure 11-1: The BILLING_CDR fact table and related dimensions. In order to load the BILLING_CDR fact table, you must first load all the tables attached to it, or the fact rows will be discarded.

The Table Management Utility

The TMU is not so much a utility as it is an application. It's an industrial-strength component that is built to address the very real issues associated with a data warehouse. What good is running a bunch of queries in seconds or less if it takes days (or in some cases, forever) to load the data in the first place?

There have been a number of instances where Red Brick Decision Server was purchased on the TMU performance alone. That says a lot for how capable it really is. The TMU is a program that runs separately from the server via the command line and uses the same configuration parameters as the other warehouse components. For a more in-depth discussion of the TMU, refer to the *Table Management Utility Reference Guide* in the Red Brick Decision Server documentation set.

Control scripts that specify the actions to be taken – the inputs and the outputs – drive the TMU. When the TMU is invoked via the command line, the control script is given as a command-line parameter, which the TMU then reads and, subsequently, performs the necessary tasks. The TMU can read data from a number of sources, including the following:

- ◆ Standard input
- ◆ Specified input files
- ◆ Unload format files

It also writes data to several output sources including these:

- ◆ Standard output
- ◆ Warehouse system tables
- ◆ Table and Index files
- ◆ Discard files
- ◆ Unload format files
- ◆ Load data control files
- ◆ Create Table DDL files

Finally, the TMU also writes messages to standard error and log entries to the appropriate log file via the UNIX log or NT log thread pointed to by rbwlogd.

TMU control files

TMU control files contain one or more statements that define the functions to be performed and the necessary information to perform them. Each control file statement must be terminated by a semicolon (;).

USER STATEMENT

This provides a mechanism whereby you can supply a user name and password as part of the control file, eliminating the need to supply it on the command line. If a user name and password are supplied on the command line, they override the values in the control file. The syntax looks like this:

```
USER username PASSWORD password;
--TMU Control file for table ...
/*The User Statement must be the first line
In the control file */
```

LOAD DATA / SYNCH STATEMENT

The LOAD DATA statement provides the necessary information to load data into the specified user table. This includes the table to load, the data source and format, and a map of the source data to the rows and columns of the table. The SYNCH statement is only used with LOAD DATA statements if the data is loaded into offline segments.

Refer to Chapter 9 for a discussion of offline segments. Here is the TMU control file for the PERIOD table from the sample database:

```
load data
inputfile'-'
start record 2
replace
format separated by ','
into table period(
PERIOD_KEY INTEGER external,
CAL_DATE DATE 'MM/DD/YYYY',
YEAR_NUMBER INTEGER external,
QUARTER_NUMBER integer external,
MONTH_NUMBER integer external,
MONTH_NAME CHAR( 20 ),
MONTH_APPR CHAR( 3 ),
WEEK_NUMBER integer external,
DAY_OF_YEAR integer external,
DAY_TYPE CHAR( 8 ),
DAY_OF_MONTH integer external,
DAY_OF_WEEK integer external,
DAY_NAME CHAR( 10 ),
DAY_NAME_ABBR CHAR( 3 ),
END_OF_MONTH CHAR( 3 ),
END_OF_YEAR CHAR( 3 ),
END_OF_QUARTER CHAR( 3 ),
HOLIDAY CHAR( 20 ),
SEASON1 CHAR( 20 ),
SEASON2 CHAR( 20 ));
```

Notice the first few lines at the top of the command file. The load data phrase is self-explanatory. The inputfile phrase (notice the spelling in the script; it's all one word) indicates that the input data is coming from standard input of a pipe. The start record phrase indicates that we want to start loading data from the second row. This is because Excel includes row headers in its exported data, which we don't want. The replace clause tells the TMU to ignore any data already in the table and treat it like it was empty, and finally, the format separated by clause identifies the separator used to delimit the data — in this case, a comma (,).

The TMU is very picky about the order (and spelling) in which the commands or keywords appear above the into table phrase. It can be very frustrating at times, so keep the *Table Management Utility Reference Guide* handy for a quick reference and pay attention to the details.

UNLOAD STATEMENT

The UNLOAD statement provides you with a way to unload data from the warehouse in several formats. This facility is useful for archive purposes, for providing data for use by other tools, or for moving data to another database. Data can be unloaded using an index, a table scan, or a set of criteria to find the rows. If the data is to be reloaded into another table, you can also include commands in the TMU control file to generate the necessary DDL and load script to reload the data. These commands produce the same output as the GENERATE command.

The TMU unload script unloads the PERIOD table in external format (ASCII-readable characters) and creates a TMU file to load the data back in:

```
unload period
external
tmufile 'per_unload.tmu'
outputfile '..\data\period.unload';
```

```
The TMU file generated looks like this:
LOAD DATA INPUTFILE '..\data\period.unload'
RECORDLEN 103
INSERT
INTO TABLE PERIOD (
  PERKEY POSITION(2) DATE(10) 'YYYY-MM-DD' NULLIF(1)='%',
  CAL_DAY POSITION(13) INTEGER EXTERNAL(6) NULLIF(12)='%',
  CAL_MONTH POSITION(20) INTEGER EXTERNAL(6) NULLIF(19)='%',
  CAL_YEAR POSITION(27) INTEGER EXTERNAL(11) NULLIF(26)='%',
  CAL_DAY_ABBREV POSITION(39) CHARACTER(3) NULLIF(38)='%',
  CAL_DAY_NAME POSITION(43) CHARACTER(8) NULLIF(42)='%',
  CAL_MONTH_ABBREV POSITION(52) CHARACTER(3) NULLIF(51)='%',
  CAL_MONTH_NAME POSITION(56) CHARACTER(12) NULLIF(55)='%',
  QUARTER POSITION(69) INTEGER EXTERNAL(4) NULLIF(68)='%',
  QUARTER_ABBREV POSITION(74) CHARACTER(6) NULLIF(73)='%',
  WEEK_DAY POSITION(81) INTEGER EXTERNAL(11) NULLIF(80)='%',
  WEEK_ENDING POSITION(93) DATE(10) 'YYYY-MM-DD' NULLIF(92)='%');
```

Notice how it keeps track of NULL values and knows where the input file was created. The following are the first few rows of the data file generated:

```
1990-01-02 000002 000001 00000001990 Tue Tuesday Jan January
0001 1Q1990 00000000003 1990-01-07
1990-01-03 000003 000001 00000001990 Wed Wednesday Jan January
0001 1Q1990 00000000004 1990-01-07
1990-01-04 000004 000001 00000001990 Thu Thursday Jan January
0001 1Q1990 00000000005 1990-01-07
```

GENERATE STATEMENT

The GENERATE statement enables you to automatically create the CREATE TABLE or LOAD DATA statements based on the current table. These are very handy for reloading data created with the TMU UNLOAD statement. If you unload data for archive purposes and have an idea that you may want to reload the data later (next year?), be sure to create the CREATE TABLE and LOAD DATA statements because your table may look entirely different next year than it does today. This will allow you to bring back the data into either a separate table or into a segment of the old table with a minimum of fuss.

REORG STATEMENT

The REORG statement allows the reorganization of a table or segment. This includes RI checking and rebuilding any specified index to improve internal storage. The TMU REORG can run in parallel in a segment-wise fashion, which in many cases can be faster than a create index statement. This is what the DEFFERED keyword in the CREATE INDEX syntax takes advantage of. If you create a number of deferred indexes, you would then use the TMU REORG to build them all at once, segment by segment.

UPGRADE STATEMENT

The UPGRADE statement is used to upgrade an existing database of one version of Red Brick Decision Server to the next. Note that not all versions require an actual upgrade operation. In those instances where the UPGRADE command is necessary, all the information necessary to perform the task is built into the UPGRADE command itself. It's a good idea to back up your database and system tables before you start, and you should always read the release notes prior to executing any upgrade procedures.

SET STATEMENTS

Like its query counterpart, the TMU also supports a number of SET statements that can be issued at the top of your TMU command files to change the behavior of the TMU for the current session. Each of the parameters is summarized here. You can find more information in the *Table Management Reference Guide*. The following parameters can be controlled via TMU SET statements:

LOCK WAIT, NO WAIT   This controls TMU behavior when the database or database tables are locked. The TMU automatically locks the database or the affected tables during its operations. If SET LOCK WAIT is used, the TMU will wait until it is granted the locks it has requested for the server.

TMU_BUFFERS   Discussed earlier, these are the memory pages used for loading operations. Note that using a SET TMU_BUFFERS command can only increase the number of buffers. You cannot use it to decrease the value set in the rbw.config file. To decrease the number of TMU buffers, you must edit the rbw.config file directly.

INDEX_TEMPSPACE DIRECTORY   While a load operation is going on, the TMU stores intermediate results in memory until they reach a threshold value. At this point, the information is spilled (written) to disk This parameter and the following two control how temporary space is used and apply to both memory and disk space. The TEMPSPACE_DIRECTORY determines where the spill files will be created.

INDEX_TEMPSPACE THRESHOLD   This entry determines how much index information can be kept in memory before it is spilled to disk.

INDEX_TEMPSPACE MAXSPILLSIZE   This parameter determines how big each spill file is allowed to grow on disk. If a spill files exceeds this size, the load aborts.

TMU_CONVERSION_TASKS   When the PTMU is loading data, it can use multiple tasks to accomplish specific parts of the job. This is true even on a single CPU machine. The conversion tasks are those that convert input data to the platform-specific internal format used to represent the data. These tasks are also responsible for uniqueness and referential checking. These are also the tasks referred to earlier when using international character sets and delimited input data. The default value is half the number of processors on the machine and determined by probing the hardware.

TMU_INDEX_TASKS   These are the tasks that are responsible for writing index entries for all nonunique indexes on the table being loaded. Each nonunique index can have one task assigned to it. The number specified is the maximum number of tasks that can be used to process all nonunique indexes on the table, and the actual number used will be either the number of nonunique indexes or the values specifies in this parameter, whichever is smaller.

TMU_SERIAL_MODE   The PTMU can be forced to run in serial mode, meaning that no parallel processing will take place, effectively running as the TMU. This affects only operations that would be run in parallel. All other operations remain unaffected.

The last three parameters affect only the PTMU for parallel loading operations. Note that some of these override the global setting found in the rbw.config file.

Load modes

There are two load modes available through the TMU: online and offline. Each has its uses, as described next. Note that the type of load you perform affects the index-building process discussed later in this chapter.

ONLINE

Online loads can be run in serial or parallel and can be used to load multiple segments at a time (meaning that the input data spans multiple segments). Autorowgen is also possible in an online load, and the index build optimizations can be either on or off.

OFFLINE

An offline load, however, cannot be run in parallel and can work on only one segment at a time. Autorowgen must be off, and the index-building optimize on is the only choice.

Load types

There are several types of loads that can be performed:

◆ Insert – Adds new rows to a previously empty table.

◆ Modify – Adds new rows or updates existing rows in a table.

◆ Update – Updates only existing rows; new rows will be rejected.

◆ Append – Adds new rows to a table that already has rows.

◆ Replace – Deletes all the data in a table and performs an INSERT load.

Parallel loading

There are two versions of the loader: a serial version (TMU) and a parallel version (PTMU). Parallel loads run faster than serial loads because much of the index building is handed over to secondary processes to be done. You should consider using the PTMU when you have the following:

◆ More than one CPU

◆ Online loading

◆ Additional temporary disk space

◆ Plenty of RAM

In OPTIMIZED OFF mode, if you have set the TMU buffers high enough to reduce random I/O in index-building or presorted the data, the parallelism will generally be twice as fast. If you don't set the buffers or sort the data, then your load process will be I/O-intensive, and parallel TMU offers no significant advantage.

OPTIMIZED ON loading is generally three to four times faster than OPTIMIZED OFF loading and is suggested in most of cases. Adding parallelism to it would speed it up another two times. General recommendations include the following:

◆ Parallel OPTIMIZED OFF load with sorted, high-duplicate data

◆ Parallel OPTIMIZED ON load with low duplicate data, whether it's sorted or not

Versioned loads

On databases where TMU Versioning has been turned on, you can run your loads as versioned transactions. Versioned transactions allow queries (read) operations to occur on a previously committed version of the database while a new version is being written. To accomplish this, a blocking transaction locks all of the tables involved and does not allow query (read) operations to begin until the transaction is complete.

TMU operations that can be run as versioned transactions include the following:

◆ Online LOAD operations

◆ REORG

◆ SYNCH

Each versioned PTMU transaction requires an extra 100K of shared memory, so be sure to account for that when calculating the kernel parameters and other related values.

Prior to the introduction of versioning, all TTMU transactions ran as blocking transactions. This is the default behavior for TMU versioning set to OFF. When TMU versioning is set to ON, all TMU load and reorg operations are run as versioned transactions. You can find more information in the *Table Management Utility Reference Guide.*

Typical Load Rates

In the early days of Red Brick systems, we did a lot of benchmarking where we would have to prove to the prospective customer that the technology worked as advertised. (Go figure!) One of the outcomes of these benchmarks was a comparison of load rates between Red Brick and the other database servers so customers could get an idea of how long it would take to load the data on the frequency they required it. I mentioned earlier that a number of Red Brick licenses were sold on nothing more that the ability of Red Brick to load, check, and index the data in record time.

Often, competitors would turn off index building and/or referential integrity checking to speed up their load times in the hopes of competing. The only problem was that until the data is checked for RI and the indexes exist, no one could use it, so the faster load time didn't buy you anything. Additionally, you would sometimes hear statements about not having any need to validate the RI because it was checked as it was added to the transaction database. The following figures are actual production rates achieved by Red Brick Decision Server customers, are running today, and come from press releases and other sources.

- ◆ A telecommunications customer loading 10GB (200 million rows unsorted) per hour using an OPTIMIZE OFF load

- ◆ A retail customer loading 18GB (200–250 million unsorted rows) per hour using OPTIMIZE OFF load

In addition, several benchmarks have been conducted over the years and have shown sustained load rates of between 10 and 14GB per hour.

Setting expectations

With the loader technology as capable as it is, it's easy to set expectations too high. Yes, you will get good load times – perhaps better than anyone else in the industry. However, load rates are subject to a number of things that can have a negative impact, including hardware configuration, data sort order, and system resources. At some point, loading data comes down to basic physics, and even Red Brick can't break those rules (although we managed to break most of the other rules surrounding traditional data loading!).

Setting realistic expectations is key to loading your warehouse, especially if you have a number of data issues that are not easily solved. The load process is frequently misunderstood because the process has been oversimplified as a means of explaining it to nontechnical people. This simplification is fine as long as you communicate the complexity of the processes well. If there are eight steps, describe the process in eight steps as opposed to simply stating, "load the data."

The real benefit to you (or your DBA) is that when data problems occur (and they will), the expectations are already set as to how it all fits together, and you can spend your time addressing the problem instead of managing expectations.

Your mileage may vary

The one problem of quoting load rates is that everyone expects to get that rate or better, and as I've just stated, the load rate you experience is subject to any number of things that are beyond Red Brick Decision Server's control. Your mileage will definitely vary; however, you will, without a doubt, get the best load rate possible with Red Brick Decision Server. Period. See the sidebar for more commentary on the load performance.

A Word to the Skeptical

I feel it necessary to say a word to the skeptics concerning the loader and its performance. When I was first introduced to Red Brick Decision Server (version 2.0), I did not believe the rates I was being quoted. In my life as a Red Brick Decision Server customer, I had a manager to answer to and budget dollars to be responsible for. However, I became a believer when, on my first attempt to load my data into a development database, I loaded over 10GB of scanner data in less than an hour. You owe it to yourself to give it a try because there is nothing like it! It really does work as advertised.

Query response times

Oddly enough, load rates can give you some insight into the response times you can expect when running queries. Although load times are impacted (to some extent) by the number of indexes being built, most other aspects of the load (disk layout, hardware configuration, and so forth) remain constant at query time. Therefore, once you know how long it takes to load a certain number of rows to a fact table, you can usually get a good idea of how long it will take to query that same number of rows back out, as long as you consider concurrent user load and memory resources available at query time.

It's not perfect but should give you an idea to work from. Generally speaking, your query times will be no faster than the corresponding load times for the table in question. This estimation technique is just that — an estimation. Technically, there isn't any direct relationship between the load speed and the query time other than the fact that both are tied to the underlying hardware configuration, which affects the overall performance of the system.

There are situations where it doesn't work so well, especially where there are a large number of indexes on the fact table being loaded and you have a limited number of system resources (CPU or memory), the load is being run in a serial fashion, or you are running in a versioned environment.

Discussion of Sample Data and Load Scripts

I have provided a sample set of data that you can use to build the sample database. This sample data contains a full set of dimension data and a relatively small set amount of fact table data. This is due to the physical constraint of how much information can be placed on a single CD. However, having a data warehouse with just a little data is perhaps directionally correct, but marginally useful. As such, I have also provided Perl scripts that you can use to generate as much fact data as you have room for. Hopefully, you will take advantage of this and build as large a sample as you can afford to really try out many of the tips and techniques presented in this book.

To make it simple, all the data with the exception of the PERIOD table was generated using the Perl scripts, so whether you load only the sample data or generate more, you need only one set of TMU scripts – the data is in the same format. The period table, however, was generated using the Excel spreadsheet, which is also included on the CD. To load this data, the information was exported out of Excel as comma (,) delimited and loaded in that fashion. This not only provides an opportunity to show you a delimited TMU control file, but also gives you the opportunity to customize the PERIOD table to match your specific situation and generate data accordingly. This is possible because I have used generic primary keys for all dimensions.

All the data provided with the sample database is generated. You can see from the Perl scripts what the seeds are (if any) and can adjust as necessary if you care to. The Perl scripts are written to generate data over the entire set of dimension values. If you add more dimension values, you will have to edit the fact table Perl scripts to make them aware of it. Except for the fact table data, all the dimension data has been generated in sorted order and can be loaded in OPTIMIZE ON mode. The fact table data is sorted by period key, but only if you load the files in order.

Since all the data is generated, there is a chance that you will encounter duplicate rows when loading the fact table data. In testing the material for the book, we ran in to about a 1 percent duplicate rate for the fact tables. Given the nature of the book, we felt that this was acceptable.

Note that you need to load the dimension tables first and the fact tables next. If you have the resources and time available, you might want to experiment with the autorowgen feature and see what it can do for you.

Lessons from the Trenches

And now for this chapter's hard-earned lessons.

Make sure segmentation ranges are correct

This is the issue that gets almost everyone at least once, especially when loading segmented fact tables. When the ranges are incorrect or the segments are incorrectly sized, you end up running out of space when you don't expect it. If you have implemented guard segments as outlined in Chapter 9, you may find this situation early, before you've loaded a bunch of data.

In any event, if you run out of space because the segment is sized wrong, that's not too difficult to fix. If, on the other hand, the ranges are wrong, you must fix the ranges, which may be as easy as dropping and recreating a segment or as complicated as dropping and recreating the table.

Sort data if possible

This is one of the best things you can do to help the overall performance of the database. The sort order of the input data not only impacts the size of the indexes, but it also affects how often a block must be read from disk while running a query. Recall that the data is written to the PSUs in a segment in the order in which it is read from the input stream. In addition, the PSUs for a given segment are written to in the order in which they occur in the segment.

If the data is totally unordered, you will have larger indexes because of the split index nodes necessary to account for future entries, and the data will be spread all over the place inside the PSUs. If you run a query over data spread out in this fashion, if the server is using an index, not only is the index fat, but it is very likely that the server will have to reread a significant number of data blocks. The ideal situation is to have the data appear in sorted fashion so that the server has to read only one data block once. Obviously, this is not possible in those situations where there are multiple indexes, so the best sort order is the most frequently used STARindex.

TMU is your friend

The TMU is a very capable utility and can be used for all sorts of things. Traditional databases may take a different view of the bulk loading process, but Red Brick is designed to address the real loading/maintenance issues associated with a data warehouse. You should look to leverage the functionality of the TMU as often as possible because it will make your life easier.

Summary

Data is the final frontier and includes bad data, missing data, and ETL issues as well. All of these combined together can create a number of issues when trying to load the warehouse in a timely manner.

Data preparation is another issue that warrants close attention and includes issues such as duplicates, sort order, and the like. The sort order of the input data directly affects the performance of both loads and queries. Even partially sorted data will improve optimized off loading and query performance for those queries fetching data in a sorted nature.

Red Brick Decision Server databases must be loaded from the outside, meaning that outrigger tables (if any) are loaded first, dimension tables are loaded next, and finally, the fact tables are loaded.

Be sure to consider the number of expected duplicates when loading and use the most appropriate optimized setting for your situation.

Chapter 12

Red Brick Query Processing

IN THIS CHAPTER

- ◆ How Red Brick processes queries

- ◆ Red Brick join algorithms

- ◆ Scanning technologies

- ◆ The EXPLAIN function

- ◆ SET STATS output

- ◆ Query performance

- ◆ Running queries

- ◆ Sample database queries

- ◆ Lessons from the trenches

THE RED BRICK QUERY engine is quite an impressive piece of technology. It is the place where all the other technology comes together in the form of exceptional performance and capability. Queries that would run for hours or days in the merchant databases are reduced to minutes and seconds in Red Brick. It's common to see queries that run in subseconds as well. Not every query you ever write will run in under two seconds, but if everything is done correctly, you won't get better performance anywhere.

We'll start this chapter by providing an overview of how queries are processed in Red Brick. From there, we'll discuss the query engine and the operator model it's based on, along with the operators themselves. This will give you the knowledge necessary to read, understand, and use the EXPLAIN function both to understand how your queries are being processed and to look for ways to tune them. There is also a discussion of subselects, or subqueries, which are a very powerful feature in Red Brick. The ability to place a subquery almost anywhere you can use a column name is a tremendous advantage in tuning your queries. Although it's assumed that you have a working knowledge of SQL and relational databases, there is also a discussion on the join algorithms used inside the server – including STARjoin and TARGETjoin. STARjoin technology is the centerpiece of Red Brick's technology and is extremely powerful if used correctly.

The last part of this chapter is devoted to the EXPLAIN function, how it works, what it generates, and how to read its output. In the days before EXPLAIN, query tuning was definitely an art that required lots of experience to do well. Those of you who have used earlier versions of will recall how hard it was to interpret what the server is doing just from the query statistics. The good news is that now there is a facility that can generate query plans, and — together with the query statistics — it's now possible to do some pretty slick performance tuning in a short amount of time. The key is being able to read, understand, and use the EXPLAIN information.

How Red Brick Processes Queries

Traditional relational database servers use table/column statistics and cost-based techniques at query compile time to generate query evaluation plans. Red Brick Decision Server does not rely solely on statistics or cost-based techniques at compile time because statistics, estimated costs, and therefore, the resulting plans produced by these methods are often inaccurate.

Instead Red Brick Decision Server runs partial query plans to completion, and on the basis of these intermediate results, decisions about algorithms, indexes, join orders, and parallelism are made dynamically during the queries evaluation. This approach produces correct choices regardless of the accuracy of any data statistics.

At a conceptual level, Red Brick query processing is very simple. In actual practice, there are several steps to it, and the mechanics of choosing the best retrieval method can get a little confusing. Before getting into the details, however, you should understand the components of a Red Brick query. A Red Brick query specification must contain the following elements:

◆ The SELECT keyword

◆ A select list

◆ The FROM keyword

◆ A from clause

Other optional clauses don't necessarily have to exist in order to process the query. However, if one or more optional clauses are included, they must occur in the following order:

1. WHERE where_clause

2. GROUP BY group_by_clause

3. HAVING having_clause

4. WHEN when_clause

5. ORDER BY order by clause

6. Set operations (such as UNION, INTERSECT, and EXCEPT)

When a SELECT statement is issued, the server processes the query in a series of steps:

1. **Evaluate the FROM clause.** The server evaluates the FROM clause and determines the tables involved in the query and what join conditions were requested.

2. **Evaluate the WHERE clause.** The WHERE clause is evaluated next to identify the columns being filtered. Of these, it next looks to see which predicates apply to dimension tables. Each predicate is evaluated across its associated dimension and produces a list of rows that meet the criteria. This is done for each dimension in turn. What you end up with after this step is a list of rows for each dimension that satisfy that dimension's WHERE clause criteria.

3. **Evaluate and select indexes.** The next step is to evaluate the list of row IDs from each dimension and determine which indexes could be used to go get the fact table rows. Once this is done, the server selects the most appropriate retrieval method, be it a STARjoin, TARGETjoin, relation scan, or some other method.

4. **Retrieve rows.** Next the server retrieves the rows of data from the tables specified in the FROM clause, joins the rows from separate tables as necessary, and, depending on the type of join, generates an intermediate result table. The server tries to avoid instantiating intermediate results where possible, and so most of the time, intermediate results flow a row at a time between operators. An exception to this is STARjoin preliminary plan results, which are always instantiated (materialized). If a WHERE clause is present, the server returns only rows from the result table that satisfy the criteria; otherwise, it returns the entire result table.

5. **Perform GROUPING functions.** In this step, if a GROUP BY clause is present, the intermediate result table is divided into the appropriate groups as specified in the GROUP BY clause. Note that Aggregate functions (such as SUM and COUNT) are applied to the entire intermediate result generated up to this point, regardless of the GROUP BY clause.

6. **Evaluate HAVING clause.** If the HAVING clause is present, the server retains only those groups that satisfy the HAVING criteria; otherwise, all groups are retained.

7. **Evaluate SUPPRESS BY clause.** If this clause is present, the server removes the appropriate rows from the result table; otherwise, everything is retained.

8. **Evaluate ORDER BY clause.** If ORDER BY is present, the server sorts the resultant rows in the order specified in the clause.

9. **Perform RISQL display functions.** The next step is to apply any RISQL display functions requested to the query result set. This includes things like RANK and NTILE. In addition, this step is also where any RESET BY values are computed as defined in the RESET BY subclause of the ORDER BY clause.

10. **Evaluate WHEN clause.** If a WHEN clause is present in the query, the server retains only those rows that satisfy the specified conditions.

11. **Evaluate DISTINCT keyword.** If the DISTINCT keyword is specified in the select list, duplicate rows are eliminated here.

12. **Create BREAK BY rows.** If the BREAK BY subclause of the ORDER BY clause is present, the server creates the BREAK BY rows. These rows are the sub-total rows — they are not part of the base data. They are calculated in accordance with the criteria in this subclause.

Subselects

At this point, it's appropriate to discuss subselects at a high level. Red Brick allows you to place a subquery almost anywhere you can use a column name. Read that again: You can place a subquery almost anywhere a column can be used. That's a powerful statement. As a practical matter, uncorrelated subqueries are generally processed before correlated subqueries; however, it all depends on when the columns required to evaluate the subquery are available in the query plan. There are several types of subselects:

◆ SELECT clause subselects

◆ FROM clause subselects

◆ WHERE clause subselects

◆ CASE statements

Subqueries have some specific performance-enhancing behavior. Not all of these optimizations are available in all situations; it depends on where the subquery exists and what it returns. For example, subqueries that appear in the SELECT list *must* return one row. Subqueries in the FROM clause can return a set of rows.

The optimizations that may be taken advantage of during a query are as follows:

◆ Subqueries that return multiple rows are able to cache result rows — reducing the number of times the subquery must be run.

◆ Red Brick executes only the part of subquery that is necessary. For subqueries that are evaluated row by row, once the server finds what it's looking for (the matching row), execution of the subquery stops. In some cases the subquery will never need to run to completion – potentially saving a lot of processing time. The behavior depends on the predicate relating the subquery to the outer (or containing) query. For example, a NOT IN (subselect) might require examining every subquery value produced.

There are many other subquery-related optimizations: caching of correlated subquery correlation values and associated results, subquery-to-join transformations, and prerunning of subquery components.

◆ Caching of correlated subquery results. For *scalar* (subqueries that return one or zero rows) correlated subqueries, the server caches some of the correlation values and results; for *vector* (subqueries returning more than one result row) correlated subqueries, the server caches one set of correlation values and a result.

◆ Subquery-to-join transformations. In STARjoin preliminary plans, (uncorrelated) subqueries related by IN or = ANY predicates are converted to joins whenever the result set of the subquery is provably distinct – for example, SELECT DISTINCT . . . , or GROUP BY, or a primary key definition, and so forth. More generally, in RB 6.10, IN and NOT IN (uncorrelated) subqueries are transformed to joins regardless of their application in the plan. Large in lists (of literal values) – such as 10,000+ literals – are also converted to joins.

◆ Subqueries and their subexpressions may be prerun and the results saved for reuse whenever they may have been evaluated multiple times, for example, when they were part of a parallel subplan or nested inside a correlated subquery.

SELECT clause subselects

These subselects appear in the SELECT list. This type of subquery is iterative – meaning that the subquery must be run once for every row returned from the WHERE clause. If the subquery is uncorrelated, then the performance is likely to be good. However, if the query is correlated, then a better approach might be to move the subquery to the FROM clause.

FROM clause subselects

This class of subselect is very powerful. When the server sees a subquery in the FROM clause, it runs that query first. The server always uses virtual tables to store intermediate results. If the subselect contains operations like SELECT DISTINCT, GROUP BY (or aggregate functions), certain RISQL functions, sorts, or other blocking operations, then a virtual table is built. Otherwise, rows flow through the query plan one at a time, and there is no virtual table. In many cases, FROM clause subselects can be composed or rolled into the containing SELECT statement where possible.

If the virtual object exists, there are no indexes on this table, and it exists only for the life of the query. If the results of this subquery are small enough to fit into memory, then the join process is a memory scan as opposed to a disk scan. Generally speaking, the virtual table containing the results is joined using the HASHjoin operator, unless the intermediate result is computed first and then joined to a single table, in which case index-based joins are possible.

WHERE clause subselects

These subselects look like the following:

```
...
WHERE x in (select y from usr_table)
...
```

These types of subqueries perform reasonably well, especially if the table referenced in the subselect (usr_table in previous example) is narrow. Evaluation of the inner select in a subquery is optimized in the same manner as the outer select. The resulting plan depends on the presence of predicates, indexes, and so forth, just like the outer select.

Case statements

The CASE statement is a row operator, meaning that it is evaluated for every row returned out of the WHERE clause. This operator doesn't cost you anything except in two situations:

◆ Situations where components of the CASE statement require lots of data manipulation (DATEPART to DATEDIFF to INT, for example).

◆ Any situation where the row would not have been needed except for the CASE statement.

Other optimizations

Red Brick employs several other technology components that help reduce the query processing time. These are invoked by the server as it processes a query wherever possible. They are not tunable in the sense that you can turn them on or off; rather they are invisible, and you'd never know they were there if you hadn't read about them.

◆ Dynamic reorder – As the server evaluates the WHERE clause criteria, it reorders the sequence in which the constraints are evaluated to throw out as many rows as possible as early as possible in the process. In other words, the most restrictive constraint is evaluated first, the next most restrictive is evaluated second, and so forth. This dynamic reordering occurs only for TARGETscan operations.

◆ Early exit – As the server is returning rows during a TARGETscan operation, the server is looking at the cost of processing the remaining index entries versus the cost of scanning the remaining intermediate result set. When the scan is cheaper, the server abandons the index processing, scans the remaining intermediate result set, and returns the rows.

◆ Internal query rewrite – This is discussed in Chapter 7 in conjunction with Vista, Red Brick's aggregate navigator; however, there are several other instances where the query is rewritten by the server in order to process faster. In addition to the subquery-related transformations previously described and the discussion on FROM clause subselects, the other transformations include:

  ■ Common subexpression analysis – The compiler tries to avoid making redundant computations by computing only one instance of a function. For example, two SUM() functions of the same column data could be replaced by a single computation.

  ■ Compile-time expression simplification – The compiler evaluates constant expressions at compile time.

  ■ Pushing predicates – In release 6.10, predicates are pushed through set operations such as UNION. The optimization enables effective use of a UNION of fact tables in place of a single fact table.

  ■ Constraint projection – Constraint projection is used in conjunction with database views. As you know, in the merchant databases, if you submit a query against a view, the server must create the instance of the view or populate it with data. Only then can the query be evaluated against it. Red Brick (wherever possible), will look at the constraints on the outer query and will project constraints into the view query. This is not always possible, but when the server is able to do it, it reduces the size of the view results, thereby increasing the query performance.

As you just discovered, the server goes through many phases while processing a query. You should note that the run-time criteria have a lot to do with how a query is processed – based on the number and type of indexes present (or absent). The following sections list the join algorithms Red Brick Warehouse uses, illustrate the phases of query processing, and discuss how to use the EXPLAIN command. This command shows you what phases a particular query will go through and what steps you can take to optimize query performance.

Red Brick Join Algorithms

Red Brick employs a number of join algorithms to answer your queries. Many of these join technologies were pioneered by Red Brick and have grown up over the years to be extremely effective. You should already possess a working knowledge of standard SQL and have a basic understanding of the join types provided by an ANSI standard database.

The purpose of a relational database is to relate data in one table to the data in another table. The process of joining tables is the mechanism that accomplishes the relationship. Red Brick takes advantage of a number of specialized joins to deliver fast query response times. The selection of the join method is controlled by the presence or absence of the different index types; you cannot explicitly ask for a specific join when writing your queries. Consider the server to be a radio of sorts that you tune by using the index knob.

NOTE

The selection of the join method is controlled by the presence or absence of the different index types; you cannot explicitly ask for a specific join when writing your queries.

When evaluating a query, Red Brick looks at all the available indexes and determines which index/join method will yield the best (fastest) time. The server evaluates the join possibilities in the order they are listed.

STARjoin

This is Red Brick's premier technology for processing data warehouse queries. STARjoins operate on STARindexes. As you know, a STARindex is a multitable, join-accelerating index that inherently minimizes the I/O necessary to retrieve data for a query. The STARjoin technology allows you to do a multitable join in a single pass, as opposed to the standard pairwise joins found in other databases. The STARjoin is still Red Brick's sweet spot for query performance and is most successful when the right STARindex is in place. In general, STARjoins outperform all other Red Brick join operators for multitable joins, and Red Brick Decision Server will do its best to use a STARjoin if possible.

There are two types of STARjoins — single fact table joins and multi-fact table joins. In the case of a single fact table, the STARjoin is performed in a straightforward manner: As you know, a STARindex is made up of some or all of the foreign keys on a fact table and contains the row IDs of the dimension table rows in question. Figure 12-1 shows a single fact table and its related dimensions from the sample database.

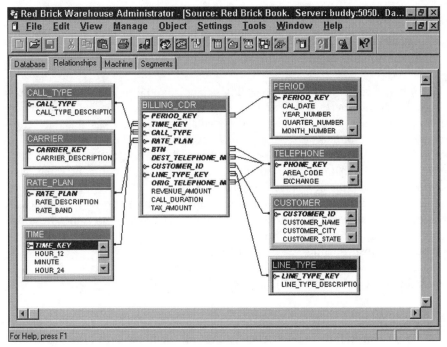

Figure 12-1: The BILLING_CDR fact table and related dimensions

When the server processes a query over this simple STARindex, it first determines the rows from each of the dimensions in question that match the WHERE clause criteria. At that point, the server starts to probe the STARindex for the combination of row IDs previously identified. As it finds an entry in the STARindex, it retrieves the Fact table row from the pointer.

In the case of multiple fact tables, things are a little different. A multi-fact table STARjoin is performed in a manner similar to a single fact table STARjoin. The main difference is that the join is performed against a virtual STARindex that is made up of the indexes of the individual fact tables. Consider two STARindexes for two fact tables. Index1 has dimensions [[A, X, B]]. Index2 has dimensions [[AA, X, BB]]. X is a shared dimension; that means that X is a referenced table in the declaration of foreign keys of both fact tables. The virtual index used to do a multi-fact table join is created in three steps:

1. Concatenate all dimensions in all indexes resulting in [[A, X, B, AA, X, BB]]. The two STARindexes in question are put end-to-end.

2. Eliminate duplicate references to all shared dimensions, resulting in a virtual index of [[A, X, B, AA, BB]]. Because the X dimension is shared, there is no need to probe it more than once, so redundant references to X are removed.

3. Reserve the *relative* order of the dimensions in the individual indexes in the virtual index as well. In this case, dimension AA in Index2 preceded X, whereas it is behind X in the virtual index; therefore, AA is moved after A and in front of X [[A, AA, X, B, BB]].

If you take a closer look a the preceding example, you'll notice that the indexes in question do not necessarily result in a well-behaved join because the shared dimension is smack in the middle of the virtual star. This means that any constraints on X will not be as effective as they might be. It's clear from the preceding discussion that there must be at least one shared dimension and that the shared dimensions of all STARindexes participating in the join must be in the same relative order. However, the position of the shared dimension now becomes important. Joins involving multiple STARindexes can be messy at times; however, it is possible to design the indexes for well-performing joins. The messiness comes from the fact that calculations required to identify the next entry in the virtual STARindex must be accomplished using just the components of the index.

There are a few guidelines you can follow in building STARindexes that will result in better performing virtual stars for fact-to-fact joins:

◆ Keep all the common dimensions in the same *absolute* order.

◆ If the constraints on the shared dimensions are tight, put the shared dimensions at the beginning of all STARindexes participating in a query.

◆ If the constraints on the shared dimensions are loose (the dimensions are used only for the purpose of the join), put the shared dimensions at the end of the first STARindex and at the beginning of the other index(es).

◆ The first STARindex should have its leading dimensions as tightly constrained as possible, although the server will analyze the expected performance of alternative join orders at run time and potentially reorder their evaluation.

If you have multiple STARindexes on a fact table, the order of the foreign key constraints in the query determines which index is used. In other words, Red Brick uses the STARindex built on columns with the closest match to the query constraints to do the join.

TARGETjoin

TARGETjoin is the latest of the Red Brick indexing technologies. TARGETjoin join processing is enabled by creating TARGET or b-tree indexes on the foreign key columns of a fact table. You create TARGET indexes on single-column foreign keys and multicolumn b-tree indexes on multicolumn foreign keys. TARGETjoin is most useful in those situations where the number of STARindexes would become excessive.

This situation is frequently encountered when there are a large number of dimensions, and none are used any more frequently that any of the others – thereby forcing you to create a large number of STARindexes to accommodate the user analysis.

You will get a TARGETjoin in three situations:

♦ No STARindex indexes – There are no STARindexes on the fact table in question, and TARGET indexes exist on the foreign key columns.

♦ STARindex index – In this situation, there is one STARindex on the fact table that contains all the foreign keys. If the STARindex index is wide (has lots of columns), a small number of STARindex columns are constrained, and the constraints on those STARindex index columns are tight (perhaps returning a single value), then you will likely see a TARGETjoin. The more you tightly constrain the trailing columns of the STARindex, the more likely you are to get a TARGETjoin.

♦ Multiple STARindex indexes – This case is much more iffy in that with multiple STARindexes the chances of a TARGETjoin are less because there are many more options available for STARjoin, and the TARGET options usually evaluate to be more costly. You will see TARGETjoins in the query plan, but they are less likely to be chosen at run time.

 The more STARindex indexes you have, the less likely you are to see a TARGETjoin executed when running the query.

Nested loops join (B11M)

The Nested loops join is refereed to in several ways: B-Tree 1-1 Match or B11M for short. This is your standard b-tree join-processing algorithm. It looks up key values in an index, and you will see it when joining to dimension tables not in the STARindex or when joining to "outboard" tables. B11M is also used to process Left Outer Joins.

HASH join

The HASH join algorithm used in Red Brick is a tremendous piece of technology. In terms of performance, it sits between b-tree processing and the Cartesian product and provides for some spectacular performance improvements in the right situations because it actually builds a hash index on the fly and then uses that hash index to join to other database objects.

This join type is most effective when the HASH table (left table) fits in memory, that is, when the "build table" is small. The "probe table" (right table) does not need to fit into memory. You will see this join type used in situations where there are no indexes at all on the joining columns. One nice feature of this algorithm is that it decides which table will be the build table and which will be the probe table in order to build the temporary index. Note that this is used only where the join is an equi-join: (T1.col_a = T2.col_b). Also note that RIGHT OUTER and FULL OUTER joins are performed using the HASH join and that the build and probe tables are explicitly set according to which side of the RIGHT or FULL OUTER phrase each table appears.

Naïve 1-to-1 match (cross join)

Generally speaking, you don't want to see these types of joins too often if you can help it. This is the standard cross product, or Cartesian product, between two tables. As you know, the bigger the tables, the worse this gets both in terms of number of rows returned and the time it takes to return them; however, the actual number of rows returned is not determined by the *use* of cross join, but by the predicates being *evaluated* in the cross join.

You will see this join type only when there are no indexes on the joining columns and the join being performed is not an equijoin. This is by far the poorest performing operator in Red Brick, but it can be easily avoided by adding appropriate indexes; however, note that the requirement to use a cross join is determined more by the predicates relating the tables to be joined than by the absence of indexes. In other words, if cross join is turned OFF and you get a cross-join message, you have most likely forgotten to write one or more join criteria statements in the WHERE clause. You must have cross join set to ON in the rbw.config file for this join to be considered.

In order for the server to consider using a cross join, you must enable cross join in the configuration file rbw.config.

To reiterate just a little, the warehouse server's choice of join method depends on which indexes are available. At run time, the server evaluates the query and makes decisions about the query execution plan according to the following criteria:

1. If the appropriate STARindex exists to join the tables, the query uses the STARjoin algorithm. An appropriate STARindex contains some or all of the keys that are constrained in the query.

2. If the appropriate STARindex exists to join the tables and if TARGET or b-tree indexes exist on the foreign key columns in the referencing (fact) table, the query will use either the STARjoin or TARGETjoin algorithm, depending on which has the best indexes available for the join operation. This decision is made at run time. If there is a column that participates in a STARindex and has a TARGET index on it also, the server will most likely execute the STARjoin.

3. If the appropriate STARindex does not exist but TARGET indexes exist on the foreign key columns in the referencing (fact) table, then the query will use the TARGETjoin algorithm.

4. If the appropriate STARindex does not exist but either a b-tree or a TARGET index is present over the joining columns, that index is used with the b-tree one-to-one match algorithm. If both a b-tree and a TARGET index exist, the server chooses the best index for the join operation.

5. If no indexes are present over the joining columns and the join is an equijoin (the query constraints are equality conditions), the hybrid HASH join algorithm is used.

6. If no indexes are present over the joining columns and the join is not an equijoin, the cross-join algorithm is used. The cross-join algorithm calculates all possible combinations of the joining columns (the Cartesian product). Therefore, cross joins are disallowed unless the OPTION CROSS JOIN parameter is set to ON. This requirement ensures that users do not issue cross-join queries inadvertently, by omitting a join condition, for example.

These criteria are somewhat simplified for the purpose of this discussion, but be aware that there are many other variables that add complexity to the choices the Red Brick Warehouse server makes; they include (but are not limited to) available indexes, memory, work load, and segmentation.

Scanning in Red Brick

Although Red Brick Decision Server tries its best to resolve queries using one of the join methods just described, there are times when the correct answer is to scan the table or index in question. Traditional Red Brick teaching holds that table scans are bad, and for the most part that is true, unless you really want all the data in the table.

However, there are situations where scanning a table or index (or parts of them) may actually be to your advantage. The following descriptions outline Red Brick Decision Server scanning technology and how it is used to further improve query performance when scanning is necessary.

Smartscan

Smartscan is a feature that optimizes data access from tables that are segmented by range of values. Smartscan is aimed specifically at queries containing particular predicates on the segmenting column of the table. Suppose table T is segmented by range on an integer column A and that table T has 3 segments with ranges (min:1000), (1000:2000), (2000:max).

The first segment will contain all rows in T where the value of column A is strictly less than 1000, the second segment will contain all rows of T having A between 1000 (inclusive) and 2000 (exclusive), and the third segment will contain all rows with A greater than or equal to 2000.

The Smartscan optimization will be of great benefit in two situations: those instances where you are doing a table scan and instances where you are doing an index scan.

Tablescans

With the Smartscan optimization on, the following queries will scan exactly one segment of T:

```
select * from T where T.A < 1000;
(returns all rows of the first segment.)

select * from T where T.A => 1000 and T.A < 2000;
(returns all rows from the 2nd segment.)

select * from T where T.A => 2000;
(returns all rows from the 3rd segment.)
```

In general, for queries that involve a tablescan (no indexes are involved), Smartscan will eliminate segments from the scan whenever the predicate in the WHERE clause has an AND clause that contains a comparison between the segmenting column and a literal value that disqualifies all the rows in that segment. If the WHERE clause has an OR clause that contains only comparisons of the segmenting column with literal values, then segments that don't satisfy any of the predicates will not be scanned. In other words, only those segments that match the predicates will be scanned.

For example:

```
select * from T where T.A < 1000 or T.A => 2000;
(smartscans first and third segments)
```

In situations where the predicates contain nested ANDs and ORs, none of the segments in questions will be Smartscanned, and the server will do a traditional scan on them:

```
select * from T where T.A < 1000 or (T.A >= 1000 and T.A < 2000);
(scans all segments in the traditional fashion)
```

Index scans

For queries that would normally be evaluated using an index, and a STARindex in particular, the requirements for doing Smartscan are more stringent. Suppose that T is a fact table, and the column A is foreign key referencing primary key column A of table D. If a STARindex is built on T and contains column A, then certain queries that could be answered by scanning a subset of the segments of T will be performed with a STARjoin instead. This is the traditional behavior.

Now, Smartscan may use a restricted tablescan to evaluate such queries, for example:

```
select * from T, D where T.A = D.A and D. A < 1000;
(scans first segment of table T.)
```

In general this substitution will occur only in the event that the predicate on A falls exactly on the segment boundary (that is, A < 1000 or A => 1000) and there are no other predicates on the dimension. For example:

```
select * from T,D where T.A = D.A and D.A < 1000;
(scans first segment of table T)

select * from T,D where T.A = D.A and D.A <= 1000;
(executes a STARjoin plan)

select * from T,D where T.A = D.A and D.A < 1000 and D.B = 'value';
(Executes a STARjoin plan)
```

The first example scans the first segment only because the predicate falls exactly on a segment boundary. The second example does a traditional STARjoin because the "<=" condition falls across segments. (Recall that segment ranges are read as "From x_value up to but not including y_value.") The third example executes a traditional STARjoin plan because there is an additional predicate on column B of dimension D.

Similar transformations will take place for queries that involve an index scan using a b-tree or TARGET index. In these cases there is an additional restriction that the query must contain a predicate constraining on a column not in the index. For example, if there is a b-tree index on T.A only, then:

```
select * from T where T.A < 1000;
(executes a btreescan)

select * from T where T.A < 1000 and T.B = 'value';
(scans first segment of table T)
```

Smartscan is OFF by default. To enable the Smartscan feature, add a line to your rbw.config file OPTION Q_SMARTSCAN ON, or from a RISQL session, you may turn it on with the command set q smartscan on.

You've now seen the types of joins that Red Brick can do, have seen how Red Brick scans, and have a basic understanding of when you might expect to see each one. The next step in understanding not only how queries are processed but also how to change their processing behavior is to understand how the query engine is built and how to use the EXPLAIN function.

Understanding the EXPLAIN Function

Red Brick uses an object-oriented operator model to evaluate and process a query. Each query is broken down into stages, and each stage is further reduced to operators. These operators taken together are what are known as the query execution plan. This plan describes all possible options with which to process the query. The EXPLAIN command is the mechanism that puts the plan into a readable form for you to use in understanding and tuning the query.

The operator model

The Red Brick operator model consists of over two dozen operators. In release 6.10, there are 31 active operators. These operators are designed to return data (rows) and are demand driven in that operators are invoked in response to another operator's demand for data, not the presence of the data itself. The operator model employed by Red Brick provides for a standard external interface so that it's relatively easy for the developers to add new functionality as customers continue to push the technology envelope.

Every Red Brick query can be broken down into combinations of these basic components. Understanding the operators and their functions is the first step to reading, understanding, and using the EXPLAIN output. Once you understand the EXPLAIN output, you then have the ability to improve your queries by:

- Rewriting the query

- Adding or dropping indexes

◆ Modifying the Schema

◆ Modifying tuning parameter values

◆ Changing the physical layout of your database

There are two advantages of the Red Brick operator model: it provides a platform for the EXPLAIN functionality (EXPLAIN is actually an operator), and it provides for a true plug-and-play environment for the developers to add new functions as they are developed.

The list that follows shows each of the operators and gives a short description of what it does.

◆ Advisor – This operator produces advisor information for the Vista option.

◆ B11M – This is the b-tree 1-to-1 Match operator and is used to perform a standard pairwise join.

◆ B-Tree Scan – This is the standard index lookup for b-tree indexes and scans a b-tree index for key value(s) or ranges of key value(s).

◆ Bit Vector Sort – This operator sorts the rows that satisfy the constraints on the dimension tables and passes the sorted list to the STARjoin join operator. The MERGE SORT operator is also used for this same purpose, depending on the cardinality of the dimension table and the amount of memory allocated to the query.

◆ Check – This operator performs consistency checking of tables and indexes; it replaces the utilities tblchk and ixvalid of previous releases.

◆ Choose Plan – This operator represents a decision point that will be taken by the server at run time. As each query is processed, there are decision points that can't be determined prior to running the query. When a Choose Plan operator exists, there will be at least two options for the server from which to choose. Which one the server will choose is based on the results found up to that point and the number and types of indexes available. Only one of the available choices will be selected and run. This operator is also used to sequence the query plan, so for example, when subquery are prerun, the CHOOSE PLAN operator will appear in the plan to ensure that the prerunning operation occurs before the portions of the plan that depend on the prerun result. In this instance, the operator will have only a single choice.

◆ Delete – This operator removes rows from a table and any corresponding index entries it may have.

◆ Delete Cascade – This operator locates the rows in the referencing tables that would no longer pass referential integrity when the referenced row is deleted.

◆ Delete Refcheck — This operator checks to see if there is data in the referencing table that corresponds to the data to be deleted from the referenced table. If there are rows in the referencing tables that would violate referential integrity when the referenced row is deleted, then the referencing row is not deleted.

◆ Exchange — This operator manages the parallel processing for a query. Several of the other operators are capable of running in parallel, and this operator spawns the other tasks. Note that when you see the EXCHANGE operator in your query plan, that does not mean the query will go parallel, only that it is eligible to go parallel. Whether it is processed in parallel or not is dependent on the number of parallel resources available, system workload, and other system resources. Parallelism is also data dependent, based on the results of the preliminary plans. The EXCHANGE operator is data driven; that is, when data are available, they flow across the EXCHANGE operator.

◆ Execute — This is always the first operator in a query plan (EXPLAIN output). This operator initiates evaluation of the query plan.

◆ Explain — This is the operator that produces the query plan that shows all the possible ways to run the query, based on the state of the database at the time it is generated. The query plans will change as tables and indexes are added, modified, or removed from the database.

◆ Functional Join — This operator reads a row of data using Segment and Row information passed to it from other operators. This is the fetch mechanism that retrieves the data rows.

◆ General Purpose — A "catch-all" operator that substitutes performance-efficient routines for some standard types of queries such as SELECT COUNT (*) FROM tablename.

◆ Hash 1-1 Match — This operator creates a hash table using the values from the table on the left side of the join while it searches for those values in the table on the right. The order of the tables matters.

◆ Hash Avl Aggregate — This operator performs all aggregation functions used inside a query including GROUP BY, DISTINCT, SUM, and AVG. SELECT DISTINCT may often be computed using MERGE SORT.

◆ Insert — This operator is used to insert rows into a table.

◆ Merge Sort — This operator sorts lists of row pointers.

◆ Naijve 1-1 Match — This operator is used to compute the cross join (or Cartesian product) of two tables. This is the only poorly performing join operator in Red Brick.

- ◆ `RISQL Calculate` — This operator processes all the RISQL display functions including `RANK`, `NTILE`, and `TERTILE`.

- ◆ `Sample Scan` — This operator is new in version 6.0 and performs true random sampling functions.

- ◆ `Simple Merge` — This standard merge operator takes two input lists and combines them.

- ◆ `Sort 1-1 Match` — This operator performs a matching sort between two sorted lists and is used in queries that contain the `UNION`, `INTERSECT`, or `EXCEPT` keywords.

- ◆ `STARjoin` — This multitable, parallel-enabled join operator performs STARjoin processing.

- ◆ `Subquery` — This operator is used to process both scalar and correlated subqueries.

- ◆ `Table Scan` — This operator scans a table by performing a standard sequential (top to bottom) read of a table.

- ◆ `TargetJoin` — This multitable join operator performs TARGETjoin processing.

- ◆ `Target Scan` — This operator performs TARGET index processing.

- ◆ `Update` — This operator is used to update a row in a table.

- ◆ `Virtual Table Scan` — This operator manages temporary internal results stored in virtual memory.

These are the basic operators in Red Brick. By combining each of these building bricks, the server can process the most complex query you can pose. You now have enough information to begin to understand the output of the `EXPLAIN` command.

The EXPLAIN command

The output of the `EXPLAIN` command lists the operators that are used in a given query execution plan. Those of you who were using Red Brick before this functionality became available can perhaps recall how challenging it was trying to figure out what the query was doing by considering the statistics generated at the end of the query. Things have come a long way since then, and you now have a powerful facility to understand your queries and query environment.

Becoming an expert in reading `EXPLAIN` output is not an easy task. It takes time and practice. Keep in mind that query plans can become quite complicated, and it's almost impossible to discuss every possible situation you might run into. If you are having trouble, break the query into several smaller parts to understand how the server wants to process them.

Reading EXPLAIN output

There are two ways to generate and read EXPLAIN output — from within the Warehouse Administrator and from within a RISQL session. If you are using the Administrator, you have an option of getting a graphical representation of the EXPLAIN output, or you can generate the traditional text-based output using the EXPLAIN keyword at the top of your query. If you are using a RISQL session, then you can generate only the text version of the output. You'll have a chance to examine both, but the Administrator seems to be much easier to work with. The query plan is actually a tree of operators, and the EXPLAIN statement output is a linear representation of that tree.

The text-based example that follows is based on the sample database, with the primary indexes only on the dimensions, along with the following indexes on the BILLING_CDR fact table:

A primary key of

```
PERIOD_KEY
TIME_KEY
CALL_TYPE
RATE_PALN
BTN
CUSTOMET_ID
LINE_TYPE_KEY
```

And a STARindex of

```
PERIOD_KEY
TIME_KEY
CALL_TYPE
RATE_PALN
LINE_TYPE_KEY
CUSTOMET_ID
BTN
```

In any case, the EXPLAIN output is generated by placing the EXPLAIN keyword in front of the SQL text like this:

```
explain
select customer_state state, quarter_number quarter, sum(revenue_amount) revenue
from customer natural join period natural join billing_cdr
where customer_state='NJ'
and quarter_number=1
and year_number=1999
group by state, quarter;
```

Notice that the constraints are on the dimensions PERIOD and CUSTOMER – the leading and training sides of both the primary index and the STARindex. When you execute this query, you get the following information back:

```
[
- EXECUTE (ID: 0) 8 Table locks (table, type): (PERIOD, Read_Only), (CUSTOMER,
Read_Only), (BILLING_CDR, Read_Only), (TIME, Read_Only), (CALL_TYPE, Read_Only)
, (RATE_PLAN, Read_Only), (LINE_TYPE, Read_Only), (TELEPHONE, Read_Only)
--- HASH AVL AGGR (ID: 1) Log Advisor Info: FALSE, Grouping: TRUE, Distinct: FA
LSE;
----- CHOOSE PLAN (ID: 2) Num prelims: 2; Num choices: 2; Type: StarJoin;

Prelim: 1; Choose Plan [id : 2] {
BIT VECTOR SORT (ID: 3)
-- TABLE SCAN (ID: 4) Table: PERIOD, Predicate: ((PERIOD.YEAR_NUMBER) = (1999) )
&& ((PERIOD.QUARTER_NUMBER) = (1) )
}

Prelim: 2; Choose Plan [id : 2] {
BIT VECTOR SORT (ID: 5)
-- TABLE SCAN (ID: 6) Table: CUSTOMER, Predicate: (CUSTOMER.CUSTOMER_STATE
) = ('NJ')
}

Choice: 1; Choose Plan [id : 2] {
FUNCTIONAL JOIN (ID: 7) 1 tables: PERIOD
-- FUNCTIONAL JOIN (ID: 8) 1 tables: CUSTOMER
---- FUNCTIONAL JOIN (ID: 9) 1 tables: BILLING_CDR
------ STARJOIN (ID: 10) Join type: InnerJoin, Num facts: 1, Num potential
dimensions: 7, Fact Table: BILLING_CDR, Potential Indexes: CDR_STAR_1;
Dimension Table(s): PERIOD, TIME, CALL_TYPE, RATE_PLAN, LINE_TYPE, CUSTOMER,
TELEPHONE
}

Choice: 2; Choose Plan [id : 2] {
FUNCTIONAL JOIN (ID: 11) 1 tables: PERIOD
-- BTREE 1-1 MATCH (ID: 12) Join type: InnerJoin; Index(s): [Table: PERIOD
, Index: PERIOD_PK_IDX]
---- FUNCTIONAL JOIN (ID: 13) 1 tables: CUSTOMER
------ BTREE 1-1 MATCH (ID: 14) Join type: InnerJoin; Index(s): [Table: CU
STOMER, Index: CUSTOMER_PK_IDX]
-------- TABLE SCAN (ID: 15) Table: BILLING_CDR, Predicate: <none>
}

]
```

Notice several things about the output:

◆ Each operator is indicated by one or more dashes, followed by its name in capital letters. This is how (in the text version anyway) you keep track of where you are.

◆ Each operator is followed by an ID number unique to the query. These ID numbers uniquely identify each step and correspond to the statistics generated after the query is run, so you can determine exactly which step was taken.

◆ There are a couple preliminary steps: Prelim1 and Prelim2. If you recall the earlier discussion of how Red Brick queries are processed, the server works on the dimensions first. The Prelim steps are where this takes place.

◆ The server has generated two choices to run the main part of the query: Choice 1 and Choice 2. One (and only one) of these will be used to execute the query.

So, how do you read and interpret all this stuff? Start at the top with the EXECUTE operator:

```
[
- EXECUTE (ID: 0) 8 Table locks (table, type): (PERIOD, Read_Only), (CUSTOMER,
Read_Only), (BILLING_CDR, Read_Only), (TIME, Read_Only), (CALL_TYPE, Read_Only)
, (RATE_PLAN, Read_Only), (LINE_TYPE, Read_Only), (TELEPHONE, Read_Only)
--- HASH AVL AGGR (ID: 1) Log Advisor Info: FALSE, Grouping: TRUE, Distinct: FA
LSE;
----- CHOOSE PLAN (ID: 2) Num prelims: 2; Num choices: 2; Type: StarJoin;
```

To properly read this section, you start at EXECUTE, which identifies the tables, and then go to the CHOOSE PLAN operator. Recall from the discussion of the operators and the order in which things are processed, the HASH AVL AGGR operator processes the GROUP BY portion of the query, which can't happen until the rows have been identified.

Looking at the CHOOSE PLAN operator (ID: 2), you will notice there are two preliminary steps and two choices. The preliminary steps must be processed before the server can decide which choice to use to continue with the query. Once these are processed, the server will choose one and only one of the choices to process the query.

The preliminary steps are as follows:

```
Prelim: 1; Choose Plan [id : 2] {
BIT VECTOR SORT (ID: 3)
-- TABLE SCAN (ID: 4) Table: PERIOD, Predicate: ((PERIOD.YEAR_NUMBER) = (1999) )
&& ((PERIOD.QUARTER_NUMBER) = (1) )
}
```

```
Prelim: 2; Choose Plan [id : 2] {
BIT VECTOR SORT (ID: 5)
-- TABLE SCAN (ID: 6) Table: CUSTOMER, Predicate: (CUSTOMER.CUSTOMER_STATE
) = ('NJ')
}
```

Notice that immediately following the Prelim: 1 identifier is a Choose Plan identifier — in this case [id : 2]. This tells you which Choose Plan operator is dependent upon this preliminary step. It is possible to have many Choose Plan operators in a given query due to subqueries and other things, and there must be a mechanism to associate them correctly.

To read the preliminaries correctly, start at the bottom and read up. The first step would then be the TABLE SCAN on the PERIOD table, looking for the rows with a QUARTER_NUMBER = 1 and YEAR_NUMBER = 1999. Once the rows are identified, they will be sorted via the BIT VECTOR SORT step.

Preliminary 2 is read the same way — start at the bottom and read up. We're going to do a table scan of the CUSTOMER table and look for all the rows in New Jersey. Once the server finds them, it will sort them by row ID, again with the BIT VECTOR SORT operator.

Now it's time to evaluate the two choices generated for this query:

```
Choice: 1; Choose Plan [id : 2] {
FUNCTIONAL JOIN (ID: 7) 1 tables: PERIOD
-- FUNCTIONAL JOIN (ID: 8) 1 tables: CUSTOMER
---- FUNCTIONAL JOIN (ID: 9) 1 tables: BILLING_CDR
------ STARJOIN (ID: 10) Join type: InnerJoin, Num facts: 1, Num potential
dimensions: 7, Fact Table: BILLING_CDR, Potential Indexes: CDR_STAR_1;
Dimension Table(s): PERIOD, TIME, CALL_TYPE, RATE_PLAN, LINE_TYPE, CUSTOMER,
TELEPHONE
}
```

Choice 1 is the STARJOIN plan. Like the preliminaries, you start at the bottom and read up to determine the order of the steps. Notice the indentation with the dashes. This will also help you read the plans within a section. This plan will do a STARjoin on the BILLING_CDR table. As it retrieves rows, it does a FUNCTIONAL JOIN to each of the dimensions to get the appropriate dimension data. If the server chooses this plan, then the output would be fed to the HASH AVL AGGR you saw earlier at the top of the plan.

Now look at choice 2:

```
Choice: 2; Choose Plan [id : 2] {
FUNCTIONAL JOIN (ID: 11) 1 tables: PERIOD
-- BTREE 1-1 MATCH (ID: 12) Join type: InnerJoin; Index(s): [Table: PERIOD
, Index: PERIOD_PK_IDX]
```

```
---- FUNCTIONAL JOIN (ID: 13) 1 tables: CUSTOMER
------ BTREE 1-1 MATCH (ID: 14) Join type: InnerJoin; Index(s): [Table:
CUSTOMER, Index: CUSTOMER_PK_IDX]
-------- TABLE SCAN (ID: 15) Table: BILLING_CDR, Predicate: <none>
}
```

Choice 2 is a TABLE SCAN plan. This choice will scan the entire BILLING_CDR
table and do a BTREE 1-1 MATCH back to each dimension to determine if the row
should be returned or not. You may be tempted to think this is the slower choice;
however, depending on the query, the database structure, and other factors, it may
be the faster choice. Otherwise, there would be no reason to have it be an alternative plan.

As indicated earlier, it is possible to have more than one Choose Plan operator
in a query. This situation happens most often with subqueries, so the next example
is one that has a scalar subquery. This query is being run against the sample database with the same indexes available as the previous example.

 A scalar subquery returns only a single row. If it returns more than that, the
server reports an error.

```
explain
select customer_state state, sum(revenue_amount) revenue_Q198,
 (select sum(revenue_amount) from customer natural join period natural join
billing_cdr
where year_number=1999 and customer_state='NJ') as revenue_Q199
from customer natural join period natural join billing_cdr
where year_number=1998
and customer_state='NJ'
group by state;
```

In this example, the revenue for the state of New Jersey is being reported for the
years 1998 and 1999. The outer query produces the data for 1998, and the inner
query (or subquery) produces the data for 1999. This query produced the following
EXPLAIN:

```
[
- EXECUTE (ID: 0) 8 Table locks (table, type): (PERIOD, Read_Only), (CUSTOMER,
Read_Only), (BILLING_CDR, Read_Only), (TIME, Read_Only), (CALL_TYPE, Read_Only)
, (RATE_PLAN, Read_Only), (LINE_TYPE, Read_Only), (TELEPHONE, Read_Only)
--- SUBQUERY (ID: 1) Scalar: TRUE, Correlated: FALSE;
----- HASH AVL AGGR (ID: 2) Log Advisor Info: FALSE, Grouping: TRUE, Distinct:
```

```
FALSE;
------- CHOOSE PLAN (ID: 3) Num prelims: 2; Num choices: 2; Type: StarJoin;

Prelim: 1; Choose Plan [id : 3] {
BIT VECTOR SORT (ID: 4)
-- TABLE SCAN (ID: 5) Table: PERIOD, Predicate: (PERIOD.YEAR_NUMBER) = (1998)
}

Prelim: 2; Choose Plan [id : 3] {
BIT VECTOR SORT (ID: 6)
-- TABLE SCAN (ID: 7) Table: CUSTOMER, Predicate: (CUSTOMER.CUSTOMER_STATE
) = ('NJ')
}

Choice: 1; Choose Plan [id : 3] {
FUNCTIONAL JOIN (ID: 8) 1 tables: CUSTOMER
-- FUNCTIONAL JOIN (ID: 9) 1 tables: BILLING_CDR
---- STARJOIN (ID: 10) Join type: InnerJoin, Num facts: 1, Num potential
dimensions: 7, Fact Table: BILLING_CDR, Potential Indexes: CDR_STAR_1;
Dimension Table(s): PERIOD, TIME, CALL_TYPE, RATE_PLAN, LINE_TYPE, CUSTOMER, TE
LEPHONE
}

Choice: 2; Choose Plan [id : 3] {
FUNCTIONAL JOIN (ID: 11) 1 tables: PERIOD
-- BTREE 1-1 MATCH (ID: 12) Join type: InnerJoin; Index(s): [Table: PERIOD
, Index: PERIOD_PK_IDX]
---- FUNCTIONAL JOIN (ID: 13) 1 tables: CUSTOMER
------ BTREE 1-1 MATCH (ID: 14) Join type: InnerJoin; Index(s): [Table: CU
STOMER, Index: CUSTOMER_PK_IDX]
-------- TABLE SCAN (ID: 15) Table: BILLING_CDR, Predicate: <none>
}

----- HASH AVL AGGR (ID: 16) Log Advisor Info: FALSE, Grouping: FALSE, Distinct
: FALSE;
------- CHOOSE PLAN (ID: 17) Num prelims: 2; Num choices: 2; Type: StarJoin;

Prelim: 1; Choose Plan [id : 17] {
BIT VECTOR SORT (ID: 18)
-- TABLE SCAN (ID: 19) Table: PERIOD, Predicate: (PERIOD.YEAR_NUMBER) = (1
999)
}

Prelim: 2; Choose Plan [id : 17] {
BIT VECTOR SORT (ID: 20)
```

```
-- TABLE SCAN (ID: 21) Table: CUSTOMER, Predicate: (CUSTOMER.CUSTOMER_STAT
E) = ('NJ')
}


Choice: 1; Choose Plan [id : 17] {
FUNCTIONAL JOIN (ID: 22) 1 tables: BILLING_CDR
-- STARJOIN (ID: 23) Join type: InnerJoin, Num facts: 1, Num potential dim
ensions: 7, Fact Table: BILLING_CDR, Potential Indexes: CDR_STAR_1;
Dimension Table(s): PERIOD, TIME, CALL_TYPE, RATE_PLAN, LINE_TYPE, CUSTOMER, TE
LEPHONE
}


Choice: 2; Choose Plan [id : 17] {
FUNCTIONAL JOIN (ID: 24) 1 tables: PERIOD
-- BTREE 1-1 MATCH (ID: 25) Join type: InnerJoin; Index(s): [Table: PERIOD
, Index: PERIOD_PK_IDX]
---- FUNCTIONAL JOIN (ID: 26) 1 tables: CUSTOMER
------ BTREE 1-1 MATCH (ID: 27) Join type: InnerJoin; Index(s): [Table: CU
STOMER, Index: CUSTOMER_PK_IDX]
-------- TABLE SCAN (ID: 28) Table: BILLING_CDR, Predicate: <none>
}


]
```

Now, there are two Choose Plan operators (ID: 3 and ID: 17) and a SUBQUERY operator. Each of these Choose Plan operators has preliminary steps associated with it, and if you examine the EXPLAIN output closely, you will see that each preliminary step identifies the Choose Plan to which it belongs:

```
------- CHOOSE PLAN (ID: 17) Num prelims: 2; Num choices: 2; Type: StarJoin;

Prelim: 1; Choose Plan [id : 17] {
BIT VECTOR SORT (ID: 18)
-- TABLE SCAN (ID: 19) Table: PERIOD, Predicate: (PERIOD.YEAR_NUMBER) = (1
999)
}


Prelim: 2; Choose Plan [id : 17] {
BIT VECTOR SORT (ID: 20)
-- TABLE SCAN (ID: 21) Table: CUSTOMER, Predicate: (CUSTOMER.CUSTOMER_STAT
E) = ('NJ')
}
```

and

```
------- CHOOSE PLAN (ID: 3) Num prelims: 2; Num choices: 2; Type: StarJoin;

Prelim: 1; Choose Plan [id : 3] {
BIT VECTOR SORT (ID: 4)
-- TABLE SCAN (ID: 5) Table: PERIOD, Predicate: (PERIOD.YEAR_NUMBER) = (1998)
}

Prelim: 2; Choose Plan [id : 3] {
BIT VECTOR SORT (ID: 6)
-- TABLE SCAN (ID: 7) Table: CUSTOMER, Predicate: (CUSTOMER.CUSTOMER_STATE
) = ('NJ')
}
```

This query is processed in the same manner as the previous example by starting with the EXECUTE operator:

```
- EXECUTE (ID: 0) 8 Table locks (table, type): (PERIOD, Read_Only), (CUSTOMER,
Read_Only), (BILLING_CDR, Read_Only), (TIME, Read_Only), (CALL_TYPE, Read_Only)
, (RATE_PLAN, Read_Only), (LINE_TYPE, Read_Only), (TELEPHONE, Read_Only)
--- SUBQUERY (ID: 1) Scalar: TRUE, Correlated: FALSE;
----- HASH AVL AGGR (ID: 2) Log Advisor Info: FALSE, Grouping: TRUE, Distinct:
FALSE;
------- CHOOSE PLAN (ID: 3) Num prelims: 2; Num choices: 2; Type: StarJoin;
```

Notice the SUBQUERY operator – this exists to process the subquery in the select list. As in the first example, you start at the EXECUTE operator – move down the Choose Plan operator and read up. The outer part of this query is processed exactly like the previous example in that for Choose Plan (ID: 3) the preliminaries are executed, and depending on the results, the server will execute one of the choices defined for that Choose Plan step.

Once Choose Plan (ID: 3) has been executed, the rows returned are fed the HASH AVL Aggregate for the SUM() function (ID: 2). At this point, the SUBQUERY (ID: 1) is executed, taking you down to the HASH AVL AGGR (ID: 16) and Choose Plan (ID: 17). In this example, the SUBQUERY operator will project the result of operator (ID: 16).

The HASH operator is necessary because of the group by in the subquery. From Choose Plan (ID: 17), you have the following:

```
----- HASH AVL AGGR (ID: 16) Log Advisor Info: FALSE, Grouping: FALSE, Distinct
: FALSE;
------- CHOOSE PLAN (ID: 17) Num prelims: 2; Num choices: 2; Type: StarJoin;
```

```
Prelim: 1; Choose Plan [id : 17] {
BIT VECTOR SORT (ID: 18)
-- TABLE SCAN (ID: 19) Table: PERIOD, Predicate: (PERIOD.YEAR_NUMBER) = (1
999)
}


Prelim: 2; Choose Plan [id : 17] {
BIT VECTOR SORT (ID: 20)
-- TABLE SCAN (ID: 21) Table: CUSTOMER, Predicate: (CUSTOMER.CUSTOMER_STAT
E) = ('NJ')
}


Choice: 1; Choose Plan [id : 17] {
FUNCTIONAL JOIN (ID: 22) 1 tables: BILLING_CDR
-- STARJOIN (ID: 23) Join type: InnerJoin, Num facts: 1, Num potential dim
ensions: 7, Fact Table: BILLING_CDR, Potential Indexes: CDR_STAR_1;
Dimension Table(s): PERIOD, TIME, CALL_TYPE, RATE_PLAN, LINE_TYPE, CUSTOMER, TE
LEPHONE
}


Choice: 2; Choose Plan [id : 17] {
FUNCTIONAL JOIN (ID: 24) 1 tables: PERIOD
-- BTREE 1-1 MATCH (ID: 25) Join type: InnerJoin; Index(s): [Table: PERIOD
, Index: PERIOD_PK_IDX]
---- FUNCTIONAL JOIN (ID: 26) 1 tables: CUSTOMER
------ BTREE 1-1 MATCH (ID: 27) Join type: InnerJoin; Index(s): [Table: CU
STOMER, Index: CUSTOMER_PK_IDX]
-------- TABLE SCAN (ID: 28) Table: BILLING_CDR, Predicate: <none>
}
```

This query will be processed the same way as the outer query in that the preliminaries must be processed prior to the server's selecting one of the choices to process the main part of the query. Notice that this subquery is executed only once because it is not correlated to the outer query.

Reading TARGETjoin EXPLAIN output

Now look at what happens to the EXPLAIN output once you enable TARGETjoins. TARGETjoins are enabled by building TARGET indexes on all the foreign keys of the fact table. Accordingly, six TARGET indexes are built on all the foreign keys of the BILLING_CDR table in addition the indexes that were listed earlier.

Recall the first example query looked like this:

```
explain
select customer_state state, quarter_number quarter, sum(revenue_amount) revenue
from customer natural join period natural join billing_cdr
```

```
where customer_state='NJ'
and quarter_number=1
and year_number=1999
group by state, quarter;
```

When you run it against the database with the TARGET indexes, you get the following EXPLAIN output:

```
[
- EXECUTE (ID: 0) 8 Table locks (table, type): (PERIOD, Read_Only), (CUSTOMER,
Read_Only), (BILLING_CDR, Read_Only), (TIME, Read_Only), (CALL_TYPE, Read_Only)
, (RATE_PLAN, Read_Only), (LINE_TYPE, Read_Only), (TELEPHONE, Read_Only)
--- HASH AVL AGGR (ID: 1) Log Advisor Info: FALSE, Grouping: TRUE, Distinct: FA
LSE;
----- CHOOSE PLAN (ID: 2) Num prelims: 2; Num choices: 3; Type: StarJoin;

Prelim: 1; Choose Plan [id : 2] {
BIT VECTOR SORT (ID: 3)
-- TABLE SCAN (ID: 4) Table: PERIOD, Predicate: ((PERIOD.YEAR_NUMBER) = (1
999) ) && ((PERIOD.QUARTER_NUMBER) = (1) )
}

Prelim: 2; Choose Plan [id : 2] {
BIT VECTOR SORT (ID: 5)
-- TABLE SCAN (ID: 6) Table: CUSTOMER, Predicate: (CUSTOMER.CUSTOMER_STATE
) = ('NJ')
}

Choice: 1; Choose Plan [id : 2] {
FUNCTIONAL JOIN (ID: 7) 1 tables: PERIOD
-- FUNCTIONAL JOIN (ID: 8) 1 tables: CUSTOMER
---- FUNCTIONAL JOIN (ID: 9) 1 tables: BILLING_CDR
------ STARJOIN (ID: 10) Join type: InnerJoin, Num facts: 1, Num potential
dimensions: 7, Fact Table: BILLING_CDR, Potential Indexes: CDR_STAR_1;
Dimension Table(s): PERIOD, TIME, CALL_TYPE, RATE_PLAN, LINE_TYPE, CUSTOMER, TE
LEPHONE
}

Choice: 2; Choose Plan [id : 2] {
FUNCTIONAL JOIN (ID: 11) 1 tables: PERIOD
-- BTREE 1-1 MATCH (ID: 12) Join type: InnerJoin; Index(s): [Table: PERIOD
, Index: PERIOD_PK_IDX]
---- FUNCTIONAL JOIN (ID: 13) 1 tables: CUSTOMER
------ BTREE 1-1 MATCH (ID: 14) Join type: InnerJoin; Index(s): [Table: CU
STOMER, Index: CUSTOMER_PK_IDX]
```

```
-------- TABLE SCAN (ID: 15) Table: BILLING_CDR, Predicate: <none>
}


Choice: 3; Choose Plan [id : 2] {
FUNCTIONAL JOIN (ID: 16) 1 tables: PERIOD
-- BTREE 1-1 MATCH (ID: 17) Join type: InnerJoin; Index(s): [Table: PERIOD
, Index: PERIOD_PK_IDX]
---- FUNCTIONAL JOIN (ID: 18) 1 tables: CUSTOMER
------ BTREE 1-1 MATCH (ID: 19) Join type: InnerJoin; Index(s): [Table: CU
STOMER, Index: CUSTOMER_PK_IDX]
-------- FUNCTIONAL JOIN (ID: 20) 1 tables: BILLING_CDR
---------- TARGETJOIN(ID: 21) Table: BILLING_CDR, Predicate: <none> ; Num
indexes: 2 Index(s): Index: TARGET1 ,Index: TARGET7
------------ FUNCTIONAL JOIN (ID: 22) 1 tables: PERIOD
-------------- VIRTAB SCAN (ID: 23)
------------ FUNCTIONAL JOIN (ID: 24) 1 tables: CUSTOMER
-------------- VIRTAB SCAN (ID: 25)
}


]
```

Notice the addition of a completely new choice to run the main part of the query. The preliminary steps are the same, as are the STARjoin and TABLE SCAN choices, but now there is a third choice: TARGETjoin. TARGETjoin processing can show up in your query plans in a number of ways. At first glance, you might not recognize it as a TARGETjoin, so careful examination is necessary.

In Choice 3, the following things are happening. First, notice the VIRTAB SCAN. This operator is scanning the results of Preliminary 2, getting all the customers in New Jersey. The second VIRTAB SCAN is scanning the results of Preliminary 1 that found all the PERIOD table rows for Q1, 1999.

The next step is a TARGETjoin to the BILLING_CDR table to retrieve the fact rows in question. As each fact table row is retrieved, the server does a FUNCTIONAL join back to the dimensions to retrieve the relevant fact data – in this case Quarter, Year, and State.

There is one important thing to note with TARGETjoin processing. During the preliminary steps when the server is evaluating the dimensions, it retains the ROW_Ids of the dimension rows in anticipation of doing a STARjoin query. If the server determines that there is a less expensive way to process the query using some other join method, the ROW_Ids must be turned back into key values. Remember that STAR-indexes are made up of ROW_Ids; all the other index types contain that actual key value. That is the reason for the FUNCTIONAL JOIN steps (ID: 24) and (ID: 22) in Choice 3 .

TARGETindexes contain key values and lists of row pointers in the table the TARGETindex exists on; STARindexes contain row references of the dimensions and ROW_Ids to the facts.

SET STATS Output

The other side to the `EXPLAIN` information is the `STATS` information. There are several flavors of `SET STATS` information, as well as some undocumented ways to get lots of detail.

Using an undocumented feature means that you know and understand that the behavior is undefined and can go away at any time. Don't use them and then call Informix Tech Support to complain about a problem caused by its use — you're on your own. <End Commercial>

The most often used `SET STATS` command is `SET STATS FULL`. This is technically not supported; however, it provides a lot of information. I believe that if you ask technical support, they will tell you to use `SET STATS ON` and `SET STATS INFO` — both of which will give you subsets of what you see here.

What is not generally known is what all the text means and how to interpret what it's telling you. Consider the following `SET` output:

```
** STATISTICS ** (499) Compilation = 00:00:00.01 cp time, 00:00:00.02 tot cp
time, 00:00:00.02 agg tot cp time, 00:00:00.07 elapsed time, 00:00:00.07 agg
elapsed time, Logical Reads/Writes:16/0, Pageflts=0, Blk Reads=5, Blk Writes=0
** STATISTICS ** (1299) Block Cache Reads/Writes: 2/0 Mem used: 0 Spill
count: 0 Spill used: 0 Parallel count: 0
** STATISTICS ** (499) Time = 00:00:00.01 cp time, 00:00:00.02 tot cp time,
00:00:00.04 agg tot cp time, 00:00:00.01 elapsed time, 00:00:00.08 agg
elapsed time, Logical Reads/Writes:26/0, Pageflts=0, Blk Reads=0, Blk Writes=0
** STATISTICS ** (1299) Block Cache Reads/Writes: 4/0 Mem used: 0 Spill
count: 0 Spill used: 0 Parallel count: 0
** INFORMATION ** (256) 59 rows returned.
RISQL>
```

This is what it all means:

◆ Compilation cp time = time it takes to convert ASCII SQL into understandable code the server can process.

- ◆ tot cp time = total time it took to process this step of the query.

- ◆ agg tot cp time = sum total of all of the "tot cp time" numbers for this query (all steps up to this one inclusive).

- ◆ elapsed time = amount of elapsed time to process this step.

- ◆ agg elapsed time = sum total of all the "elapsed time" numbers for this query (all steps up to this one inclusive).

- ◆ Logical Reads/Writes: = the number of times Red Brick Decision Server asked UNIX for information. If UNIX can get the information from its own disk caching system, it will, and it still counts as a logical I/O. If UNIX has to go out to hard disk, that also counts as a logical I/O. Red Brick keeps its own internal cache too. If the data requested in the query can be fetched from the Red Brick cache, then they will be, and no Logical I/O count will be generated for that bit of information. So running the same query again and again, you will see this number jump around, but typically it will go down after each query until it levels off. However, even when this is the case, there is no direct connection between the number of logical I/Os and time because Red Brick has no way of knowing or controlling if UNIX gets the data from hard disk or from the UNIX disk cache system.

- ◆ Pageflts = the number of times Red Brick received a bad block of data from the OS and had to request a resend.

- ◆ Blk Reads / Blk Writes = the number of times the OS read from or wrote to the hard disk. This is not OS disk cache but a physical I/O.

- ◆ Block Cache Reads/Writes: = the number of times Red Brick read from or wrote to the Red Brick Warehouse data cache.

- ◆ Mem used: = the amount of memory used for this step of the query.

- ◆ Spill count: = the number of times the query temp space threshold was reached, forcing a spill to disk.

- ◆ Spill used: = the amount of disk space used by query tempspace temporary files.

- ◆ Parallel count: = the number of parallel processes used for processing this query.

Improving Query Performance via SQL/EXPLAIN

The next logical step is to be able to use the EXPLAIN output to improve your query performance. There are as many ways to improve your specific queries as there are people reading this book. Determining when and how to make these changes requires an in-depth knowledge of SQL, but the following examples provide some limited suggestions.

UNION versus OR

Often, queries that contain an OR condition can be rewritten into a UNION query that results in better performance.

```
Select prod_name, cust_state, sales_dollars
From product, customer, sales
Where prod_name like 'M%'
Or cust_state in ('NJ', 'DE')
Order by prod_name, cust_state;
```

can be rewritten as:

```
Select prod_name, cust_state, sales_dollars
From product, customer, sales
Where prod_name like 'M%'
UNION
Select prod_name, cust_state, sales_dollars
From product, customer, sales
Where cust_state in ('NJ', 'DE')
Order by prod_name, cust_state;
```

FROM clause subquery versus correlated subquery

A query that has a subquery in the FROM clause often runs faster than the equivalent (returning the same result set) query with a correlated subquery in the SELECT list.

This is primarily because the FROM clause query is run once and the results are joined, as opposed to running a query for every single row that is passed out of the WHERE clause.

Avoid table scans

At one level this seems intuitive, and indeed, it's true. About the only times table scans are good are if you really want the whole table or if the table is so small it costs more to process the indexes.

Change DISTINCT to GROUP BY

You may often be able to gain a performance advantage by changing SELECT DISTINCT to a GROUP BY. This is possible because SELECT DISTINCT A, B, C is equivalent to GROUP BY A, B, C because the grouping operation by definition produces the distinct combinations of A, B, and C.

Running Queries

In a production environment, most users submit their queries from some front-end tool in a point-and-click type of environment. Many don't have any idea what gets sent to the server and perhaps don't care, so long as they get the information they are looking for in a timely fashion. However, you or the DBA for your Red Brick Warehouse will need another facility to submit queries and capture the EXPLAIN output.

There are two ways to interface with the server to get this information: by a RISQL session and through the Warehouse Administrator. After many years of dealing with the RISQL command line, I've found it much easier to work through the Administrator, in part because the average query generates so much EXPLAIN output that it's hard to manage from the command line. Even if vi is your friend, it's so nice to be able to use a scroll bar to page through it.

Sample Database Queries

Back in Chapter 2, I introduced the sample database and outlined some of the analysis that could be done. As part of the sample database, I've included a number of queries to help illustrate a number of query components. The business questions are posed here as English text. The SQL text is included on the CD; however, feel free to take a crack at writing the queries and check you work against the material on the CD.

- ◆ What is the total revenue and number of distinct originating phone #s by call type and customer age band for holiday morning calls?

- ◆ What is the total January revenue and average January duration by carrier description for customers who churned 1/10/99?

- ◆ What is the # distinct residential customers, # distinct business customers, and # distinct phone numbers in Delaware?

- ◆ What is the average credit limit and total outstanding balances by reason description for married homeowners that churned in the first half of January 1999?

- ◆ What is the number of customers and average outstanding balances by rate plan description for business customers who churned in January 1999 for Lower Cost?

- ◆ Rank the line types in revenue order, highest to lowest, for both residential and business customers.

- ◆ What is the # of customers and average outstanding balances by rate plan description for residential customers who churned in January 1999?

- What are the heaviest call days for business customers? For residential customers?

- Which geographical area generates the most revenue?

- What is the average and total revenue for residential customers for each quarter in 1999, by income band, analyzed by area code and state?

Lessons from the Trenches

The lessons from the trenches for this chapter sound simple, but require some work on your part to be successful. Perhaps the biggest hurdle Red Brick Decision Server customers have is learning how to read, understand, and use the EXPLAIN information to tune their warehouse. This task can be complicated even more if you don't have a reasonable command of SQL and the basics of how queries are processed.

Know your SQL

There is no substitute for knowing your SQL. Red Brick is capable of processing extremely complex queries. I recall a customer who had written a single query that generated something on the order of 100 or so operators. It was so amazing at the time that the EXPLAIN output was sent to the development people so they could get a look at it. It was really something. Actually, query plans composed of several hundred operators are common now.

One of the reasons this was so amazing is because the gentleman who generated it really knew his SQL and was able to do extraordinary things with the engine. SQL is a skill that comes only with practice, so don't get too frustrated if it doesn't come right away. Obviously, not everyone will have the skills to write queries that are as complicated as the one just mentioned, but you can, with practice, become quite adept at expressing complex business questions using SQL and the Red Brick RISQL extensions.

I might also mention that the Red Brick documentation set comes with a *RISQL Self Study Guide*. This self-paced study guide walks you through the basics of SQL, the RISQL extensions, and how to use them. If you are new to SQL, you will find it very useful. Those who are already competent in SQL but new to Red Brick will find it a quick study on the RISQL functions.

Learn to read EXPLAIN output

This has a double meaning. First, you must learn to understand how to navigate the information and make sense out of it. Second, you must develop a sense of reasonableness and priority in determining what's bad and good. Keeping track of preliminaries, subqueries, or, sometimes, nested subqueries makes it hard to see the bricks for the building as it were. Consequently, you may see a TABLE SCAN operator, and before you understand its consequences, you may go solve something that isn't a problem in the first place.

It pays to be methodical and deliberate in reading the EXPLAIN output and to understand not only what the server is doing, but on what amount of data it's doing it. Very often, operations that would be considered bad on large amounts of data are acceptable on smaller amounts and vice versa.

Developing this higher skill comes only with practice, but it is possible to develop it to the point where you can determine with amazing accuracy and frequency which plan will be used and how long it will take the query to process. I've been trying to explain just how I do this to a colleague of mine for years, but I still can't articulate all that well – it just happens. Unfortunately, the technology to figure it out for you hasn't been invented yet, which means that you've got no other choice but to use due diligence, take the offending queries apart if necessary, and understand what's going on.

Strive to understand the query processing engine

This point is related to the previous one and is just as important. The query engine is a complicated but very capable piece of technology. Designed to run business queries, it's based on the dimensional model concepts discussed earlier. It is dependent on the indexes and environment resources available when deciding how to process a query. An in-depth discussion of the query engine would fill a book by itself, but for the most part things work as advertised. Don't be afraid to experiment with different memory allocations and index definitions and to see what the server does. Don't forget that the EXPLAIN output shows you how the query might be processed, not how it was processed. To understand what the server actually chose, use the SET STATS FULL command. This will append the necessary statistics to the end of the result set.

Summary

The Red Brick query engine is the centerpiece to Red Brick Decision Server technology and is designed from the ground up to run Data Warehouse queries. It is based on an object-oriented model and provides the basic building blocks to answer extremely complex queries as well as provide new functionality as customer requirements evolve.

You have seen how the Red Brick joins work and know enough now to examine your queries, know what they are doing, and determine how to improve their performance. Query tuning is an entire subject in its own right; however, these are the building blocks that make it all happen.

The EXPLAIN output is perhaps the most valuable information you have in trying to work out problems with the query environment. Every minute spent in understanding what that information is trying to tell you is well worth the effort.

Chapter 13

Parallel Queries

IN THIS CHAPTER

◆ How parallel queries are processed

◆ Parallel operators

◆ Factors that limit parallelism

◆ Enabling parallel query processing

◆ Enabling parallel aggregation

◆ Evaluating parallel performance

◆ Lessons from the trenches

THE PREVIOUS CHAPTER DISCUSSED how queries are processed in Red Brick Decision Server and touched briefly on the concept of parallel queries. This chapter focuses on turning parallel queries "on" and discusses initial configuration settings to get you started. We'll also look at the differences between UNIX and NT in processing parallel queries and provide a basic configuration for NT platforms that you can use as a starting point.

Query Engine: How Parallel Queries Are Processed

Parallel queries are processed in the same fashion as their serial counterparts as far as the overall strategy and planning goes. The mechanisms that govern the eligibility of a query to run in parallel are few but very integrated, meaning that a change to one often means reevaluating changes to one or more of the others. The difference lies in that there are a few operators that are capable of spawning children processes (UNIX) or other threads (NT). These operators are discussed in detail shortly, but you must understand some fundamental differences between UNIX and NT as they relate to Red Brick Decision Server parallel processing.

On a UNIX platform, Red Brick Decision Server invokes a separate process for each parallel task it allocates to a given parallel query. Each of these extra processes has its own memory allocation. On NT systems, there is one process with multiple threads. These threads share a common address space between them. This is the fundamental difference between UNIX and NT; however, queries that run in parallel in a UNIX environment will also run in parallel in an NT environment (assuming the governing parameters are set appropriately). NT has one process with multiple threads that share address space between them. This is also true for any parallel loader operations performed with the PTMU.

There are several ways to monitor parallelism on NT platforms:

◆ Windows NT Task Manager – Seen as an increase in the number of active threads.

◆ Red Brick Decision Server rb_show utility – Show up as the number of active connections.

◆ Dynamic system tables – You are able to query the DSTs and get information on the current commands, databases, locks sessions, and users currently attached to the server instance you are working with.

The execution mode for Red Brick Decision Server parallel queries and loads is the same for both UNIX and NT; however, the implementation is slightly different because of fundamental operating-system design elements. However, queries that run in parallel on UNIX systems will run in parallel in an NT environment.

Parallel Operators

The previous chapter documented the query operators that Red Brick Decision Server uses to break down and process queries. Most operators are designed not to care about parallel processing; however, a few are capable of working in parallel. The EXCHANGE operator is the only operator capable of spawning child processes. All the parallel operators are subject to a number of configuration parameters.

Just because a query is eligible to go parallel does not mean that it will be processed that way. Parallel operations are subject to machine capacity, current user workload, the threshold configuration parameters, and data dependencies — that is, on the output of the STARjoin preliminary plans.

For the balance of this chapter, any reference to the generic term "process" (meaning operating system process) applies equally well to a UNIX process or an NT thread. In cases where a distinction is necessary, it will be clearly indicated.

All parallel operations are governed by the EXCHANGE operator. The existence of this operator in the EXPLAIN output of a query indicates that the query is eligible to run in parallel, but it's not guaranteed to do so. If you do not see the EXCHANGE operator in the query plan, then the query will not (under any circumstances) run in parallel.

The EXCHANGE operator spawns multiple processes for the parallel operators:

Functional Join	Uses a segment ID and a row number to read a data row from a table
STARjoin	A multitable join operator
TARGETjoin	Parallelizes TARGETjoin processing
TABLE Scan	Performs a standard sequential read of a database object
HASH 1-1 Match	Works on nonindexed objects that create a hash table from the left side of the join
Lower Hash 1-1 Match	
Upper Hash 1-1 Match	Parallelizes partitioned parallel aggregation

Multiple processes will be generated for nonparallel operators if the compiler attaches them to parallel operators in the previous list.

For example, the HASHAVLAGGR operator (a serial operator) in the following plan does not originate parallelism, but it is parallelized. Since the compiler attaches the HASHAVLAGGR operator to the functional join and the exchange initiates multiple functional join processes, then each functional join process will have its own HASHAVLAGGR process; hence, the HASHAVLAGGR operator has been parallelized.

In other words, if the EXCHANGE operator determined that it could spawn three functional join tasks, then each functional join task would have its own HASHAVLAGGR operator in order to group the rows coming from its partner functional join. Another way to think about this might be "parallelism by the company the other query operators keep." Many other normally serial operators, including B11M, can be parallelized in a similar manner.

From an EXPLAIN perspective, this output fragment shows you what you will see in the output:

```
...
    Choice: 1; Choose Plan [id : 1] {
      HASH AVL AGGR (ID: 4) Grouping: TRUE, Distinct: FALSE;
    -- EXCHANGE (ID: 5) Exchange type: Functional Join
    ---- HASH AVL AGGR (ID: 6) Grouping: TRUE, Distinct:FALSE;
    ------ FUNCTIONAL JOIN (ID: 7) 1 tables: MS
    -------- FUNCTIONAL JOIN (ID: 8) 1 tables: UB
    ---------- EXCHANGE (ID: 9) Exchange type: Star Join
    ------------ STARJOIN (ID: 10) Join type: InnerJoin, Num
...
```

Notice the two EXCHANGE operators: (ID: 9) and (ID: 5). Recall that query plan segments are read from the bottom up. In this example, the server is going to do a STARjoin and has determined that the operation can be run in parallel; hence, the EXCHANGE operator (ID: 9).

The other parallel opportunity in this fragment is (ID: 5), near the top. The (ID: 5) EXCHANGE operator will define the number of parallel processes used for operator (ID: 6) and for (ID: 7), the functional join operator. Notice that the EXCHANGE would be present even if no aggregation were necessary.

Since (ID: 6) is being processed in parallel, as just discussed, (ID: 4) is necessary to combine the results of the multiple groupings produced by each of the HASHAVLAGGR processes.

EXCHANGE operators can appear anywhere that one of the basic parallelizable operators can appear. This includes select list subqueries, FROM clause subqueries, and queries that include UNION, OR, EXCEPTS, and so on.

A word about reasonable values

Before we venture off into parameter and configuration settings that govern parallel query operations, it's necessary to make a few comments on reasonable values. No one set of tuning values applies to all customer situations across all queries. The dynamic nature of Red Brick Decision Server, the hardware resources available, and the differences in the way the users access and use the warehouse make it impossible to define a "one-size-fits-all" set of parameter values.

However, based on many years of field experience, it's possible to provide you with a good place to start. In all cases, you will have to adjust these recommendations based on your specific situation.

The following parameters govern the parallel query operations of Red Brick Decision Server. Some of these items were discussed briefly in Chapter 10; however, they are included here as well for ease of reference and to help illustrate how they are related to each other.

TUNE FILE_GROUP

TUNE FILE_GROUP is the facility that allows you to group file systems that share the same physical file system. For example, you might have a single disk that has several file systems on it. At the file-system level, Red Brick Decision Server knows nothing about the underlying disk subsystem and how it's configured. If left alone, Red Brick Decision Server would spawn a read process for each PSU. In these instances where several file systems share the same physical spindle and you have PSUs on those file systems, spawning multiple read processes to a single physical device can be counterproductive. The TUNE FILE_GROUP parameter provides you with a way to tell Red Brick Decision Server about the physical structure of your disks.

To determine which group a file belongs to, the file name (as specified in CREATE SEGMENT statements) is converted to an absolute file name (corresponding to either a link or an actual file). Then the longest pathname prefix that is a left substring of the file name is located. The disk_group_id associated with this pathname prefix is the ID of the group to which the file belongs.

The most important point to note is that parallelism is bounded by the number of groups in which the index and/or data reside. In general, the system does not allocate more processes than there are groups affected by the query. If left alone, the server will allocate one process per file group per query. The next parameter provides a way to limit the number of processes per FILE GROUP.

TUNE GROUP

The TUNE GROUP parameter determines how many processes per query will access a given file group. In a nonredundant disk situation (meaning there is no mirrored or RAID technology), it is generally considered best to have one process per physical device. In those cases where there are several file systems sharing a single device, the TUNE FILE_GROUP parameter just discussed keeps the server from spawning too many readers to the device.

In redundant disk situations (RAID or mirror does exist), it is possible for the disk subsystem to support multiple readers via the TUNE GROUP parameter. This provides a way to allow some parallel processing to occur within a disk group. In cases where queries are CPU-intensive rather than I/O-bound and there is excess CPU capacity, you can use the GROUP parameter to allow additional parallelism to take advantage of all the CPU capacity. Note that you will need to enter a separate GROUP parameter for each disk group you want to modify.

TUNE TOTALQUERYPROCS

The TOTALQUERYPROCS parameter specifies the maximum number of processes available for parallel queries at one time on all the servers controlled by a single daemon (or instance of Red Brick Decision Server), providing a mechanism to control the system load imposed by parallel queries. This allows you to control the number of processes available for parallel query processing and the allocation of those processes in a multiuser environment.

TUNE QUERYPROCS

The QUERYPROCS parameter specifies the maximum number of concurrent parallel processes to be used in processing a single parallel query. This mechanism controls the resources allocated to a single query. The algorithm that allocates processes to queries employs a "graceful decrease" allocation mechanism to ration remaining processes when the demand is high.

Although the allocation of parallel processes to queries is rather complicated, it is best described as follows: After approximately 50 percent of the total available processes (as defined by TOTALQUERYPROCS) have been allocated, subsequent queries are allocated fewer and fewer processes per query. These process allocations apply only to parallel queries and have no effect on any serial queries that might be in process on the server. This number is an upper bound; other factors such as the ROWS_PER_TASK and FORCE_TASKS parameters (discussed next) and the TOTALQUERYPROCS parameter can also limit the number of processes available for a single query. Also note that the distribution of data might result in some processes completing before others, which might reduce the amount of parallelism to less than expected because there was much less work to do.

For example, assume a system with a TOTALQUERYPROCS value of 12 and a QUERUYPROCS value of 3. You might be tempted to think you can run only four parallel queries. This is not necessarily true. With no other query activity on the system, the first parallel query will most likely get three processes assigned to it. While query one is running, the second parallel query will most likely get three as well. The third and fourth parallel queries might only get two each, with the fifth and sixth parallel queries perhaps receiving one each. This is an extremely oversimplified example, but it illustrates how the processes are allocated.

If all six queries are running and query one completes, those three processes are then available to be reallocated to other parallel queries currently running or allocated to new queries being submitted, depending on who makes the first request. At each phase in the query plan, when the server needs parallel resources, it looks to see what's available. If resources are available at the time of the request, then the server will allocate resources to the process. If you are watching your queries run with SAR or some like-minded system-monitoring tool, what you will observe is that for a given parallel query, processes come and go, depending on where you are in the query plan.

> During the execution of a query, parallel processing comes and goes, depending on where you are in the plan. Only the phases of a query that contain the EXCHANGE operator are able to run in parallel. Everything else is done in a serial fashion.

The QUERYPROCS value must be a non-negative integer in the range of 0 to 32767. A value of 0 or 1 effectively disables parallel query execution. Changing this parameter might also require operating-system parameters to be changed, as described in the *Installation and Configuration Guide.*If multiple TOTALQUERYPROCS or QUERYPROCS statements are present, the last such entry is used and all others are discarded. With the exception of duplicate elimination, the order of the entries has no impact.

TUNE ROWS_PER_SCAN_TASK

You can provide thresholds to be used by the server in determining how much parallelism to use. If the number of rows to be processed is small, the overhead of parallel processes outweighs the benefits. In a simplified sense, queries estimated to produce a total row count below the threshold values will not go parallel whereas queries estimated to produce a total row count at or above the threshold values *may* go parallel if resources are available. The following three parameters are used to set threshold values for different types of queries:

- ◆ ROWS_PER_SCAN_TASK
- ◆ ROWS_PER_FETCH_TASK
- ◆ ROWS_PER_JOIN_TASK

ROWS_PER_SCAN_TASK is the minimum estimated number of rows to be scanned by a relation scan before a parallel relation scan is performed. If the expected number of rows to be scanned exceeds this number, parallel scan processes are used. The number affects that part of a query where parallelism was originated by a table scan. There may be other parts of the query that use indexes, and there may even be index-based operations, like B11M, that are parallelized because they are necessary to complete the part of the plan that includes the table scan that is now being run in parallel. (See the previous parallel discussion.)

The server uses the ROWS_PER_SCANTASK parameter value as follows to determine the maximum number of processes to use for a relation scan query:

- ◆ .Each disk group with at least the number of rows specified by ROWS_PER_SCAN_TASK is assigned a process.

- ◆ The number of rows in each disk group containing fewer than the specified number of rows is added together. This total row number is then divided by the number of rows specified by ROWS_PER_SCAN_TASK to determine how many additional processes to allocate.

 The number of rows (in a disk group) refers to the number of rows for which space has been allocated in a PSU, and this number might exceed the number of rows visible to a query; for example, space might be allocated for rows that have since been deleted.

These parameters can be set for all sessions with entries in the rbw.config file, which are read at server startup; therefore, changes are effective only for new server sessions started after the change is made. If multiple values for a given parameter are specified, the last entry of each type is used and all others are discarded. With the exception of duplicate elimination, the order of the entries has no impact. These parameters can also be set for a specific session with a SET command.

TUNE ROWS_PER_FETCH_TASK, ROWS_PER_JOIN_TASK

The ROWS_PER_FETCH_TASK and ROWS_PER_JOIN_TASK parameters determine how many parallel processes are used to process queries that use a STARindex. ROWS_PER_FETCH_TASK is the minimum estimated number of data rows that must be returned during the fetch portion of a STARjoin before parallel fetch processes are used, and ROWS_PER_JOIN_TASK is the minimum number of rows to be joined before parallel join processes will be allocated.

Because the amount of work done during the index-probing phase and the row-data-processing phase varies from query to query, you can set different limits for each phase. For example, if your queries tend to require a lot of processing after each row is fetched (GROUP BY, SUM, MIN, and so on), you should assign fewer rows per process for the fetch phase than for the join phase so that more processes are used for the fetch phase. These parameters allow you to control parallel processing for queries that use a STARindex based on the following guidelines:

- ◆ The more tightly constrained a query is on the columns that participate in the STARindex, the smaller the number of parallel processes needed to probe the index efficiently during the join phase. The ROWS_PER_JOIN_TASK parameter defines how many processes to use during the join phase.

- ◆ The more rows to be returned and/or the more processing of row data to be done, the larger the number of parallel processes that can be used effectively during the fetch phase. The ROWS_PER_FETCH_TASK parameter determines how many processes to use during the fetch phase.

When setting these parameters, remember that the settings in the rbw.config file apply to all users and all databases that are serviced by that instance of Red Brick Decision Server.

TUNE FORCE_SCAN_TASKS

The ROWS_PER_TASK parameters just discussed require that you determine a minimum number of rows needed to justify starting a parallel process, which is an implicit limit. The TUNE FORCE parameters allow you to set an explicit number of tasks to be used for a given query. This facility provides an easy way to override the default settings for these "one off" queries that require a different level of support. Except for the FORCE_HASHJOIN_TASKS parameter, the next few are analogous to the ROWS_PER_TASK parameters in their target queries.

The FORCE_SCAN_TASKS parameter controls the number of parallel tasks for relation scans of tables, just as if it's the cousin of ROWS_PER SCAN_TAKS. If the FORCE option is used, it will be assigned the lowest of the following three values:

- The FORCE_SCAN_TASKS value

- The number of PSUs over which the table is distributed

- The number of processes that can be allocated from the QUERYPROCS /TOTALQUERYPROCS pool

Using the FORCE_SCAN_TASK option does not guarantee that a certain number of parallel processes will be used. For example, assume the following settings:

FORCE_SCAN_TASKS	16
PSUs in table	18
QUERYPROCS	18
TOTALQUERYPROCS	24

Whether the FORCE_SCAN_TASKS value is used or not depends on the number of processes available from the TOTALQUERYPROCS pool. If 6 processes are already allocated, 18 processes will be available, so the FORCE_SCAN_TASKS value of 16 will be used. However, if 14 processes are currently allocated to other parallel queries, leaving only 4 available, then the FORCE value of 16 will be ignored, and you may end up with only 1 or 2 at the most. The FORCE parameters abide by the same rules of allocation as the ROWS_PER parameters in that after about 50 percent of the TOTALQUERYPROCS pool has been allocated subsequent queries are allocated fewer processes per query. This is intentional in that as the system load goes up, everyone gets a share of the resources and no one query hogs it all.

TUNE FORCE_FETCH_TASKS, TUNE FORCE_JOIN_TASKS

These parameters are used to override the setting for STARjoin processing. If either of these values is greater than or equal to 1, it will override the corresponding value set for ROWS_PER_FETCH_TASK or ROWS_PER_JOIN_TASK. However, the FORCE_FETCH_TASKS and FORCE_JOIN_TASKS values do not guarantee that a certain number of parallel processes will be used. The actual number of processes used to fetch rows will be the lowest of these three values:

◆ The FORCE_FETCH_TASKS value

◆ The number of PSUs over which the table is distributed

◆ The number of processes available from the QUERYPROCS /TOTALQUERYPROCS pool

In rare cases, the FORCE_JOIN_TASKS value might be greater than the number of STARindex rows that match the constraints in the query; therefore, it will not be possible to logically divide and process the query by the specified number of tasks. Instead, the number of matching rows will be used to set the limit on parallel join tasks.

TUNE FORCE_HASHJOIN_TASKS

The value set for FORCE_HASHJOIN_TASKS controls the number of parallel tasks for hybrid hash joins. However, the FORCE_HASHJOIN_TASKS value does not guarantee that a certain number of parallel processes will be used. The actual number of processes used will be the lowest of these following values:

◆ The FORCE_HASHJOIN_TASKS value

◆ The number of processes that can be allocated from the QUERYPROCS /TOTALQUERYPROCS pool

Also, note the following points regarding task allocation for parallel hybrid hash joins:

◆ The PARALLEL_HASHJOIN option must be set to ON, either with a SET PARALLEL_HASHJOIN ON command or a TUNE PARALLEL_HASHJOIN ON parameter, to get any parallelism from hybrid hash joins.

◆ You must have at least two more than the value you specify in FORCE_ HASHJOIN_TASKS available from the QUERYPROCS/TOTALQUERYPROCS pool to achieve that level of parallelism. For example, to get 8 parallel hash join processes, you must specify FORCE_HASHJOIN_TASKS to 8 and have at least 10 tasks available from the QUERYPROCS/TOTALQUERY PROCS pool.

Recommended NT configuration

By and large, when we talk about parallel processing, it's natural to instinctively assume that the platform is one of the UNIX flavors. However, Red Brick Decision Server can do parallel processing on an NT platform if it has the resources to do so. The next question is, "What's an appropriate NT platform?"

Outlined next is what I consider to be a reasonable platform for an NT installation of Red Brick Decision Server. Note that much of the sample database material has been written and tested on a single CPU NT workstation, with 32MB of memory and 12GB of disk, so obviously, it will run in a minimal environment.

In any event, when configuring an NT server for Red Brick Decision Server, the following configuration is perhaps a good place to start.

◆ Separate disk drives/controllers with SCSI disks.

◆ 2–4 or more CPUs depending on capacity of hardware system bus.

◆ 64–128MB RAM per CPU.

◆ High page file size (swap file recommended – between 256 to 512MB).

◆ High clock speed CPUs.

◆ Control Panel settings: network → services → Server → maximize Throughput for network applications.

◆ System performance. Set the boost performance of foreground applications to NONE.

Once the machine is configured, enabling parallel processing on NT functions as previously described. The only difference is in how you set the QUERY PROCS and TOTALQUERY PROCS parameters.

To evoke parallelism on an NT platform:

QUERY PROCS	Set to the number of CPUs.
TOTALQUERY PROCS	Each thread takes up 6 to 7MB of address space, so memory is a limiting factor here. You might start by dividing total memory by 7 to yield a maximum number and then reduce it by 20 percent to allow the system to be able to do it's housekeeping activity.

From this point on, everything else works as advertised and should be approached in much the same manner as you would a UNIX platform. I would use the initial settings previously indicated, see where you are, and adjust as necessary.

Factors That Limit Parallelism

Now that you've learned how to make the server process in parallel, it's time to talk about how to limit that processing to reasonable levels. Parallel processing for the sake of parallel processing is not only a waste of resources, it just plain doesn't make any sense. It's a balancing act between system load, user expectations, and system resources.

File groups

The FILE_GROUP parameter definitions tell a warehouse server what PSUs are on the same disk to reduce seek contention on individual disk devices; these groups of PSUs are referred to as *disk groups*. This parameter limits the amount of parallelism. In general, at most, one process will be allocated per disk group for each operation (such as a scan), unless the TUNE GROUP parameter is used to specify that more than one process can be used for a specific group.

Because of the SuperScan technology used for disk I/O, processes from multiple servers performing relation scans on tables can access the same data with a single read operation, which can reduce seek contention across server processes. These entries are read at server startup so changes will be in effect for all sessions started after a change to the rbw.config file.

The number of processes applied to index join tasks is also limited by the number of file groups in which the segments for the selected STARindex reside. For example, for two processes to be used to perform a STARjoin, the index must be spread over at least two file groups. If it is fewer than two file groups, only one process will be applied (unless you force parallelism with the FORCE_JOIN_TASKS parameter or specify more than one disk group process with the GROUP parameter. In this instance, the extra processes will be created, but may not do any work at all). In general, if you examine the segments in which the STARindex resides, the limit on the amount of parallelism used in the join tasks is the number of file groups covered by those segments.

The number of groups that the data object resides over is generally considered the maximum number of processes that can be used to process that object. In other words, the fewer number of groups the data is spread across, the lower the number of processes that can be used.

System load and resources

Another limitation is the possibility that the system might be unable to allocate the number of desired processes because of constraints on one or more of the following:

- ◆ I/O activity

- ◆ Memory

- ◆ CPU availability

- ◆ Available parallel system tasks

Enabling Parallel Query Processing

To enable parallel processing, you must set the QUERYPROCS and TOTALQUERYPROCS parameters in the rbw.config file to a value greater than 1.

To recap briefly, you can control the extent of parallelism for query processing in either of two ways:

- ◆ Specify the minimum number of rows you want a task to process with the ROWS_PER_TASK parameters, which prevent incurring the overhead of parallel processing for trivial queries. These parameters are intended to handle the general-purpose, day-to-day processing.

- ◆ Specify the number of parallel tasks you want to use to process a query regardless of the number of rows per task by using the FORCE_TASKS parameters. These parameters, which allow you more control over CPU resources, are designed for use on specific queries on which you want to specify the number of parallel processes to be used to get the query processed quickly, regardless of the resources used. These parameters override the ROWS_PER_TASK parameters.

All parameters can be entered as TUNE parameters in the rbw.config file so they affect all server sessions; the order of these parameters in the rbw.config file is not significant. Alternatively, you can enter them as SQL SET statements, in which case they affect only the current session.

In any case, all these parameters are subject to the allocation process discussed in detail previously. Setting or forcing a particular parameter value in no way guarantees that a specific number of processes will be allocated to the query.

Enabling Parallel Aggregation

Partitioned parallel aggregation is a Red Brick Decision Server facility in which queries that involve aggregation functions (SUM, MIN, MAX, COUNT) over groups specified in the GROUP BY clause can have the grouping functions done in parallel. For this to be beneficial and pay for itself, there must be a significant number of groups to aggregate over – for example, hundreds of thousands or millions. This is because parallel tasks are expensive, and there should be enough work to make them cost-effective.

Note that even if this option is not enabled, the server *may* still compute aggregates and group by operations in parallel.

For relatively small numbers of groups, the performance is generally better with PARTITIONED PARALLEL AGGREGATION set to OFF. With PARTITIONED PARALLEL AGGREGATION set to on, the number of processes can potentially double because you now have to take into account the number of processes needed for the parallel aggregation plus the number of processes needed for the rest of the query processing. Therefore, to ensure that the same amount of resources are available to parallel query operations as before, you should consider increasing the values of the QUERYPROCS and TOTALQUERYPROCS parameters as discussed in the next section.

Partitioned parallelism is also very effective when you are populating tables with INSERT INTO...SELECT...FROM...GROUP BY operations and is particularly effective when there are a large number of groups. Consider this option when creating aggregate tables based on feedback from the Vista advisor.

Evaluating Parallel Performance

Getting the best performance on parallel queries depends on the degree to which you can exploit concurrency and load balancing across a system, a task that requires careful planning even before you load the database. It's very difficult to provide rules for evaluating performance because there are so many tradeoffs to be made, and each situation is different. There are, however, three general comments that will help you keep everything in perspective.

Parallel everything isn't the answer

Parallel processing is expensive. It costs something to spawn and manage parallel tasks and shouldn't be used indiscriminately. Parallel query processing is really a method to manage queries that require a larger amount of work to be done than normal. The definition of "normal" is site-specific; however, the expectations should be that not every query sent to the server would process in parallel. In the final analysis, most of the users probably don't care whether the query was parallel, as long as the results are right and the time to get them is reasonable (within the expectation you've been setting all along).

Considerations for multiuser environments

Multiuser environments bring with them several areas for you to pay attention to when evaluating queries in general and parallel queries in particular. Although few in number, these issues can have a large impact on the performance of your system. In a multiuser environment consider the following:

◆ Disk contention

◆ File groups

◆ Concurrent users

◆ CPU availability

DISK CONTENTION

To reduce disk contention and increased I/O activity, I/O load should be distributed evenly across as many physical disks as there are parallel processes. The object is to reduce the time a query waits because its processes are blocked on I/O. Ideally, no more than one disk group, as defined by the FILE_GROUP parameter, should be assigned to one physical disk. Disk arrays or disks grouped together using a logical volume manager facility are exceptions; in these cases, there are always multiple physical disks grouped together as one logical disk.

FILE GROUPS

If there are multiple files (PSUs) per physical disk, these files should normally be organized into a single disk group using the FILE_GROUP parameter. Such an organization ensures that I/O can be scheduled evenly and reduces excessive head movements on the disk, which is especially important for parallel scans where it is desirable to have an orderly sequential access on the file and to take advantage of any available read-ahead capability as much as possible. In some cases where disk arrays or disks are grouped together, such as striped disks or RAID systems, or where the query workload is CPU-intensive rather than I/O-bound and there is excess CPU capacity, better performance might result from allowing more than one process per disk group. If you want to allow parallel processes within a disk group for a query, use the TUNE GROUP parameter to specify the number of processes.

CONCURRENT USERS

The number of concurrently active users will determine the memory demand and paging/swapping activities in the system at any one time. Three users probably will not introduce heavy paging/swapping activities in the system. However, if there are 50 concurrently active users, examine carefully whether there is enough memory to support them. If there is not enough memory, thrashing will occur, resulting in very heavy paging/swapping activities. When the system is up and running, monitor the paging/swapping activities.

Acceptable values for paging and swapping vary depending on system size and speed. Rather than using generic values that may or may not apply to your system, a better approach is to monitor the system when it is not performing optimally; the paging/swapping disks will indicate when the settings are not right. The two indicators to monitor are the waiting for I/O (WIO) percentage in the System Activity Report (SAR) or an equivalent performance-monitoring tool and the disk service time.

You can also evaluate disk usage based on busy percentage, disk request queue, and disk waiting time. If all these indicators are high, users are probably kept waiting while the system is busy paging or thrashing in memory. To decrease the wait time, you can add more paging /swapping devices, reduce parallelism, or add memory.

CPU AVAILABILITY

The degree of concurrency in parallel processing largely depends on how many CPUs are available. Although allocating all the CPUs in the system might yield the best results, this option is often impractical because other work in the system could be competing for CPU resources. If the CPUs are used for parallel query processing, other users would experience a slowdown because CPU resources are less available to them. Therefore, each administrator must decide how the CPU resources are to be distributed. Of course, if all the CPUs are already saturated (that is, 100 percent busy), there will be no gain and perhaps even a slight degradation from parallel processing.

After you have determined the number of CPUs to use for parallel query processing, you can derive an initial value for the number of parallel processes (QUERYPROCS) as follows:

◆ For queries that are CPU-intensive, set the QUERYPROCS parameter to the number of CPUs divided by the number of concurrently active users.

◆ For queries that are not very CPU-intensive but are I/O-intensive, set the QUERYPROCS parameter to two or three times the value derived for CPU-intensive queries. Monitor the CPU-busy statistic to determine whether more parallel processes are needed.

The following suggestions provide some basic guidelines for setting "reasonable" values. Remember, however, each system and workload is unique, so you must experiment to determine what works best at your site:

◆ Set the ROWS_PER_JOIN, ROWS_PER_FETCH, and SCAN_TASK values fairly high.

◆ Set the values for ROWS_PER_JOIN_TASK and ROWS_PER_FETCH_TASK to the same value.

◆ Set QUERYPROCS as just discussed.

◆ Set TOTALQUERYPROCS to at least two to three times QUERYPROCS, or even higher if memory is available.

◆ If multiple PSUs for the same table are on the same disk device, define a disk group (file group) for those PSUs.

◆ In most cases, you do not need to set the TUNE GROUP parameter: generally, only one process per disk group is best.

Lessons from the Trenches

Parallel processing is perhaps the least understood component of Red Brick Decision Server technology. Although the mechanics may seem a little on the technical side, the basic fundamentals of how it was designed to work are quite simple. Much of my performance tuning activities while at Red Brick were centered around parallel queries and the configuration parameters that control them.

There are only three lessons from the trench for this chapter; however, they are of paramount importance. These are based on a tremendous amount of firsthand tuning experience and have been proven time and time again.

Don't over-parallelize

One of the most frequent mistakes people make is to over-parallelize their environment. The best approach is to configure your system as defined in Chapter 10, and then, based on query performance and user loads, adjust as necessary. If you over-parallelize right from the start, you will have a much harder time trying to determine exactly where the performance problems are coming from. Being able to pinpoint the source of a problem is necessary in order to take the correct actions to resolve it. Over-parallelized environments often lead to resolutions to nonexistent problems because the real issue was masked by the parallel processing activity.

Start conservatively

This is related to over-parallelization in that whatever you do, you should start with conservative settings. A little parallel resource can go a long way towards addressing performance problems. Again, it's not about using every last ounce of resources on the machine, but rather about providing the right amount of resources for the task at hand without penalizing other users or processes.

Parallelism won't fix everything

The other mistake frequently made is the assumption that increased parallelism can compensate for every and all types of problems. This is not true. Parallel processing will not fix bad data models, poor or nonexistent indexes, or poorly formed queries. If you parallelize a bad query, what you end up with is a bad parallel query. Yes, it might be a bit faster, but it's still less than it could be if the underlying problems were addressed.

Parallelism and scalability go hand in hand, and they are not a panacea. Red Brick Decision Server gives you the ability to implement parallelism on demand. Often, you will hear from other vendors that if you want faster response time, you should add more processors. However, if you take an inherently poor join algorithm like pairwise join and multiply it by eight processors, it just ends up making the problem worse. It will give you short-term relief, but you haven't addressed the real problem. Perhaps the best way to think of parallel processing in a multiuser scalable environment is as a mechanism for maintaining a consistent level of performance for large volumes of users.

Summary

There are a number of ways to control the amount of parallelism in the Red Brick Decision Server environment. The settings in the rbw.config file apply to all databases and users attached to that server instance. You can override these settings with the TUNE parameters for those queries that require more work to process than normal.

The execution of parallel queries on UNIX and NT platforms is the same, although the implementation is operating-system-specific. Parallelism is largely limited to the number of file groups over which the data object is spread. In general, the number of file groups represents an upper limit.

You should approach parallel processing conservatively – it's too easy to mask and/or hide (for a while, anyway) more fundamental system flaws by applying more resources to the problem. This is a temporary fix, and once you've exhausted the available resources and need more performance, there is no place left to get it. This is a very painful place to be. Parallelism is not a fix-all, but rather a tool to provide reasonable performance across the concurrent user base while at the same time applying more resources to queries that really need it.

Chapter 14

Maintaining a Red Brick Decision Server Warehouse

IN THIS CHAPTER

◆ New Dimensions

◆ Altering tables and indexes

◆ Managing segments

◆ Segments and time-cyclic data

◆ Validating tables and indexes

◆ Copying and moving a database

◆ Maintaining the sample database

◆ Lessons from the trenches

ONCE THE WAREHOUSE IS up and running, you will almost always need to add new data, enhance system performance, or modify the schema in one way or another to accommodate new or more complicated requests from the user community. This is normal and should be expected. Unfortunately, however, little is said about how to accomplish these maintenance types of tasks, especially with a large warehouse. Most often, the issues suggesting that such adjustments are needed are either ignored completely or glossed over in such a way as to imply they are not crucial. As in every other step in this process, you must consider implications associated with maintenance issues and functions before blindly going off and adding tables and indexes to an otherwise perfectly working warehouse.

In this chapter, I address some of the most common issues that arise in a post-production environment. Some issues to be aware of in making changes include adding new dimensions, altering tables and indexes, adding columns, changing data types, and managing segments to roll data into and out of the warehouse.

We'll also review the implications of using check table and check index functions, as well as learn how to move a database using copy management. We'll also briefly discuss planning scheduled downtime as a way to accommodate changes,

341

perform maintenance, and add functionality such that everyone should be able to live with it (or at least accept it).

New Dimensions

Frequently, one of the first things that happens after the warehouse is live and accessible to the users is that somebody says, "If I only had this extra data, I'd have it made." If I had a nickel for every time I've heard that, I'd buy myself an island and retire. Once the user community learns how to use the warehouse, they begin to leverage it in their workday routines, and this is what drives new features, new data, new performance requirements, and new functionality.

Perhaps the most frequently asked question is, "How do I put new data into the warehouse?" Well, it depends on which type of data it is (facts or dimensions) and what you want to do with it. If you stop to think about it, this is no different than identifying the data sources for the original project, except that where no database existed before, you now have a warehouse in which it all has to fit. Most importantly, any new data added must not change the meaning or grain of existing tables.

Adding new dimensions

Do not be misled by the perceived simplicity of adding new dimensions to an existing warehouse. Build a table and load the data into it — simple. On the surface, it is; however, there is more to it than that. Specifically, if you're adding a new dimension, how is it connected to the existing fact table(s)?

It's not enough to simply add a new table; you must also be able to provide a valid foreign key reference to any existing fact tables with which you wish to connect the new dimension. Additionally, you must also be sure that the new dimension does not change the grain of the fact table. It's okay if the grain is at a higher level than the facts, but it cannot be lower.

Connecting to existing fact tables

The second and usually more work-intensive step is to create the appropriate foreign key reference between the fact table and the new dimension. This can be as simple as creating a new constraint on the fact table in question, to unloading, updating, re-creating, and reloading the fact table data. If the data objects are large, this can be very time consuming.

For example, let's assume that we want to expand the sample database and keep track of the carrier for all long-distance calls made. To accommodate this change, we would have to add the CARRIER table as a foreign key to the BILLING_CDR table. The CARRIER table already exists — it's a foreign key to the CHURN table — but it's not connected to the BILLING_CDR table.

If we were carrying a column on the fact row that represented the carrier key, it would be a simple matter of creating the appropriate constraint on the BILLING_CDR table back to the CARRIER table and we'd be finished. This is an oversimplified example, but it illustrates the point.

If the data doesn't exist in the fact table to begin with, then you have a much bigger job on your hands. In effect, you have to add a new column to the fact table and populate it with appropriate foreign key values.

This means that for every existing fact table row, once you have created the new column (as would be the case if we were attaching CARRIER to BILLING_CDR), you would have to update each fact row. To update each fact row, you would have to find the data with which to populate the new column in each of the 30 million existing fact rows.

The larger the table fact table in question is, the more resource-intensive the process will be. Frequently, it's better to unload the data in external format, update, drop, and re-create the table, and then update the data and reload it into the new table, all with the proper constraints already in place.

Altering Tables and Indexes

This business of altering tables in your warehouse has a mystique about it that I don't quite understand. Many folks shudder at the thought of having to do it, and some even go so far as to add extra columns to their tables just in case. This is a practice I don't recommend, as it generally just leads to as much or more work than adding columns as you go. Fortunately, thanks to many of the early Red Brick customers, early on, Red Brick was able to understand the impact of large data objects in terms of both query processing and performing "routine" maintenance.

Adding columns

You can also add new data to the warehouse by adding columns to your tables and populating them as appropriate. Like anything else, there are implications to this process that you must take into account.

NONKEY COLUMNS
Nonkey columns are the easiest type of column to add (although easy is indeed a relative term). If you look at the ALTER TABLE command in the *SQL Reference Guide*, you will see the following syntax diagram for the ALTER TABLE command:

```
ALTER TABLE table_name add column column_name;
```

PRIMARY AND FOREIGN KEY COLUMNS
You cannot add primary key constraints to an existing table. The only way to accomplish this is to unload, drop, and re-create the table with the appropriate primary key definition, and then reload the data. You can, however, add and drop a foreign key column. Perhaps the best way to accomplish this is through the Administrator.

IN PLACE

The IN PLACE phrase refers to where the columns are to be added (or dropped) in the segment that currently contains the row or into a completely new segment. IN PLACE means exactly that — modify the rows in the place they currently reside (read segment). If you are adding columns to a table, each segment must be large enough to hold all of its newly expanded rows. If not, you will get an error.

IN SEGMENT

The IN SEGMENT phrase provides a mechanism that allows you to modify the table and write the resulting modified rows to a new set of segments. This is your only option when the result of adding a column will exceed the size of the segment. As a practical matter, all rows are copied from the old segments and written to the new segments with the ADD (or DROP) operation applied as the rows are being written.

Using the IN SEGMENT phrase has two stipulations regarding how many new segments the data can be written to. If the table existed in a single segment prior to adding or dropping a column, then the IN SEGMENT clause can reference only a single new segment. If the table existed in multiple segments prior to the ADD or DROP operation, then the IN SEGMENT clause must reference the same number of new segments as old segments. Note that the original segments are dropped or detached, depending on what type of segments they are. Named segments are detached (separated from the table but still existing as a data object to be reused), and default segments are dropped (that is, erased completely).

The new or existing segments of a table must always be large enough to hold the resulting rows produced by an ADD COLUMN or DROP COLUMN operation. If not, you will receive an error.

Changing column data type

Changing a column's data type is the most time-consuming operation associated with modifying your tables. There are several reasons for this, all of them physical in nature. As you saw from the discussion on object sizing, every data type has an internal storage size associated with it. Different data types have different sizes, which impacts data and index storage. Changing data types once the table exists and is loaded with data can lead to disastrous results for your segmentation. Two options are available to you to accomplish this.

Unload/reload the table	This option is the most time-consuming and requires you to unload the data, edit the DDL required to create the table, drop and re-create the table, and then reload its data.

Alter the table

This option requires you to add the new column (perhaps with a temporary name) with the correct data type using an ALTER TABLE statement. Next, you issue an UPDATE statement to copy the data from the old column to the new column. Next, you issue an ALTER TABLE statement to drop the old column, and finally, you issue another ALTER TABLE statement to rename the new column as required.

Be sure that the data that existed in the column prior to changing the data type is consistent with the new data type, or you'll have to add a conversion step to accommodate the change. You don't want to do this on a regular basis, and as I've pointed out in other chapters, a little planning goes a long way.

If you choose the second option, you must first make sure that the table segmentation is large enough to hold both the old column and the new column. If it's not, you will have to add the appropriate space to the segments to perform the operation. If you don't, the process will run out of space and abort with an error.

Changing MAXROWS and MAXSEGMENTS

Sometimes it becomes necessary to adjust either the number of segments that a table has, the maximum number of rows allowed in a segment, or both. The server uses these two values to calculate the size of STARindexes and to validate the segmentation of those indexes. Changes to these values can have far-reaching effects, and you should consider them carefully.

MAXROWS PER SEGMENT

This value determines the maximum number of rows that can exist in any given segment. It applies equally to all segments and is defined when the table is created. STARindex space is allocated in bits, with as many bits as necessary to represent the actual number of rows expected in the segment. Because the space is allocated in this way, you must understand the concept of bit boundaries to fully appreciate the next few points.

A bit boundary is the highest value that can fit in a given number of bits and is nothing more than powers of 2:

```
2^2 = 4
2^3 = 8
2^4 = 16
2^5 = 32
```

and so on.

This means that if a dimension table has eight values, the server will allocate 3 bits to store the references. Sixteen values get 4 bits. As you can see, it is an exponential function. Let's say you have a table with an initial MAXROWS PER SEGMENT value of 12, meaning that there will only ever be a maximum of 12 rows per segment. Then let's assume that there is a business reason to add more rows to the table, perhaps because you just developed some new products to bring the total to 15.

If you change the MAXROWS PER SEGMENT to 15, everything should be fine because the value of 12 is stored in the same number of bits as the value of 15. On the other hand, if you added eight new products, then it gets interesting.

The value of 20 can be stored in only 5 bits. The initial value was stored in 4 bits. When the MAXROWS PER SEGMENT crosses this bit boundary, all the STARindexs will be invalid. In fact, if you attempt to change the value past the range specifications, you will get an error message identifying the STARindexs in question. The only real solution for this is to unload the table, drop the table, change the MAXROWS PER SEGMENT value, re-create the table, and reload the data. This is not my idea of the best way to spend a Saturday.

Changing either the MAXROWS or the MAXSEGMENTS values impacts the space the server thinks is allocated to the table. One easy way to check the effects of any changes to these values is to multiply the new MAXROWS PER SEGMENT value by the MAXSEGMENTS value. Then compare the result to the value stored in the MAXSIZE_ROWS column of the RBW_TABLES system table for the table you are working on. If the new parameters yield a value higher than MAXSIXE_ROWS, you will have to add space to the segments because you will run out of space before you have reached the new limit.

Your best bet is to determine the number of rows expected, and, depending on the growth you expect, either designate the maximum MAXROWS value for the number of bits necessary to hold your data or specify a maximum value of the next higher number of bits.

Don't be in a huge rush to plug in large MAXROWS values as a way to reduce your maintenance time. Remember, everything costs something. You will have to make some tradeoffs as the data objects in question get larger and larger. It can be very misleading when you use examples with just a few rows, but consider the following.

It takes 19 bits to hold 524,288 values, 20 bits gets you 1,048,576 values, and 21 bits yields 2,097,152 values that can be stored. Relative to a STARindex, 21 bits is not exactly the skinniest index section in the world, and it costs you something to traverse a STARindex section this wide.

The best STARindex performance occurs when the MAXROWS PER SEGMENT value accurately represents the number of rows in the largest segment you expect to have. The largest segment might be a history segment you already have data for, it could be a segment, or it could be a segment of data for a future time period. You must consider the growth of the data over the planning horizon because the MAXROWS value applies to all segments.

Generally speaking, the MAXROW PER SEGMENT value is arrived at by calculating the sum of the number of rows you plan to load initially, and then factoring in the growth expected over the planning horizon. Once this value is known, you can calculate the number of bits required to store the calculated number of rows. Once the number of bits required is known, you can then increase the MAXROWS PER SEGMENT value to the maximum number of rows the calculated number of bits can represent. This is a slight departure from past Red Brick thinking. See the Sidebar for more information.

Later in this chapter, I'll discuss planning horizon and routine maintenance, but for now, I strongly caution you against supplying artificially large MAXROWS values as a way to minimize your maintenance tasks.

MAXSEGMENTS

The MAXSEGMENTS parameter has much the same function as the MAXROWS PER SEGMENT parameter, and indeed, they are usually referred to as a pair in most of the Red Brick Decision Server documentation. This parameter indicates the maximum number of segments that a table will have. For dimension tables, this value is usually 1. Fact tables are usually more.

This parameter is defined when the table is created and is also used to create STARindexes. Space is allocated in the index to keep track of the segment in which the row pointed to in the index resides.

Much of the discussion about MAXROWS PER SEGMENT applies to MAXSEGMENTS, although the frequency of change is much smaller and you don't have so much trouble with the bit boundary issues represented by the MAXROWS PER SEGMENT parameter discussed above. However, it is still possible to create a problem if you decide to double the number of segments you want to keep. Proper planning is the key to avoiding this issue.

Managing Segments

Managing segments will most likely take up the most time in warehouse administration because you're always adding new data and archiving older data. Red Brick Decision Server has a very robust and flexible segmentation management capability that provides a simple yet effective means of managing potentially large amounts of data as a single object.

You accomplish segment management by using the ALTER SEGMENT command. *The SQL Reference Guide* contains a more in-depth discussion of the ALTER SEGMENT command; however, using this facility, you can perform a number of operations including the following:

- ◆ DETACH segments – Separates a segment from a table with the content intact.

- ◆ VERIFY – Examines the PSUs in the specified segment and determines if they are damaged in some way.

- ◆ FORCE INTACT – Forces a segment to be viewed by the server as intact and ready to go. Use this with caution: unlike the VERIFY option, FORCE INTACT does not interrogate the PSUs.

- ◆ Adjust the SEGMENT BY and RANGE values – Specifies the column to segment by, and the range of values in that column that apply to each segment.

- ◆ ONLINE – Makes a previously OFFLINE segment available to the database.

- ◆ CLEAR – Deletes all the rows in a data segment and all index entries from all indexes that reference that data segment.

- ◆ RENAME – Changes the name of the specified segment. This is very useful when rolling data in and out of the system.

- ◆ CHANGE MAXSIZE – Allows you to change the maximum size of a PSU. You cannot change the MAXSIZE of a PSU if the next PSU contains data.

- ◆ CHANGE EXTEND SIZE – Changes the amount of space by which a PSU will expand each time it needs to expand. It will expand by this increment until the MAXZISE value has been reached.

- ◆ CHANGE PATH – Changes the location of the specified PSU. Using the ALTER SEGMENT CHANGE PATH command does not physically move the PSU; it only updates the LOCATION column in the RBW_STORAGE table. You must use the appropriate operating system command to physically move the PSU.

- ◆ MIGRATE TO – Allows you to copy an entire segment to another location.

- ◆ Add COMMENTs – Adds a comment to the segment.

- ◆ Add new PSUs to the segment – Allows you to add new PSUs to accommodate the new data as the segment grows.

This list, although brief in its descriptions, illustrates just how powerful the segmentation concept is and how Red Brick Decision Server provides the necessary tools to manage it. *SQL Guide* and the *Warehouse Administrator's Guide* contain more detailed information in the ALTER SEGMENT command, and you should review it the first few times you need to perform an operation on a segment.

 TIP You might want to think about maintaining a backup of the segment you plan to work on in case you have a problem while working with it. I realize that these segments can get quite large, but it's nice to have a safety net.

Segments and Time-Cyclic Data

Chapter 9 discussed segmentation as a data management tool with performance benefits, but we didn't spend a lot of time discussing the mechanics of exactly how this management is practiced. If you recall from the earlier segmentation discussions in Chapter 9, the whole idea is that data will flow into and out of the warehouse regularly, but on an infrequent basis to provide a rolling time frame effect to the data.

For example, the sample database is initially set up to be rolling four weeks; no fact table data will be more than four weeks old. When week five comes along, week one goes away, week six replaces week two, week seven replaces week three, and so forth.

Roll-Off

The process of taking the oldest data out of the warehouse is called *rolling off*. In most instances, the data doesn't actually go away; it is archived in some way so that it is available to be brought back at a later date, perhaps for some special research or other one-time analysis. The data is rolled off in single segment-size chunks, meaning that if I segment by month, I generally roll the data off by month. This is not a hard-and-fast rule but a general observation. It's possible to segment your data by week, and at the end of the month, roll off four weeks' worth of data. It's a tradeoff among administration, data size, and environment, to name a few.

The big assumption here is that you have segmented your data and indexes in the same way, meaning that for every data segment, there is a corresponding index segment. This means that the column used to segment the data is the first column in all the STAR indexes attached to the fact table. If this assumption is not true, then the time and effort to accomplish a roll-off will be much higher, primarily because the server will have to interrogate each entry in each index to determine whether it can be removed. The other option is to drop the indexes and rebuild them once the data has been removed, but that is rarely a valid option.

Assuming you have backed up the data in the segment prior to this step, the procedure to roll data off looks like this:

1. Take the segment to be rolled off offline with the ALTER SEGMENT command:

   ```
   ALTER SEGMENT segment_name OF TABLE table_name OFFLINE;
   ```

2. Clear the segment (remove all the data from it) by using the DETACH option like this:

   ```
   ALTER SEGMENT segment_name of TABLE table_name DETACH
   OVERRIDE FULLINDEXCHECK ON SEGMENTS (star_index
   segment_name);
   ```

The OVERRIDEFULLINDEXCHECK option takes advantage of data and indexes that are segmented in the same way. It assumes that all index entries for the data segment (segment_name) exist in the STARindex segment (star_index_segment_name). This means that the server does not have to interrogate each index entry to see if it should be removed or not — it already knows where all the index entries are.

If you do not have identically segmented STARindexes and data, then do not use the OVERRIDEFULLINDEXCHECK option. If this clause is absent, then each index is probed and the appropriate index entries are removed.

3. Take the index segment offline with:

```
ALTER SEGMENT star_index_segment_name OF INDEX index_name
OFFLINE;
```

4. Detach this segment and remove all the index entries from the index with:

```
ALTER SEGMENT index_segment_name OF INDEX index_name DETACH;
```

5. Rename the old data and index segments so they accurately represent the data they will eventually hold using the following:

```
ALTER SEGMENT old_data_segment_name RENAME
new_data_segment_name;
```

and

```
ALTER SEGMENT old_index_segment_name RENAME
new_index_segment_name;
```

At this point, you may want to investigate to be sure that newly renamed segments will be large enough to hold the new data coming in. To that end, you may want to add PSUs, change maxsize values, or change path or locations.

6. Attach the renamed segments to the table and index, being sure to use the correct range definitions and references as follows:

```
ALTER SEGMENT new_data_segment_name  ATTACH TO TABLE
table_name
Range (DATE'1999-02-01':DATE'1997-02-8');
```

The index segment is attached like this:

```
ALTER SEGMENT new_index_segment_name ATTACH TO INDEX
index_name
Range(28:35);
```

Recall that star indexes are built using row references (or row numbers), so the implication is that the segmenting table (in this case, PERIOD) actually contains those rows necessary. If not, when you load the new segment, the data rows will be discarded for RI.

Notice that attaching a segment table of index sets the segment to an ONLINE mode and makes it available.

7. At this point, you can load your new data via the TMU or use SQL insert commands to populate the new segment. This is what's known as an ONLINE load, meaning that the data and index segments are attached to the table while the load is in progress.

If you are in a situation where you must perform off-line loads, the procedure is slightly different; however, you can follow the previous procedure up to the point where the newly renamed segments are reattached to the table. From that point, you must do the following:

1. Be sure the segment in question is truly off-line with the following:

```
ALTER SEGMENT NEW renamed_data_segment_name OFFLINE;
```

2. Create a working segment to provide space to build the index entries for the offline data segment as follows:

```
CREATE SEGMENT working_segment STORAGE path/filename MAXSIZE
maximum_space_required;
```

3. Create a TMU file to load the data. You will also need to perform a TMU SYNCH operation once the data is loaded, but because the SYNCH operation actually locks the table, thereby preventing others from running queries against it, you may want to load the data with one TMU control statement and perform the SYNCH statement with another TMU control statement at a time better suited to locking the table.

4. Load the new data and set the data segment to ONLINE mode using:

```
ALTER SEGMENT data_segment_name OF TABLE table_name ONLINE;
```

5. Perform the SYNCH operation prior to placing the data segment online. The SYNCH operation is what merges the index entries in the work segment into the existing index(es) of the table.

6. Drop the work segment.

Adding and extending PSUs and segments

You add PSUs to a segment by using the ALTER SEGMENT ADD STORAGE command. A segment can contain multiple PSUs, and each PSU can be a different size. You can also change the maxsize or extendsize of a PSU, provided that the PSU following the one you want to work on (the PSU with the next highest sequence number than the PSU you are working with) is empty.

Recovering a damaged segment

You will inevitably encounter situations in which a segment becomes damaged. The damage actually occurs to one or more PSUs within the segment because, as explained in Chapter 9, a segment is really a virtual object. This damage can be caused by one or more of the following:

- ◆ A missing PSU

- ◆ Inadequate file system permissions

- ◆ I/O errors

- ◆ Operating system errors or conditions

- ◆ Network conditions or errors

- ◆ Improper process termination

 One of the most frequent cautions issued to Red Brick Decision Server DBAs is not to terminate warehouse processes outside the server unless it's absolutely necessary. This indiscriminate process termination has created a much larger problem for the DBA than he or she might have expected, and, as usual, termination generally comes at the worst possible moment. Red Brick Decision Server provides the facility to terminate a process should that become necessary. You should not undertake any other termination procedures without the direction of Informix technical support.

Determining which segments are damaged is the first step. Often, if the problem is large enough, you may have more than one segment with a problem, and you should verify the extent of the problem before you go about fixing anything. You can do this by running the following simple queries that look through the RBW_SEGMENTS table and report all those with an intact value of N:

```
Select name, tname, iname, intact from rbw_segments
Where intact='N';
```

You can also find damaged tables of indexes by running these simple queries:

```
Select name, intact from rbw_tables where intact='N';
Select name, intact form rbw_indexes where intact='N';
```

Once you have identified the PSUs in question, you must then determine if the PSUs are indeed damaged. If the cause of the problem is minor, such as network connections, file permissions, or other temporary issues, you can force the segment to be intact with the following command:

```
alter segment segment_name of table table_name force intact;
```

For index segments, the command looks like this:

```
alter segment segment_name of index index_name force intact;
```

Use the FORCE command carefully and only after you have determined that the PSUs in question are indeed okay. The FORCE command updates the intact column in the systems tables and does nothing to validate the physical status of the PSU.

If, on the other hand, the segment is physically damaged in some way, you have more steps to go through. You must decide whether or not to take the segment offline and provide partial availability to the user community. This allows queries to continue to run against the table but not against the broken segment. Any queries that require data contained in the broken segment receive a warning message indicating that some of the data is unavailable.

Next you must determine the cause of the damage by using the ALTER SEGMENT VERIFY command, as follows:

```
alter segment segment_name of table table_name verify;
```

For index segments, the command looks like this:

```
Alter segment segment_name if index index_name verify;
```

Once the VERIFY procedure has completed, you will have the necessary information to determine the root cause of the problem. Addressing all the causes that can render segments invalid would be a daunting task; however, as indicated earlier, they can run from simple problems such as file permissions to complex and sometimes irreparable problems such as a disk crash or other hard system error.

This example only serves to point out that you should be prepared to restore the segment from a backup, or otherwise reload the segment data. The whole question of backup and recovery is too complex to adequately address here; however, it tends to be much more involved and complicated in a warehouse situation because the data objects are so large.

Validating Tables and Indexes

Two utilities you need to be aware of when performing maintenance on your data warehouse are Ixvalid and Tblchk. Both are critical tools in detecting and repairing indexes and tables should you have a problem that results in some amount of corruption.

IXVALID

IXVALID checks the indexes for corruption and can be used on any type of Red Brick Decision Server index: STARindex, TARGETindex, or b-tree indexes. Ixvalid works by scanning the index in question and checking for corrupted entries. Ixvalid also reports configuration and size information for the index that includes the following:

- ◆ Size and type of the index key

- ◆ The maximum number of entries per index block

- ◆ The number of segments that the index is in

When operating on STARindexes, ixvalid reports the MAXROWS PER SEGMENT value for each dimension table referenced in that particular index. The size information for STARindexes also includes the following:

- ◆ The number of index entries

- ◆ The number of index blocks used as leaf nodes and inner nodes for each segment of the index

To use ixvalid, you must run it from an account that has read permissions on the system tables and the files that make up the index being checked. Perhaps the easiest way to ensure that ixvalid has the required access rights is to run it as the warehouse administrative user. You must also set the RB_PATH environment variable to point to the directory containing the database.

Ixvalid is invoked as follows:

```
Usage:  ixvalid [-summarize] [-check_rows] [-dump_rows] [-
dump_keyinfo] <indexname> [segmentname]
```

where

- ◆ <indexname> specifies the index to be checked.

- ◆ [segmentname] specifies a segment of the index that needs to be checked. [segmentname] can be used in conjunction with all of the listed options.

When specified, ixvalid validates only the specified index segment and displays results pertaining only to that segment. It should be specified as the last argument.

Note that to run ixvalid over an index with a delimited identifier (meaning that there is a space or other special character in the index name), you must put single quotes (') around the delimited identifier. For example:

```
$ ixvalid '"My Index"'
```

performs an ixvalid operation on an index named My Index.

Additionally, you can use a number of command-line switches with ixvalid. Here is what they do:

summarize	Displays the configuration information quickly and then terminates without validating the index or calculating the size information. Use the summarize option if you are interested only in the configuration information because ixvalid takes a significant amount of time to validate a very large index.
check_rows	Traverses the index and, for each index key, fetches the row from the table that the index references. It compares the key in the row to the key in the index to ensure that they match, and it also ensures that each index entry points to a unique row and that every row in the referenced table is pointed to by one index entry. This is a very slow operation, even on modestly sized tables, because the entire index is read and checked, top to bottom, and every row it references is read. In many cases, it's much easier (and faster) to drop the index in question and re-create it. You can specify the deferred keyword and then use the parallel reorganization feature to build it even faster.
dump_rows	Prints out each index entry in the index. It prints from one to three lines per index entry and therefore can generate a lot of output.
dump_keyinfo	Prints the key, the key representation for the index, and the number of rows represented by that key. This option is most useful for TARGET indexes. For b-tree and STAR indexes, it might generate a lot of output.

-et_index_valid_flag	Indicates index validity by using a flag kept in the RBW_INDEXES system table. You can force an index marked invalid to be valid by using this option on the ixvalid command line. Using this option only sets the flag; it doesn't do anything to physically correct the index.
[segmentname]	ixvalid can be run on a specific segment of an index. To do this, specify the segment you want ixvalid to check as the last parameter in the ixvalid command, and it will only check that segment. Note that since you are only checking one segment, ixvalid cannot guarantee that every row in the table is only pointed to by only one index entry because entries in other segments could point to rows in the segment being examined and index entries in the current segment could point to the data rows in other segments. ixvalid will do all the other validations as described.

TBLCHK

The TBLCHK utility checks and optionally repairs certain types of damage to a table. If any repairs are done, the table must be reorganized using the TMU REORG command. In addition, you must be the administrator to run this utility.

The command is invoked as follows:

```
$tblchk <tablename> [-d|-s] [-f] [-w] [segmentname]
```

where

- ◆ <tablename> is the name of the table whose data is to be scanned.

- ◆ [segmentname] is the name of the segment that needs to be checked for consistency. If a segment name is specified, the utility reports only on that segment, thereby saving a considerable amount of time when validation is required only on a specific segment.

There are several command line options that can be used as follows:

- ◆ Detailed or summary mode — Either -d or -s can be specified on the command line, with the -d option as the default. These options indicate whether the analysis should result in a detailed (-d) or summary (-s) report.

- ◆ Fix damage — The -f option indicates that you want tblchk to try to repair any damage it finds.

- ◆ Lock wait — The -w option instructs tblchk to wait for the appropriate table locks to be granted before proceeding. Without the -w option, if locks are asked for and denied, tblchk terminates.

Copying and Moving a Database

Early in Red Brick Decision Server history, our consultants and SEs found a need to make copies of tables or whole databases for testing purposes or for training and porting to another operating system. You might think that just copying the required files would be sufficient; however, Red Brick Decision Server is able to store pathnames as either full pathnames or relative pathnames.

 A full pathname starts with a backslash (\); a relative pathname does not start with a backslash.

This ability to store full pathnames makes a simple copy of the database unwise unless you are sure there are only relative pathnames. To determine which types of pathnames are stored in your system tables, run the following query for NT:

```
select segname, pseq, location
from rbw_storage
where substr(location,2,2)=':\';
```

Run this query for UNIX:

```
select segname, pseq, location
from rbw_storage
where substr(location,1,1)='/';
```

If you get any results from this query, you cannot simply copy the files; you must use either the copy management utility or a combination of TMU unload/load routines to accomplish the move.

Red Brick Decision Server is able to transfer database information in internal or external formats. The internal format is specific to the hardware platform you are on, and data transferred in internal format cannot be read or loaded on any other type of platform than the one from which it came. External format, however, is very transportable because everything is moved as ASCII files. This facility allows you to migrate to other hardware platforms.

Lessons from the Trenches

There are only two lessons from the trenches for this chapter. Each of them was driven home by an actual experience where the customer failed to consider the point and ended up paying the price.

A day of planning is worth two weeks of maintenance

Planning routine maintenance tasks for your warehouse is a necessary activity. It can't be an afterthought. If not addressed, you may end up one of those "make-you-instantly-famous" situations that everyone dreads. Plan your load windows. Plan your recovery strategy. Plan the major changes that are bound to happen as the warehouse matures, and the users become more effective in leveraging its content and functionality.

No one plans to fail; however, you must plan for the unexpected. It's like your car. It'll probably run well for a while without a tune up, but it runs much better if you perform regular maintenance on it. By performing regular maintenance, you also have the opportunity to fix little problems before they become big problems.

Schedule routine maintenance downtime

Scheduling routine downtime can be a little difficult, especially in a 24x7 environment. This is one of the reasons that parallel reorganization is such a great addition to the TMU. If at all possible, try to schedule some maintenance time at least once a year during which you have total ownership of the system and can do the necessary work in the shortest amount of time possible. You will surely have unscheduled maintenance times. Some will come from hardware issues, some from operator error, and perhaps some from simple oversight. In any event, it's nice to be able to schedule those occurrences that you can control.

Don't rush to a solution

Often, when an unexpected event occurs that requires maintenance, you may be faced with a tremendous amount of pressure to fix the problem as fast as possible. Situations like these are opportunities to practice your expectation skills. There is a definite need to have the warehouse back in an appropriate amount of time; however, try as much as possible to think through your steps before you execute.

Rushing in with a solution to the problem before the size and scope of the issue are understood have often made a bad situation worse. Restoring files from a backup without really knowing what is wrong can result in an invalid table, instead of a segment. Killing a load process in an inappropriate manner can result in invalid indexes or tables or both.

If you are unsure of what to do to solve a problem, get on the telephone with tech support, a consultant, or other colleagues who have had the experience to guide you.

Maintaining the Sample Database

At this point, maintaining the sample database is largely up to you. Continue to experiment and try new ideas and methods to manage your warehouse. You have the ability to make the warehouse as large as you want it to be; therefore, you should be able to create any number of different situations to test and validate your approach in resolving a problem. You should also be able to test drive the different component technologies in the Red Brick Decision Server technology. Drop me an e-mail and let me know how much data you generated.

By the time you reach this part of the project, you are perhaps looking at building another warehouse, or expanding the one you've just built. Warehouses are not static; they evolve with time. I hope that you have gotten more value from this book than you expected. That was the goal. As always, I'm open to questions and comments, and I'll do the best I can to reply. As with everything else in business, being courteous and constructive is always in style.

Summary

Maintaining your data warehouse is largely a matter of going through the predefined steps of loading data on an incremental schedule, rolling some off every now and again, and examining what (if anything) you should be doing to improve the system performance.

In addition, there is the routine query tuning, index analysis, and maintenance associated with an ever-evolving data warehouse. It's worthwhile to pay some attention to how you go about adding data and functionality to your existing warehouse — not everything will be painless, but you can certainly make it as pain-free as possible by thinking things through before you start.

You will have unexpected problems that will cause you to perform unscheduled maintenance and repair on the warehouse. When these things happen, try not to get too excited, but rather work with deliberate and measured steps.

Appendix A

What's on the CD-ROM

THE CD THAT ACCOMPANIES this book has a number of things on it that you may find valuable – including templates and example documents as well as all the DDL and load scripts necessary to create and load the sample database.

Having a database engine that is designed and built to manage large amounts of data is only as useful as the amount of data you have to put into it. Unlike most other books of this nature, I wanted to provide a mechanism that allowed you to build a database as large as your available space. To that end, there is also a complete set of Perl scripts that you can use to generate as much data as you'd like. This gives you a chance to take a hard look at some of the interesting problems a large database represents and see how Red Brick Decision Server manages the task with features such as segmentation, query performance, index selection, and – most of all – Vista. With the amount of data that fits on a CD, almost anything you do will be fine. After all, you need a sizable amount to really understand the problems. What follows below is a description of each item on the CD, as well as a directory layout to help navigate. Good luck!

Documents Directory

The documents directory contains all the templates and other document examples mentioned throughout the book:

- ◆ Design Document.doc – a sample design document that has many of the sections completed with the information from the sample database. You can use this as a template for your project and expand it where necessary to address the specific issues your project presents.

- ◆ Out of Scope.doc – A sample out of scope document that you can use to keep track of enhancement requests or other issues that fall outside the scope of your project.

- ◆ PERIOD.xls – Period table spreadsheet used to generate the data for the period table.

- ◆ Status Report.doc – A sample status project status report.

- ◆ Readiness Assessment.doc – A Data Warehouse readiness assessment document.

- ◆ Project Notebook Outline.doc – An outline of the basic sections of a project notebook that you can use as it stands or expand upon to accommodate your requirements.

- ◆ Data map.xls – A sample data mapping spreadsheet.

Data Directory

The data directory contains all the data necessary to build the sample database discussed throughout the book. Note that all the files are zipped. This is primarily due to the limitation of how much information can be placed on a single CD. The data files included can be found on the readme file.

DDL Directory

The DDL directory contains the necessary scripts to create all the database objects including tables, indexes, explicit hierarchies, and precomputed views for the sample database. The following scripts are included:

- ◆ aggregate_cdr.sql – Creates the aggregate_cdr table used by Vista as discussed in Chapter 7.

- ◆ agg_cdr_view.sql – Creates the aggregate_cdr precomputed view as required by Vista.

- ◆ areacode_state.sql – Creates the areacode_state derived dimension as discussed in Chapter 7.

- ◆ areacode_state_hier.sql – Creates the explicit hierarchy between area codes and states.

- ◆ areacode_state_view.sql – Creates the precomputed view as required by Vista.

- ◆ billing_cdr.sql – Creates the BILLING_CDR central detail fact table.

- ◆ call_type.sql – Creates the CALL_TYPE dimension.

- ◆ carrier.sql – Creates the CARRIER dimension.

- ◆ cdr_day_agg_view.sql – Creates a precomputed view over the daily billing aggregate table to be used by Vista.

- ◆ cdr_week_agg_view.sql – Creates a precomputed view over the weekly billing aggregate table to be used by Vista.

- ◆ churn.sql – Creates the CHURN fact table.

- churn_reason.sql – Creates the CHURN_REASON dimension table.

- customer.sql – Creates the CUSTOMER dimension table.

- line_type.sql – Creates the LINE_TYPE dimension table.

- period.sql – Creates the PERIOD dimension table.

- rate_plan.sql – Creates the RATE_PLAN dimension table.

- telephone.sql – Creates the TELEPHONE dimension table.

- time.sql – Creates the TIME table.

- weekly_cdr.sql – Creates the weekly aggregate table.

- wk_to_yr_heir.sql – Creates the explicit hierarchy in the period table that rolls weeks to months to quarters to years.

Perl Directory

The Perl directory contains the Perl scripts necessary to generate extra data over and above the basic set of data provided. The build_database.txt file provides step-by-step instructions on building and loading the data into your database. The PERL scripts include the following:

- Build_database.txt – Provides instructions on using the Perl scripts to generate date additional data

- Billing_cdr_res.pl – Generates residential call rows for the BILLING_CDR table

- Billing_cdr.bus.pl – Generates business call rows for the BILLING_CDR table

- Call_type.pl – Generates the CALL_TYPE dimension data

- Carrier.pl – Generates the CARRIER dimension data

- Churn_reason.pl – Generates the CHURN_REASON data

- Customer.bus.pl – Generates the business customers for the CUSTOMER dimension

- Customer.res.pl – Generates residential customer data for the CUSTOMER dimension

- Line_type.pl – Generates the line type information for the LINE_TYPE dimension

- Rate_plan.pl – Generates RATE_PLAN dimension data

◆ Telephone.pl – Generates the TELEPHONE dimension data

◆ Time.pl – Generates the data for the TIME dimension

SQL Directory

This directory contains the business questions written in SQL:

◆ Query1.sql

◆ Query2.sql

◆ Query3.sql

◆ Query4.sql

◆ Query5.sql

◆ Query6.sql

◆ Query7.sql

◆ Query8.sql

◆ Query9.sql

◆ Query10.sql

ActivePerl Directory

This directory contains ActivePerl, which must be installed if you plan to use thePERL scripts to generate extra fact table data.

Commercial support for ActivePerl is available through the PerlClinic at http://www.PerlClinic.com. Peer support resources for ActivePerl issues can be found at the ActiveState Web site under support at http://www.activestate.com/support/.

The ActiveState Repository has a large collection of modules and extensions in binary packages that are easy to install and use. To view and install these packages, use the Perl Package Manager (PPM) which is included with ActivePerl.

ActivePerl is the latest Perl binary distribution from ActiveState and replaces what was previously distributed as Perl for Win32. The latest release of ActivePerl as well as other professional tools for Perl developers are available from the ActiveState Web site at http://www.activestate.com.

Appendix B

Sample Database

THIS APPENDIX SUPPLIES sample database information. The data is organized into 11 tables.

TABLE B-1 BILLING CDR FACT TABLE

Column Name	Description
Period Key	Foreign key reference to the PERIOD table.
Time Key	Foreign key reference to the TIME table.
Call Type	Foreign key reference to the CALL TYPE table.
Rate Plan	Foreign key reference to the RATE PLAN table.
BTN	Foreign key reference to the TELEPHONE table. This is the Billing Telephone Number.
Destination Telephone Number	Foreign key reference to the TELEPHONE table. This is the number that was called.
Customer ID	Foreign key reference to the CUSTOMER table. This is the customer who pays the bill for the BTN.
Line Type Key	Foreign key reference to the LINE TYPE table. This indicates the type of phone line. Example: 800 line, WATTS line, and so on.
Origination Telephone Number	Foreign key reference to the TELEPHONE table. This is the number that the call was made from.
Revenue Amount	This is the amount the customer was charged for the call.
Call Duration	The number of minutes the call lasted.
Tax Amount	The amount of tax charged for the call.

TABLE B-2 CALL TYPE DIMENSION

Column Name	Description
Call Type Key	Primary key to the CALL TYPE table.
Call Type Description	The description of a call types. Examples: Person-to-Person, Collect, and so on.

TABLE B-3 CARRIER DIMENSION

Column Name	Description
Carrier Key	Primary key to the CARRIER table.
Carrier Description	These are the other carriers a customer might switch to. Example: AT&T, Bell Atlantic, and so on.

TABLE B-4 CHURN FACT TABLE

Column Name	Description
Churn Key	Foreign key reference to CHURN REASON table.
Carrier Key	Foreign key reference to CARRIER table.
Customer ID	Foreign key reference to CUSTOMER table.
Phone Number	Foreign key reference to TELEPHONE table.
Churn Date	Date this phone number churned.
Credit Limit	Customer Credit Limit the day phone number churned.
Outstanding Balance	Outstanding balance due from prior periods.
Current Bill	Balance due for current period.

TABLE B-5 CHURN REASON DIMENSION

Column Name	Description
Churn Reason Key	Primary key.
Churn Reason	The reason the customer dropped service with Local-Tel and acquired service from another provider. Example: Cost, Better Hours, Rebate, and so on.

TABLE B-6 CUSTOMER DIMENSION

Column Name	Description
Customer ID	Primary key.
Customer Name	Name of customer.
Customer City	Customer location city.
Customer State	Customer location state.
Customer Postal Code	Customer location zip code.
Billing City	City where bill is sent.
Billing State	State where bill is sent.
Billing Postal Code	Zip code where bill is sent.
Credit Limit	Limit on how much credit can be extended.
Customer Type	Residential or Business.
Age Band	Age ranges for residential customers. NA for business customers.
Household Count Band	Ranges of household members. NA for business customers.
Home Owner	Yes, No.
Marital Status	Married, Single, Widowed, Divorced.
Annual Income Band	Annual Income ranges for residential customers. NA for business customers.

Continued

TABLE B-6 CUSTOMER DIMENSION *(Continued)*

Column Name	Description
Number Employees Band	Number of employee ranges for business customers. NA for residential customers.
Annual Revenue Band	Annual revenue ranges for business customers. NA for residential customers.
SIC Code	Standard industry Code for business customers. NA for residential customers.

TABLE B-7 LINE TYPE DIMENSION

Column Name	Description
Line Type Key	Primary key.
Line type Description	Describes the type of phone line: T1, 800, 900, WATTS, ISDN, and so on.

TABLE B-8 PERIOD DIMENSION

Column Name	Description
Period Key	Primary key
Date	Full date value for this date (mm/dd/yyyy)
Day Number	Day number of the year: 1–365
Calendar Week Number	Number of the calendar week; 1–52
Day Name Long	Long day name: Monday, Tuesday, and so on
Calendar Month Number	Number of the calendar month: 1–12
Day Name Short	Short day name: Mon, Tue, Wed, Thr, Fri, Sat, Sun
Calendar Quarter Number	Calendar Quarter this day belongs to: 1–4

Column Name	Description
Calendar Month Name	Month Name: January, February, and so on
Calendar Year	Example: 1998, 1999, 2000
Day Type	Description of the day: Holiday, Weekday, Weekend
Fiscal Week Number	Fiscal week this day belongs to: 1–52
Fiscal Month Number	Fiscal month this day belongs to: 1–12
Fiscal Year	Fiscal year: 1999, 2000
Fiscal Period Number	Fiscal period this day belongs to: 1–12

TABLE B-9 RATE PLAN DIMENSION

Column Name	Description
Rate Plan Key	Primary key.
Rate Plan Description	Description of the rate plan. Example: $.05 Evening Rate, Family Calling Plan, and so on.

TABLE B-10 TELEPHONE DIMENSION

Column Name	Description
Phone Number	Primary key to the TELEPHONE table
Area Code	Area code for the number
Exchange	3-digit exchange
Number	4-digit number
City	City of this number's location
State	State of this number's location

TABLE B-11 TIME DIMENSION

Column Name	Description
Time Key	Primary key
Hour 12	Hour value in 12-hour format: 1–12
Minute	Minute Value 1–60
Hour 24	Hour value in 24-hour format: 1–24
Second	Second value 1–60
AM PM	AM/PM indicator
Time Description	Description of periods of the day: Morning, Evening, Weekend, Holiday, Late Night, Overnight, Early Morning, Afternoon

Index

Symbols

IDG Books Worldwide, Inc.
End-User License Agreement

READ THIS. You should carefully read these terms and conditions before opening the software packet(s) included with this book ("Book"). This is a license agreement ("Agreement") between you and IDG Books Worldwide, Inc. ("IDGB"). By opening the accompanying software packet(s), you acknowledge that you have read and accept the following terms and conditions. If you do not agree and do not want to be bound by such terms and conditions, promptly return the Book and the unopened software packet(s) to the place you obtained them for a full refund.

1. **License Grant.** IDGB grants to you (either an individual or entity) a nonexclusive license to use one copy of the enclosed software program(s) (collectively, the "Software") solely for your own personal or business purposes on a single computer (whether a standard computer or a work-station component of a multiuser network). The Software is in use on a computer when it is loaded into temporary memory (RAM) or installed into permanent memory (hard disk, CD-ROM, or other storage device). IDGB reserves all rights not expressly granted herein.

2. **Ownership.** IDGB is the owner of all right, title, and interest, including copyright, in and to the compilation of the Software recorded on the disk(s) or CD-ROM ("Software Media"). Copyright to the individual programs recorded on the Software Media is owned by the author or other authorized copyright owner of each program. Ownership of the Software and all proprietary rights relating thereto remain with IDGB and its licensers.

3. **Restrictions On Use and Transfer.**

   (a) You may only (i) make one copy of the Software for backup or archival purposes, or (ii) transfer the Software to a single hard disk, provided that you keep the original for backup or archival purposes. You may not (i) rent or lease the Software, (ii) copy or reproduce the Software through a LAN or other network system or through any computer subscriber system or bulletin-board system, or (iii) modify, adapt, or create derivative works based on the Software.

   (b) You may not reverse engineer, decompile, or disassemble the Software. You may transfer the Software and user documentation on a permanent basis, provided that the transferee agrees to accept the terms and conditions of this Agreement and you retain no copies. If the Software is an update or has been updated, any transfer must include the most recent update and all prior versions.

business interruption, loss of business information, or any other pecuniary loss) arising from the use of or inability to use the Book or the Software, even if IDGB has been advised of the possibility of such damages.

(c) Because some jurisdictions do not allow the exclusion or limitation of liability for consequential or incidental damages, the above limitation or exclusion may not apply to you.

7. **U.S. Government Restricted Rights.** Use, duplication, or disclosure of the Software by the U.S. Government is subject to restrictions stated in paragraph (c)(1)(ii) of the Rights in Technical Data and Computer Software clause of DFARS 252.227-7013, and in subparagraphs (a) through (d) of the Commercial Computer – Restricted Rights clause at FAR 52.227-19, and in similar clauses in the NASA FAR supplement, when applicable.

8. **General.** This Agreement constitutes the entire understanding of the parties and revokes and supersedes all prior agreements, oral or written, between them and may not be modified or amended except in a writing signed by both parties hereto that specifically refers to this Agreement. This Agreement shall take precedence over any other documents that may be in conflict herewith. If any one or more provisions contained in this Agreement are held by any court or tribunal to be invalid, illegal, or otherwise unenforceable, each and every other provision shall remain in full force and effect.

my2cents.idgbooks.com

Register This Book — And Win!

Visit **http://my2cents.idgbooks.com** to register this book and we'll automatically enter you in our fantastic monthly prize giveaway. It's also your opportunity to give us feedback: let us know what you thought of this book and how you would like to see other topics covered.

Discover IDG Books Online!

The IDG Books Online Web site is your online resource for tackling technology — at home and at the office. Frequently updated, the IDG Books Online Web site features exclusive software, insider information, online books, and live events!

10 Productive & Career-Enhancing Things You Can Do at www.idgbooks.com

- Nab source code for your own programming projects.

- Download software.

- Read Web exclusives: special articles and book excerpts by IDG Books Worldwide authors.

- Take advantage of resources to help you advance your career as a Novell or Microsoft professional.

- Buy IDG Books Worldwide titles or find a convenient bookstore that carries them.

- Register your book and win a prize.

- Chat live online with authors.

- Sign up for regular e-mail updates about our latest books.

- Suggest a book you'd like to read or write.

- Give us your 2¢ about our books and about our Web site.

You say you're not on the Web yet? It's easy to get started with IDG Books' *Discover the Internet,* available at local retailers everywhere.

CD-ROM Installation Instructions

The CD-ROM that accompanies this book contains all the necessary scripts and data to build the sample database. Appendix A describes what's on the CD, and Appendix B contains the discussions of the sample database from each chapter. To generate extra data, install the Perl scripts from the CD as follows:

Create the following directories:

```
<parent>/scripts/
<parent>/scripts/lib
<parent>/output/
```

Place all the *.pl scripts in <parent>/scripts/ and the *.pm files in <parent>/scripts/lib.